A Computational Theory of

This book breaks new ground by developing, for the first time, a formal computational theory of writing systems. It offers specific proposals about the nature of the linguistic objects that are represented by orthographic elements; what levels of linguistic representation are involved and how they may differ across writing systems; and what formal constraints hold of the mapping relation between linguistic and orthographic elements. Sproat demonstrates that this mapping relation is regular in the technical sense that it can be implemented computationally using the simplest class of computational devices, namely finite-state machines. He also argues that the level of linguistic representation reflected in written forms is always consistent within a given writing system. This level may be "shallow" (the language is "spelled as it sounds") or "deep," but in any case it extends over the entire vocabulary. Based on his insights as to what linguistic elements can be represented in writing, Sproat proposes a new taxonomy of writing systems. The treatment of theoretical linguistic issues and their computational implementation is complemented with discussion of empirical psycholinguistic work on reading and its relevance for the computational model developed here. Throughout, the model is illustrated with a number of detailed case studies of writing systems around the world.

This innovative book will be of interest to students and researchers in a variety of fields, including theoretical and computational linguistics, the psycholinguistics of reading and writing, and speech technology.

Richard Sproat has done published research in numerous areas of linguistics and computational linguistics. He is currently a Technology Consultant in the Human/Computer Interface Department at AT&T Labs – Research.

Studies in Natural Language Processing

Series Editor: Branimir Boguraev, IBM T. J. Watson Research

Also in the series

Douglas E. Appelt, *Planning English Sentences*
Madeleine Bates and Ralph M. Weischedel (eds.), *Challenges in Natural Language Processing*
Steven Bird, *Computational Phonology*
Peter Bosch and Rob van der Sandt (eds.), *Focus*
T. Briscoe, Ann Copestake, and Valeria Paiva (eds.), *Inheritance, Defaults and the Lexicon*
Ronald Cole, Joseph Mariani, Hans Uszkoreit, Giovanni Varile, Annie Zaenen, Antonio Zampolli, and Victor Zue (eds.), *Survey of the State of the Art in Human Language Technology*
David R. Dowty, Lauri Karttunen, and Arnold M. Zwicky (eds.), *Natural Language Parsing*
Ralph Grishman, *Computational Linguistics*
Graeme Hirst, *Semantic Interpretation and the Resolution of Ambiguity*
András Kornai, *Extended Finite State Models of Language*
Kathleen R. McKeown, *Text Generation*
Martha Stone Palmer, *Semantic Processing for Finite Domains*
Terry Patten, *Systemic Text Generation as Problem Solving*
Manny Rayner, David Carter, Pierrette Bouillon, Vassilis Digalakis, and Mats Wirén, *The Spoken Language Translator*
Ehud Reiter and Robert Dale, *Building Natural Language Generation Systems*
Michael Rosner and Roderick Johnson (eds.), *Computational Linguistics and Formal Semantics*
Patrick Saint-Dizier and Evelyn Viegas (eds.), *Computational Lexical Semantics*

A Computational Theory of Writing Systems

Richard Sproat
AT&T Labs – Research

CAMBRIDGE UNIVERSITY PRESS
Cambridge, New York, Melbourne, Madrid, Cape Town, Singapore, São Paulo

Cambridge University Press
The Edinburgh Building, Cambridge CB2 2RU, UK

Published in the United States of America by Cambridge University Press, New York

www.cambridge.org
Information on this title: www.cambridge.org/9780521663403

First published 2000
This digitally printed first paperback version 2006

A catalogue record for this publication is available from the British Library

Library of Congress Cataloguing in Publication data

Sproat, Richard William.

A computational theory of writing systems / Richard Sproat.

p. cm. – (Studies in natural language processing)

ISBN 0-521-66340-7

1. Written communication – Data processing. I. Title. II. Series.

P211.4.S67 2000
411′.0285 – dc21 99-058467

ISBN-13 978-0-521-66340-3 hardback
ISBN-10 0-521-66340-7 hardback

ISBN-13 978-0-521-03422-7 paperback
ISBN-10 0-521-03422-1 paperback

For Lisa, who is learning to read

Contents

List of Figures

List of Tables

Preface

Most general books on writing systems are written or edited by scholars who are specialists in a small subset of the writing systems that they cover and who have developed their views on writing in general based on their own experience in their particular specialized area.

This book is different: I cannot claim to be an expert on *any* particular writing system. My interest in writing systems stems in part from my interest in text-to-speech synthesis systems, and in particular the problem of converting from written text into a linguistic representation that specifies how that text would be read. Given that problem, it is natural to inquire about the formal nature of the relationship between the written form and the linguistic representation that the written form encodes: What linguistic elements do written symbols encode? Do writing systems differ in the abstractness of the linguistic representation encoded by orthography, and if so how? What are the formal constraints on the mapping between linguistic representation and writing? Some of these issues have, of course, been addressed elsewhere, though usually in an informal fashion. This book is an attempt to answer these questions in the context of a formal, computational theory of writing systems.

One point that needs to be made at the outset is that this book is not intended as an introduction to the topic of writing systems. There are many excellent books that serve that purpose, including Sampson (1985), Coulmas (1989), and DeFrancis (1989). Special mention must be given to the superb collection in Daniels and Bright (1996), without which the present book would not have been possible. Thus, while I do discuss aspects of several writing systems in some amount of detail, there are also a number of writing systems that are discussed in less detail. The reader unfamiliar with the general properties of the writing systems discussed here is urged to consult one of the many general introductions to the topic, such as those cited above.

In preparing this work, I have benefited greatly from discussions with and comments from a number of colleagues, listed here in alphabetical order: Harald Baayen, Alan Black, Wayles Browne, Roy Harris, Leonard Katz, George Kiraz, Martin Jansche, Kazuaki Maeda, Mark-Jan Nederhof, Anneke Neijt, Elena Pavlova, Geoffrey Sampson, Chilin Shih, Brian

Stowell, Robert Thomson, J. Marshall Unger, and Jennifer Venditti. I would especially like to thank Steven Bird, who read through two whole drafts of this work and gave me extensive comments on both. I also acknowledge an anonymous reviewer for Cambridge University Press. Portions of this work were presented at the University of Arizona and at Charles University in Prague, and I thank audiences there for useful comments and questions. I also thank Juergen Schroeter for help in using his recording setup for the experiment reported in Section 3.3.

The technical production of this book depended heavily upon several free or public domain resources including databases and software. I am indebted to Rick Harbaugh (developer of `www.zhongwen.com`) for kindly allowing me access to his data on Chinese character structure. Several of the more detailed analyses in this book, including the treatment of English in Section 3.2 and of Chinese in Section 2.3.4, were implemented, and these implementations depended upon the *fsm* library developed by my colleagues at AT&T Labs, Michael Riley, Fernando Pereira, and Mehryar Mohri. Chinese characters were incorporated into LaTeX using Stephen Simpson's *PMC* package; for Devanagari I used Frans Velthuis's *devtex* package; Visible Speech fonts are due to Mark Shoulson. Editing of figures and graphics were done using Vectaport Inc.'s *idraw*, John Bradley's *xv*, and Davor Matic's *bitmap*.

Finally I would like to thank my editor at Cambridge University Press, Christine Bartels, for her support for this project.

1 Reading Devices

Our starting point for this study of writing systems is text-to-speech synthesis – TTS, and more specifically the computational problem of converting from written text into a linguistic representation. While the connection between TTS systems on the one hand and writing systems on the other may not be immediately apparent, a moment's reflection will make it clear that the problem to be solved by a TTS system – namely the conversion of written text into speech – is exactly the same problem as a human reader must solve when presented with a text to be read aloud. And just as writing systems, their properties, and the ways in which they encode linguistic information are of interest to psycholinguists who study how people read, so (in principle) should such considerations be of interest to those who develop TTS technology: At the very least, it ought to be of as much interest as, for example, understanding the physiology and acoustics underlying speech production, something that early speech synthesis researchers such as Fant (1960) were heavily involved in.[1]

Since my starting point is TTS, and since I assume that most readers will not be familiar with this field, I will start this chapter with a review of some of the issues relevant to the development of TTS systems, particularly as they relate to the problem of analyzing input text. This will be the topic of Section 1.1. In Section 1.2 I will informally introduce, by way of a simple example, the model that I shall be developing throughout the rest of this book. Finally, Section 1.3 will introduce some aspects of the formalism and the conventions that will be used throughout this book.

[1] It will perhaps come as no surprise that TTS researchers have *not*, in fact, generally been overly interested in writing systems. This is undoubtedly due in part to the relatively low interest in text-analysis issues in general in the TTS literature, at least as compared to the high level of interest in such matters as prosody, intonation, voice quality, and synthesis techniques. It also is undoubtedly related to the fact that much of the work on TTS is driven by rather practical aims (e.g., building a working system), where an overactive interest in theories of writing systems might appear to be an unnecessary luxury.

1.1 Text-to-Speech Conversion: A Brief Introduction

As noted above, the task of a TTS system is to convert written text into speech. Normally the written representation is in the form of an electronic text – coded in ASCII, ISO, JIS, UNICODE, or some other standard depending upon the language and system being used; this circumvents one problem that humans must solve, namely that of visually recognizing characters printed on a page.[2] Similarly the output is a digital representation of speech. Between these two representations are numerous stages of processing, which can be profitably classified into two broad stages. The first stage is the conversion of the written text into an internal linguistic representation; the second is the conversion from that linguistic representation into speech. The latter consists of computing various phonetic and acoustic parameters, including segmental duration, F_0 ("pitch") trajectory, properties of the output speech such as spectral tilt or glottal open quotient, and (in concatenative speech synthesis systems) selection of appropriate acoustic units or (in formant-based synthesis systems) the generation of vocal-tract transfer functions appropriate to the intended sounds. We will have nothing further to say about these issues here; the reader is referred to Dutoit (1997) for a good general introduction to these issues and also to Allen, Hunnicutt, and Klatt (1987) and Sproat (1997b) for an overview of how two particular systems (the MITalk system and the Bell Labs TTS system) work.

In any TTS system the output speech will be generated from an annotated linguistic representation, which is in turn derived from input text via the first stage of processing defined above. How rich a linguistic representation is presumed (and in terms of which linguistic theories and assumptions it is couched) differs from system to system, of course, but we may at least assume that the linguistic representation will include information on the sequence of sounds to be enunciated (usually allophones of phonemes, but in some systems whole syllable-sized units); lexical stress or tone information; word and phrase-level accentuation and emphasis; and the location of various prosodic boundaries, including syllable and prosodic phrase boundaries. Thus for an input such as that in (1.1), we might presume as a plausible (partial) linguistic representation, the representation in Figure 1.1.

(1.1) I need 2 oz. of Valrhona and 6 anchos for the mole.

In the particular rendition of the sentence presumed in Figure 1.1 there are two intonational phrases (denoted by ι) grouped into a single utterance (U). Lexical stress is indicated by a metrical tree dominating individual

[2] Of course, it is possible to hook up a TTS system to an *optical character recognition* (OCR) system; such systems have in fact been available for several years in the form of page-readers for the blind (e.g., Kurzweil's reader); and there has been much recent interest in conversion of FAX into speech, which adds yet a further complication, namely messy input.

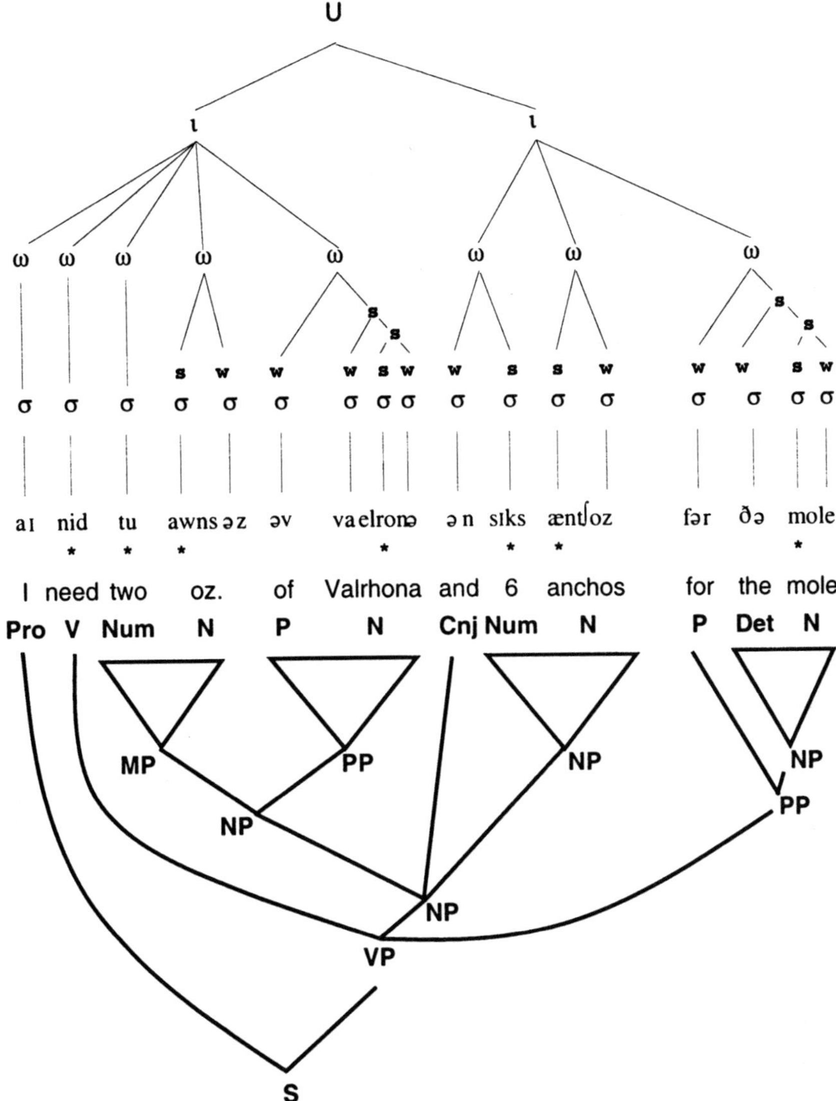

Figure 1.1. A partial linguistic representation for the sentence in (1.1). Shown are a phonetic transcription, a prosodic analysis into two intonational phrases (ι) and one utterance (U), accent assignment ($\underline{*}$), a set of part of speech tags, and a simple phrase-structure analysis. Phonetic symbols are IPA. Note that 'MP' means 'measure phrase'.

syllables (σ) and dominated itself by a prosodic word (ω); we assume that proclitics form a prosodic word with the following content word. Also indicated are lexical accents for the words *need, two, ounces, Valrhona, six, anchos*, and *mole.*

To produce this representation, or any equally plausible representation, for this sentence, a reader must "reconstruct" a great deal of linguistic information that is simply not represented in the written form. Naturally all syntactic information, including both the morphosyntactic part of speech tags as well as phrase structure, must be computed. So must a great deal of the phonological information. In particular, the sequence of phonetic segments are only somewhat indirectly represented in English orthography; in some written forms such as *2, 6*, and *oz.* they cannot be said to be represented at all. In the latter case the linguistic form must be reconstructed entirely from the reader's knowledge of the language and often depends upon information about context (does one say *ounce* or *ounces*?). In some cases readers may need to make educated guesses about the pronunciations of some words, though if these follow the normal pronunciation conventions of the language they will usually guess correctly: Even readers who had not previously seen the words *anchos* or *Valrhona* could nonetheless probably have guessed the correct pronunciation. For *mole* – in the sense of a Mexican sauce, and pronounced /ˈmoleɪ/ – the situation is more complex since the pronunciation here does not follow standard English conventions: In this case one would simply have to be familiar with the word. But there is of course an additional problem here in that, as in the case of *oz.*, one must also disambiguate this word, so that one does not pronounce it as the homographic /ˈmol/ (e.g., in the sense of a species of insectivore).

Prosodic phrasing is rarely represented; note that punctuation is only partly used in this function (Nunberg, 1995), and in any case it is by no means consistently used in every case where one might plausibly find a prosodic boundary. Lexical accentuation is almost never indicated.[3]

Thus, if one is designing a TTS system that can handle arbitrary text in a given language, it is generally necessary for the system to possess a large

[3] It is generally true that suprasegmental and prosodic information is systematically omitted from the orthographies of a large variety of languages. This is particularly true for high level prosodic information such as prosodic phrase boundary placement, and accentuation and prominence. But it extends to purely lexically determined features such as lexical tone. Thus while some languages, such as Thai, Vietnamese, or Navajo, *do* indicate lexically distinctive tone in their orthographies, it seems to be far more common to omit this feature: For example many orthographies developed for tonal languages of Africa omit marks of tone, though it should be noted that many of these scripts were developed by European missionaries who had no understanding of tone; see Bird (1999) for a discussion of more recently developed African orthographies where tone is marked.

A related point, as Geoffrey Sampson has noted (personal communication), is that Latin did not mark length in vowels (though gemination in consonants was marked).

amount of linguistic knowledge, including knowledge about the lexical and phrasal phonology of the language in question, and at the very minimum a set of heuristics for determining plausible locations for accents and prosodic phrase boundaries (Dutoit, 1997; Sproat, 1997b).

If one, furthermore, is developing a TTS system that is intended to be adaptable to more than one language, then there is an additional consideration: Not only do the written forms of utterances systematically fail to indicate many aspects of the spoken forms, but different writing systems present different sets of problems. Thus, if one designs a TTS system with European languages in mind, one might reasonably assume (as many have done) that words in the input text are separated by whitespace. But this assumption will fail with writing systems such as those of Chinese, Japanese, or Thai, where word boundaries are never written. (See the discussion of various Asian scripts in Daniels and Bright (1996), and see Sproat et al. (1996) for a discussion of the issue in a computational setting.) Similarly, for many languages one may assume that abbreviations and numbers can be expanded in a "preprocessing" phase prior to full linguistic analysis. For English (or Chinese) this (almost) works in that an abbreviation such as *oz.* has only two plausible translations, namely *ounce* or *ounces*, and in most cases some simple heuristics based on the context can tell you which one it should be. But as I have discussed at length elsewhere (Sproat, 1997a,b), such a simple approach cannot work for Russian, where in order to decide how to pronounce a seemingly innocuous sequence such as *5%*, one needs to determine such things as whether the percentage expression is modifying a following noun ('a 5% discount') or not ('I need 5%'). In the former case the '5%' phrase is an adjective agreeing in case, number, and gender with the following noun; in the latter case, it is a noun, and its case number and gender is determined by the syntactic context in which it occurs. Thus the expression **5% скидка** <5% skidka> '5% discount', is read as *pjat+i*-**procent+n+aja** *skidka* (five+Gen[itive]-percent+Adj[ective]+Nom[inative]Fem[inine] discount), with an adjectival form *procentnaja* agreeing in number, gender, and case with the following noun. The simple expression <5%> on its own would be read as *pjat'* **procent+ov** (five+Nom percent+GenPl[ural]), with a nominal *procentov* in the genitive plural form. If the example were <4%>, the word for 'percent' would have to be in the genitive *singular* form: *četyre* **procent+a** (four+Nom percent+GenSg[=Singular]). If the "percent phrase" is governed by an element, such as a preposition, requiring an oblique case, then the entire phrase, including the number and word for 'percent', must appear in that oblique case: Thus **с 5%** <s 5%> 'with 5%', is *s pjat'ju* **procent+ami** (with five+Instr[umental] percent+InstrPl).

Considerations such as these inevitably lead one to ask what commonalities there are among the diverse written representations of language, and whether a single computational model can encompass all systems that one might encounter. A model of this kind for TTS text analysis, one that has been applied to languages and writing systems as diverse as German, Spanish, Russian, Hindi, Chinese, and Japanese, is discussed elsewhere (Sproat, 1997a,b). The purpose of this book is to present a computational theory of writing systems that was motivated by the work on TTS and that is at least to some extent consistent with the model presented in this previous work.

1.2 The Task of Pronouncing Aloud: A Model

We turn now to sketching the model of the relation between written and linguistic form that we will develop in this book. As implied by our discussion in the last section, we will, at least initially, be concerned with specifying a computational model whose task is to pronounce text aloud. Thus the problem we start out with is essentially what psychologists who study reading term *naming* – the pronunciation aloud of a written form. This is in principle a different task from the task of *lexical access* via a written form, and from the task of deciding how to *spell* a given linguistic form. The computational model of writing that we will propose will nonetheless have implications for these issues also: Indeed a large portion of the discussion in Chapter 3 will focus on a model of spelling for English. We start here with an example that will illustrate the model to be developed.

1.2.1 A Simple Example from Russian

Most literate people, even those who are monolingual, are broadly aware that some orthographies are more "regular" than others, that, for example, Spanish orthography is highly regular ("written as it sounds"), and that English orthography, in contrast, is highly irregular. This naive notion of regularity corresponds roughly to what psychologists term *orthographic depth*. That is, psychologists often refer to an orthography as deep if it is not generally possible to reconstruct the pronunciation of a word by simply looking at the string of symbols and applying general "letter-to-sound" rules; see Frost, Katz, and Bentin (1987); Besner and Smith (1992); Katz and Frost (1992); Seidenberg (1992), inter alia, as well as the discussion in Chapter 5.[4] Thus, in terms of the metaphor of depth, the orthography of Spanish, is shallower than that of English (or Hebrew). With some legitimacy we can consider Spanish and English as being near two ends of a spectrum of possible orthographic depths.

[4] An alternative term to *orthographic depth*, namely *orthographic transparency*, is gaining some currency (Leonard Katz, personal communication).

Russian falls somewhere in between these two extremes: It is not nearly as irregular as English, but at the same time it is not possible to do as one can in Spanish and predict the pronunciation of a word purely by looking at the orthographic string. Russian orthography is often described as *morphological* (Cubberley, 1996, page 352), meaning that the spelling system attempts to represent morphologically related forms consistently, abstracting away from at least some phonological changes. As a corollary, a reader of Russian needs access to this morphological information to pronounce words correctly.

To see what is meant by this, consider the problem of pronouncing a particular letter string, say **города** <goroda>. As it happens, this can represent one of two lexical forms in standard Russian: 'of a city' (city+gen.sg.), in which case it is pronounced with initial stress /ˈgorədʌ/; or 'cities' (city+pl.nom./acc.), in which case it is pronounced with final stress /gərʌˈda/. That there are two possible pronunciations for the string **города** <goroda> shows immediately that it is not possible to pronounce this string merely by looking at the sequence of letters: One must have access to lexical information, and in this case one presumably needs access to some information about the context in which the word occurs, since the reader needs to determine whether the genitive singular or plural nominative/accusative is the more appropriate interpretation.[5] Not surprisingly, given the high degree of lexical competence needed to be able to assign lexical stress in Russian words, pedagogical grammars of Russian routinely mark stress placement. Thus the genitive singular form would be written **го́рода** <góroda>, whereas the genitive plural form would be written **города́** <gorodá>. But such marks of stress are rarely used in nonpedagogical contexts. In not marking stress, Russian orthography thus fails to mark information that is important for getting the reading correct; to use a term suggested to me by Anneke Neijt, its *coverage* of the phonological information is incomplete.

But Russian orthography, in addition to its incomplete coverage, is also relatively "deep" in that there are stress-related vowel reductions that are not marked in Russian orthography. Note for example, that the first /o/ in **города** <goroda> shows up as /o/ when stressed, as in the genitive singular form, but as /ə/ when destressed (more correctly, when in the syllable antepenultimate to the stress (Wade, 1992)), as in the nominative/accusative plural. These alternations are quite regular and predictable, but they are never marked in the orthography, which means that Russian orthography represents a level that is somewhat more abstract than a surface phonemic

[5] Note also that this particular ambiguity between genitive singular and plural nominative/accusative – with concomitant shift in lexical stress – is by no means general in Russian: Only a subset of nouns show this particular ambiguity, though other cases of stress-related minimal pairs are rife in the language.

level. As we shall see in Section 3.1, the standard orthography for Belarusian *does* orthographically represent these vowel reductions, and it is therefore somewhat more shallow than the orthography of standard Russian. (Belarusian is like Russian in terms of coverage, though, in that it too fails to mark stress in the orthography.)

Before we proceed further, we need to define a little more precisely what we mean when we speak of an orthographic object *representing* a linguistic object. Let us start with what I take to be a fairly uncontroversial (partial) representation of the genitive singular form *goroda* 'of a city', namely the Attribute-Value Matrix (AVM) in (1.2):

(1.2)
$$\begin{bmatrix} \text{PHON} & \langle g\text{ˈ}oroda \rangle \\ \text{SYNSEM} & \begin{bmatrix} \text{CAT} & noun \\ \text{GEN} & masc \\ \text{CASE} & gen \\ \text{NUM} & sing \\ \text{SEM} & city \end{bmatrix} \end{bmatrix}$$

(On the use of AVMs in phonological representations see, inter alia, Bird and Klein (1994), Mastroianni and Carpenter (1994) and Bird (1995).) First of all, a few comments on (1.2) are required. The primary stress on the first syllable is indicated here with the standard diacritic 'ˈ', rather than by an explicit hierarchical prosodic structure within the AVM; this is purely a notational convenience. For similar reasons of notational convenience, the phonological representation is given, in this example, as a list of segments, with no indication of higher level prosodic structure, such as syllables or feet. (Indeed, we are taking some amount of liberty by even allowing *segments* into our ontology, given the growing body of phonological work that views segments as epiphenomena of temporally overlapping collections of features. We return to this point in Section 1.2.4.2.) Also noteworthy is that the segmental representation presented would be traditionally termed a relatively "deep" representation, since it abstracts away from various low-level phonological processes, such as the vowel reductions we have discussed; this is intentional, since I shall argue that it is this deep phonological level that is represented by the orthography of Russian. Finally, the representation in (1.2) fails to indicate that *goroda* is morphologically complex, arguably consisting of a stem *gorod-* and an inflectional affix *-a*. Perhaps surprisingly, I will have relatively little to say about morphology in this book, though I will return briefly in Section 3.4 to the relation between orthography and morphological structure.

Where does orthography fit into (1.2)? An obvious first cut at a representation would be simply to assume another attribute "ORTH" with an associated list of orthographic elements:

(1.3)

$$\begin{bmatrix} \text{PHON} & \langle \textit{g'oroda} \rangle \\ \text{ORTH} & \langle \textbf{города} \rangle \\ \text{SYNSEM} & \begin{bmatrix} \text{CAT} & \textit{noun} \\ \text{GEN} & \textit{masc} \\ \text{CASE} & \textit{gen} \\ \text{NUM} & \textit{sing} \\ \text{SEM} & \textit{city} \end{bmatrix} \end{bmatrix}$$

But this representation is inadequate for several reasons. First, although it represents the fact that **города** <goroda> is the orthographic representation of *goroda*, it fails to indicate the obvious fact that the individual letters of the orthographic representation each correspond to a particular linguistic unit, in this case a segment: Thus г <g> clearly represents /g/, and о <o> clearly represents /o/. Second, it fails to represent the *kind* of relation between (in this case) the phonological portions of the representation and the orthographic portion. It seems reasonable to view this relation as one of *licensing*, where particular (sets of) linguistic elements *license* the occurrence of (sets of) orthographic elements. Thus /g/ licenses the occurrence of г <g> in this example. Third, and finally, by presenting the value of ORTH as an *ordered* list, we are redundantly specifying information that is specified elsewhere in the AVM: The phonological segments are ordered with respect to one another, and the linear ordering of the licensed orthographic elements ought to follow in some fashion from that.

These considerations lead us to propose, instead, the representation in (1.4):

(1.4)

$$\begin{bmatrix} \text{PHON} & \langle g_{1*}\, 'o_{2*}\, r_{3*}\, o_{4*}\, d_{5*}\, a_{6*} \rangle \\ \text{ORTH} & \{\text{г}_1, \text{о}_2, \text{р}_3, \text{о}_4, \text{д}_5, \text{а}_6\} \\ \text{SYNSEM} & \begin{bmatrix} \text{CAT} & \textit{noun} \\ \text{GEN} & \textit{masc} \\ \text{CASE} & \textit{gen} \\ \text{NUM} & \textit{sing} \\ \text{SEM} & \textit{city} \end{bmatrix} \end{bmatrix}$$

We represent licensing using numerical coindexation, where the index of the licenser is marked with an asterisk. The value for ORTH is itself an unordered list of objects; we indicate this using the standard curly-brace notation for sets.

As we have seen, we have assumed a relatively abstract phonological representation in the Russian example that we have been discussing. In general we will assume that the orthography of a language represents a particular linguistic *level* of representation. For phonological information that is orthographically encoded we can speak of this level as being relatively "deep" compared to a "surface phonemic" representation; or we can refer to it as relatively shallow. We will term the linguistic level represented by the orthography of a language the *Orthographically Relevant Level* – ORL.[6] Note that we are *not* claiming that every symbol in the spelling of a word necessarily has a (nonorthographic) linguistic counterpart at the ORL. So as we shall argue in Section 3.2, many aspects of the spellings of words in English are arbitrary and simply must be listed as part of the word's spelling. Nonetheless even in an orthography as irregular as that of English there are regular correspondences between linguistic elements and their orthographic expression: The ORL is simply that linguistic level of representation at which those regular correspondences are most succinctly stated. Note that for expository reasons we will typically present as the ORL just that portion of the linguistic representation that is relevant to the particular orthographic phenomenon under discussion. Thus, for most purely phonographic scripts, information associated with the SYNSEM portion of the AVM is not typically relevant (though in some cases it might be, as for example in German where capitalization is sensitive to whether or not the word is a noun). In such cases the SYNSEM information would be omitted from the representation. It should be understood, however, that the information is still present, just not germane to the discussion at hand.

Returning to (1.4), we note that there is still some redundancy that can be removed. Russian orthography is largely regular in the sense that a given (abstract) phoneme is typically only spelled in one way. This in turn implies that we should not need to explicitly list the orthographic elements in the AVM; indeed in the example in (1.4) all of the letters are completely predictable and could be derived via a set of rewrite rules as follows:

(1.5) g → г <g>
o → о <o>
r → р <r>
d → д <d>
a → а <a>

Such rules can be viewed as filling positions in the orthography portion of the AVM and hence licensing the material in those positions. Of course

[6] This level is roughly equivalent to what I have referred to as the *morphologically motivated annotation* (MMA) in previous work on text-analysis for TTS (Sproat, 1997a,b).

even in fairly regular spelling systems – and certainly in complex systems such as English – some lexical specification of spelling is necessary. This can be handled either by simply listing the irregular spelling, or else by using a lexically specific spelling rule. Thus for the English word *knit*, for instance, we might assume a lexical representation as in (1.6a), or else a rule as in (1.6b), in either case specifying the spelling of /n/ as <kn>; we assume that the remaining /it/ is regularly spelled:

(1.6) (a)

$$\begin{bmatrix} \text{PHON} & \langle n_{1*}\,\text{ɪ}t \rangle \\ \text{ORTH} & \{kn_1\} \\ \text{SYNSEM} & \begin{bmatrix} \text{CAT} & \textit{verb} \\ \text{SEM} & \textit{knit} \end{bmatrix} \end{bmatrix}$$

(b) n → <kn> in *knit*

As we will discuss further, we will follow Nunn (1998) in assuming that rules are used not only in the initial *graphemic licensing* phase that we have been discussing but also in a subsequent phase of what Nunn terms *autonomous spelling rules.* We will expand her notion of autonomous spelling rule to include what we will term *surface orthographic constraints*; see Section 3.5.

1.2.2 Formal Definitions

In this section we expand the formalism further, introducing some additional formal notations, as well as some axioms that control the mapping between linguistic information and orthography. We will also introduce the central theses of this study.

1.2.2.1 AVMs and Annotation Graphs

Let us return to the AVM representation from (1.4), repeated here as (1.7):

(1.7)

$$\begin{bmatrix} \text{PHON} & \langle g_{1*}\,{}'o_{2*}\,r_{3*}\,o_{4*}\,d_{5*}\,a_{6*} \rangle \\ \text{ORTH} & \{\text{г}_1, \text{о}_2, \text{р}_3, \text{о}_4, \text{д}_5, \text{а}_6\} \\ \text{SYNSEM} & \begin{bmatrix} \text{CAT} & \textit{noun} \\ \text{GEN} & \textit{masc} \\ \text{CASE} & \textit{gen} \\ \text{NUM} & \textit{sing} \\ \text{SEM} & \textit{city} \end{bmatrix} \end{bmatrix}$$

In the Russian example, orthographic elements are licensed purely by phonological elements. In partly logographic writing systems such as Chinese, we propose that part of a complex glyph may be licensed by a portion of the SYNSEM part of the representation. Thus consider the character 蟬 <INSECT+CHÁN> *chán* 'cicada' (see Section 1.3 for a detailed discussion of our conventions for glossing Chinese characters) where the INSECT component 虫 (left-hand portion of the character) is the so-called semantic radical and the right-hand component 單 *chán* cues the pronunciation. For this case we assume an AVM as in (1.8), where the INSECT portion is licensed by the SEM entry, and the phonological portion is licensed by the syllable:

(1.8)

$$\begin{bmatrix} \text{PHON} & \begin{bmatrix} \text{SYL} & \begin{bmatrix} \text{SEG} & \left\langle \begin{bmatrix}\text{ONS } \textit{ch}\end{bmatrix}\begin{bmatrix}\text{RIME } \textit{an}\end{bmatrix} \right\rangle \\ \text{TONE } 2 & \end{bmatrix} \end{bmatrix}_{1*} \\ \text{SYNSEM} & \begin{bmatrix} \text{CAT } \textit{noun} \\ \text{SEM } \textit{cicada}_{2*} \end{bmatrix} \\ \text{ORTH} & \{\text{虫}_2, \text{單}_1\} \end{bmatrix}$$

An equivalent representation that we will use – and which will more directly form the basis for our axioms – is the *annotation graph*; see Bird and Liberman (1999) and also Bird (1995). The annotation graphs in (1.9) and (1.10) are equivalent (omitting some detail) to the AVMs in (1.7) and (1.8), respectively.

(1.9)

SEM:	*city*					
PHON:	g : г	o : о	r : р	o : о	d : д	a : **а**

(1.10)

SEM:	*cicada* : 虫	
TONE:	2	
SYL:	*σ* : 單	
ONS-RIME:	*ch*	*an*

The representations of the annotation graphs in (1.9) and (1.10) are to be interpreted as follows. First, the annotations such as "SEM", "SYL", and so forth in the left-hand column mark arc sequences that encode values of the thus-named attribute(s) in the corresponding AVM. Thus in (1.10), for instance, the SEM arc represents the value *cicada* for the attribute SEM. Second, the vertical marks indicate vertices of the graph out of which the horizontal arcs emanate. The vertices are assumed to be temporally anchored, with vertices on the left preceding vertices on the right. Thus the *source* vertex of the ONS arc labeled *ch* in (1.10) – *source*(*ch*) – precedes its destination vertex (*dest*(*ch*)); it also precedes the destination vertex of the SEM arc *cicada*: 虫. We will denote precedence in the standard fashion with "$\prec$" so that $a \prec b$ is read "*a* precedes *b*"; "$\preceq$" will be used to mean "precedes or is cotemporaneous with"; finally "$\succ$" and "$\succeq$" will also be used with the obvious meanings.

Sets of arcs that are in a dominance relation (i.e., form a *graph-based hierarchy* in the sense of Bird and Liberman (1999)) are (vertically) adjacent to each other and are joined at at least one vertex. Sets of arcs that are not in a dominance relation are separated by a blank line. These dominance relations correspond to relations of dominance in the corresponding AVM. So, in (1.10) the SYL and ONS-RIME arc sequences are in a dominance relation: This corresponds to the fact that in the AVM in (1.8), the SYL attribute has an AVM containing the onset and rime AVMs and thus dominates the AVMs. (Similarly, SYL dominates TONE, though TONE is not in a dominance relation with ONS-RIME, a point not well represented in the graph.) However, SEM is not in a dominance relation with SYL. Rather the SEM and SYL arcs merely temporally overlap (Section 1.2.2.2). Finally, we indicate licensing by placing the licensed element on the same arc as its licenser. Thus 'g:r' means that the phoneme /g/ licenses the letter r <g>.

1.2.2.2 Definitions

We now state some definitions and axioms over the annotation graph representation that we have just developed.

First we need some definitions, starting with two versions of temporal overlap:

Definition 1.1 (Overlap) *Arc* α overlaps *arc* β $(\alpha \bigcirc \beta)$ *if either:*

1. $source(\alpha) \preceq source(\beta)$ *and* $dest(\alpha) \succ source(\beta)$, *or*
2. $dest(\alpha) \succeq dest(\beta)$ *and* $source(\alpha) \prec dest(\beta)$.

Definition 1.2 (Complete Overlap) *Arc* α completely overlaps *arc* β $(\alpha \bigcirc_c \beta)$ *if:* $source(\alpha) \preceq source(\beta)$ *and* $dest(\alpha) \succeq dest(\beta)$.

Note that while overlap is symmetric, complete overlap is not. (Note that we use the symbol "$\bigcirc$" for overlap, rather than the more normal $\circ$; this latter symbol is used here for composition.)

Following Bird and Liberman's notion of graph-based hierarchy, we define immediate dominance both in terms of the graph and in terms of the types of arcs involved.

> **Definition 1.3 (Immediate Dominance)** *Arc* α immediately dominates *arc* β *(*$\alpha >_{dom} \beta$*) if* $\alpha \bigcirc_c \beta$ *and the type of* β *is (a list element of) a value of an attribute in AVMs of type* α.

Thus a SYL arc that completely overlaps an ONS arc would immediately dominate the ONS arc assuming in the associated AVM the SYL AVM has an attribute (e.g., SEG) whose value is a list containing the AVM for ONS; cf. (1.8). However, SEM would not dominate ONS.

We will also need a definition of path-precedence on arcs, denoting a situation where two arcs join at the same vertex, such that the second immediately follows on the first within the same path through the graph.

> **Definition 1.4 (Immediate Path-Precedence)** *Arc* α immediately path-precedes *arc* β *(*$\alpha \prec_P \beta$*) if* $dest(\alpha)$ *is identical to* $source(\beta)$.

1.2.2.3 Axioms

This section introduces the axioms that form the core of the theory that we will be defending. Before we do that, we will formalize a few ideas somewhat further. We have already introduced the notion of Orthographically Relevant Level (ORL) as being the level of linguistic representation encoded orthographically by a particular writing system. We will denote the output of the mapping from the ORL to spelling (i.e., the spelling itself) as Γ. As we have already said, we follow Nunn (1998) in assuming that this mapping can be decomposed into a set of graphic encoding rules and a set of autonomous spelling rules; again, see Section 3.5. Each of these sets of mapping rules implements a relation (we will be more specific on what kind of relation momentarily), the former of which we'll notate as M_{Encode} and the latter as M_{Spell}. The entire mapping, which we will denote as $M_{ORL \rightarrow \Gamma}$, is simply the composition of these two relations: $M_{ORL \rightarrow \Gamma} = M_{Encode} \circ M_{Spell}$.

We will use the expression $\gamma(\alpha)$ to denote the *image* of linguistic element α under $M_{ORL \rightarrow \Gamma}$.

The axioms make use of two further concepts. The first is the notion of *catenation*. Informally, α catenates with β, denoted $\alpha \cdot \beta$ if α is adjacent to β. The most familiar notion of catenation is the string-based notion of *concatenation* in formal language theory (Harrison, 1978; Hopcroft and Ullman, 1979; Lewis and Papadimitriou, 1981) where $\alpha \cdot \beta$ constructs a string by concatenating α with β, in that order. In Chapter 2, we will generalize this notion to planar (two-dimensional) catenation. In the discussion in this section, for simplicity's sake, we will assume what we shall later term *left-to-right catenation*, denoted $\vec{\cdot}$: $\alpha \vec{\cdot} \beta$ simply denotes a string $\alpha\beta$, where α immediately precedes β.

The second concept is the idea that the spellout of a linguistic sequence under $M_{ORL \to \Gamma}$ may be lexically specified, as already introduced above. We illustrate this point immediately after the statement of Axiom 1.1.

Axiom 1.1 *If* $\alpha \prec_p \beta$ *then if* $\gamma(\alpha\beta)$ *is not otherwise defined,* $\gamma(\alpha\beta) = \gamma(\alpha) \cdot \gamma(\beta)$. *(If* α *immediately path-precedes* β*, then the image of* $\alpha\beta$ *under* $M_{ORL \to \Gamma}$ *is simply the catenation of* $\gamma(\alpha)$ *with* $\gamma(\beta)$*.)*

Thus in English, the spellout of the phoneme sequence /bo/ would, according to Axiom 1.1, be $\gamma(b) \vec{\cdot} \gamma(o)$, or <bo> (assuming the default ways of spelling those phonemes). However, lexical specification may override this: /ks/ is frequently spelled <x>, preempting spellout as $\gamma(k) \vec{\cdot} \gamma(s)$.

The second axiom describes the mechanism of inheritance of graphical spellout for a complex linguistic construction that immediately dominates other (possibly complex) linguistic constructions:

Axiom 1.2 *If* $\alpha >_{dom} \beta$ *(*β *possibly a sequence) then if* $\gamma(\alpha)$ *is not otherwise defined,* $\gamma(\alpha) = \gamma(\beta)$. *(If* α *immediately dominates* β*, then the image of* α *under* $M_{ORL \to \Gamma}$ *is simply the image of* β *under* $M_{ORL \to \Gamma}$*.)*

Thus, for instance, the spellout of the syllable dominating /kæt/ would consist of the spellout of the onset dominating /k/ and the spellout of the rime dominating /æt/. In turn, the former consists of the spellout of /k/, and the latter the spellout of the sequence /æt/.

Finally, we introduce Axiom 1.3, which defines the spellout of two overlapping elements. The functionality of this axiom will be illustrated with data from Chinese in Section 4.2.

Axiom 1.3 *If* $\alpha \bigcirc \beta$*, then* $\gamma(\alpha, \beta) = \gamma \cdot \beta$. *(If* α *overlaps* β*, then the image of* α *together with* β *under* $M_{ORL \to \Gamma}$ *is simply the image of* α*, catenated with the image of* β*.)*

An important point to note about these axioms is that they do not preclude regular (i.e. nonlexically specified) context-dependent spellout. For instance, the default spelling of /k/ before <i>, <e>, or <y> in English is as <k>, whereas in other contexts it is <c>. Axiom 1.1 merely requires that *whatever spells out /k/* catenate with *whatever spells out the vowel.*

1.2.3 Central Claims of the Theory

We now come to the core proposals that I wish to defend in the remainder of this work:

- **Regularity**: *The mapping* $M_{ORL \to \Gamma}$ *is a regular relation.*
- **Consistency**: *The ORL for a given writing system (as used for a particular language) represents a consistent level of linguistic representation.*

We describe these claims in the next two sections. Here, and elsewhere in this work, I will capitalize the terms "Regular," "Regularity," "Consistent," and "Consistency" when they are used in these technical senses, and otherwise lower case them.

1.2.3.1 Regularity

The first of the core proposals states that $M_{ORL \to \Gamma}$ is a regular relation or, equivalently, that $M_{ORL \to \Gamma}$ can be implemented as a *finite-state transducer* (FST); readers not familiar with FSTs may wish to consult Appendix 1.A, though a short synopsis is given immediately below.

Our route to the claim of Regularity comes about in two ways. First, we have assumed that the mapping between linguistic representation and orthography can be handled by context-sensitive rewrite rules, an assumption held by others including Venezky (1970) and Nunn (1998), and it is one which naturally fits well with the standard notion of "spelling rule." Now, as has been shown in Johnson (1972) and Kaplan and Kay (1994), as long as certain constraints on nonapplication to their own output are observed, such rules are formally equivalent to regular relations and can therefore be implemented using FSTs. Indeed, practical compilers have been built that compile from rewrite rule representations into transducers (Karttunen and Beesley, 1992; Kaplan and Kay, 1994; Karttunen, 1995; Mohri and Sproat, 1996). An instance of an FST – one implementing the simple set of rules in (1.5) – is shown in Figure 1.2.

Second, Regularity follows from the axioms introduced in Section 1.2.2.3. To see this, consider that each of the axioms states that in $\gamma(\alpha\beta)$, composed of $\gamma(\alpha)$ and $\gamma(\beta)$, $\gamma(\alpha)$ is catenated with $\gamma(\beta)$. The definition of regular relations (see Appendix 1.A.2) states first that a mapping between a pair of symbols is a regular relation, and furthermore that the concatenation of two regular relations is itself a regular relation. It is therefore easy to see that one can provide a constructive proof whereby Regularity follows from the stated axioms. In one sense, the axioms provide a rather restrictive notion of Regularity. Consider a writing system in which a linguistic object $\alpha\beta\delta\zeta$ is spelled out as $\gamma(\alpha)\gamma(\delta)\gamma(\zeta)\gamma(\beta)$. For example, the writing system might have the (bizarre) property that the second phoneme is always spelled out at the end of the word. This would certainly be a violation of the axioms insofar as the spelled string is not formed by concatenating either $\gamma(\alpha)$

Figure 1.2. A simple FST implementing the rewrite rules in (1.5). In this example the machine has a single state (0), which is both an initial and a final state. The labels on the individual arcs consist of an *input label* (to the left of the colon) and an *output label* (to the right). Here, capital Roman letters are used to represent the equivalent Cyrillic letters.

or $\gamma(\delta)$ with $\gamma(\beta)$. However, this example can be handled by a regular relation that in effect maps a symbol – here β – to nothing (ϵ) on the output side, "remembers" that it has seen β, and then spells it out as $\gamma(\beta)$ at the end of the string. But such "memory" comes at some cost in finite-state machinery, since such a machine must represent intervening material multiple times: In addition to mapping δ to $\gamma(\delta)$ and ζ to $\gamma(\zeta)$, the machine must also remember which second phoneme (β) it had seen, and the only way to do this is to have separate paths through the remaining portions of the transducer, one path for each phoneme that might have been deleted. Memory in finite-state devices can only be encoded in states: If one wishes to delete β with a view to inserting $\gamma(\beta)$ later on, then one must have the arc that deletes β end in a state s_1 distinct from the state s_2 that terminates an arc that, for instance, deletes θ (inserted later on as $\gamma(\theta)$). The states s_1 and s_2 would in turn be the source for arcs that map δ to $\gamma(\delta)$ and ζ to $\gamma(\zeta)$, and they would each have their own private copies of these arcs. Writing systems generally do not seem to require this kind of memory. At first one might think such cases are common. Consider, for instance, the spelling of English /eɪ/ as <aCe>, where 'C' is a consonant (*make*) or sequence of consonants (*taste*). If <e> is somehow part of the spelling of /eɪ/, then this would seem to be a violation of the axioms. However, it seems perfectly reasonable to assume that /eɪ/ is in fact spelled by <a> and that <e> is merely introduced by rule to "support" the spelling of /eɪ/ as <a> in certain environments; see Cummings (1988).

An important feature of regular relations is that they are closed under *composition*. Suppose we have two regular relations R_1 and R_2, and suppose that the domain of R_1 is (the set of strings) x, with its range y, and suppose further that the domain of R_2 is y and its range is z. Then the composition of these two relations, denoted $R_1 \circ R_2$, is also a regular relation whose domain is x and range is z. (The notion of composition here is exactly the same notion as that of function composition in algebra.) This property of closure under composition has an important implication. Since single rewrite rules can be represented computationally as FSTs, one can also represent an ordered series of such rewrite rules as a single FST, by merely composing together the FSTs for the individual rules.

A second important property of regular relations and FSTs is that they are *invertible*. That is, by switching the input and output labels, one switches the domain and range of a relation. In the case at hand, if one has a transducer M that maps from ORL to Γ, then the inverse of M, denoted M^{-1}, will map from Γ to the ORL. This is clearly a useful property since it means that a model of spelling can also serve (inverted) as a model of reading – in the limited sense of decoding a linguistic structure from a written text.

In addition to using regular relations and FSTs to implement the mapping between the ORL and Γ, one can also implement constraints using regular *languages* and finite-state acceptors (FSAs). Finite-state constraint-based systems have been used widely in other areas of linguistic description, such as phonology (Bird and Ellison, 1994) and syntax (Voutilainen, 1994; Mohri, 1994). In writing systems, surface spelling constraints can be modeled in this fashion. For instance, if a certain written symbol l is disallowed in word-final position one might write a constraint such as the following (where '#' denotes a word boundary):

(1.11) $\neg\, l\, \#$

See Section 3.5 for some discussion of real examples of surface orthographic constraints.

As we have already discussed, we follow Nunn (1998) in our assumption that the relation Γ can be decomposed into a composition of the set of graphic encoding rules M_{Encode} and the set of autonomous spelling rules M_{Spell}. At this point we can be more specific in our claim: M_{Encode} and M_{Spell} both implement regular relations and Γ is the composition of those two regular relations: $M_{Encode} \circ M_{Spell}$. Surface orthographic constraints are clearly a component of M_{Spell}: One can factor M_{Spell} into two components, one that implements a mapping $M_{Spell_{map}}$, and the other that implements a set of constraints $M_{Spell_{constr}}$. M_{Spell} itself is then just the composition of these two, or more formally:

(1.12) $M_{Spell} = M_{Spell_{map}} \circ Id(M_{Spell_{constr}})$.

Here, Id is an operation that converts an FSA into an equivalent FST, where the input and output labels on each arc are identical (Kaplan and Kay, 1994, page 341).

Finally, we have been implicitly assuming in this discussion a model of regular relations that contains a standard string-based "left-to-right" concatenation operator. As we have already noted, we will need to extend the notion of catenation to handle various forms of two-dimensional combination. We will discuss this in Chapter 2.

1.2.3.2 Consistency

In Section 1.2.1 we introduced the notion of the Orthographically Relevant Level, and we suggested that depending upon the writing system, the ORL could represent a relatively deep or relatively shallow orthographic level. The thesis of Consistency simply states that this level is consistent across the entire vocabulary of the language. As should be clear, and as we will discuss further, this notion presumes a classical derivational model of phonology.

Consider a sequence of phonological rules $R_1 R_2 \ldots R_n$, which applies in the derivation of every word of some language. We will define U to be the input level to the sequence of rules. For such a system, there are $n + 1$ consistent levels of representation, namely U itself and U composed with $R_1 \ldots R_i$, $i \leq n$. The Consistency hypothesis requires the ORL to be picked from one of these consistent levels i. A violation of Consistency would be a system where one portion of the vocabulary (e.g., all nouns or all words having a particular phonological structure) picks a level i, and the remainder of the vocabulary picks a level j, $i \neq j$.

The model described in the last paragraph could be expanded to support more intricate notions of consistency. For instance, in a Lexical Phonology-based theory (Mohanan, 1986), instead of sequences of rules, we might think in terms of sequences of strata. The ORL could then be picked to be either the input level or else the output of one of the strata. This would of course be a more constrained theory of consistency, and probably one that should be favored over the looser model previously described. We will not, however, attempt to choose between these variant models here. Note that a similar question was raised by Klima (1972), who asked (page 67) "which levels of linguistic structure ... are then *most readily accessible* to the process of reading and writing?" (italics original).

An additional issue is cyclicity. If a morphologically complex word is constructed in a cyclic fashion, might it be the case that orthographic features of the morphemes are also added cyclically? In what sense then could we speak of orthography mapping to a single level? See Section 3.4 for further discussion.

Consistency will be exemplified in Chapter 3 with a comparison of Russian and Belarusian orthographies, as well as a discussion of (American) English orthography. We will also examine an apparent counterexample to Consistency from Serbo-Croatian. As we shall see, Consistency forces a reanalysis of the Serbo-Croatian data, which leads in turn to a more insightful description of the phenomenon than the traditional description. Even in quite regular systems such as Russian, one does in fact find cases where the orthography would appear to map to a deeper or shallower level of representation than would be expected on the basis of the posited ORL for the remainder of the vocabulary. We shall see such examples in the discussion of Russian and Belarusian in Chapter 3. As long as the exceptions constitute a small minority – as is the case in the Russian and Belarusian examples that we shall discuss – they can always be handled by means of lexical marking, though naturally this device comes at some cost. The examples in Chapter 3 will thus be seen generally to support Consistency, but we will necessarily leave it as a topic for future research to determine whether Consistency is supported more broadly across the world's writing systems.

The assumption that orthography may represent a particular level – deep or shallow – of a language is implicit in many discussions of reading in the psycholinguistics literature; it is arguably implicit in Venezky's 1970 classic analysis of English orthography; and it is a claim also made in *The Sound Pattern of English* (Chomsky and Halle, 1968), where English orthography is described as a "near perfect" representation of an underlying phonological representation.

As we have already noted, we take as the basis for Consistency a traditional derivational model of phonology. This is surely a controversial move: Naturally it would seem desirable in light of modern nonderivational theories of phonology to cast our analysis in terms of a nonderivational paradigm. For example, it would be natural to seek an account of the phenomena that we will discuss in terms of a monostratal theory such as those of Bird and Ellison (1994), Bird and Klein (1994) and Bird (1995). Similarly, one might desire an account in terms of Optimality Theory (Prince and Smolensky, 1993), where the only linguistic level in effect is the output level at which the rank-ordered constraints are evaluated (at least on one version of the theory). It is not at present clear to me how to do this. While I do not doubt, for example, that an analysis of the Russian and Belarusian facts to be discussed in Chapter 3 could be recast in terms of such a framework, they seem to be describable most naturally within a model wherein one can speak of different levels of representation. Once again, I leave it as a topic for future research to work out analyses within more current phonological frameworks.

1.2.4 Further Issues

In this section we discuss two issues that the current work and the model presented herein raise. The first issue (Section 1.2.4.1) concerns the following question: Given that writing, unlike natural language, is an artefact, one that – again unlike natural language – must be explicitly taught, why should one believe that a constrained model of the kind typically applied to language would apply to writing? The second issue (Section 1.2.4.2) relates to our adoption of a phonological model that includes segments: Given that many phonographic writing systems are essentially "segmental" (the basic symbols representing segment-sized units), this is certainly a convenient choice, yet it seems to fly in the face of more recent models of phonology that eschew segments.

1.2.4.1 Why a Constrained Theory of Writing Systems?

It may have occurred to the reader to wonder why a constrained theory of writing systems should have any chance of being correct. To be sure, such models have been applied in linguistics with great success. But writing is crucially different from other aspects of linguistic knowledge. Language occurs naturally in all human communities. Writing, in contrast, is a technological development that was apparently only independently invented four times in history (in Egypt, Sumer, China, and Central America) and has only been used by a minority of languages and people throughout most of history. With few exceptions all humans learn to speak (or sign) at least one language without any special instruction; in contrast, reading and writing must be taught explicitly and in many cases takes years of special instruction to master. Writing is therefore not "natural" in the same sense as language.

One might even go further than this: Writing systems are *developed* for particular languages, with more or less care being taken to ensure that they reflect the linguistic properties of the language in question. Furthermore, at least a few writing systems have undergone reforms over the years, to attempt to bring the system more in line with the language (see Section 6.2). Orthography, then, can be thought of as a kind of practical linguistic theory.

This latter view has been expressed perhaps best by Aronoff (1985) in a paper describing the punctuation system of Masoretic Hebrew. Masoretic annotations evolved as a way of marking various information about Biblical Hebrew text, in particular information about how to pronounce and accent or intone the text. The system was based on diacritics, with annotations being added to, but not altering, the core consonantal text, which was considered sacred. The system for marking vowels survives as the (optional) vowel points of Modern Hebrew. The notation for accent, which is the topic of Aronoff's discussion, is only used in the Bible. Aronoff argues that the accentual marking system in fact marks "a complete unlabeled binary phrase-structure analysis of every verse" of the Bible (page 28). It thus represents the end product of conscious linguistic analysis and thus in effect encodes a linguistic theory of what the phrase structure of Hebrew should look like. Furthermore, like any linguistic theory, the Masoretic annotation system can be incorrect in the structures it presumes for particular constructions. Indeed Aronoff argues that the analysis implicit in the annotation is in some cases incorrect.

As Aronoff notes, the Masoretic system is quite unusual in the richness of linguistic structure that is marked. Certainly no orthographic system that is in wide use has conventions for marking constituent structure. (One might think of normal punctuation symbols as marking some level of syntactic or phonological phrasing, but Nunberg (1995) effectively argues against this.) And of course the Masoretic system is atypical in another respect: It was not an orthographic system used by native speakers of a language for everyday communication, but rather a system designed specifically to give precise guidance in the pronunciation of sacred texts to nonnative speakers (since Hebrew was, during the relevant period, nobody's mother tongue). From that point of view, the system has more in common with systems of annotation for marking scansion in poetry than it does with the orthographic system of, say, Modern English. Nonetheless, to the extent that conscious effort goes into the design of more typical orthographies, Aronoff's points remain valid. These considerations would thus appear to argue against applying the same kinds of methods in the study of writing as in the study of language more generally. There are however at least a couple of basic reasons why such pessimism is ill-founded.

Firstly, while writing surely must be learned, and while writing systems are often consciously designed, they must also be used, which means that to be practical they must bear some sensible relation to the languages that they represent. Presumably by "sensible" we imply nonarbitrary, and by "nonarbitrary" we mean that it should be possible to state formal constraints. Whether Consistency and Regularity, introduced in Section 1.2.3, are reasonable constraints is an empirical question. What is not in doubt, in my view, is that some such constraints must exist.

Secondly, while orthographic systems certainly depend upon the linguistic knowledge of their creators, influences in the other direction are also found. First of all, as Wells (1982) notes, the orthographic representation of words is often the basis for speakers' *conscious* beliefs about their pronunciation: naive English speakers may believe that *tow* and *toe* are pronounced differently because they are spelled differently. Secondly, there are so-called spelling pronunciations, such as /vˈɪktʃuəlz/ (rather than /vˈɪtəlz/) for *victuals*, where the phonological representation of individual words has been modified over time on the basis of spelling. Thirdly, one also finds more systematic effects on the phonology on the basis of written form. Thus, according to Serianni (1989), Northern Italian dialects historically lack gemination – termed *raddoppiamento* in the Italian literature – both within words and across words – the so-called *raddoppiamento sintattico*. Cross-word gemination is not written in standard Italian orthography, and Northern dialects continue to lack *raddoppiamento sintattico*. However, word-internal *raddoppiamento* as in the second /m/ of *mamma* 'mama,' is consistently spelled. As a result, northern dialects, which historically lacked word-internal *raddoppiamento* now possess it. Linguistic knowledge is often assumed to be in some sense primary, or at least more basic than orthographic knowledge. Spelling pronunciations and examples like those in Italian show that in some cases particular bits of linguistic knowledge can best be explained on the basis of orthography. This in turn suggests the need to understand the relation between orthography and linguistic structure, as well as the formal constraints on that relation.

1.2.4.2 Orthography and the "Segmental" Assumption

In the discussion above, we assumed that the graphemes in a segmental phonographic system such as Russian are licensed by phonological segments in the traditional sense. In making this assumption, we may seem to be taking two steps backwards. Several strands of work in phonology over the past decade and a half, including Feature Geometry (Clements, 1985; Sagey, 1986), Declarative Phonology (Coleman, 1998), and Articulatory Phonology (Browman and Goldstein, 1989), have converged on the conclusion that segments are epiphenomena, the result of overlapping gestures. Indeed, there seems to be a widely accepted dogma that the very notion of segment in Western phonological tradition derives from segmental alphabetic writing.

We should note at the outset that in one sense this issue is orthogonal to the model being developed here. That is, I have chosen to represent the licenser of Russian г <g> as the segment /g/, but I could just as easily not have. If we have instead a set of overlapping gestures (e.g., VELAR, +VOICE, −CONTINUANT, −NASAL), each on its own arc in an annotation graph representation, then we can assume that this collection of features together licenses г <g>. One implementation of this idea would be to assume that the timing slot or syllable position that is linked to the overlapping set of features is the licenser of г <g> and can only license this grapheme by virtue of the collection of features that it is associated with. Those who are bothered by my use of segmental phonological representations are invited to think of them as a shorthand for the more articulated view I have just sketched.

The view that the notion "segment" in phonology derives from segmental writing is overly facile, and should not be uncritically accepted, I believe. Perhaps the best articulated presentation of this concept is a paper by Faber (1992) where she sets herself the task of explaining the following paradox: The notion of segment is unnatural and derives in part from alphabetic writing: "investigations of language use suggest that many speakers do not divide words into phonological segments unless they have received explicit instruction in such segmentation comparable to that involved in teaching an alphabetic writing system" (page 111). But alphabetic writing systems do exist. How could they have come about in the first place if the principles upon which they are based are so unnatural?

Faber's answer makes use of the standard view that when the Greeks adopted the Phoenician script, they misinterpreted some of the consonantal symbols as representing vowels. Thus the use of *alpha* to represent /a/ was a misinterpretation of Phoenician /ʔalpa/, representing /ʔ/. This much is widely accepted, and it therefore is possible that the Greek inventors of the segmental alphabet did not have an a priori notion of segment: On the contrary, they *thought* they were borrowing a system of writing that represented both vowels and consonants.

A reasonable question at this point is why Faber is focusing on the Greek alphabet (and its derivatives). After all, there are many apparently segmental systems in the world, including numerous South Asian scripts such as Devanagari (see Section 2.3.2), Korean Hankul (Section 2.3.1), and Ethiopic (Haile, 1996). Some of these, such as the South Asian scripts, may have had a Semitic origin (Salomon, 1996), like Greek – though surely independently of Greek. For others, such as Hankul, which is a totally endemic Korean invention, the external inspiration (if any) for designing a segmental system is unclear (King, 1996). Indeed, even unvocalized Semitic writing systems could be considered segmental, though they traditionally omit marks for vowels: As with the nonrepresentation of lexical stress in Russian (Section 1.2.1) we can say that the *coverage* of traditional Semitic scripts is incomplete.

Faber concentrates on Greek because she takes a rather narrow view of the notion of "alphabetic writing," and it is only "alphabetic writing," according to Faber, that engenders the paradoxical situation introduced above. For her an alphabet is a "segmentally linear script" that represents "vowels and consonants both as separate and equal." The latter requirement, of course, eliminates traditional Semitic scripts from consideration: They do not represent vowels. "Segmentally linear" scripts are scripts where the elements are arranged in a more or less linear fashion, without any significant use of two-dimensional layout: Only in such scripts are all elements on a par with each other. Thus South Asian scripts and Hankul scripts are eliminated, since in both cases the consonant and vowel symbols are laid out in two-dimensional (syllable-sized) chunks (Sections 2.3.2 and 2.3.1); furthermore in many South Asian scripts (though not so clearly in the case of Hankul), the vowels are frequently diacritic symbols written around the consonantal core, and thus they are not on a par with each other. If one narrows the field in this fashion, then, it would seem that segmental writing was really only invented once, by accident, and we do not need to attribute any "naturalness" to the notion of segment.

Still, one might wonder about the justification for the limitations that Faber imposes. Why is Devanagari any less segmental than Greek? Just because it happens to represent /e/ as a stroke above the temporally preceding /k/, whereas Greek arranges the symbols by left-to-right concatenation? Faber's point, not surprisingly, is that scripts such as Devanagari (or Ethiopic, or Hankul) arrange their segmental elements in syllable-sized chunks (in Chapter 2 we will say that in such scripts the *Small Linguistic Unit* is the syllable), which are themselves linearly arranged ("segmentally coded, syllabically linear"). In other words, the syllable has a special status in such scripts that is seemingly lacking in Greek-derived ("segmentally coded, segmentally linear") scripts.

Now, one cannot deny the importance of the syllable as an organizing principle in orthographies. We will see several instances of this in Chapter 2, and syllables even show themselves to be important in "segmentally linear" scripts; see Section 3.5 and Nunn (1998). But Ethiopic, South Asian scripts, Hankul, and other scripts also encode segmental information. This point, it seems to me, is not nullified by the fact that the scripts also encode syllabic information. Segmental systems have evolved, or been developed, in a variety of different cultures, speaking a wide variety of languages, and under a variety of different conditions. The notion "segment" may be an unnatural epiphenomenon, but if so, then at least it is one that is fairly widespread.

1.3 Terminology and Conventions

This section outlines the terminology and conventions that we use throughout this book.

We will use the terms "script," "orthography," and "writing system" in their conventional senses as follows: A "script" is just a set of distinct marks conventionally used to represent the written form of one or more languages. Crucially, one can speak of a script without implying its use for a given language. Thus we will speak of the "Roman script" or the "Chinese script." A writing system however is a script used to represent a particular language. Thus "writing system" implies "writing system for a given language."[7] We will use the terms "orthography" and "writing system" interchangeably;[8]

[7] One could go further and define the notion of writing system at a more abstract level whereby, for example, the Braille encoding of the Roman alphabet, as used for English, is an instance of the same writing system as is used in printed English – though obviously the script is quite different. (Actually to make this connection, one would have to gloss over the fact that braille has various lexical and string-based abbreviatory conventions that have no direct counterpart in standard print.) We will not be concerned with this level of abstraction here.

[8] Though properly an orthography is really merely one type of writing system; see Mountford (1996).

in some of the literature, the term "orthography" implies "standardized orthography," such as the standard system of spelling used in American English, and this implicitly excludes systems of writing that have not been standardized (as was the case in, say, Elizabethan English). Though we will primarily be discussing standardized orthographies in this work, we do not intend the term to carry with it any implication of standardization.

The following notational conventions will be observed:

- Angle brackets will be used to enclose orthographic representations in Roman script. Note that this will *only* be the case when in the discussion at hand the focus is on the orthographic representation. For example in a discussion of a linguistic example containing the word *frog*, that word will be italicized as per normal linguistic convention, if we are merely referring to the linguistic object (word, morpheme, ...) *frog*. However if we are specifically interested in the string of characters 'f', 'r', 'o', and 'g', then angle brackets will be used: <frog>.
- Examples in non-Roman scripts will generally be transliterated, with the transliteration given in angle brackets. Phonemic transcriptions and translations will be given where relevant. Inevitably some single characters of a non-Roman script will need to be transliterated with a sequence of characters in Roman script; in such cases, the sequence of characters will be underlined in order to indicate that it is a unit. For example: (Cyrillic) я <ja>.
  For scripts that run from right-to-left, I will indicate this by marking the string of graphemes with the symbol '←'.
  For Chinese writing I will adopt a slightly more complex strategy, at least in cases where the internal structure of Chinese characters is under discussion. As many as 97% of Chinese characters can be analyzed as being composed of a semantic radical plus a phonetic component (DeFrancis, 1984). In cases where this decomposition is feasible I will "gloss" the character in small capitals: <SEMANTIC+PHONETIC>. Here SEMANTIC will be a conventional term to describe the semantic radical in question, and PHONETIC will be a phonetic transcription in pinyin of the pronunciation of the phonetic component; more on the transcription of the phonetic component will be presented momentarily. Following this will be given a phonetic transcription in pinyin of the whole character, and an English gloss where possible and relevant.
  Choosing the appropriate transcription for the phonetic component is not as straightforward as it might seem. First, many phonetic components have more than one pronunciation as

independent characters. For example, the phonetic component of 蟬 *chán* 'cicada', namely 單, has two independent pronunciations, namely *dān* and *chán*. Secondly, in a number of cases, no independent pronunciation of the phonetic component is particularly similar to the pronunciation of the semantic–phonetic compound, but a significant fraction of the characters that contain that phonetic component have an identical pronunciation, possibly ignoring tone, to the character of interest. A particularly striking instance involves the phonetic component 丑, which as an independent character is pronounced *chǒu*, but as a phonetic component is always pronounced *niu* (with various tones). In such a case, one is arguably justified in transcribing the phonetic component as *niu* rather than *chǒu*.

In deciding how to transcribe the phonetic component of a character we therefore adopt the strategy of finding the closest match between the pronunciation of the semantic–phonetic compound among:

- the attested *independent* pronunciations of the phonetic and
- the pronunciations of well-populated subsets of those characters sharing the same phonetic component.

In case we make use of the second of these options, we indicate the ratio of:

- the number of characters listed in Wieger (1965) with the phonetic component *and* the pronunciation of interest and
- the total number of characters in Wieger's lists with that phonetic component.

We also list the page number(s) in Wieger where one can find the characters with that phonetic component. If the tones differ among the members of the subset, and only in that case, we omit tonemarks from the transcription.

For instance, for 蝗 *huáng* 'locust' the transcription would be <INSECT+HUÁNG>[9] where *huáng* happens to be the independent pronunciation of the phonetic component 皇 'emperor'. For 蟬 *chán* 'cicada' we transcribe <INSECT+CHÁN>, where *chán* is one of the independent pronunciations of 單, though not the most frequent. For 醍 *tí*, the phonetic component is 是, whose only independent pronunciation is *shì*. However, a significant number of characters listed in Wieger (1965) with 是 as a phonetic component have the pronunciation *tí*, and thus we transcribe 醍 as <WINE+TÍ$_{9/19\ p.498}$>, meaning that in nine out of nineteen characters with 是 as a phonetic component (page 498), Wieger lists the pronunciation as

[9] I.e., 虫+皇.

tí. This method of transcription, while surely not uncontroversial, is at least replicable.

In cases where the internal structure of the Chinese character is not at issue, I will in general dispense with the detailed character-structure gloss and merely give a phonetic transliteration in pinyin and (where possible or relevant) an English gloss.[10]

- I will use the term *grapheme* to denote a basic symbol of a writing system, despite the valid objections to the use of that term outlined in Daniels (1991a,b). However, note that Daniels's objections are aimed at the use of the term *grapheme* as an implicit parallel of *phoneme*: His contention is that there is no "systematic graphemics" parallel to a systematic phonemic level. I do not wish to contend this point and merely use the term *grapheme* as a convenient short way of saying "basic symbol of a writing system."

  Note that in discussing some writing systems we may use the term grapheme in slightly different ways depending upon how fine-grained an analysis is being assumed. For instance, it is convenient to refer to a single Chinese character as being a grapheme in some contexts. In particular, in the electronic coding of texts it is invariably the case that single Chinese characters constitute separate codes, and thus from the point of view of a computational system (such as a TTS system), Chinese characters are unanalyzable basic units. However, there is clearly important internal structure in Chinese characters (cf. the semantic+phonetic composition of Chinese characters alluded to above) and from the point of view of a finer-grained analysis of Chinese writing, these smaller units would certainly be called graphemes.

  I will also use the term *glyph* conventionally to refer to a written symbol with a particular shape, independently of whether it corresponds to a single grapheme or multiple graphemes. Thus in my discussion of Korean Hankul (Section 2.3.1) I will refer to "syllable-sized glyphs" as well as consonant and vowel glyphs; the latter correspond to single graphemes, whereas the former are polygraphemic.
- Where there is unlikely to be confusion I will use the name of language X to denote "the orthography of language X." Thus "Chinese" will denote Chinese orthography, except where this usage is likely to be confusing.

[10] Note that throughout this work, I will use traditional Chinese characters as used in Taiwan and Hong Kong and eschew the use of simplified characters as used on the Mainland and Singapore, except where the structure of such simplified characters is at issue.

1.A Appendix: An Overview of Finite-State Automata and Transducers

This appendix gives an overview of regular languages and relations and their associated computational devices, finite-state automata, or acceptors (FSAs), and finite-state transducers (FSTs). The coverage here is necessarily brief, and for further discussion other sources are recommended. Finite-state acceptors and regular languages are discussed in any good introduction to the theory of computation; see, for example Harrison (1978), Hopcroft and Ullman (1979), or Lewis and Papadimitriou (1981). There are fewer introductory works on transducers. One reasonably accessible discussion (dealing with transducers) can be found in Kaplan and Kay (1994). One might also consult the third chapter of Sproat (1992) for an in-depth introduction to the use of finite-state transducers in computational phonology and morphology. For transducers (as well as weighted acceptors), there is a recent paper by Mohri (1997) that discusses various formal properties and algorithms, and various other relevant works are cited therein. See also Mohri (2000) for in-depth discussion of algorithms and other properties of FSTs.

1.A.1 Regular Languages and Finite-State Automata

Basic to the theory of automata is the notion of an *alphabet* of symbols; the entire alphabet is conventionally denoted Σ. The *empty string* is denoted by ϵ, which is *not* an element of Σ; also, the empty string is distinct from the *empty set* $\emptyset$. Σ^* denotes the set of all strings – including ϵ – over the alphabet Σ.

It is usual to define a *regular language* with a recursive definition such as the following (modeled on that of Kaplan and Kay (1994, page 338)):

1. $\emptyset$ is a regular language.
2. For all symbols $a \in \Sigma \cup \epsilon$, $\{a\}$ is a regular language.
3. If L_1, L_2, and L are regular languages, then so are
   (a) $L_1 \cdot L_2$, the *concatenation* of L_1 and L_2: for every $w_1 \in L_1$ and $w_2 \in L_2$, $w_1 w_2 \in L_1 \cdot L_2$;
   (b) $L_1 \cup L_2$, the *union* of L_1 and L_2;
   (c) L^*, the *Kleene closure* of L. Using L^i to denote L concatenated with itself i times, $L^* = \cup_{i=0}^{\infty} L^i$.

While the above definition is complete, regular languages observe additional *closure* properties:

- *Intersection*: If L_1 and L_2 are regular languages then so is $L_1 \cap L_2$.
- *Difference*: If L_1 and L_2 are regular languages then so is $L_1 - L_2$, the set of strings in L_1 that are not in L_2.

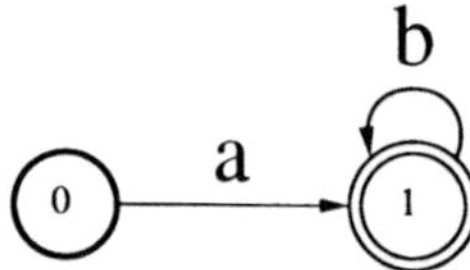

Figure 1.3. An acceptor for ab^*. The heavy-circled state (0) is (conventionally) the initial state, and the double-circled state is the final state.

- *Complementation*: If L is a regular language, then so is $\Sigma^* - L$, the set of all strings over Σ that are *not* in L. (Of course, complementation is merely a special case of difference.)
- *Reversal*: If L is a regular language, then so is $Rev(L)$, the set of reversals of all strings in L.

Regular languages are sets of strings, and they are usually notated using *regular expressions*. A fundamental result of automata theory are the so-called Kleene's theorems, which demonstrate that regular languages are exactly the languages that can be recognized using *finite-state automata*, where this computational device can be defined as follows (Harrison, 1978; Hopcroft and Ullman, 1979; Lewis and Papadimitriou, 1981):

A finite-state automaton is a quintuple $M = (K, s, F, \Sigma, \delta)$ where:

1. K is a finite set of states,
2. s is a designated initial state,
3. F is a designated set of final states,
4. Σ is an alphabet of symbols, and
5. δ is a transition relation from $K \times \Sigma$ to K.

As a simple example, consider the (infinite) set of strings: $\{a, ab, abb, abbb \ldots\}$ (i.e., the set consisting of a followed by zero or more bs). The most compact regular expression denoting this set is ab^*. Furthermore, the language can be recognized by the finite-state machine given in Figure 1.3.

1.A.2 Regular Relations and Finite-State Transducers

Regular n-relations can be defined in a way entirely parallel to regular languages. Again, the definition given here is modeled on that of Kaplan and Kay (1994):

1. $\emptyset$ is a regular n-relation.
2. For all symbols $a \in [(\Sigma \cup \epsilon) \times \ldots \times (\Sigma \cup \epsilon)]$, $\{a\}$ is a regular n-relation.

3. If R_1, R_2, and R are regular n-relations, then so are
   (a) $R_1 \cdot R_2$, the *(n-way) concatenation* of R_1 and R_2: for every $r_1 \in R_1$ and $r_2 \in R_2$, $r_1 r_2 \in R_1 \cdot R_2$;
   (b) $R_1 \cup R_2$;
   (c) R^*, the *n-way Kleene closure* of R.

One can think of regular n-relations as *accepting* strings of a relation stated over an m-tuple of symbols, and mapping them to strings of a relation stated over a k-tuple of symbols, where $m + k = n$. We can therefore speak more specifically of $m \times k$-relations. As in the case of regular languages, there are further closure properties that regular n-relations obey:[11]

- *Composition*: If R_1 is a regular $k \times m$-relation and R_2 is a regular $m \times p$-relation, then $R_1 \circ R_2$ is a regular $k \times p$-relation. Composition will be explained below.
- *Reversal*: If R is a regular n-relation, then so is $Rev(R)$.
- *Inversion*: If R is a regular $m \times n$-relation, then R^{-1}, the *inverse* of R, is a regular $n \times m$-relation.

One computes the inverse of a transducer by simply switching the input and output labels. The fact that regular relations are closed under inversion has an important practical consequence for systems based on finite-state transducers, namely that they are fully bidirectional. Thus, as we noted in Section 1.2.3.1, a model of spelling (mapping from the ORL to Γ) can be turned into a model of reading (mapping from Γ to the ORL) by simply inverting the FST implementing $M_{ORL \to \Gamma}$.

For most practical applications of n-relations $n = 2$ (so that k and m are obviously both 1).[12] In this case we can speak of a relation as mapping from strings of one regular language into strings of another. In this work we will be concerned exclusively with 2-relations, and we will use the term *regular relations* with that meaning throughout.

The computational device corresponding to a regular relation is a *finite-state transducer*. The definition of FST can be modeled on the definition of FSAs given above, so we will merely illustrate by example, rather than essentially repeat the definition. Say we have an alphabet $\Sigma = \{a, b, c, d\}$ and a regular relation over that alphabet expressed by the set: $\{(a, c)$, (ab, cd), (abb, cdd), $(abbb, cddd) \ldots\}$. The relation thus consists of a mapping to c followed by zero or more bs mapping to d. This relation can be represented compactly by the *two-way regular expression* $a{:}c\ (b{:}d)^*$. Figure 1.4 depicts an FST that computes this relation. We refer to the expressions on the

[11] The omission of difference, complementation, and intersection is intentional. In general, regular relations are *not* closed under these operations, though some important subclasses of regular relations are. See Kaplan and Kay (1994) for further discussion.

[12] One exception is the work of Kiraz (forthcoming).

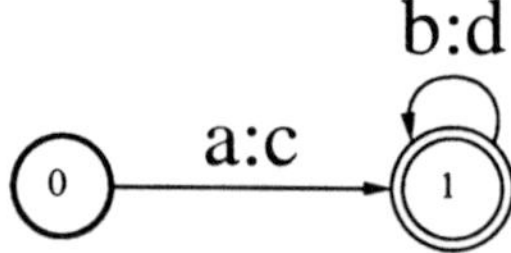

Figure 1.4. An FST that accepts *a:c (b:d)**.

left-hand side of the ':' as the input side; the expressions on the right-hand side is the output side. Thus, in Figure 1.4, the input side is characterizable by the regular expression ab^*, and the output side by the expression cd^*.

Composition of regular relations has the same interpretation as composition of functions: If R_1 and R_2 are regular relations, then applying $R_1 \circ R_2$ to an input expression I is the same as applying R_1 to I first and then applying R_2 to the output. Figure 1.5 depicts two transducers, labeled T_1

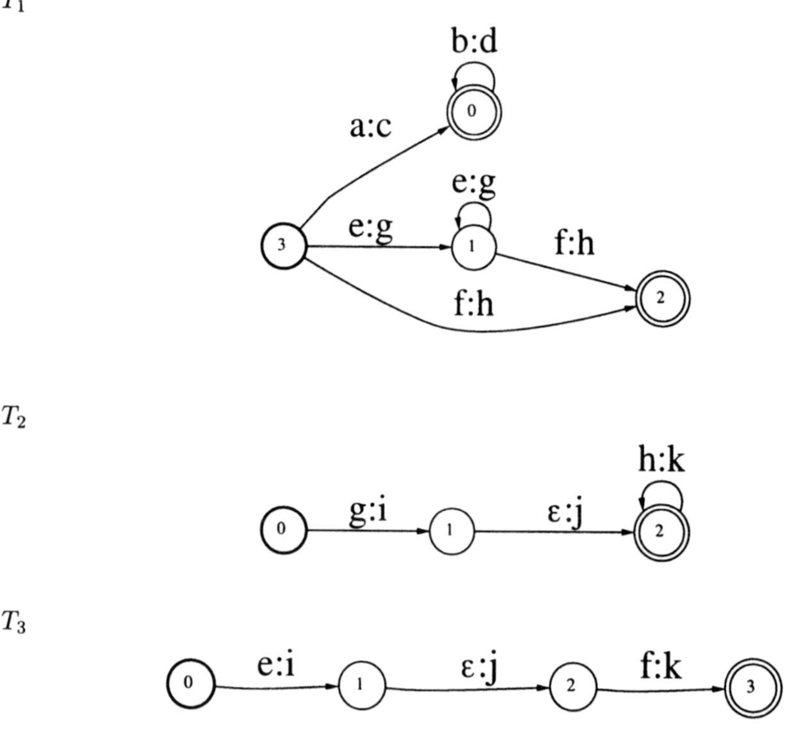

Figure 1.5. Three transducers, where $T_3 = T_1 \circ T_2$.

and T_2. T_1 computes the relation expressable as $(a{:}c\ (b{:}d)^*)\ |\ ((e{:}g)^*\ f{:}h)$ (where | denotes disjunction), whereas T_2 computes $g{:}i\ \epsilon{:}j\ h{:}k^*$ (with the $\epsilon{:}j$ term inserting a *j*). The result of composing the two transducers together ($T_1 \circ T_2$) is a transducer that computes the trivial relation, $e{:}i\ \epsilon{:}j\ f{:}k$. In this particular case, though both T_1 and T_2 express relations with infinite domains and ranges; the result of composition merely maps the string *ef* to *ijk*.

One other notion worth mentioning is that of *projection* onto one dimension of a relation. For example, for a 2-way relation R, $\pi_1(R)$ projects R onto the first dimension and $\pi_2(R)$ projects onto the second dimension. Projection applied to an FST produces an FSA corresponding to one side of the transducer. Thus the first projection (π_1) of the transducer in Figure 1.4 is the acceptor in Figure 1.3.

2 Regularity

In this chapter we defend the first hypothesis that was introduced in Section 1.2.3, namely Regularity.

It is obvious at the outset that the normal notion of a regular language, where the catenation operator '·' denotes simple left-to-right concatenation, will not suffice. This can be seen easily enough with the Chinese character 醬 <WINE+JIÀNG> *jiàng* 'sauce' where the semantic radical 酉 <WINE>[1] occurs below the phonetic portion 將 <JIÀNG>. This contrasts with the case of 鯉 <FISH+LǏ> *lǐ* 'carp', where the semantic radical 魚 <fish> occurs to the left of the phonetic component 里 <LǏ>; with 鴨 <BIRD+JIǍ> *yā* 'duck', where the semantic radical 鳥 <BIRD> occurs to the right of the phonetic component 甲 <JIǍ>; with 草 <GRASS+ZǍO> *cǎo* 'grass' where the semantic radical <GRASS> 艸 occurs above the phonetic component 早 <ZǍO>; and with 國 <SURROUND+HUÒ> *guó* 'country', where the semantic radical 口 <SURROUND> *surrounds* the phonetic component 或 <HUÒ>. These data are summarized in Table 2.1.

Clearly we need a more powerful notion than simple concatenation to handle such cases. We will therefore introduce the notion of *planar regular languages*, which differ from ordinary (string-based) regular languages only in defining a richer set of concatenation operations. The definition of planar regular languages will be given immediately in Section 2.1; we will also introduce (in Section 2.2) the notion of *Small Linguistic Unit* (SLU), the linguistic unit within which variation from the macroscopic – line- and document-level – order of a script is possible. In subsequent sections we will show the applicability of the expanded formalism to various phenomena that arise in a variety of scripts. It will be clear that the extended formalism is capable of providing straightforward analyses of these phenomena, which lends support to the Regularity hypothesis. Problematic examples from Ancient Egyptian will be discussed in Section 2.3.5. In Section 2.4 we briefly survey the possible instantiations of the SLU in different writing systems. Finally, we end the chapter with the implications of the theory for the macroscopic arrangement of scripts, and in particular for the instantiations of *boustrophedon* writing.

[1] Used alone, this character, pronounced *yǒu*, is used mostly as a term in the calendrical cycle, though in archeological usage it retains its original meaning of 'amphora'.

Table 2.1 *Chinese characters illustrating the five modes of combination of semantic (underlined) and phonetic components*

鯉 = <u>魚</u> left of 里	鴨 = <u>鳥</u> right of 甲
草 = <u>艸</u> above 早	醬 = <u>酉</u> below 將
國 = <u>口</u> surrounding 或	

2.1 Planar Regular Languages and Planar Regular Relations

Planar grammars of various kinds have been used both in two-dimensional pattern recognition and in building generative models of two-dimensional layouts. For instance two-dimensional *context-free* grammars have been used in the recognition of printed mathematical equations (Chou, 1989) and in formal descriptions of Chinese character construction (Fujimura and Kagaya, 1969; Wang, 1983). Planar finite-state models have also been used, mainly in pattern recognition. For instance Levin and Pieraccini (1991) developed a *planar hidden Markov model* approach to optical character recognition. A comprehensive review of two-dimensional finite-state models and their properties is given in Giammarressi and Restivo (1997). Their discussion focuses on two-dimensional languages – also termed, for obvious reasons, *pictures* – that can be represented with symbols on a rectangular grid. For instance, the following would be a picture over the alphabet $\{a, b\}$:

(2.1)
```
a a a a a a b
a a a a a b a
a a a a b a a
a a a b a a a
a a b a a a a
a b a a a a a
b a a a a a a
```

This view is not really adequate for our purposes, however, since we would like to view the primitive elements of the alphabet as being, in effect, geometrical figures that might occupy more than one "square" in such a two-dimensional grid. For example, in Figure 2.2, the basic element $\gamma(\alpha)$ is left-adjoined with the entire complex consisting of $\gamma(\beta)$, $\gamma(\zeta)$, and $\gamma(\delta)$ – and in particular is directly to the left of both $\gamma(\beta)$ and $\gamma(\zeta)$ – something that is not easily represented in an arrangement such as that in (2.1).

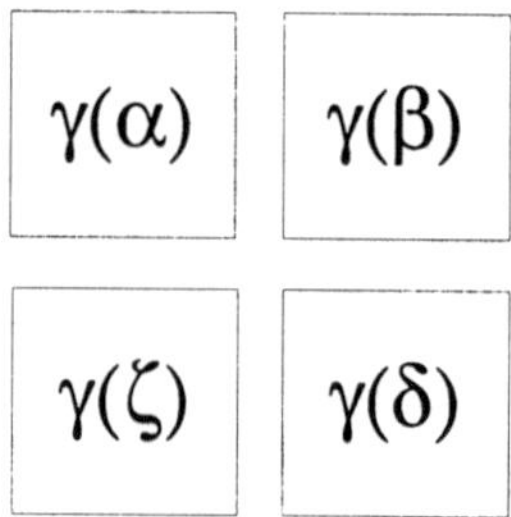

Figure 2.1. $\gamma(\alpha) \overset{\rightarrow}{\cdot} \gamma(\beta) \overset{\downarrow}{\cdot} \gamma(\zeta) \overset{\rightarrow}{\cdot} \gamma(\delta)$.

The notion of planar regular languages that we have in mind here can be described informally as follows. Suppose you have a set of two-dimensional figures arranged in some fashion on a flat surface. Consider for example the four rectangles labeled $\gamma(\alpha)$, $\gamma(\beta)$, $\gamma(\zeta)$, and $\gamma(\delta)$ in Figure 2.1. We assume for simplicity's sake that we are told what the subfigures are and where they are relative to one another. That is, our task is not to compute that there are four blocks in Figure 2.1, and that they are arranged in some pattern, but rather, given a predetermined layout, to describe that layout in formal terms. The analogy in the one-dimensional case is between, say, optical character recognition and string matching; in the former case one must discover what characters are in a text; in the latter case one already knows the characters and their relative orders, and one merely has to, for example, find patterns in this already known sequence of characters.

There are a number of ways in which one could describe Figure 2.1, but supposing we start in the upper left-hand corner, we might say that $\gamma(\alpha)$ *left catenates* with $\gamma(\beta)$; that this pair *downwards catenates* with the pair $\gamma(\zeta)\gamma(\delta)$; and that $\gamma(\zeta)$ left catenates with $\gamma(\delta)$. If we use '$\overset{\rightarrow}{\cdot}$' for 'left catenates with' and '$\overset{\downarrow}{\cdot}$' for 'downwards catenates with,' we could describe the layout succinctly as $\gamma(\alpha) \overset{\rightarrow}{\cdot} \gamma(\beta) \overset{\downarrow}{\cdot} \gamma(\zeta) \overset{\rightarrow}{\cdot} \gamma(\delta)$. Of course other patterns are consistent with this formula (consider Figure 2.2). This brings up the point that unlike the case of one-dimensional concatenation, planar catenation

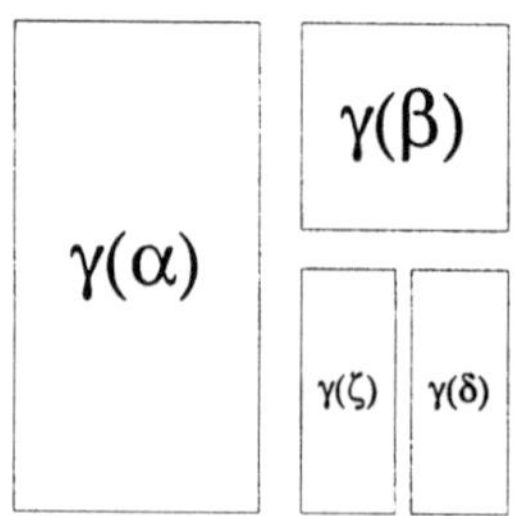

Figure 2.2. Another figure described by $\gamma(\alpha) \overset{\rightarrow}{\cdot} \gamma(\beta) \overset{\downarrow}{\cdot} \gamma(\zeta) \overset{\rightarrow}{\cdot} \gamma(\delta)$.

operators are not in general associative. More specifically, a sequence of *within* operator catenations is associative: $[\gamma(\alpha) \overset{\downarrow}{\cdot} \gamma(\beta)] \overset{\downarrow}{\cdot} [\gamma(\zeta) \overset{\downarrow}{\cdot} \gamma(\delta)]$ is equivalent to $\gamma(\alpha) \overset{\downarrow}{\cdot} [\gamma(\beta) \overset{\downarrow}{\cdot} \gamma(\zeta)] \overset{\downarrow}{\cdot} \gamma(\delta))$; but cross-operator catenations are not in general associative. There are a couple of possible solutions that allow us to more precisely describe a particular layout. One approach is to make brackets an explicit part of the formalism. Thus Figure 2.1 could be described as $[\gamma(\alpha) \overset{\rightarrow}{\cdot} \gamma(\beta)] \overset{\downarrow}{\cdot} [\gamma(\zeta) \overset{\rightarrow}{\cdot} \gamma(\delta)]$, as distinct from $\gamma(\alpha) \overset{\rightarrow}{\cdot} [\gamma(\beta) \overset{\downarrow}{\cdot} [\gamma(\zeta) \overset{\rightarrow}{\cdot} \gamma(\delta)]]$, which would describe Figure 2.2. An alternative that can be adopted in some cases (see Section 2.3.1, for instance) is to define a precedence on operators. So Figure 2.1 can be described as simply $\gamma(\alpha) \overset{\rightarrow}{\cdot} \gamma(\beta) \overset{\downarrow}{\cdot} \gamma(\zeta) \overset{\rightarrow}{\cdot} \gamma(\delta)$, if we have the understanding that '$\overset{\rightarrow}{\cdot}$' has precedence over '$\overset{\downarrow}{\cdot}$', so that the groups $\gamma(\alpha) \overset{\rightarrow}{\cdot} \gamma(\beta)$ and $\gamma(\zeta) \overset{\rightarrow}{\cdot} \gamma(\delta)$ will form first, and only then will $\overset{\downarrow}{\cdot}$ join the two groups together. Such an approach would not allow us to describe Figure 2.2, since no definition of precedence between '$\overset{\rightarrow}{\cdot}$' and '$\overset{\downarrow}{\cdot}$' will allow us to group the components appropriately. In such cases one would have to resort to bracketing. For example, the Chinese 鱗 *lín* 'fish scale' is composed of the components, 魚, 米, 夕, and 㐄, arranged as follows: 魚 $\overset{\rightarrow}{\cdot}$ [米 $\overset{\downarrow}{\cdot}$ [夕 $\overset{\rightarrow}{\cdot}$ 㐄]].

We turn now to a formal definition of planar regular languages. The definitions of regular languages introduced in Appendix 1.A carry over directly to planar regular languages, the only novel feature being the splitting of concatenation '$\cdot$' into five operations – each of which is needed to describe the Chinese character component layouts illustrated in the introduction to this chapter:[2]

- Left catenation: $\overset{\rightarrow}{\cdot}$
- Right catenation: $\overset{\leftarrow}{\cdot}$
- Downwards catenation: $\overset{\downarrow}{\cdot}$
- Upwards catenation: $\overset{\uparrow}{\cdot}$
- Surrounding catenation: $\odot$

Note that $\odot$ does not have a dual; we discuss this point further in Section 2.3.4.

Thus, we can amend the relevant portions of the definition of regular languages given in Appendix 1.A.1 to read as follows:

3. If L_1 and L_2 are planar regular languages, then so are
   (a) $L_1 \overset{\rightarrow}{\cdot} L_2$; $L_1 \overset{\leftarrow}{\cdot} L_2$; $L_1 \overset{\downarrow}{\cdot} L_2$; $L_1 \overset{\uparrow}{\cdot} L_2$; $L_1 \odot L_2$.

Each of these catenation operations is illustrated in Figure 2.3.

[2] Note that Coleman (1998, pages 27–28) uses downwards concatenation (which he terms *cocatenation*) as part of his description of the formal syntax of IPA symbols.

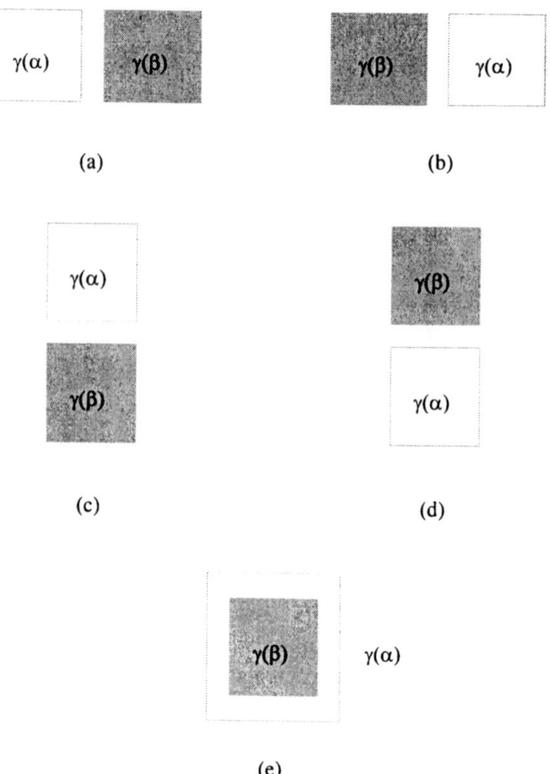

Figure 2.3. The five planar concatenation operations: (a) $\gamma(\alpha) \stackrel{\rightarrow}{\cdot} \gamma(\beta)$; (b) $\gamma(\alpha) \stackrel{\leftarrow}{\cdot} \gamma(\beta)$; (c) $\gamma(\alpha) \stackrel{\downarrow}{\cdot} \gamma(\beta)$; (d) $\gamma(\alpha) \stackrel{\uparrow}{\cdot} \gamma(\beta)$; (e) $\gamma(\alpha) \odot \gamma(\beta)$.

Of course, for the implementation of $M_{ORL \to \Gamma}$ in a given writing system, we will not only be interested in planar regular languages, but more generally in *planar regular relations*. On the orthographic side of the mapping, one is clearly mapping to planar objects built using some combination of planar catenation operations. On the linguistic side things are perhaps less clear. Although linguistic objects such as the annotation graphs introduced in Section 1.2.2 are displayed in two dimensions, they are not really planar objects: There is no sense in which the SEM arc is, say, above the TONE arc in (1.10). For the sake of the present discussion we will assume for simplicity that graph-theoretic objects such as (1.10) have been "linearized" into strings, so that we can think of their construction as being in terms of simple string concatenation '·'. So, in the present discussion we will be interested in planar regular relations that involve mappings between strings constructed using '·' and planar objects using some combination of planar catenation operations. Thus we might want to state, for instance, that $\alpha \cdot \beta \cdot \delta$ transduces to $\gamma(\alpha) \overset{\downarrow}{\cdot} \gamma(\beta) \overset{\rightarrow}{\cdot} \gamma(\delta)$. We can straightforwardly redefine the normal notion of concatenation in regular relations to implement the case we are interested in (Appendix 1.A.2):

3. If R_1 and R_2 are planar regular relations, then so are:
   (a) $R_1 < \cdot, \overset{\rightarrow}{\cdot} > R_2$; $R_1 < \cdot, \overset{\leftarrow}{\cdot} > R_2$; $R_1 < \cdot, \overset{\downarrow}{\cdot} > R_2$; $R_1 < \cdot, \overset{\uparrow}{\cdot} > R_2$; $R_1 < \cdot, \odot > R_2$.

Here, the notation $<oper_1, oper_2>$ means that we combine the input side of the relation using $oper_1$ and the output side using $oper_2$.

It should be stressed that the planar catenation operations are not generally intended to describe the *exact* placement of one element relative to another. Thus stating a formula such as $\gamma(\alpha) \overset{\downarrow}{\cdot} \gamma(\beta)$ merely entails that $\gamma(\alpha)$ is placed somewhere above $\gamma(\beta)$, but it says nothing about whether the center of gravity of the visible glyph representing $\gamma(\alpha)$ is exactly centered on the visible glyph representing $\gamma(\beta)$ or is perhaps, say, a little to the right. Of course sometimes such differences correlate with a difference in meaning. To take an obvious example, in a number of scripts the apostrophe <'> and the comma <,> are almost identical or completely identical in form; the only difference is the vertical placement. In both <Jones'> and <Jones,> we would say that the comma/apostrophe is catenated to the right of <s>, so it would seem as if the current formalism can say nothing about how these two cases are distinguished. The solution, of course, is to assume that glyphs are not merely a collection of black bits but in general also include a block of white bits within which the black bits are situated. Thus apostrophe and comma are really represented as in (2.2) and (2.3), respectively:

(2.2) ’

(2.3) ,

Thus we can preserve the simple statement that apostrophes and commas alike catenated in a left-to-right fashion with their neighbors and, at the same time, guarantee that they will be positioned appropriately in the vertical dimension relative to those neighbors. In many other cases, though, issues of exact placement of glyphs relate to written stylistics, and in general placements may vary substantially depending upon the style of font and whether one is dealing with ordinary printed text, ordinary handwritten text, or calligraphy. Such stylistic concerns are outside the scope of the present study.

A further point needs to be made about the use of brackets to indicate association, discussed above. In principle, the unbounded use of paired brackets introduces nonregularity, since nonfinite sets of well-formed bracketings are well-known to require context-free power; see, for example, Harrison (1978, pages 312ff.). We can keep the language within the set of regular languages, however, if we limit the depth d of bracketing that we allow, thus also limiting the number of switches between catenation operators that we allow. (Since bracketing is not involved when we combine elements within a given catenation operator – e.g., when we combine $\gamma(\alpha) \stackrel{\rightarrow}{\cdot} \gamma(\beta)$ and $\gamma(\delta) \stackrel{\rightarrow}{\cdot} \gamma(\zeta)$ using $\stackrel{\rightarrow}{\cdot}$ – there are no restrictions on "depth" of combination in such cases.) It is unclear what the setting for d should be, but a reasonable setting might be seven.[3] This would be more than sufficient to allow for an exhaustive structural analysis of the most complex Chinese characters (Rick Harbaugh, personal communication); see Section 2.3.4.

The computational devices corresponding to planar regular languages and relations are planar (or "two-dimensional") finite-state automata (2FSA) and planar finite-state transducers (2FST), respectively. We can define a planar finite-state acceptor along the lines of the definition of (one-dimensional) finite-state automata from Appendix 1.A.1, adding to the definition a set of directions, a start position, and a set of grouping brackets; computationally it is easier to define the machines using brackets rather than in terms of operator precedence.

> *A planar finite-state acceptor is an octuple* $M = (K, s, p, B, F, d, \Sigma, \delta)$ *where:*
>
> 1. K *is a finite set of states,*
> 2. s *is a designated initial state,*
> 3. p *is the starting position (in the planar figure) for* s*, chosen from the set* {*left, top, right, bottom*}*,*
> 4. B *is the set of grouping brackets* $\{\ [\ ,\ ]\ \}$*,*
> 5. F *is a designated set of final states,*
> 6. d *is the set of directions* {*R(ight), L(eft), D(own), U(p), I(nwards)*} *(corresponding to the catenation operators* $\stackrel{\rightarrow}{\cdot}$, $\stackrel{\leftarrow}{\cdot}$, $\stackrel{\downarrow}{\cdot}$, $\stackrel{\uparrow}{\cdot}$, *and* $\odot$*, respectively),*
> 7. Σ *is an alphabet of symbols, and*
> 8. δ *is a transition relation between* $K \times (\Sigma \cup \epsilon \cup B) \times d$ *and* K*.*

To recognize the figure in Figure 2.2 we effectively need to have a 2FSA that recognizes the description $\gamma(\alpha) \stackrel{\rightarrow}{\cdot} [\gamma(\beta) \stackrel{\downarrow}{\cdot} [\gamma(\zeta) \stackrel{\rightarrow}{\cdot} \gamma(\delta)]]$. So we need to have a machine where scanning begins at the left-hand side of the figure, proceeds rightwards reading $\gamma(\alpha)$, reads rightwards across one grouping bracket, reads rightwards across $\gamma(\beta)$, reads downwards across one grouping bracket, reads rightwards across $\gamma(\zeta)$, reads rightwards across $\gamma(\delta)$, and finally reads rightwards across two grouping brackets. A 2FSA that accomplishes this is given in Figure 2.4.

A 2FST can be defined similarly to a 2FSA. For our purposes we are interested in machines that map from expressions constructed using string

[3] In a similar vein, Church (1980) proposed a hard limit on the depth of embedding in syntactic structure in order to be able to implement a finite-state syntactic analyzer.

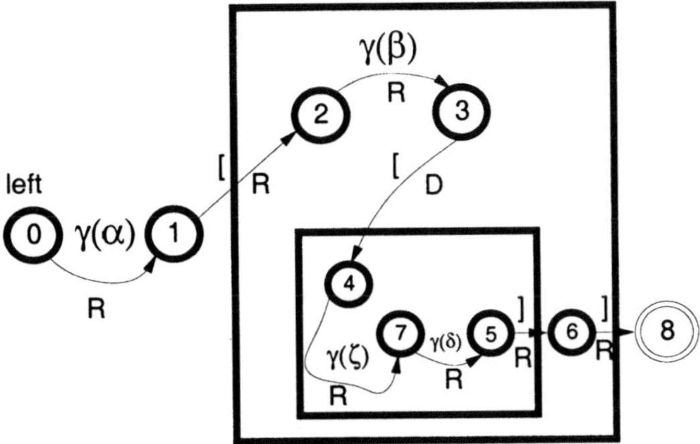

Figure 2.4. A 2FSA that recognizes Figure 2.2. The labels "R" and "D" on the arcs denote reading direction; "left" on state 0 (the initial state) denotes the position at which scanning begins.

catenation, to expressions constructed using planar catenation operators. The only part of the definition that changes is 8:

A planar finite-state transducer is an octuple $M = (K, s, p, B, F, d, \Sigma, \delta)$ where:

1. *K is a finite set of states,*
2. *s is a designated initial state,*
3. *p is the starting position (in the planar figure) for s, chosen from the set {left, top, right, bottom},*
4. *B is the set of grouping brackets { [,] },*
5. *F is a designated set of final states,*
6. *d is the set of directions {R(ight), L(eft), D(own), U(p), I(nwards)} (corresponding to the catenation operators $\overset{\rightarrow}{\cdot}$, $\overset{\leftarrow}{\cdot}$, $\overset{\downarrow}{\cdot}$, $\overset{\uparrow}{\cdot}$, and $\odot$, respectively),*
7. *Σ is an alphabet of symbols, and*
8. *δ is a transition relation from $K \times (\Sigma \cup \epsilon) \times (\Sigma \cup \epsilon \cup B) \times d$ to K.*

In general arcs that are labeled with brackets on the "planar side" will be labeled with ϵ on the "string side" of the transduction. A 2FST that maps the expression $\alpha\beta\zeta\delta$ to $\gamma(\alpha) \overset{\rightarrow}{\cdot} [\gamma(\beta) \overset{\downarrow}{\cdot} [\gamma(\zeta) \overset{\rightarrow}{\cdot} \gamma(\delta)]]$ (Figure 2.2) is given in Figure 2.5.

2.2 The Locality Hypothesis

How are the various catenation operators actually distributed in a writing system that uses more than one? Invariably one finds a situation such as the following. At a macroscopic level, the script runs in a particular direction, say left to right ($\overset{\rightarrow}{\cdot}$) or top to bottom ($\overset{\downarrow}{\cdot}$) (see Section 2.5); the particular choice may be somewhat free, as it is in Chinese, but whatever is chosen is fixed for a given text. Alterations of this macroscopic order occur

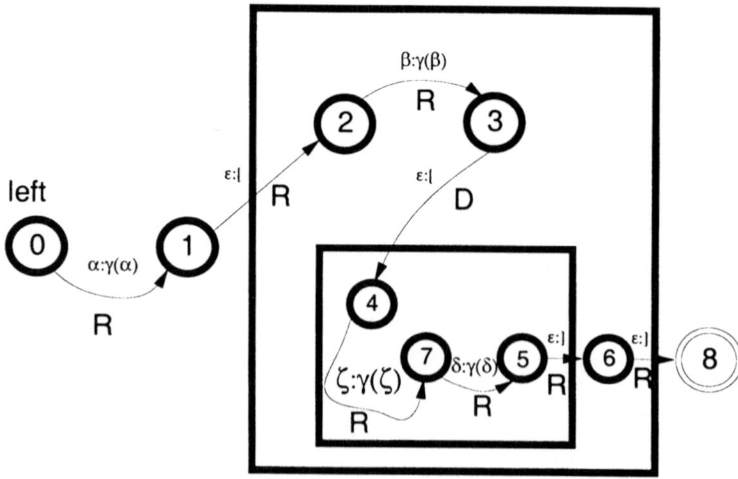

Figure 2.5. A 2FST that maps the expression $\alpha\beta\zeta\delta$ to $\gamma(\alpha) \overset{\rightarrow}{\cdot} [\gamma(\beta) \overset{\downarrow}{\cdot} [\gamma(\zeta) \overset{\rightarrow}{\cdot} \gamma(\delta)]]$.

only locally. Thus in Chinese, the construction of a particular character may involve various combinations of the catenation operators that we have described, but there is (for a given text) only one choice available for catenating that character with the following one. This observation leads to the following claim, which we shall term *Locality*:

(2.4)

> **Locality**
>
> *Changes from the macroscopic catenation type can only occur within a graphic unit that corresponds to a small linguistic unit (SLU).*

As we shall see, in many writing systems, the SLU in question is the syllable, though in some cases (Section 2.3.2) the "orthographic syllable" is nonisomorphic to the phonological syllable; in other cases the unit seems to be the word (as we shall see in a case from Aramaic in Section 4.4.1). This issue is further discussed in Section 2.4.

In the remaining sections of this chapter, we turn to an application of the formalism and theory developed here to various phenomena found in writing systems.

2.3 Planar Arrangements: Examples

In this section we discuss four writing systems – Korean Hankul, Devanagari, Pahawh Hmong, and Chinese – that make substantial use of more than one planar catenation operator. In each of these cases the SLU is the syllable, though in Devanagari, the relevant notion of "syllable" is orthographically rather than phonologically defined. In the final subsection we discuss an apparent counterexample to the claim of regularity from Ancient Egyptian.

2.3.1 Korean Hankul

The discussion of Korean Hankul here draws upon the description presented by King (1996) (and see also Sampson (1985)). The following summarizes the facts discussed in detail by King. The letters of Hankul are arranged into "syllable-sized" glyphs.[4] The syllable-sized glyphs are catenated with either left-catenation or downwards-catenation. Within the syllable-sized glyphs, however, both left- and downwards-catenation are used in ways that are predictable given the particular segments being combined. Vowel and diphthong glyphs are classified into two classes, VERTICAL and HORIZONTAL; examples of each of these will be given momentarily. All orthographic syllables in Hankul must have onsets. If the corresponding phonological syllable lacks an onset, then a "placeholder" glyph ㅇ is used to represent the empty onset.[5] That is, $\gamma(\emptyset_{\mathrm{onset}}) =$ ㅇ.

As examples of the construction of Hankul orthographic syllables, consider the glyphs 못 <mos> and 잘 <cal>. The first is constructed out of three components arranged in vertical descending order as follows:

ㅁ <m>
ㅗ <o>
ㅅ <s>

For 잘 <cal>, the component glyphs are as follows, with the first two arranged horizontally with respect to each other, but above the third glyph:

ㅈ <c>
ㅏ <a>
ㄹ <l>

[4] Note that by "syllable," here we mean syllable at a morphophonemic (rather than surface phonemic) level of representation. In many cases, units that are represented orthographically as syllables do not represent single syllables in the surface phonology. The ORL in Modern Korean orthography would appear to be fairly deep. King observes (page 223) that:

> Hankul orthography drifts from a more or less consistently phonemic approach in the fifteenth century, to an increasingly morphophonemic one by the twentieth century.

Sampson (1985, pages 135ff.) gives a detailed discussion of this issue.

[5] In coda position, this symbol represents /ŋ/, which does not occur in syllable-initial position.

The glyph ㅗ <o> belongs to the horizontal class whereas ㅏ <a> belongs to the vertical class (note the largely horizontal orientation of ㅗ <o> as opposed to ㅏ <a>) and this in turn correlates with the fact that <o> is arranged vertically with respect to the preceding onset, whereas <a> is arranged horizontally.

The macroscopic arrangement of Hankul syllable glyphs is traditionally top-to-bottom, though left-to-right arrangement is becoming much more common. Deviations from this macroscopic order only occur within the syllable, prompting the following statement for Hankul:

(2.5) The *SLU* is the *syllable.*

A set of rules for the arrangement of glyphs in Hankul can be given as follows; see Sampson (1985, page 132) and King (1996, page 222). In this version of the rules, we assume that syllable-sized units are arranged in a left-to-right fashion:

- For syllables σ_1 and σ_2, $\gamma(\sigma_1 \cdot \sigma_2) = \gamma(\sigma_1) \overset{\rightarrow}{\cdot} \gamma(\sigma_2)$.
- For onset-nucleus cluster $\omega\nu$ and coda κ, $\gamma(\omega\nu \cdot \kappa) = \gamma(\omega\nu) \overset{\downarrow}{\cdot} \gamma(\kappa)$.
- If coda κ is complex, consisting of (maximally) two consonants κ_1 and κ_2, then $\gamma(\kappa) = \gamma(\kappa_1 \cdot \kappa_2) = \gamma(\kappa_1) \overset{\rightarrow}{\cdot} \gamma(\kappa_2)$.
- For onset ω and nucleus ν,
  - if ν belongs to the VERTICAL class then $\gamma(\omega \cdot \nu) = \gamma(\omega) \overset{\rightarrow}{\cdot} \gamma(\nu)$
  - else $\gamma(\omega \cdot \nu) = \gamma(\omega) \overset{\downarrow}{\cdot} \gamma(\nu)$.

The principles of Hankul graphic syllable construction are illustrated in Figure 2.6, again using the syllables /mos/ and /cal/. Recall that <o> belongs to the horizontal class, whereas <a> belongs to the vertical class. Figure 2.6 makes use of brackets to indicate grouping. Thus, in <cal>, <c> is catenated to the left of <a>, and then this whole group is catenated on top of <l>; the alternative bracketing would result in a different arrangement of symbols. However, for the rules given above it is possible to dispense

[ㅁ	$\overset{\downarrow}{\cdot}$	ㅗ]	$\overset{\downarrow}{\cdot}$	ㅅ	=	못
<m>		<o>		<s>		<mos>
[ㅈ	$\overset{\rightarrow}{\cdot}$	ㅏ]	$\overset{\downarrow}{\cdot}$	ㄹ	=	잘
<c>		<a>		<l>		<cal>

Figure 2.6. The syllables <mos> /mo/ 'cannot' and <cal> /čal/ 'well' in Hankul.

with brackets in favor of operator precedence, as discussed in Section 2.1: Giving leftwards catenation higher precedence than downwards catenation ($\stackrel{\rightarrow}{\cdot} \gg \stackrel{\downarrow}{\cdot}$) yields the desired result.

2.3.2 Devanagari

The Devanagari script is a modern Indian script derived originally from the Brahmi script (Bright, 1996). It is used to represent Hindi, Nepali, and Marathi, as well as a variety of local languages of North India; it is also the usual script used in representing Sanskrit. In the present discussion, we will assume the use of the Devanagari script as a writing system for Hindi, though everything that we will discuss carries over, mutatis mutandis, to the script's use for other languages.

Bright describes Devanagari as an *alphasyllabary*, meaning that the system is basically alphabetic, but that the symbols are arranged in syllable-sized units. As we shall see momentarily, the relevant syllables for the orthography are not isomorphic to phonological syllables.

The basic features of the script that will concern us here are the following:

- (Phonological) syllable-initial vowels are represented as full symbols, but when combined with a preceding consonant they appear in diacritic forms that appear above, below, before, or after the consonant in question. The vowel /ə/ has no diacritic form, so that a consonant without a vowel mark has an inherent schwa. The forms of the independent and diacritic vowels (with onset consonant क <k>) are given in Table 2.2.
- Consonant clusters are represented by ligatured groups, which behave as units for the purposes of vowel placement. Thus स <s> + क <k> yields स्क <ska>; क <k> + ष <š> + म <m> yields क्ष्म <kšma>.[6] A sequence /skɪ/ is represented स्कि <i+sk>, with the <i> occurring in the position before the cluster. The ligatured-unit-plus-vowel combination forms an *orthographic syllable.*
- A preconsonantal initial /r/ in an orthographic syllable is represented by a superscript symbol occurring at the *end* of the orthographic syllable. Thus /vərma/ is represented as वर्मा <vəma+r>.

A procedure and a set of mapping rules for Devanagari that handles these facts are as follows:

6 The rules for ligature formation are somewhat complex and will not concern us here.

Table 2.2 *Full and diacritic forms for Devanagari vowels, classified by the position of expression of the diacritic forms. Thus "after" means that the diacritic occurs after the consonant cluster, "below," below it, and so forth*

Expression	Full form		Diacritic form	
Null	अ	<ə>	क	<kə>
After	आ	<a>	का	<ka>
	ओ	<o>	को	<ko>
	औ	<ɔ>	कौ	<kɔ>
	ई	<i>	की	<ki>
Above	ए	<e>	के	<ke>
	ऐ	<ɛ>	कै	<kɛ>
Below	उ	<U>	कु	<kU>
	ऊ	<u>	कू	<ku>
	ऋ	<r̲i̲>	कृ	<kr̲i̲>
Before	इ	<I>	कि	<kI>

- Divide the phonological string into orthographic syllables by placing a syllable boundary $_{syl}$:
  - at the beginning of the word;
  - between each pair of adjacent vowels;
  - before the first consonant of a cluster.

  The *SLU* in Devanagari is the *orthographic syllable.*
- Assume a function *Lig*, which forms the ligatured form of a sequence of consonant glyphs. Then $\gamma(C_1C_2\ldots C_n) = Lig(\gamma(C_1)\gamma(C_2)\ldots\gamma(C_n))$.
- Let $Full_j$ be the full vowel glyph for vowel V_j; then $\gamma(V_j) \rightarrow Full_j/\ {}_{syl}\_\_\_$.
- For consonant cluster κ and vowel υ, then

$$\gamma(\kappa \cdot \upsilon) = \begin{cases} \gamma(\kappa) & \text{if } \upsilon = \text{ə}, \\ \gamma(\kappa) \overset{\rightarrow}{\cdot} \gamma(\upsilon) & \text{if } \upsilon = /\text{a,o,ɔ,i}/, \\ \gamma(\kappa) \overset{\uparrow}{\cdot} \gamma(\upsilon) & \text{if } \upsilon = /\text{e,ɛ}/, \\ \gamma(\kappa) \overset{\downarrow}{\cdot} \gamma(\upsilon) & \text{if } \upsilon = /\text{u,ʊ,ri}/, \\ \gamma(\kappa) \overset{\leftarrow}{\cdot} \gamma(\upsilon) & \text{if } \upsilon = /\text{ɪ}/. \end{cases}$$

- For an orthographic syllable starting with /r/ and remainder $\kappa\upsilon$ with non-null consonant κ, $\gamma(/\text{r}/ \cdot \kappa\upsilon) = \gamma(/\text{r}/) \overset{\downarrow}{\cdot} \gamma(\kappa\upsilon)$.

The properties of Devanagari that we have just analyzed are common among other Indian and Indian-derived scripts. Indeed, compared with those of some other scripts, Devanagari diacritic vowels are relatively simple: Thai for example (Diller, 1996) has vowel symbols that not only occur above, below, before, and after the consonant symbol but also has vowel diacritics that surround the consonant symbol.

2.3.3 *Pahawh Hmong*

The Pahawh Hmong messianic script invented in 1959 by Shong Lue Yang, a Hmong peasant, is described at length in a fascinating study by Smalley, Vang, and Yang (1990); a more concise description can be found in Ratliff (1996). There were actually four stages of the script, which evolved as Shong Lue Yang refined his original design. We will be concerned with the Third Stage, which is the version that received the widest acceptance and use. There are two sets of glyphs in Pahawh, the first representing onset consonant clusters, and the second the rime (i.e., the vowel plus the lexical tone).[7] Pahawh is thus sometimes described as a *demisyllabic* system, though this is really a misnomer. The writing runs from left to right, with spaces separating syllables, making the syllable-sized chunks quite easy to identify. What is notable about Pahawh is that the glyph representing the rime is systematically written *to the left of* the glyph representing the onset, in contravention to the overall left-to-right order of the script. For example Shong Lue's name is written <ɔ́ŋ> + <š> <î> + <l> /šɔ́ŋ lî/ in Pahawh Hmong writing. Clearly, as others have noted, one can view this as a generalization of the property of many Indian and Indian-derived Southeast Asian scripts, to allow *some* vowel glyphs to precede consonant clusters that, on the basis of phonological ordering, they logically follow; we

[7] In the final (fourth) stage, the vowel and tone symbols had become completely separate, and even in the Third stage, there is a partial separation, with some tonal information being represented by diacritic symbols written over the vowel symbol. We will not be concerned with the representation of tone here, and for the purposes of this discussion, we will consider the vowel-plus-tone combination as a single unit.

saw an example of this with Devanagari in the previous section. However, Pahawh is the only known writing system that consistently has this reversal.[8]

While the origin of this unique feature of Pahawh is mysterious, its implementation within the current framework is simple. As for Hankul, the SLU is the syllable:

(2.6) The *SLU* in Pahawh Hmong is the *syllable*.

The rules describing Hmong glyph arrangements are as follows:

- For syllables σ_1 and σ_2, $\gamma(\sigma_1 \cdot \sigma_2) = \gamma(\sigma_1) \overset{\rightarrow}{\cdot} \gamma(\sigma_2)$.
- For onset ω and nucleus ν, $\gamma(\omega \cdot \nu) = \gamma(\omega) \overset{\leftarrow}{\cdot} \gamma(\nu)$.

2.3.4 *Chinese*

As will be recalled from Section 1.2.2 (and see also Section 4.2), Chinese is a partly logographic writing system where most individual characters are made up of a component that gives some information about the pronunciation (the "phonetic" component) and another component (the "semantic" component) that gives clues to the meaning. These two components can be arranged in a number of ways relative to each other, as we discussed briefly in the introduction to this chapter. From the annotation-graph representation of a Chinese morpheme such as that in (1.10), repeated below as (2.7), we have assume that the semantic information associated with that morpheme overlaps, but does not dominate, the phonological information:

(2.7)

SEM:	*cicada* : 虫	
TONE:	2	
SYL:	σ : 單	
ONS-RIME:	*ch*	*an*

Given Axiom 1.3 from Section 1.2.2, it follows that the image of the semantic portion under $M_{ORL \rightarrow \Gamma}$ must catenate with the image of the phonological portion under $M_{ORL \rightarrow \Gamma}$. The SLU in Chinese, like the three writing systems we have just discussed, is the syllable, and (with a single exception that need not concern us here) syllables are in turn implemented using single characters. In principle therefore, the catenation operator chosen to implement

[8] Furthermore, since Shong Lue Yang was illiterate when he first began to create the script, it is hard to see how he could have known about this tendency to reverse the logical order in the region's writing systems.

the within-character combination of the semantic and phonetic elements can differ from the macroscopic catenation, whether that be the traditional downwards catenation or the more modern left-to-right catenation. In fact, the particular catenation operator chosen depends upon a relatively complex set of rules and lexical specifications. This section presents a preliminary analysis of the internal structure of Chinese characters in terms of the present planar grammar formalism.

There has been a long history of structural analysis for Chinese characters starting with the A.D. 200 *Shuō Wén Jiě Zì*; see Wieger (1965) for a brief history. One important point in the history of Chinese character studies is the compendious dictionary compiled during the reign of the Kang-Xi emperor (r. 1661–1722). The modern classification of characters according to semantic radicals largely follows the usage in that dictionary. In more modern times, there have been various generative analyses. One such study was that of Fujimura and Kagaya (1969), who constructed a program that was capable of generating (and outputting on an oscilliscope) not only real Chinese characters but also *possible* characters – that is, characters that are nonexistent but obey the structural constraints of Chinese characters. Wang (1983) presented a generative-grammar-based model of Chinese character structure that predicted the relative placement of semantic "classifiers" and phonetic "specifiers" within characters and also provided a model of the actual writing of the characters, with special attention being paid to the analysis of the stroke order; we will discuss Wang's analysis in more depth momentarily.

An interesting study by Myers (1996) argues for the relevance of prosodic *headedness* in Chinese character construction. By assuming that the structural head of a character is (depending upon the overall composition of the character) on the bottom, the right, or the bottom right, Myers is able to explain several robust features of Chinese characters. For instance, the largest component or stroke tends to be on the bottom or on the right (i.e., in the head position); the leftmost stroke in a character with a significant amount of structure to its right is curved (i.e., a nonhead vertical stroke is curved); and there is a strong preference for semantic components to occur on the left or on the top (i.e., in a nonhead position). This latter point is completely in accord with our observations, reported below. Finally, Myers notes a tendency for reduced forms of radicals (see page 82) to occur on the top or the left (i.e., in nonhead position).

Finally, there is a website (`www.zhongwen.com` (Harbaugh, 1998)) that produces structural analyses for selected characters. One of the points that is nicely brought out in this website is the fact that Chinese characters are tree-structured objects, and complex characters can be analyzed into many levels. Thus in the character 楓 <TREE+FĒNG> *fēng* 'maple', which is analyzed at the level we are interested in as 木<TREE> $\overrightarrow{\cdot}$ 風<FĒNG>, we can further break down the right-hand component into the components 凡 and 虫. Thus an exhaustive analysis would be 木 $\stackrel{\rightarrow}{\cdot}$ [凡 $\stackrel{\downarrow}{\cdot}$ 虫]; examples more complex than this are not hard to find (cf. the example 鱗 *lín* 'fish scale', introduced earlier). In the present discussion we will only be concerned with the top level, namely the combination of semantic with phonetic, or semantic with semantic, in characters that have such analyses.

We return now to the study by Wang (1983). The analysis of semantic–phonetic component placement in Wang's study is feature based, using the features [high], [low], [left], and [right]. A semantic component such as 門 <DOOR>, which typically takes its phonetic component inside (e.g., 閨 <DOOR+GUĪ> *guī* 'door to women's apartments'), is analyzed as [+high,+left,+right]. Similarly 力 <FORCE>, which typically occurs on the right (勁 <FORCE+JĪNG> *jìn* 'strength'), is analyzed as [+right]. Finally $口_{big}$ <SURROUND>, which completely surrounds its phonetic (國 <SURROUND+HUÒ> *guó* 'country'), is analyzed as [+high,+low,+right,+left]. Phonetic components may also have specifications: 壯 *zhuàng*, as in 裝 <CLOTHING+ZHUÀNG> *zhuāng* 'pack, contain', is [+high,−low]. Wang assumes a series of rules that use the feature specifications to determine the actual placement of the components:

- If neither component is specified, a default semantic-left, phonetic-right placement is used.
- If one component is specified, the opposite features are filled in for the other component.
- If both components are specified, and if there is a conflict, the semantic component wins.

There are various interesting aspects to Wang's analysis, and on the whole it seems to be on the right track. It is certainly true, for example, that the semantic-left/phonetic-right placement is in some sense the default. This is shown in Table 2.3, which shows the frequencies, for 12,728 characters from the Taiwan Big5 character set, of various semantic radical placements.[9] One problem with Wang's analysis, though, is that it is too powerful. In particular, the featural system he develops would predict that one might have a component that is specified [−left,−right,−high,−low] and would thus *select* to be in the *middle* of whatever it combines with. However, the only cases where such placement occurs is in fossilized forms. Thus 東 *dōng* 'east' is traditionally analyzed as being composed of 日 *rì* 'sun, day' placed in the middle of 木 *mù* 'tree, wood', but 日 *rì* does not in fact select for this position: There is no productive character-formation process that can account for 東 *dōng*. This is why the surrounding catenation operator $\odot$

[9] Here, I took at face value the traditional 214 Kang-Xi radicals, assuming that these are in fact the correct semantic components in all cases. Occasionally this assumption is misguided.

Table 2.3 *Distribution of placement of semantic component (Kang-Xi Radical) among 12,728 characters from the Taiwan Big5 character set*

left	8,303
top	1,964
bottom	1,246
right	882
surround	159
other	174

does not have a dual; the notion of "inside catenation" does not appear to be necessary.

It also seems that the difference between 門 <DOOR> as [+high,+left, +right] versus 口$_{\text{big}}$ <SURROUND> as [+high,+low, +left,+right] is rather redundant. Presumably the fact that the latter completely surrounds its sister component, whereas the former only partially does so, follows from the shapes of the two components. To handle both cases, it ought to be sufficient to say that they *surround* their sister.

We therefore dispense with the featural approach and present instead a preliminary analysis based on the catenation operators introduced in this chapter. Our analysis is based upon 2,588 characters from the Taiwan Big5 character set for which we know the breakdown into semantic and phonetic/semantic components.[10] As we see in Table 2.4, the relative magnitudes of the different placements of the components is roughly the same as for the fuller Big5 character set (Table 2.3), so this smaller sample may be taken as representative.[11]

We now turn to a description of the rules developed to handle these characters. In the following discussion, we will dispense with the normal glosses, except where critical, so as not to overly clutter the text. Note that some semantic radicals are marked as *full* or *red* (*reduced*). In these cases there are alternative forms – "full" and "reduced" for the radical, and

[10] These breakdowns were taken from the raw data used in the www.zhongwen.com (Harbaugh, 1998) website. I am grateful to Rick Harbaugh for making these data available to me.

[11] For the purposes of the present discussion, we eliminated characters, such as 東 *dōng* 'east', which do not belong to one of the five categories in Table 2.4. Invariably such characters are old constructions that are not built out of their supposed components by any productive process.

Table 2.4 *Distribution of placement of semantic component (Kang-Xi Radical) among 2,588 characters from the Taiwan Big5 character set*

left	1,745
top	313
bottom	313
right	166
surround	51

these two forms behave differently. Thus 心 *xīn* 'heart' has two forms as the radical <HEART>, one being more or less the same shape as the full character (placed underneath the second component), and the other a reduced three-stroke component, as in the left-hand portion of 忙 *máng* 'busy' (placed to the left of the second component). We assume for the present that it is part of the lexical orthographic specification of a morpheme whether a particular character has the full or reduced variant, though to some extent one can predict this by the position of the radical in the character (Myers, 1996). Which of the two options – "full" or "red" – is marked depends upon which one is reasonably regarded as the default; only the nondefault is marked in the glosses. Finally, as indicated in the descriptions below, we assume that one of the components – usually the semantic radical, but sometimes the phonetic radical – is the "determining component": It is the one that will be listed *first* in the formulae, so that an expression such as $A \overset{\downarrow}{\cdot} B$, with A the determining component, will unambiguously mean that A occurs above B:

(2.8) (a) The following, as phonetic components, take precedence (i.e., determine the placement of the components in the character): 皿, 爿, 厂, 厭, 麻, 攸, 厤, 尚. In other cases the semantic component determines the placement. As noted above, the "determining component" occurs to the left of the catenation operator in the formulae.

(b) $\cdot \Rightarrow \overset{\downarrow}{\cdot}$, if any of the following is the determining component: 艸, 竹, 尸, 戶, 厂, 人$_{\text{full}}$, 大, 虍, 雨, 羊, 穴, 玨, 网, 羽, 厭, 麻, 攸, 厤, 尚.

(c) $\cdot \Rightarrow \overset{\leftarrow}{\cdot}$, if any of the following is the determining component: 刀, 鳥, 頁, 邑, 隹, 殳, 斗, 見, 欠, 力, 弋, 戈.

(d) $\cdot \Rightarrow \overset{\uparrow}{\cdot}$, if any of the following is the determining component: 貝, 心$_{\text{full}}$, 虫虫,[12] 寸, 皿, 火$_{\text{red}}$, 臼, 子, 儿, 手$_{\text{full}}$, 刀$_{\text{full}}$, 皿.

(e) $\cdot \Rightarrow \odot$, if any of the following is the determining component: 門, 行 匚, 口$_{\text{big}}$ (= <SURROUND>), 鬥.

(f) Otherwise $\cdot \Rightarrow \overset{\rightarrow}{\cdot\,\cdot}$.

The current set of rules can analyze 88% of the 2,588 characters, leaving the remaining 12% to be lexically specified exceptions; examples of 196 of the analyzed and 38 of the unanalyzed characters are given in Appendix 2.A. Although further tuning of the rules could undoubtedly increase the coverage further, it must be borne in mind that some amount of lexical specification is always going to be necessary. For example, 目 <EYE> and 亡 <MÁNG$_{16/21}$ *p*.404> can combine in two ways, yielding the characters 盲 *máng* 'blind' and 盳 *máng*, a variant spelling of 盲.

One interesting observation about these data is that if one considers only the characters for which the phonetic component is a *perfect* predictor of the pronunciation (including tone) of the whole character – 624 characters in this set – the accuracy of the rules presented increases to 92%. This means that "regularly pronounced" characters are also more regular in structure. This result is perhaps not surprising since it parallels commonly observed patterns in morphology where semantically transparent and morphologically productive constructions also tend to be the ones that are more phonologically regular. Presumably this increase in regularity for phonologically regular compounds is useful for the Chinese reader. As we discuss elsewhere (Section 5.2), there is psycholinguistic evidence that Chinese readers make use of the phonetic component of characters when they are useful; in order to be able to reliably locate and identify the phonetic component, it helps if the placement of this component is more regular, and less subject to idiosyncratic lexical specifictions. In Appendix 2.A, regularly pronounced characters are indicated with '◊'.

One additional topic discussed by Wang (1983) and for which we need to provide an account is what he terms *classifier raising*: In some cases the semantic classifier of the phonetic component is "raised" to become the semantic classifier of the entire character. This is a relatively rare phenomenon, restricted in part to spelling variants of certain characters. However, there are a couple of phonetic components that seem to undergo this process as a matter of course. One such component is the top portion of 螣 <INSECT+TÉNG$_{7/12}$ *p*.505> *téng* 'serpent', 縢 <SILK+TÉNG$_{7/12}$ *p*.505> *téng* 'bind', or 騰 <HORSE+TÉNG$_{7/12}$ *p*.505> *téng* 'mount'. The phonetic component in each case consists of the portion above the semantic radical, plus the

[12] I.e., double 虫 <INSECT>.

lefthand component 月, which is at least structurally the phonetic component's own semantic radical. This 月 has been raised to become the semantic radical of the whole character. To account for this in the current formalism, we need to assume a rule such as the following, which reassociates the components of characters containing this phonetic:[13]

(2.9) Semantic $\cdot$ [月 $\cdot$ 关] $\rightarrow$ 月 $\overset{\rightarrow}{\cdot}$ [关 $\overset{\downarrow}{\cdot}$ Semantic].

2.3.5 *A Counterexample from Ancient Egyptian*

The hieroglyphic writing system of Ancient Egyptian (Gardiner, 1982; Ritner, 1996) presents one case that is problematic for regularity. In Old Kingdom Egyptian, plural number was indicated in the orthography by the double copying of the base word, or a portion thereof. The copying could be implemented in various ways including duplicating the entire phonographically written word as in (2.10), duplicating the entire logograph as in (2.11), or duplicating only the semantic classifier of the word as in (2.12):

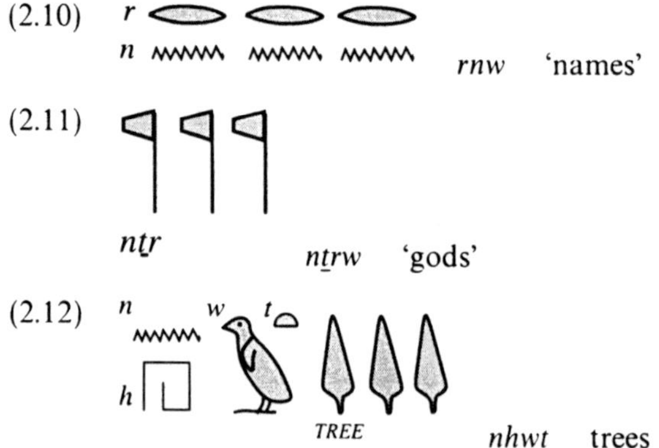

The problem lies in the fact that the Egyptian plural was morphologically marked by suffixation, *-w* with masculine nouns and *-wt* with feminine nouns.[14] This suffix *-wt* is actually spelled out in the orthography in the representation in (2.12), though it was not in general required to spell out the plural suffix. Since the orthographic duplication does not represent any linguistic duplication, it must be part of the mapping between linguistic

[13] In this and similar cases, then, we actually need to delve slightly deeper than the top-level componential analysis that we have dealt with in this section and at least recognize a second tier of structure.

[14] The same point can be made for the orthographic representation of dual number, which was also represented by copying, in this case a single copy. As in the case of the plural, the dual was encoded morphologically via suffixation.

representation and orthography, or in other words it must be handled by $M_{ORL \to \Gamma}$. Given that regular relations are not powerful enough to handle arbitrary copying, this orthographic practice stands as a counterexample to the claim of Regularity.

It is interesting to note that this copying was only used during the Old Kingdom (prior to 2240 B.C.); by the Middle Kingdom it had been replaced (except in religious texts) by a logographic symbol involving three strokes (Gardiner, 1982, page 59), apparently derived from the original repetition. An example (from Gardiner, page 59) is given in (2.13):

(2.13)

nṯr Pl *ntrw* gods

One assumes that this device was introduced by the scribes as an abbreviatory aid to save them writing (or carving) three copies of a set of glyphs. But it is interesting that this abbreviatory device also rendered Egyptian orthography more Regular, in the formal sense defined here.

The most similar example I am aware of in a modern orthography is the encoding of plurality in Spanish initials by doubling the letters corresponding to the plural noun: Thus *Estados Unidos* 'United States' is abbreviated as *EE.UU.*, and *Fuerzas Armadas* 'armed forces' is *FF.AA.*. But although this process is productive in Spanish, since it only involves doubling individual letters of the alphabet it is feasible to simply list all doubled letters with an indication that these doubles are to be used to abbreviate plurals. (Alternatively one could write a rule that copies individual letters of the alphabet, and this rule could be represented as a transducer; note though that this would be computationally equivalent to simply listing the doubles.)

Apart from the Spanish example, which is easily handled within the theory, I am aware of no other cases of such duplication in a modern writing system. It is tempting therefore to conclude that the Egyptian example was marked, as the theory predicts, and that the rarity of such cases is a consequence of this markedness.

2.4 Cross-Writing-System Variation in the SLU

All of the writing systems that we have examined in the previous section involve syllable-sized SLUs. This is no accident. Writing systems where basic glyphs are organized into syllable-sized units seem to be quite prevalent among the world's writing systems, as has often been noted in the literature. For instance, Faber (1992) assigns a node in her arboreal taxonomy of

Table 2.5 *Linguistic units corresponding to Mayan complex glyphs, from Macri (1996); glossing conventions follow those of Macri. In some phrasal cases it is unclear whether the unit in question is really a constituent: Such cases are indicated with a question mark*

Element	Gloss	Size of element
y-ak'aw	he.presents	word
u-pi(s)	his-cycle	word
pixol	hat	word
u-ha(l)	his-necklace	word
u-tup	his-earrings	word
yax	green	word
u-kawaw	his-helmet	word
ch'ok	young.one	word
Kawil	(a name)	word
y-ak'a-w	it.is.given	word
u-sak hunal	his-white headband	(adjective–noun) phrase
chan tun	sky stone	(noun–noun) phrase
hun winik	one twenty	phrase?
yax ch'ul	green sacred	(adjective–adjective) phrase?

writing systems to what she terms *segmentally coded, syllabically linear* scripts, which include Hankul and Devanagari.

However, larger SLUs certainly seem to be possible. For example, Mayan writing appears to have had an SLU at the level of the word or small phrase. Mayan complex glyphs were typically arranged in paired columns that were to be read left to right, top to bottom (Macri, 1996). Thus, the reading order of the following schema, would be *A B C D E F*:

A B
C D
E F

The basic reading order is therefore left-to-right, with each line of text consisting of two glyphs. Within each glyph, the arrangement of basic glyphs was somewhat freer, with signs running "loosely from upper left corner to lower right corner, with generous allowances for artistic convention" (Macri, 1996, page 178). The complex glyph is therefore clearly the graphic unit corresponding to the SLU, but what kind of linguistic unit is this? The single example presented in Macri's discussion (1996, page 178) suggests that in many cases the SLU is a single – potentially morphologically complex, usually polysyllabic – word, but in some cases it seems to be an a small phrase. Table 2.5 lists each of the linguistic elements corresponding

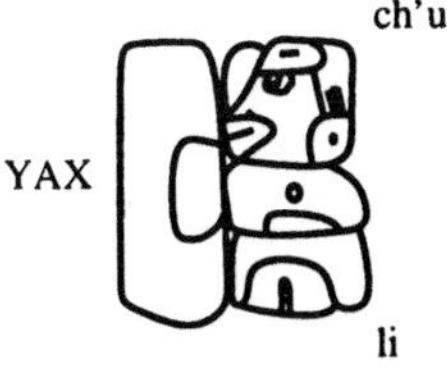

Figure 2.7. A two-word Mayan glyph representing the adjective sequence *yax ch'ul* 'green sacred', after Macri (1996, page 179), with the arrangement $YAX \overset{\rightarrow}{\cdot}$ [*ch'u*$\overset{\downarrow}{\cdot}$*li*]. Per convention, the capitalized gloss represents a logographic element, and the lower case glosses phonographic elements.

to a single complex glyph in Macri's sample text. Figure 2.7 illustrates the two-word glyph *yak ch'ul* 'green sacred'.

Needless to say, a more thorough survey of the deciphered corpus of Mayan texts will be necessary to determine the maximal size of the SLU in that writing system and what constraints, if any existed, on valid SLU's.[15] This small text does, however, at least show that the SLU in Mayan is larger than a single syllable.

Not only is the size of the SLU writing-system dependent, but it seems also to be construction dependent: One finds cases where the catenation operator is changed only in certain kinds of (local) constructions. One example of such construction-particular reordering is found in Ancient Egyptian. This is the example of "honorific inversion" (Ritner, 1996, page 80) whereby terms for gods or kings would be written before terms that they logically follow.[16] Thus the phrase *mdw nṯr* (words god) 'god's words' would be written as in (2.14), with the logograph for 'god' being written before the duplicated (hence plural) phonograph for /md/ (Ritner, 1996, page 81):

(2.14) 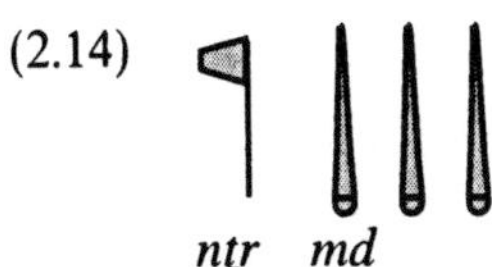

15 The data that would allow one to investigate this question already exist as part of the Maya Hieroglyphic Database Project at the University of California, Davis, Department of Native American Studies. I had hoped to be able to examine some of these data and had on more than one occasion requested access to a portion of the database, unfortunately to no avail. The resolution of this question will therefore have to wait until these potentially valuable data are made available to a wider range of scholars.

16 Additional rearrangements of symbols for artistic reasons were also found (Ritner, 1996). Plausibly such cases are due to stylistic considerations and thus fall outside the range of the present theory.

This can be accounted for if we assume that the SLU can be a word or small phrase. In that case we can assume that there is simply reversal within that SLU of the overall catenation operator in use for the text. Thus if the text is being written from left to right, and therefore generally uses the catenation operator $\overrightarrow{\cdot}$, we can assume a special principle like that in (2.15) that in honorific contexts implements $\cdot$ as $\overleftarrow{\cdot}$ rather than $\overrightarrow{\cdot}$:

(2.15) $\gamma(\alpha \cdot \beta) = \gamma(\alpha) \overleftarrow{\cdot} \gamma(\beta)$, if β is to be honored.

As Ritner notes, the Egyptian example is really no different from the situation in many modern writing systems with currency amounts. Thus consider English examples such as <$1,000> for *one thousand dollars* or more significantly <$1 million> for *one million dollars*. The "symbolic abbreviation" (to coin a term) '$' for *dollar(s)* is written before the number phrase, which it logically follows. (Note that the currency term that is "moved" may itself be complex: *one hundred US dollars* can be written as <US$100>.) This prompts a construction-particular statement similar to (2.15) in Egyptian:

(2.16) $\gamma(\alpha \cdot \beta) = \gamma(\alpha) \overleftarrow{\cdot} \gamma(\beta)$, if:

- α is a number phrase, and $\gamma(\alpha)$ starts with a digit, and
- β is a currency term, and $\gamma(\beta)$ is a symbolic abbreviation for that currency term.

The first constraint captures the fact that symbolic abbreviations for currencies must precede a number expressed as a digit: One does not find such expressions as *<$twenty five>. Indeed this in turn suggests that the true source of the reordering may actually be a surface orthographic constraint that requires the currency symbol to immediately precede a digit:

(2.17) If $\gamma(\beta)$ is a symbolic abbreviation for a currency term β, then $\gamma(\beta)$ must precede a digit.

This constraint then forces the catenation operator to be $\overleftarrow{\cdot}$, as in (2.16). Note though, in any case, that the SLU must be defined for this construction to be the whole number-plus-currency phrase, in order to allow for the deviation from the normal ordering.

The examples discussed in this section and elsewhere in this chapter suggest that there is quite a range of variation in the definition of the SLU across writing systems, and even within different components of the same writing system. We will leave it as a topic for future research to provide a complete taxonomy of the possible instantiations of the SLU.

2.5 Macroscopic Catenation: Text Direction

> ...their manner of writing is very peculiar, being neither from the left to the right, like the Europeans; nor from the right to the left, like the Arabians; nor from up to down, like the Chinese; but aslant from one corner of the paper to the other...
>
> Swift, Jonathan. 1726. *Gulliver's Travels: A Voyage to Lilliput*, chapter 6.

Many of the examples discussed in this chapter relate to the micro-arrangement of graphical symbols. Naturally, in addition to specifying how, for example, the glyphs arrange themselves into orthographic syllables, any writing system must also specify the overall direction of the script. As Harris (1995, chapter 19) usefully points out, the notion of direction is more complex than it first appears to be. In characterizing the default directionality of text in English, for instance, the following specifications need to be made:

- Each *line* of text is composed of glyphs arranged from *left to right.*
- Each *page* of text is composed of lines arranged from *top to bottom.*
- Each *multipage document* is (when correctly bound) composed of pages bound on the *left-hand side.*

These specifications are of course script dependent. The traditional statements for Chinese run as follows:

- Each *line* of text is composed of glyphs arranged from *top to bottom.*
- Each *page* of text is composed of lines arranged from *right to left.*
- Each *multipage document* is (when correctly bound) composed of pages bound on the *right-hand side.*

In principle the three types of specification – "line" level, page level, and document level – are also logically independent of each other. Still, as Harris notes, there are plausible biomechanical or other reasons for the elimination of some combinations. So once one has fixed one's script as running in horizontal lines, the option of arranging those lines from bottom to top seems not to be generally available, presumably because the production of such text would require one to cover up what one had previously written.[17] The Lilliputians' diagonal arrangements of lines is presumably disfavored because it would force constantly changing line lengths on a rectangular page.

Similarly, multipage document binding practices are not independent of the direction of the script. If one's script runs from left to right across the page, there is a natural tendency to want to read a multipage document from "left-to-right," whereas if one's script runs from right-to-left across the page (whether right-to-left in horizontal lines as in Hebrew, or right-to-left

[17] Similar considerations presumably also account for the extreme rarity (as the survey in Daniels and Bright (1996) shows) of scripts where columns run from bottom to top.

in vertical columns as in Chinese), there is also a tendency to want to read a multipage document from "right-to-left." So, holding an English book with the spine pointing away from you, you start reading on the leftmost page and continue to the rightmost page. For a Chinese or Hebrew book, holding the book in the same configuration you start from the rightmost page.

We will have nothing further to say about binding practices here, but it will be useful to dwell for a moment on Harris's second characterization of text direction, namely the arrangement of lines on a page. We have of course dealt with the issue of the macroscopic arrangement of symbols within a line (or column) of text by assuming a single macroscopic catenation operator such as $\stackrel{\rightarrow}{\cdot}$ or $\stackrel{\downarrow}{\cdot}$ for a given script or style of writing within a script. One is therefore tempted to deal with the arrangement of lines of text in a similar fashion. Such an account for English would run as follows:

(2.18) (a) $line = \alpha_1 \stackrel{\rightarrow}{\cdot} \alpha_2 \stackrel{\rightarrow}{\cdot} \ldots \stackrel{\rightarrow}{\cdot} \alpha_n$, for α a letter, symbol, or space.
(b) $page = line_1 \stackrel{\downarrow}{\cdot} line_2 \stackrel{\downarrow}{\cdot} \ldots \stackrel{\downarrow}{\cdot} line_n$.

So a line would be an arrangement of basic symbols using $\stackrel{\rightarrow}{\cdot}$ and a page would be an arrangement of lines using $\stackrel{\downarrow}{\cdot}$.

The problem with this account is that it would appear to violate Locality: A line of text does not constitute a Small Linguistic Unit, and therefore the switch from $\stackrel{\rightarrow}{\cdot}$ to $\stackrel{\downarrow}{\cdot}$ would constitute a violation. This consideration would appear to force an alternative view, one which also has the benefit of being more intuitively appealing. Under this alternative view, text is written on a *virtual tape* in one direction only. In English this would be from left to right; in Chinese from top to bottom. This tape is then "pasted" to a physical surface, with the inevitable consequence with a sufficiently long tape that one will run out of space on a line (or column) and have to wrap the tape to the next column.

There are only three reasonable ways to perform this wrapping. The first, practiced by every modern writing system, involves "cutting" the virtual tape, and continuing on the next line or column near where one started the previous line; see (a) in Figure 2.8. The second and third methods both involve starting at the side of the page where one finished the preceding line, and heading back across the page. To do this, one must bend the tape around, with the immediate consequence that the *face of the glyphs must also be turned around*; note that the term "face" is suggested by Harris (1995, page 132). The most common way to perform this bending is to fold the tape over itself so that the glyphs – now running in the opposite direction across the physical surface – are flipped around the vertical axis; see diagram (b) in Figure 2.8. This is the standard *boustrophedon* writing found in several ancient eastern Mediterranean scripts, all of which involve this change of

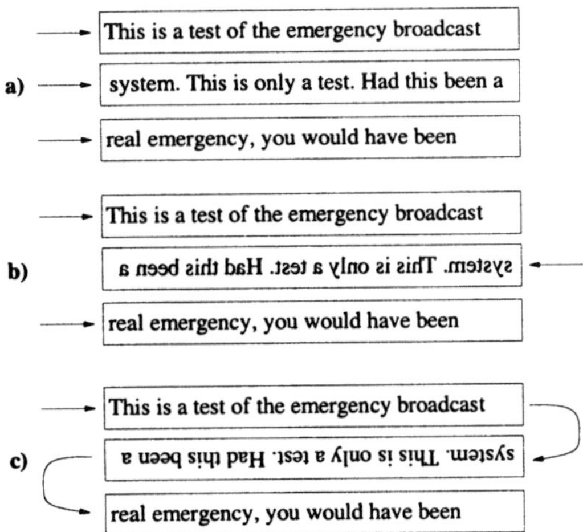

Figure 2.8. Three methods of wrapping the virtual tape: (a) standard non-boustrophedon; (b) boustrophedon; (c) inverted boustrophedon.

face around the vertical axis; see various chapters in Daniels and Bright (1996). The other way to bend the tape is to twist it around so that the glyphs running in the backwards direction are upside down. This "inverted boustrophedon" system seems to be found in only a handful of scripts, one being the Easter Island *rongorongo* script (Fischer, 1997b), and another being the ancient Italian script Venetic (Lejeune, 1974; Bonfante, 1996). See (c) in Figure 2.8; note that *rongorongo* actually runs from bottom to top across the surface, rather than top to bottom as diagrammed here. (Venetic apparently had both kinds of boustrophedon, either flipping the face of the characters when switching direction or else inverting them (Lejeune, 1974, pages 180–181).)

It is important to understand that the virtual tape model, and the consequences that follow from it, are a direct result of the theory adopted here: According to Locality one *cannot* model boustrophedon writing as a line-by-line switch of catenation type, any more than one can model the arrangement of lines on a page by modeling within-line catenation as (e.g.) $\overset{\rightarrow}{\cdot}$ and across-line catenation as $\overset{\downarrow}{\cdot}$. The flip of face in boustrophedon systems, which follows from the virtual tape model, is thus effectively forced by the theory. A boustrophedon system that does not involve a change of face would thus be a problem for the theory. It is therefore interesting to note that such systems do not appear to be common, if indeed they exist at all. Various authors, including Harris (1995) allude to the existence of such nonflipping boustrophedon systems, yet I have been unable to find specific examples of this phenomenon.

Nonetheless, one must point out that higher level script-dependent generalizations are often much freer than the microconstraints we have discussed elsewhere in this chapter. Thus, with the exception of the relatively few Chinese characters that have alternate forms, there is generally only one way to arrange the components within a Chinese character. However, modern Chinese allows two schemes for arranging the symbols on the page, the traditional one described above, and the Western-influenced left-to-right/top-to-bottom arrangement found in English; the same facts hold for other East Asian scripts.[18] Once one moves out of the domain of printed texts, other arrangements often become possible. Shop signs in English may be arranged with the characters running from top to bottom, for instance, and more novel arrangements are possible in other contexts, as long as some notion of sequentiality is preserved. This loosening of constraints as one moves from the micro to the macro level is hardly surprising and has an exact analog in linguistic structure: The syntactic possibilities for combining morphemes within words are generally highly constrained across languages, and in many "fixed word order" languages the possibilities for rearrangements of words or phrases within sentences are also limited. Beyond the sentence, however, the interrelation between units (sentences, paragraphs, turns in a dialogue, etc.) is much more loosely constrained by purely formal linguistic considerations, and much more governed by considerations of how language is used. Similarly, the macro level of written text is constrained by considerations of usage as much as by formal orthographic constraints, a point that Harris's (1995) discussion brings out nicely.

2.A Sample Chinese Characters and Their Analyses

The following pages contain a randomly selected sample of 194 Chinese characters that are accounted for by (2.8), and an additional 38 that are not. In the analyses, the determining component is listed first, after the equals sign, and before the catenation operator. The semantic component is boxed. The symbol '◇' marks characters where the independent pronunciation of the phonetic component is a perfect predictor (including tone) of the pronunciation of the complex character. This is perhaps a more stringent definition of phonological regularity than is strictly speaking necessary, but it has the advantage of being easy to compute.

Note that what is listed for the incorrectly analyzed characters is the *correct* analysis: The predicted (but incorrect) catenation operator is shown in parentheses after each example. In these examples we list the semantic component uniformly first since the determining component is unclear in many cases.

[18] A third scheme, a Semitic-style right-to-left/top-to-bottom arrangement is also found in Chinese, though this is perhaps not as common in ordinary text as the other two.

Correctly Analyzed Characters

◇伍 = 人 $\overset{\rightarrow}{\cdot}$ 五
◇兇 = 儿 $\overset{\uparrow}{\cdot}$ 凶
◇肌 = 肉 $\overset{\rightarrow}{\cdot}$ 几
◇伸 = 人 $\overset{\rightarrow}{\cdot}$ 申
◇汰 = 水 $\overset{\rightarrow}{\cdot}$ 太
◇佰 = 人 $\overset{\rightarrow}{\cdot}$ 百
◇拂 = 手 $\overset{\rightarrow}{\cdot}$ 弗
◇芽 = 艸 $\overset{\downarrow}{\cdot}$ 牙
◇俘 = 人 $\overset{\rightarrow}{\cdot}$ 孚
◇俐 = 人 $\overset{\rightarrow}{\cdot}$ 利
◇拷 = 手 $\overset{\rightarrow}{\cdot}$ 考
◇洶 = 水 $\overset{\rightarrow}{\cdot}$ 匈
◇茅 = 艸 $\overset{\downarrow}{\cdot}$ 矛
◇剛 = 刀 $\overset{\leftarrow}{\cdot}$ 岡
◇株 = 木 $\overset{\rightarrow}{\cdot}$ 朱
◇珠 = 玉 $\overset{\rightarrow}{\cdot}$ 朱
◇飢 = 食 $\overset{\rightarrow}{\cdot}$ 几
◇啃 = 口 $\overset{\rightarrow}{\cdot}$ 肯
◇淆 = 水 $\overset{\rightarrow}{\cdot}$ 肴
◇絆 = 糸 $\overset{\rightarrow}{\cdot}$ 半
◇莖 = 艸 $\overset{\downarrow}{\cdot}$ 巠
◇莉 = 艸 $\overset{\downarrow}{\cdot}$ 利
◇蚯 = 虫 $\overset{\rightarrow}{\cdot}$ 丘
◇徨 = 彳 $\overset{\rightarrow}{\cdot}$ 皇
◇惑 = 心$_{\text{full}}$ $\overset{\uparrow}{\cdot}$ 或
◇棕 = 木 $\overset{\rightarrow}{\cdot}$ 宗
◇棋 = 木 $\overset{\rightarrow}{\cdot}$ 其
◇睏 = 目 $\overset{\rightarrow}{\cdot}$ 困
◇詐 = 言 $\overset{\rightarrow}{\cdot}$ 乍

◇塘 = 土 $\overset{\rightarrow}{\cdot}$ 唐
◇塚 = 土 $\overset{\rightarrow}{\cdot}$ 冢
◇滄 = 水 $\overset{\rightarrow}{\cdot}$ 倉
◇蜓 = 虫 $\overset{\rightarrow}{\cdot}$ 廷
◇誇 = 言 $\overset{\rightarrow}{\cdot}$ 夸
◇慷 = 心 $\overset{\rightarrow}{\cdot}$ 康
◇歌 = 欠 $\overset{\leftarrow}{\cdot}$ 哥
◇筵 = 竹 $\overset{\downarrow}{\cdot}$ 延
◇蜥 = 虫 $\overset{\rightarrow}{\cdot}$ 析
◇蜴 = 虫 $\overset{\rightarrow}{\cdot}$ 易
◇酵 = 酉 $\overset{\rightarrow}{\cdot}$ 孝
◇墟 = 土 $\overset{\rightarrow}{\cdot}$ 虛
◇膛 = 肉 $\overset{\rightarrow}{\cdot}$ 堂
◇褐 = 衣 $\overset{\rightarrow}{\cdot}$ 曷
◇鞍 = 革 $\overset{\rightarrow}{\cdot}$ 安
◇餵 = 食 $\overset{\rightarrow}{\cdot}$ 畏
◇禮 = 示 $\overset{\rightarrow}{\cdot}$ 豊
◇臍 = 肉 $\overset{\rightarrow}{\cdot}$ 齊
◇藤 = 艸 $\overset{\downarrow}{\cdot}$ 滕
◇鐮 = 金 $\overset{\rightarrow}{\cdot}$ 廉
◇顧 = 頁 $\overset{\leftarrow}{\cdot}$ 雇
◇壩 = 土 $\overset{\rightarrow}{\cdot}$ 霸
◇灣 = 水 $\overset{\rightarrow}{\cdot}$ 彎
◇籮 = 竹 $\overset{\downarrow}{\cdot}$ 羅
◇鑲 = 金 $\overset{\rightarrow}{\cdot}$ 襄
◇嵋 = 山 $\overset{\rightarrow}{\cdot}$ 眉
代 = 人 $\overset{\rightarrow}{\cdot}$ 弋
佛 = 人 $\overset{\rightarrow}{\cdot}$ 弗
伯 = 人 $\overset{\rightarrow}{\cdot}$ 白
吩 = 口 $\overset{\rightarrow}{\cdot}$ 分

妞 = [女] →· 丑
扯 = [手] →· 止
折 = [手] →· 斤
汾 = [水] →· 分
使 = [人] →· 吏
固 = [口big] ⊙ 古
妹 = [女] →· 未
帖 = [巾] →· 占
抹 = [手] →· 末
拘 = [手] →· 句
法 = [水] →· 去
沸 = [水] →· 弗
治 = [水] →· 台
泊 = [水] →· 白
穹 = [穴] ↓· 弓
則 = [刀] ←· 貝
恨 = [心] →· 艮
拮 = [手] →· 吉
殆 = [歹] →· 台
珊 = [玉] →· 冊
砂 = [石] →· 少
祈 = [示] →· 斤
貞 = [貝] ↑· 卜
軌 = [車] →· 九
俾 = [人] →· 卑
剔 = [刀] ←· 易
剝 = [刀] ←· 彔
娘 = [女] →· 良
峨 = [山] →· 我
息 = [心full] ↑· 自
拿 = [手full] ↑· 合

挫 = [手] →· 坐
核 = [木] →· 亥
格 = [木] →· 各
桃 = [木] →· 兆
涕 = [水] →· 弟
特 = [牛] →· 寺
砲 = [石] →· 包
紋 = [糸] →· 文
草 = [艸] ↓· 早
袂 = [衣] →· 夬
偏 = [人] →· 扁
唱 = [口] →· 昌
婉 = [女] →· 宛
崎 = [山] →· 奇
悴 = [心] →· 卒
控 = [手] →· 空
猛 = [犬] →· 孟
現 = [玉] →· 見
符 = [竹] ↓· 付
統 = [糸] →· 充
袒 = [衣] →· 旦
袍 = [衣] →· 包
喘 = [口] →· 耑
喻 = [口] →· 俞
揭 = [手] →· 曷
揮 = [手] →· 軍
渦 = [水] →· 咼
牌 = [片] →· 卑
筆 = [竹] ↓· 聿
筍 = [竹] ↓· 旬
脾 = [肉] →· 卑

賁 = [貝] ↑: 卉
酥 = [酉] →: 禾
鈔 = [金] →: 少
鈍 = [金] →: 屯
閑 = [門] ⊙ 木
傲 = [人] →: 敖
嗓 = [口] →: 桑
嗑 = [口] →: 盍
塔 = [土] →: 荅
媽 = [女] →: 馬
嫂 = [女] →: 叟
搔 = [手] →: 蚤
楷 = [木] →: 皆
溥 = [水] →: 尃
煎 = [火$_{red}$] ↑: 前
絹 = [糸] →: 肙
綁 = [糸] →: 邦
詩 = [言] →: 寺
跨 = [足] →: 夸
鉤 = [金] →: 句
隔 = [阜] →: 鬲
嫖 = [女] →: 票
屢 = [尸] ↓: 婁
摟 = [手] →: 婁
榜 = [木] →: 旁
槍 = [木] →: 倉
蒲 = [艸] ↓: 浦
誦 = [言] →: 甬
頗 = [頁] ←: 皮
餅 = [食] →: 并
播 = [手] →: 番

璃 = [玉] →: 离
瞎 = [目] →: 害
緬 = [糸] →: 面
擇 = [手] →: 睪
篤 = [竹] ↓: 馬
罹 = [网] ↓: 惟
諷 = [言] →: 風
貓 = [豸] →: 苗
霍 = [雨] ↓: 隹
頸 = [頁] ←: 巠
頻 = [頁] ←: 步
嚏 = [口] →: 疐
壓 = 厭 ↓: [土]
嶼 = [山] →: 與
濟 = [水] →: 齊
縫 = [糸] →: 逢
蕾 = [艸] ↓: 雷
薔 = [艸] ↓: 嗇
謝 = [言] →: 射
錨 = [金] →: 苗
懣 = [心$_{full}$] ↑: 滿
瀑 = [水] →: 暴
簪 = [竹] ↓: 朁
藏 = [艸] ↓: 臧
鎮 = [金] →: 真
鵝 = [鳥] ←: 我
蟾 = [虫] →: 詹
譎 = [言] →: 矞
勸 = [力] ←: 雚
蘊 = [艸] ↓: 緼

儷 = [人] →· 麗

攜 = [手] →· 巂

灑 = [水] →· 麗

灘 = [水] →· 難

臟 = [肉] →· 藏

鷗 = [鳥] ←· 區

驗 = [馬] →· 僉

囷 = [口$_{big}$] ⊙ 禾

暌 = [日] →· 癸

糨 = [米] →· 強

常 = 尚 ↓· [巾]

當 = 尚 ↓· [田]

裳 = 尚 ↓· [衣]

掌 = 尚 ↓· [牙]

Incorrectly Analyzed Characters

◇奕 = [大] ↑· 亦 (↓·)

◇財 = [貝] →· 才 (↑·)

◇娶 = [女] ↑· 取 (→·)

◇晨 = [日] ↓· 辰 (→·)

◇壁 = [土] ↑· 辟 (→·)

◇壅 = [土] ↑· 雍 (→·)

◇禦 = [示] ↑· 御 (→·)

吉 = [口] ↑· 士 (→·)

吾 = [口] ↑· 五 (→·)

君 = [口] ↑· 尹 (→·)

岔 = [山] ↑· 分 (→·)

孤 = [子] →· 瓜 (↑·)

斧 = [斤] ↑· 父 (→·)

昏 = [日] ↑· 氏 (→·)

威 = [女] ↑· 戌 (→·)

柔 = [木] ↑· 矛 (→·)

背 = [肉] ↑· 北 (→·)

晃 = [日] ↓· 光 (→·)

隻 = [隹] ↓· 又 (←·)

曼 = [又] ↑· 冒 (→·)

崗 = [山] ↓· 岡 (→·)

斬 = [斤] ←· 車 (→·)

梟 = [木] ↑· 鳥 (→·)

紫 = [糸] ↑· 此 (→·)

翔 = [羽] ←· 羊 (↓·)

貽 = [貝] →· 台 (↑·)

暈 = [日] ↓· 軍 (→·)

甄 = [瓦] ←· 垔 (→·)

熨 = [火] ↑· 尉 (→·)

賜 = [貝] →· 易 (↑·)

曇 = [日] ↓· 雲 (→·)

燙 = [火] ↑· 湯 (→·)

嶽 = [山] ↓· 獄 (→·)

繁 = [糸] ↑· 敏 (→·)

膺 = [肉] ↑· 雁 (→·)

譽 = [言] ↑· 與 (→·)

鑒 = [金] ↑· 監 (→·)

炙 = [火] ↑· 肉 (→·)

3 ORL Depth and Consistency

In this chapter we address the second of the two proposals presented in Section 1.2.3, namely Consistency. We will first examine the orthographies of Russian and Belarusian, which form a near minimal pair from the point of view of the level of the ORL. We will show that a simple coherent analysis of the two systems can be obtained if we assume that in each case the ORL is a Consistent level, with the only difference between Russian and Belarusian being the depth of that level.

We then turn our attention to English. In light of the analysis of Russian and Belarusian, how deep is the ORL for English, and can one assume Consistency for the ORL? The evidence we will examine suggests that Consistency is possible. Not surprisingly, the analysis is simpler if we assume a relatively deep ORL, though perhaps unexpectedly the evidence is not as clearcut as in the case of Russian versus Belarusian.

An apparent counterexample to Consistency is found in the orthographic representation of obstruants in Serbo-Croatian. These data are discussed in Section 3.3, and data from a small phonetic experiment are presented that suggest that in fact the data are not a counterexample but rather offer support for Consistency.

Another potential problem for Consistency would be evidence that the spelling of a word needs to be constructed in a *cyclic* fashion, since this would seem to suggest that there might in effect be several "ORLs" for a given morphologically complex word, one for each cycle. A potential example of this is presented in Section 3.4.

Finally, as we discussed in the introduction, we assume, similar to Nunn (1998), that $M_{ORL \to \Gamma}$ can be split into two components, which we have termed M_{Encode} and M_{Spell}. One component of the latter comprises what we can term *surface orthographic constraints*, and for lack of a better place to discuss them, we turn to a short discussion of this topic in Section 3.5.

3.1 Russian and Belarusian Orthography: A Case Study

One way to illustrate the functionality of the proposed model is to compare two languages that have similar phonologies, but select different levels for the ORL. An almost ideal pair of languages for this purpose is Russian and

Belarusian. These languages share many phonological features, including strong vowel reduction in unstressed syllables and palatalization assimilation in consonant clusters. The orthographic representation of these phonological phenomena is, however, quite different in the two writing systems.

3.1.1 Vowel Reduction

One way in which the Russian and Belarusian orthographies differ is in the treatment of the vowel reduction process known in the Slavic literature by the names *akan'je*, *ikan'je*, and *jakan'je*. We have already seen an instance of *akan'je* – reduction of /a/ and /o/ – in the example **города** <goroda> /gərʌ'da/ 'cities' in Section 1.2.1. *Ikan'je* involves the reduction of /(j)e/ and /(j)a/ after soft consonants[1] to /ɩ/: Two examples are **язык** <jazyk> /jɩ'zɨk/ 'language', and **перевод** <perevod> /p,ɩr,ɩ'vot/ 'translation'. (We use a "," to denote a palatalized consonant in the phonetic transcription.) The details of Russian akan'je/ikan'je are well known (Wade, 1992, pages 5–7):

- In pretonic position (i.e., in the syllable preceding the lexically stressed syllable), word-initial in an unstressed syllable, or word-final in an open unstressed syllable, underlying /o/ and /a/ (after hard consonants) are reduced to /ʌ/.
- In all other unstressed syllables underlying /o/ and /a/ (after hard consonants) are reduced to /ə/.
- Underlying /(j)e/ and /(j)a/ (after soft consonants) are reduced to /ɩ/ in unstressed syllables.

Russian represents neither reduction process in its orthography, and so it seems reasonable to suppose, as is typically done (cf. again Cubberley (1996)), that Russian orthography is *morphological* in the sense that it represents an underlying phonological level – *UL*, though this does not necessarily represent the most abstract phonological level one could posit. The table in (3.1) gives the levels of representation for the words for 'cities' and 'translation':

(3.1)

	'cities'	'translation'
ORL (= UL)	goro'da	pere'vod
Γ	**города**	**перевод**
Φ	gərʌ'da	pɩrɩ'vot

Here, and elsewhere, Φ denotes the actual surface phonemic representation (i.e., the pronunciation). A set of spelling rules – M_{Encode} – including the

[1] Russian and Belarusian phonemically distinguish *soft* or palatalized consonants from *hard* or nonpalatalized consonants.

rules in (3.2) (copied in part from (1.5) is sufficient to accomplish this mapping:[2]

(3.2)	g	→	г <g>
	o	→	о <o> /[+*cons*, −*high*] ___
	r	→	р <r>
	d	→	д <d>
	a	→	а <a> /[+*cons*, −*high*] ___
	p	→	п <p>
	e	→	е <e> /[+*cons*] ___
	v	→	в <v>

Note the restrictions on the rewrite of vowels: /o/ and /a/ appear as **о** <o> and **а** <a> only after hard consonants ([+*cons*, −*high*]); and in the majority of Russian words, /e/ appears as **е** <e> after all consonants, whereas in syllable-initial position /e/ (as opposed to /je/) appears as the nonpalatal **э**, which we will notate here as <e> (see also Section 3.5).

Belarusian also has akan'je and ikan'je (the latter called *jakan'je*) that behave very similarly to their Russian counterparts. However, unlike the situation in Russian, Belarusian orthography generally reflects these processes; see Carlton (1990, pages 299–301). The rules can be stated as follows (following Carlton):

- In pretonic position, or word-initial in an unstressed syllable, underlying /e/ and /o/ are reduced to /a/.[3]
- In all other unstressed syllables, underlying /o/ and /e/ (after hard consonants) are reduced to /a/.

(We return at the end of this section to the case of nonpretonic unstressed /e/ after soft consonants.) Examples (from Krivickij and Podluzhnyj (1994, pages 15, 22)) are **вецер** <vecer> /ˈv,etˢ,er/ 'wind' (noun), versus **вятры** <vjatry> /v,aˈtrɨ/ 'winds'; **ногі**[4] <nogi> /ˈnogi/ 'feet', versus **нага** <naga> /naˈga/ 'foot'; and **цэгла** <cegla> /ˈtˢegla/ 'brick', versus **цагляны** <cagljany> /tˢaˈgl,anɨ/ 'made of brick'.

Similar to the table given for the Russian cases, we can assume the tables in (3.3) for the Belarusian examples we have just discussed. In this case the

[2] While we express the rules here, and elsewhere, as a set of ordered rewrite rules, there is often no crucial ordering to such rules. When ordering is not crucial they are best viewed as a set of parallel *two-level* rules in the sense of Koskenniemi (1983).

[3] It is unclear whether this is really /a/ or something more akin to /ʌ/, detailed phonetic descriptions of Belarusian akan'je having proved elusive.

[4] The Russian symbol **и** <i> is not used in Belarusian. Note also that **г**, represented phonemically here as /g/, is actually a voiced fricative, often transliterated as /h/ (Wayles Browne, personal communication).

ORL reflects the application of vowel reduction, and Φ is effectively the same as the ORL:[5]

(3.3)

	'wind'	'winds'
UL	'v,et,er	v,e'trɨ
ORL	'v,et^ser	v,a'trɨ
Γ	**вецер**	**вятры**
Φ	'v,et^ser	v,a'trɨ

	'feet'	'foot'
UL	'nogi	no'ga
ORL	'nogi	na'ga
Γ	**ногі**	**нага**
Φ	'nogi	na'ga

	'brick'	'made of brick'
UL	't,egla	t,e'gl,anɨ
ORL	't^segla	t^sa'gl,anɨ
Γ	**цэгла**	**цагляны**
Φ	't^segla	t^sa'gl,anɨ

The spelling rules necessary to map from ORL to Γ for Belarusian include those in (3.4):

(3.4)

v	→	**в** <v>
e	→	**е** <e> /[+*cons*, +*high*] ___
t	→	**т** <t>
t^s	→	**ц** <c>
r	→	**р** <r>
a	→	**я** <j̲a> /[+*cons*, +*high*] ___
ɨ	→	**ы** <y>
n	→	**н** <n>
o	→	**о** <o>
g	→	**г** <g>
i	→	**і** <i>
a	→	**а** <a> /[+*cons*, −*high*] ___
e	→	**э** <e̲> /[+*cons*, −*high*] ___
l	→	**л** <l>

The encoding of consonants and most vowels is identical to that in Russian. The only differences evident in these cases are encoding of /e/ following

[5] On the change from /t/ to /t^s/ in the form **вецер** <vecer> 'wind', which is also reflected in the orthography, see Section 3.1.2. In the underlying representations we assume an underlying /t/ for surface /t^s/.

hard consonants, which is э <e> in Belarusian (which is generally disallowed except in syllable-initial position in Russian), and the different symbol used for /i/.

It is worth noting that, at least in some versions of Belarusian, akan'je and jakan'je occur not only within words but also within clitic groups – and this is likewise reflected in the orthography. Thus in the text of Lyosik (1926), one finds examples such as the following, involving the negative clitic /ne/, in many environments written as **не** <ne>, but in the jakan'je environment written as **ня** <nja>, evidently reflecting the pronunciation /n,a/:

(3.5)	(a)	**ня то́лькі**	<nja tól'ki>	'not only'	pages 75, 83
		ня ўсе́	<nja wsé>	'not all'	page 85
		ня пі́шацца	<nja píšacca>	'is not written'	page 109
	(b)	**не маглі́**	<ne maglí>	'they were not able'	page 82
		не славя́нскі	<ne slavjánski>	'not Slavic'	page 98
		не белару́скі	<ne belarúski>	'not Belarusian'	page 95

Contrast the examples in (3.5a) with those in (3.5b).[6] However, the more recent discussion in Krivickij and Podluzhnyj (1994, page 22) explicitly denies that Lyosik's examples are correct and contrasts the behavior of **не** <ne> 'not' and **без** <bez> 'without' as separate clitics and as prefixes:

> Regularly written with **е** [<e>] are the particle **не** [<ne>] and the preposition **без** [<bez>]; if, however, they appear as prefixes, then they obey the general rule of jakan'je: **без людзей** [<bez ljudzej> 'without people'], but **бязлюдны** [<bjazljúdny> 'unpopulated'], **не шмат** [<ne šmat>] 'not much', but **няшмат** [<njašmat> 'a little'] ...

Evidently this difference is due to a change in Belarusian orthographic norms since Lyosik's day (rather than being due to an actual change in the language).[7] Krivickij and Podluzhnyj's choice of wording – "regularly written with е ... " ("**регулярно пишутся через е**") – certainly suggests this possibility. If this is the case, and this does reflect a spelling reform

[6] Nonetheless, about 25% of thirty-one examples collected from Lyosik's text seem to be inconsistent with the correct application of jakan'je for /ne/. For example he uses **ня было** <nja bylo> 'was not' (page 63). Stress must be on the second syllable of **было** <bylo> 'was' (as it is in Russian), as evidenced by nonapplication of akan'je to the /o/. Therefore, the /e/ of /ne/ should in principle be written as **е** <e>, since it is not in a pretonic syllable.

[7] It seems plausible that Lyosik's orthographic scheme was in fact experimental, since Belarusian orthography had probably not been standardized when Lyosik wrote (Elena Pavlova, personal communication).

Also, it seems that the spelling system assumed by Krivckij and Podluzhnyj was imposed by decree by Stalin in 1933, replacing an earlier popular spelling system (Maksymiuk, 1999).

in Belarusian, it is interesting to note that it is consistent with the most recent Dutch spelling reform, which we will discuss later on in Chapter 6, a reform that favors morphological, rather than phonetic regularity. As a result of this orthographic principle, **не** <ne> 'not' and **без** <bez> 'without' are spelled the same (at least when they are used as separate words), even though they may change in pronunciation. In any case, the most direct implementation of the version of Belarusian described by Krivickij and Podluzhnyj in terms of our model is to assume that *bez* 'without' and *ne* 'not' are simply lexically marked to always be spelled with **е** <e>.

Over and above the spelling conventions for **не** <ne> and **без** <bez>, and despite Belarusian's general tendency to have a shallow, phonemically based orthography, there are a few lexical exceptions to the orthographic conventions for akan'je and jakan'je. Krivckij and Podluzhnyj note that unstressed <e> is written in **дзевяты** <dzevjáty> 'ninth' (from **дзевяць** <dzévjac'> 'nine'), **дзесяты** <dzesjáty> 'tenth' (from **дзесяць** <dzésjac'> 'ten'), and in some other numerals. And etymological <o> can be found in unstressed syllables in loan words: **етымолёгiчны** <etymoljógičny> 'etymological'. Such cases must presumably simply be lexically marked. For example, for the word 'nine', we can assume a (partial) lexical representation as in (3.6a) where only the **е** <e> is lexically specified. (Recall that the orthographic specifications in the Russian example in (1.4) were redundant; we argued, that the orthographic representation of **города** <goroda> 'cities' is regularly derived.) The lexical specification will then carry over to the derived form 'ninth', as shown in (3.6b):

(3.6) (a) $\begin{bmatrix} \text{PHON}\langle {}'d^z e_{1*}\, v, at^s, \rangle \\ \text{ORTH}\{\mathbf{e}_1\} \end{bmatrix}$

(b) $\begin{bmatrix} \text{PHON}\langle d^z e_{1*}\, {}'v, ati \rangle \\ \text{ORTH}\{\mathbf{e}_1\} \end{bmatrix}$

The remaining cases of potential jakan'je, namely cases where /e/ occurs in nonpretonic unstressed syllables after a palatal consonant, are of uncertain status. In such cases, Carlton notes (1990, page 300) that Belarusian "specialists differ ... [s]ome recommend[ing] *'a* as the correct pronunciation ...," others recommending /e/, or "even a vowel between *'a* and *'e*." While the two unequivocal instances of akan'je/jakan'je are reflected in Belarusian spelling, this latter instance is not. The spelling that is chosen – **е** <e> or **я** <ja> – depends upon the spelling of the vowel in the root in question in a form where that vowel is stressed. Thus (to use Carlton's examples), we have **лес** <les> 'forest', **лясніk** <ljasník> 'woodsman', but **л**[**е**]**сніkі** <lesnikí>

'woodsman'; but ц[я]жкаваты <tsjažkaváty> 'somewhat heavy', derived from цяжка <tsjažka> 'heavily'. In any case, the pronunciation of the boxed vowels is the same, though, as we have noted, Belarusian specialists differ as to what it should be. On the face of it, then, we would appear to have a case where Belarusian spelling behaves more like that of Russian, in representing an underlying rather than surface vowel, something that would appear to be in direct violation of Consistency.

However, a possible solution to this dilemma suggests itself: Suppose that the jakan'je of nonpretonic unstressed postpalatal /e/s – call it "jakan'je-B" – is a different process than the remaining cases of akan'je/jakan'je ("(j)akan'je-A"), and suppose further that jakan'je-B occurs later than (j)akan'je-A. Then one could assume that the ORL for Belarusian represents a stage at which (j)akan'je-A has applied, but before jakan'je-B has applied. What lends plausibility to this suggestion is precisely the disagreement among Belarusian specialists as to what the vowel in such cases should be, which contrasts to their (apparent) agreement about all other instances of akan'je and jakan'je. If this disagreement reflects a true phonetic variation in the implementation of jakan'je-B – one that is not in evidence for (j)akan'je-A – then it is quite possible that these do in fact represent two stages of vowel reduction, one ((j)akan'je-A) that is firmly rooted in the phonology of the language and the other, that is less firmly established and is subject to more variation across speakers.[8] Further evidence for this position comes from the history and present distribution of akan'je and *ikan'je* in *Russian* dialects (Avanesov, 1974, and Elena Pavlova, personal communication) Ikan'je definitely postdated akan'je in Moscow dialects of Russian, due in part to the fact that the distinction between hard and soft consonants had not stabilized until quite late (fourteenth century). In modern Russian dialects there is still a great deal of variation in ikan'je, compared with akan'je, suggesting that even in Russian the two processes may be at different levels of the phonology. The ultimate correctness of this suggestion necessarily awaits further study, but if it can be maintained, then these facts do not constitute a counterexample to Consistency.

3.1.2 Regressive Palatalization

Another difference between Russian orthography and at least some versions of Belarusian orthography is in the treatment of regressive palatalization of consonants.

[8] One might suppose, along these lines, that (j)akan'je-A is a lexical phonological process, whereas jakan'je-B is a postlexical or phonetic process.

In Russian, a dental or alveolar consonant becomes palatalized if the following adjacent dental or alveolar consonant is also palatalized. More specifically (Wade, 1992, pages 9–10):[9]

- Dental stops (/t/, /d/, /n/) become palatalized before a palatalized dental or alveolar. Thus /dn,i/ 'days' is pronounced /d,n,i/.
- Alveolar fricatives (/s/, /z/) followed by a palatalized dental stop, alveolar fricative, or lateral also become palatalized; Thus /vʌ'zn,ik/ 'arose' is /vʌ'z,n,ik/.

We may assume for the sake of concreteness that the assimilation involves spreading of the feature [+high] within the sequence of consonants.[10]

Although palatalization is marked in the orthography of Russian, there is no special mark of the spreading itself. That is, the final consonant of the cluster is orthographically marked as palatal, either by virtue of its occurring before one of the "soft" vowels – **е** <(j)e>, **и** <i>, **ю** <ju>, **ё** <jo>, or **я** <ja> – or else explicitly using the soft sign **ь** <'>. But consonants internal to the cluster are not marked as palatal.[11] Thus in the word **есть** <jest'> 'is, are', the final /t/ is orthographically marked as palatal with the soft sign **ь**, but in fact the entire /st/ cluster is palatal: /jes,t,/. We assume the table in (3.7) for this case:

(3.7)

	'is, are'
ORL (= UL)	jest,
Γ	**есть** <jest'>
Φ	jes,t,

Palatalization and regressive palatalization in Belarusian is on the whole similar to that of Russian (see Krivickij and Podluzhnyj (1994, pages 55–57)), but a couple of notable differences exist. One difference in the palatalization process itself is that palatalized /t/ and /d/ become palatalized affricates, /t^s,/ and /d^z,/ respectively. Thus for Russian /d,at,ka/ 'uncle' we have in Belarusian /d^z,at^s,ka/; for Russian /t,es,t,/ 'father in law', Belarusian has /t^s,es,t^s,/.

[9] Wayles Browne (personal communication) notes that this spreading of palatalization across dental/alveolar consonant clusters is a feature of older dialects and is becoming less prevalent in contemporary Russian.

[10] Note though that words admit alternative pronunciations, including some cases that do not fall under the rubric of the two classes listed above: these include cases such as /dv,er,/ 'door', which may be either /dv,er,/ or /d,ver,/. Many such exceptions can be found in Avanesov (1983).

[11] Consonants internal to clusters *can* be marked with a soft sign, but in that case they are *lexically* palatal, and this has nothing to do with the assimilation process that we are discussing now. An example is **судьба** <sud'ba> 'fate'.

A second difference is that dental stops in Belarusian regularly palatalize before a palatalized /v/. Thus alongside the masculine/neuter form /dva/ 'two', we have feminine /d^z,v,e/ 'two'; alongside /čatyry/ 'four', we have the collective form /čat^s,v,ora/.

Once again unlike the situation in Russian, Belarusian orthographically marks regressive palatalization, at least in cases involving /t^s,/ and /d^z,/, which have a separate orthographic representation, namely ц(ь) <c(')> and дз(ь) <dz(')> respectively. Thus /d^z,v,e/ 'two (feminine)' is written as дзве <dzve>, and /čat^s,v,ora/ 'four (collective)' is written as **чацвёра** <čacvjora>. Thus although Krivickij and Podluzhnyj note that the effects of regressive palatalization are not indicated in writing (page 56), this is not strictly correct since in the case of palatalized /t/ and /d/, these are orthographically marked as affricates, though they are not followed by a soft sign ь <'>. However, for a form such as ёсць <josc,> 'is, are', which is pronounced /jos,t^s,/, the palatal /s/ is certainly not marked orthographically in any way. The explanation for the difference in behavior is presumably that the affricates /t^s/ and /d^z/, whether palatalized or not, have a standard orthographic representation as ц <c> and дз <dz>, whereas /s/, for instance, only has one representation, namely с <s>, and there is no separate symbol for a palatalized /s/. But why is the soft sign not written cluster internally?[12] We can presume that in modern Belarusian orthography, a soft sign merely marks a cluster of consonants as being palatalized. Thus we could write the following rule:

(3.8) $\phi \rightarrow$ ь $/[+cons, +high]$ ___ $(\# \,\|\, [+cons, -high])$

This rule would form part of the M_{Encode} for Belarusian and would simply insert a soft sign after a palatalized consonant, whenever it is not followed by a vowel (since in that case one uses one of the soft vowel symbols, which implicitly mark palatality) or another palatalized consonant.

The table in (3.9) gives the representations for **два** <dva> 'two' (masculine/neuter) and дзве <dzve> 'two' (feminine):

(3.9)

	'two' (masculine, neuter)	'two' (feminine)
UL	dva	dv,e
ORL	dva	d^z,v,e
Γ	два <dva>	дзве <dzve>
Φ	dva	d^z,v,e

This case is interesting, because the representation of regressive palatalization in Belarusian orthography would appear to be prima facie evidence

[12] That is, besides cases where the consonant is lexically marked as palatal, as in Russian.

against Consistency: On the one hand regressive palatalization is represented when it involves /t, d/, which become affricates; on the other hand it is not represented for any other consonant. But as we can see, the Inconsistency is only apparent. The reason that the soft sign is not used to mark regressive assimilation in general merely relates to the statement of the rule that spells out the soft sign.

Interestingly, Lyosik's usage is again different from that of Krivickij and Podluzhnyj. In Lyosik's usage, in clusters of palatal consonants, *all* assimilated consonants are marked with a soft sign. Thus whereas Krivickij and Podluzhnyj have **цвёрды** <cvjordy> /t^sv,ordy/ 'hard', Lyosik writes **цьвёрды** <c'vjordy>; for **дзве** <dzve> /d^z,v,e/ 'two (feminine)', Lyosik has **дзьве** <dz've>; for **ёсць** <josc'> /jos,t^s,/ 'is, are', he has **ёсьць** <jos'c'>. This is readily interpretable as a simplification of the rule in (3.8), which can be rewritten to describe Lyosik's spelling conventions as follows:

(3.10) $\phi \rightarrow$ **ь** $/[+cons, +high]$ ___ $\neg V$

(That is, the soft sign is inserted after a palatalized consonant, except before a vowel.) The table for the feminine form of 'two' shown above in (3.9) now becomes:

(3.11)

	'two' (feminine)
UL	dv,e
ORL	d^z,v,e
Г	**дзьве** <dz've>
Ф	d^z,v,e

3.1.3 Lexical Marking in Russian and Other Issues

Despite the regularity of Russian spelling, there are cases where one must assume lexical marking of orthographic information, and we will examine a couple of these here. We will start, however, by considering a case that might appear to involve marked orthography, but which in fact involves marked phonology, with the orthography itself being perfectly regular.

In the Slavic-derived vocabulary, sequences of hard consonants followed by nonpalatalized /e/ do not occur. Basically either one gets a palatalized consonant (e.g., *ot'ec* 'father', with a palatalized /t,/), or else one finds a hard (in this case partially palatalized) consonant, followed by /je/: *otjezd* 'departure'. There are however a large number of borrowed words that have such sequences, particularly those involving dental consonants. Consider the following examples, in which the hard consonant has been underlined: *seks* 'sex', *test* 'test', *arterioscl'eroz* 'arteriosclerosis', *g'eteromorfizm* 'heteromorphism', *d̲ekagram* 'decagram'. In each of these cases, the vowel /e/ is spelled with **е** <e>. Thus *dekagram* is spelled **декаграм** <dekagram>, and *seks* is spelled **секс** <seks>. From the point of view of the reader of Russian, these cases involve an irregular usage of the written vowel е <e>. But there is in fact nothing irregular in the spelling here: What is irregular is the phonology. The fact that the vowel is spelled with **е** <e> follows from general constraints on Russian orthography. This is because the only other way that the vowel could be spelled would be as **э** <e̲>, but this vowel symbol is generally disallowed in nonsyllable-initial position. As we shall suggest in Section 3.5, this constraint is best expressed as a surface orthographic constraint of Russian. What this entails then is that the unusual phonological structure in the cases we have been considering are spelled in the only way they can be, with **е** <e>. Note that the spelling rules that we presented in (3.2) already capture these facts, since postconsonantal /e/ is rewritten by these rules as е <e>.

One genuine case of orthographic lexical marking involves the genitive endings *-evo* and *ovo*, which are always written **его** <ego> and **ого** <ogo>. Thus for the word *bol'šovo* 'big' (masculine/neuter genitive singular) it will be necessary only to specify that the /v/ is written as г <g>.

Another and somewhat more troubling case that requires lexical specification under the present theory are prefixes such as *raz-*, or *bez-*, which assimilate in voicing to the following consonant, following regular principles of Russian phonology. Basically, word-final obstruents in Russian are always voiceless, and obstruents assimilate in voicing to a following obstruent in a cluster; this assimilation applies across words as well as within words.[13] With one class of exceptions, assimilation and devoicing of obstruents is never reflected in the orthography of Russian. Thus **город** <gorod> 'city' is thus written, even though the final /d/ is actually a /t/; similarly, the phrase **без пальца** <bez pal'ca> 'without a finger' is thus written even though the final /z/ of *bez* assimilates in voicing to the following /p/ and is therefore really /s/. The systematic class of exceptions to this generalization are the aforementioned prefixes (along with *v(o)z-* and *iz-*; see Wade (1992, page 16)). Thus we have **безбожный** <bezbožnyj> 'godless', but **беспалый** <bespalyj> 'fingerless'; **раздумье** <razdum'e> 'thought', but **расписка** <raspiska> 'receipt'. Note that this exceptional spelling is only found with prefixes ending in (underlying) voiced obstruents. Those that are underlyingly voiceless, such as *s-*, retain their expected spellings when preceding voiced obstruents (in which case their final consonants become phonologically voiced); thus *sdavat'* /zdʌvat'/ 'to hand in' is written **сдавать** <sdavat'>, not ***здавать** <zdavat'>.

13 The facts are identical in Belarusian, and the discussion here would carry over rather directly to Belarusian.

In addition to voicing assimilation, akan'je is also represented in the orthography for the prefix *raz-*: Indeed, the underlying form of *raz-* is really *roz-*. Thus, under stress it is spelled **роз** <roz> (or **рос** <ros>); thus we have **россыпь** <róssyp'> 'mineral deposit' versus **рассыпать** <rassypát'> 'spill, scatter'. The alternation is *not* marked for *bez-*. Thus one never finds the spelling ***биз** <biz>: In **беспалый** <bespályj> 'fingerless', the vowel in the prefix is /ι/, not /e/, despite the spelling.

The behavior of these prefixes would appear to require a relaxation of the Consistency assumption, since they would seem to involve an ORL that is much later than the ORL we have been assuming for the rest of the Russian vocabulary. On the face of it the facts are reminiscent of Pesetsky's (1979) unpublished but influential analysis of Russian lexical phonology, wherein he argues that prefixes are phonologically on a later cycle than suffixes. Might it be, then, that the orthography of prefixes is similarly handled at a later level, and thus reflects vowel and consonant changes that have not taken place at the point at which the spelling of stems and suffixes is handled? Under this analysis we would have to abandon Consistency in favor of a kind of *Constrained Inconsistency*. The problem with this move is that, as we noted above, the spelling irregularities are by no means common to all prefixes: Prefixes ending in voiceless consonants such as *s-* or *ot-* do not undergo these changes. Furthermore, *ot-* is always spelled **от** <ot> in Russian, even when the /o/ is reduced to /ə/ by akan'je. Thus the inconsistency would be constrained indeed, applying to just a few lexical entries.

The cleanest solution to the problem within the current framework is to assume that this class of prefixes has a special set of spelling rules that is sensitive to the voicing of the following consonant and (for *roz-*) the stress on the prefix. Thus, we assume according to the Consistency hypothesis that the ORL representation of **беспалый** <bespalyj> is /bezpalyj/. The normal spelling rule for /z/ would of course give **з** <z>, but if we assume a rule such as that in (3.12), the /z/ will instead be written **с** <s>. Similarly, the ORL representation of **рассыпать** <rassypat'> is /rossypat,/, and the spelling of /o/ as **а** <a> is accomplished by the rule in (3.13):

(3.12) z → **с** <s> / ___ [−voiced]

Condition: /z/ is in one of the prefixes *bez-*, *roz-*, *v(o)z-*, or *iz-*

(3.12) o → **а** <a>

Condition: /o/ is unstressed in the prefix *roz-*

The unusual spelling of underlying /z/ and /o/ in these cases is thus due to a form of lexical marking, this time a lexical condition on a rule. We are therefore able to preserve Consistency, though at the cost of two redundant spelling rules.

3.1.4 Summary of Russian and Belarusian

The previous discussion has offered a comparative analysis of a portion of Russian and Belarusian orthography and the relationship of those orthographic systems to the phonologies of the languages. Of course, a full evaluation of the model's applicability to these writing systems awaits a complete description of the orthography, as well as a complete description of the relevant phonological phenomena – something that is certainly beyond the scope of this work. Nonetheless, the data presented here are at least consistent with the Consistency hypothesis, which is what we aimed to show. Hence we conclude that the ORL in Russian and Belarusian are Consistent levels and that furthermore there is a great similarity in the two systems of spelling – $M_{ORL \rightarrow \Gamma}$. The main difference between Russian and Belarusian orthography lies in the depth of the ORL.

3.2 English

As we have seen, the orthographies of Russian and Belarusian are both quite regular (i.e., in the sense of being "rule-governed"); the only difference is in the level of abstractness of the ORL: In Russian, one represents in the written form a level of phonological representation that is closer to an "underlying" representation, than what one represents in Belarusian. Under that assumption, relatively little orthographic information needs to be lexically marked. In contrast, if we assumed a shallower ORL for Russian, then a large portion of the vocabulary, particularly those words with lexical /o/ or /a/, both of which surface as /ə/ or /ʌ/ in unstressed positions, would require orthographic information to be marked. That is, if the spelling **города** <goroda> is taken to represent a phonological representation such as /gərʌˈda/, then the /ə/ and the /ʌ/ will each need to be lexically marked as being written as **о** <o>, since either one could equally well have been written **а** <a>, yielding the same pronunciation. Of course, our assumption does not allow us to avoid lexical marking in Russian (or Belarusian) completely. For instance, we considered the irregularly pronounced **г** <g> /v/ in the genitive endings **его**/**ого** <ego>/<ogo>. But such items would require lexical marking of some kind in any case, since they patently fall outside the regular system of Russian spelling.

The relatively clear status of Russian as a "deep" orthography brings us to the question of how to characterize the orthography of Modern English, another phonographic writing system that has been described as "deep." Of course, even a cursory knowledge of English spelling leads one immediately to the conclusion that the system of English spelling is a great deal more chaotic than that of Russian, or indeed almost any other language that uses a script whose original design was purely phonological,[14] a fact that has not gone unnoticed by scores of spelling-reformers from the seventeenth century to the present day (Venezky 1970, pages 19ff). Nonetheless, this observation has not prevented various authors from attempting to find regularity in the system. One such enterprise was the classic work of Venezky (1970), who argued that the relation between spelling and pronunciation (he was primarily interested in the mapping in this direction, rather than the other way around) was governed by clear sets of ordered rules.[15] In Venezky's system, a spelling such as <social> was mapped to the morphophonemic representation {sosıæl}, by a set of grapheme-to-morphophoneme rules (page 46); and thence to a surface pronunciation by phonological rules. Rules in Venezky's system were arranged in ordered blocks. Thus one block states that initial <h> corresponds to morphophonemic {∅} in *heir*, (American English) *herb*, *honest*, *honor*, and *hour*; medial preconsonantal and final <h> is {∅}; and <h> is elsewhere {h} (page 74). Interestingly, Venezky says relatively little of a systematic nature about the influence of morphology: The vowel-shift-related alternations such as those exemplified in *extreme–extremity*, and which were to play so central a role in the early development of generative phonology, were treated only briefly (pages 108–109) in Venezky's discussion.

It is tempting to classify Venezky's model in our terms as being one where the ORL – his morphophonemic level – corresponds more or less to an underlying morphophonemic representation. But this is not strictly accurate: Venezky was operating within a pre-generative American structuralist set of assumptions,[16] within which such notions as underlying representation were not available.

Within the generative phonological tradition, however, such notions as deep or surface structure are explicitly assumed (or at least were until about a

[14] One exception is the orthography of Manx Gaelic, a system that is based on the orthography of English, and whose apparent arbitrariness approaches that of English in some respects; we will discuss the writing system of Manx later on in Section 6.1.

[15] Another important work that presents a rule-based account of English spelling is Cumming's (1988) treatment of American English spelling. Cumming's work is relatively unusual in the literature English orthography in that he deals, as we do in this section, with the problem of predicting spelling from pronunciation rather than pronunciation from spelling; as we have just noted, Venezky's work, for instance, dealt with the problem of inferring pronunciation from spelling.

[16] He does not even cite *The Sound Pattern of English*, even though that work appeared two years prior to the publication of his monograph.

decade ago), and it was within this set of assumptions that arguably the most radical statement about the nature of English spelling was made. Chomsky and Halle (1968) argue that English orthography is, despite appearances, a near optimal spelling system, the key assumption being that what is represented is not a surface phonemic representation, but rather a quite abstract lexical representation. The claim was made largely on the basis of such alternations as *assign–assignation*. For this pair, the surface phonemic representation /əˈsaɪn/–/ asɪgˈneɪšən/ gives no clue as to why there should be a <g> in the spelling of *assign*, or why <i> should represent two such quite different vowels. The deep representation, which would be something like /æˈsīgn/ and /ˌæsīgˈnātyon/, respectively, makes this clear, as both forms have a /g/ (removed by subsequent rules in *assign*), and both forms have the same /ī/, which undergoes vowel shift in *assign*, and reduction in *assignation*. Chomsky and Halle go so far as to claim that English orthography, far from being the unfortunate system it is usually taken to be, is in fact close to an ideal system of orthography. This is because "the fundamental principle of orthography is that phonetic variation is not indicated where it is predictable" and that "an optimal orthography would have one representation for each lexical entry" (1968, page 49) (also cited in Sampson (1985, page 200)).

Needless to say few scholars of writing systems would agree with Chomsky and Halle's rather prescriptive statement about orthographic principles, which is neither obviously true as a statistical statement about writing systems cross-linguistically, nor can it be taken as anything other than a statement of personal taste about how writing systems should be designed.[17] Furthermore, and more directly relevant to our current discussion, several authors have taken issue with the specific claim about English. For example, Sampson (1985) notes several rather serious problems with

[17] Having said that, it is certainly true that there seems to be a "tension" between what one might term *phonological faithfulness* on the one hand and *morphological faithfulness* on the other. That is, writing systems often face a choice between representing a word in a form that is representative of its (surface) pronunciation and representing the morphemes of a word in a fashion consistent with their spelling in other related words. This is hardly a new observation, and linguists have for decades made this observation in various forms. Russian orthography can be said to have addressed both problems rather elegantly in the sense that morphologically related forms – at least those that are related by fairly regular and general phonological alternations – are consistently spelled, yet going from the spelling to the pronunciation is also quite straightforward – given of course that one has certain lexical information in hand.

One might be tempted to state the notions of phonological faithfulness and morphological faithfulness as soft constraints, and explain various spellings by means of different rankings of these constraints in the manner of Optimality Theory. Indeed what we have termed morphological faithfulness is quite similar in spirit to *paradigm uniformity*, a principle that has been proposed as a phonological constraint by Steriade (1999) and others. I think, however, that these "principles" may be a little too vague and fuzzy to allow for this treatment, at least at present.

Chomsky and Halle's position. One significant problem is that even if English spelling is assumed to represent a deep level, it can hardly be said to be consistent in its representation. For instance, while *assign–assignation* shows retention of the same spelling across different derived forms, some other presumably morphologically related pairs do not, even in cases where there is no change in pronunciation. Consider the alternation in spelling for the vowel /i/ in <speech>–<speak>; or consider the alternation in spelling for the pair <collide>–<collision>, where the pronunciation of underlying /d/ as /ž/ should be predictable in this morphophonological environment, so that one ought in principle to be able to spell the word *collision* as <collidion> (Sampson 1985, page 201); or consider such minimal pairs as <race>–<racial> versus <space>–<spatial>, where the phonological alternation (/s/ versus /š/) is identical, as are the morphological environments, and yet in one case the spelling <c> is retained in the *-ial* derivative, whereas in the other the /š/ is spelled as <t>.

After discussing various other approaches to English spelling, Sampson proposes (page 203):

> We may see another kind of method in the apparent madness of our spelling, though, if we avoid letting ourselves be obsessed by the phonographic origins of the Roman alphabet and think of English spelling as at least partly logographic.

The proposal that English spelling has logographic properties is certainly a widely expressed one. For example, as Bloomfield notes (Bloomfield and Barnhart, 1961, page 27) (using the term *word writing* for *logographic*):

> Now someone may ask whether the spelling of *knit* with *k* does not serve to distinguish this word from *nit* 'the egg of a louse.' Of course it does, and this is exactly where our writing lapses from the alphabetic principle back into the older scheme of word writing. Alphabetic writing, which indicates all the significant speech sounds of each word, is just as clear as actual speech, which means that it is clear enough. Word writing, on the other hand, provides a separate character for each and every word ... Our spelling the verb *knit* with an extra *k* (and the noun *nit* without this extra *k*) is a step in the direction of word writing.

While there is certainly some merit in this view, I feel that it is important to distinguish writing systems with a true logographic component, such as Chinese or Ancient Egyptian, from the rather haphazard "pseudologographic" properties of English writing.

On the one hand, many of the logographic components (the so-called semantic radicals) of Chinese characters seem to represent semantic aspects of morphemes in a surprisingly consistent way. As we have noted elsewhere (Sproat et al., 1996), many semantic radicals in Chinese are quite consistent in the semantic information that they mark. Thus in the lists presented in Wieger (1965, pages 773–776), 254 out of 263 characters (97%) with the semantic radical 虫 <INSECT> denote crawling or invertebrate animals; for 鬼 <GHOST> (page 808), 21 out of 22 (95%) denote ghosts or spirits. The semantic information provided by these logographic elements is thus strikingly consistent. As we already proposed in Section 1.2.2, for a Chinese word such as 蟬 <INSECT+CHÁN> *chán* 'cicada', the insect radical 虫 <INSECT> represents a portion of the semantic feature set for the morpheme, whereas the phonological portion (in this case 單 <CHÁN>) represents the pronunciation associated with the morpheme.

On the other hand, it is hard to find any such consistency in the "logographic" aspects of English orthography. For instance, the set of words orthographically distinguished from other words by an initial silent <k> (*knit*, *know*, *knight*, *knave*, . . .) forms no natural class (other than that they are all of Germanic origin), and the most we can say about the <k> here is that it is an orthographic element with no corresponding phonological element. Thus the word *knit* might be represented as in (3.14), repeated in part from (1.6a). Note again that although the representation of /n/ as <kn> is idiosyncratic, the remaining spelling <it> is in this case predictable given the phonological form and does not need to be specified:

(3.14)
$$\begin{bmatrix} \text{PHON } \langle n_{1*}\, \text{ɪ}t \rangle \\ \text{ORTH } \{kn_1\} \end{bmatrix}$$

It would of course be completely unmotivated to say that the <k> or <kn> here corresponds to any nonphonological content of the feature structure of this word, and so we really have no parallel here to the Chinese case.

All of which still leaves us with the question of how best to characterize English orthography in terms of the model we are developing. The interesting question from our perspective is not how to deal with irregularities such as the <k> in *knit*, but rather how to characterize the phonological level of representation that is represented by the regular spelling. In our terms we would ask: How deep is the ORL for English spelling? A definitive answer to this question would require a complete analysis of the spelling of a large portion of the English vocabulary – something akin to Nunn's (1998) treatment of Dutch spelling, one which systematically analyzes how well the standard orthography of, say, American English, corresponds both to the standard (surface) pronunciation and to a plausible proposal for the underlying representation of each word.[18]

[18] Alternatively one might consider a data-oriented approach for measuring the relation between the spelling and various proposals for the ORL. Van den Bosch and his colleagues (van den Bosch et al., 1994) investigated three data-oriented learning methods for measuring the relative complexity of English, French, and Dutch orthographies – more specifically the complexity of the relation between the spelling and the surface phonemic representation

In this section I will describe a small analysis of a kind that should eventually be done on a more complete scale. I selected 1,169 words from an on-line dictionary with their (American) spellings and phonemic representation for a standard American pronunciation. These words consist mostly of forms that are at least in part Latin- or Greek-derived and show alternations of the kind that were central to the arguments for vowel shift, laxing, velar softening, and some other consonant alternations in Chomsky and Halle (1968) (Sound Pattern of English or SPE). Thus we find examples such as *abound–abundance* or *heliocentric–heliocentricity–heliocentricism.* In addition to the dictionary-derived surface phonemic representation, I also reconstructed an SPE-style underlying representation. Thus the underlying forms of *abound* and *abundance* are assumed to be, respectively, /æ'būnd/ and /æ'būndans/; similarly the, underlying forms of *electric* and *electricity* are, respectively, /ɛ'lɛktrɪk̲/ and /ɛlɛk'trɪk̲ɪti/. Here and elsewhere /ū/ is used to represent underlying /u/ that diphthongizes to /aʊ/; tense /u/ as in *super*, which does not diphthongize, is represented without the overbar; /k̲/ represents a /k/ that undergoes velar softening (similarly /g̲/). Where I perhaps depart from SPE is in only positing abstract forms in cases where there is plausible evidence for an alternation. Thus since there is no evidence for the first /s/ in *cervix* alternating with anything else, I represent this word underlyingly as /'sɛrvɪk̲s/ (but note the penultimate /k̲/ as evidenced by the form *cervicitis*, where the /k/ has undergone velar softening). As a general rule, I assume that there are no schwas in underlying representation, only full vowels. (Since the posited full vowels are generally posited on the basis of the orthography, this necessarily biases the analysis, and this point should be borne in mind.) The complete list of words along with their surface and posited underlying forms is given in Appendix 3.A.1 at the end of this chapter.

What other assumptions do we then need to make to predict the spelling from each of these levels? More specifically:

- What rules do we need to assume for $M_{ORL \rightarrow \Gamma}$?
- And what lexical marking of orthographic properties must we assume?

Needless to say, there are various ways in which one could juggle these two kinds of devices, and what I present here should be understood as just being one possible way, and not necessarily the best one.

---

that one would find in a dictionary. They proposed the inverse of the various models' performance as a measure of the complexity of each system. Of course, one weakness of their approach from our point of view is that they took it for granted that the surface phonemic pronunciation is the correct level to which to relate the spelling. Our thesis that the depth of the ORL differs among different languages suggests that their assumption is not necessarily valid.

Lexical specifications needed for each form are given in Appendix 3.A.1. In that list, orthographic specifications are given by subscripted letters in angle brackets. Thus: /æ'bū$_{<u>}$ndans/ denotes the fact that the /ū/ is spelled as <u>. The notation $\epsilon_{<l>}$ denotes a case where letter <l> corresponds to no phonological material. (In some cases one could alternatively have coalesced the added letter with the spellout of a preceding or following phoneme, as was done with <knit> above.) The two other main devices are the (subscripted) feature [+db], used to mark a consonant that is to be represented orthographically as double,[19] and the feature [+gk], which is used to mark words that have the Greek spellings <ph> for /f/ and <rh> for (initial) /r/. In some cases, particularly with plural *+es*, morpheme boundary information is needed to predict the appropriate spelling; the morpheme boundary is marked as '+'. The second and third columns of the table in Appendix 3.A.1 constitute proposals for deep and shallow ORLs for these English words.

The (ordered) rules corresponding to the deep and shallow ORLs are given in Appendix 3.A.2 and Appendix 3.A.3 respectively. In many cases the import of the particular rule should be clear; in cases where it is not, some commentary is added. Both of these sets of rules have been tested with their corresponding ORLs, to verify that those applied to their ORLs do indeed derive the correct spellings for all words.[20]

To illustrate the difference between the assumption of a deep versus shallow ORL, consider the word *audacity*, the AVM representations of which are given in (3.15a) (deep) and (3.15b) (shallow):

(3.15) (a)
$$\begin{bmatrix} \text{PHON} \ \langle \text{ɔ'dā}\underline{\text{k}}\text{ɪti} \rangle \\ \text{ORTH} \ \{\} \end{bmatrix}$$

(b)
$$\begin{bmatrix} \text{PHON} \ \langle \text{ɔ'dæs}_{1*}\ \text{ɪti} \rangle \\ \text{ORTH} \ \{\text{c}_1\} \end{bmatrix}$$

In this word, only a shallow ORL would require a lexical marking, namely the specification of <c> for the spelling of the /s/, indicated in Appendix 3.A.1 as a subscripted <c>. The rules needed to account for the

19 It might be believed that doubled consonants in English spelling are predictable, but in fact this is not the case. Although in general a double consonant is an indicator that the preceding vowel is lax (cf. Venezky (1970, pages 106–107), inter alia), the implication does not go the other way.

20 The system was developed and tested using the *lextools* finite-state linguistic analysis toolkit developed at AT&T Bell Labs and described in Sproat (1997a,b).

spelling given these two ORLs are listed in 3.2:

(3.16)

Spelling					Deep Rule #	Shallow Rule #
<au>:	ɔ	→	<au>		1	2
<d>:	d	→	<d>		22	24
<a>:	ā	→	<a>		45	–
	æ	→	<a>		–	48
<c>:	k̲	→	<c>		21	–
<i>:	ɪ	→	<i>		52	57
<t>:	t	→	<t>		33	35
<y>:	i	→	<y>	/__#	58	50

The numbers in the last two columns indicate the rule numbers for the Deep ORL (Appendix 3.A.2) and Shallow ORL (Appendix 3.A.3), respectively. Note that in some cases slightly different rules are needed for the two ORL levels. No rule is needed for the <c> spelling for the Shallow ORL, since this spelling is lexically specified.

We turn now to a discussion of the fragment presented in Appendix 3.A. First note the clear difference in the number of rules needed in each case, with 58 rules for the deep ORL, and 69 for the shallow ORL. (Some of these rules could have been combined; this would change the overall counts but not the relative sizes of the two sets.) More interesting are the lexical markings given in Appendix 3.A.1. We discount the [+gk] and [+db] markings, which are generally needed under either assumption of the depth of the ORL. For the deep ORL, 389 (33%) of the words require lexical marking, with 509 total marks being needed. For the shallow ORL, in contrast, 892, (76%) of the words require some lexical marking, with 1,452 total marks being used. So the shallow ORL is certainly a more costly assumption, particularly with respect to the amount of lexical marking, but also to some extent with respect to the number of required rules. This much supports Chomsky and Halle's position. However, when one considers the distribution of the marks, the situation is less convincing. The ten most common lexical specifications in the shallow ORL, covering 1,311/1,452 (90%) of the cases, are given in Table 3.1. Similarly, the ten most common lexical specifications in the deep ORL, covering 453/509 (89%) of the cases are given in Table 3.2. Among the markings for the shallow ORL, four relate to the spelling of reduced vowels /ə/ and /ɪ/ (as <e>); one involves the spelling of /s/ as <c> as in *electricity*; two involve the irregular representation (mostly in Greek-derived words) of /ɪ/ and /aɪ/ as <y>; and one involves writing /i/ as <i> (rather than the more normal <e>). Finally, we have specifications of /k/ as <ch> (in Greek words) and

Table 3.1. *The ten most frequent lexical markings for the shallow ORL in the English fragment*

Phoneme	Orthographic mark	Number of cases
/ə/	<o>	395
/s/	<c>	242
/ə/	<a>	170
/aɪ/	<y>	123
/ɪ/	<y>	112
/ɪ/	<e>	67
/i/	<i>	63
/ə/	<i>	61
/k/	<ch>	47
/z/	<s>	31

/z/ as <s>. Of these, five do not occur in some form among the top ten for the deep ORL markings: the four reduced vowel marks and the specification of /s/ as <c>. In contrast, <y> spellings for varieties of /i/, <ch> spellings for /k/, <s> for /z/, and <i> for /i/ are needed as lexically specified markings even under the assumption of a deep ORL. The need to mark the spelling of reduced vowels under the assumption of a shallow ORL is of course unsurprising. I believe it is necessary to assume that in English, as in Russian, the ORL corresponds at least to a phonological representation that contains full rather than reduced vowels. Similarly, the necessity of marking the <c> spelling of velar-softening-derived /s/ in a shallow ORL

Table 3.2. *The ten most frequent lexical markings for the deep ORL in the English fragment*

Phoneme	Orthographic mark	Number of cases
/ɪ̄/	<y>	180
/s/	<c>	84
/ɪ/	<y>	70
/k/	<ch>	47
/z/	<s>	27
/ū/	<u>	12
/i/	<i>	9
/k/	<k>	8
/i/	<e>	8
/u/	<eu>	8

would appear to provide some evidence in favor of an SPE-style deep level for the ORL. However, some other aspects of deep structure, which were important in the analysis in SPE, turn out to have much less importance than one might expect. It makes little difference, for example, that there is a vowel alternation in the pair *chaste–chastity*, an alternation that is abstracted away from in the underlying representation: In the case of a deep ORL, the underlying vowel of the stem /ā/ is mapped to <a>; with a shallow ORL, we simply have rules that map the two distinct vowels /æ/ and /eɪ/ to <a>. No lexical marking is required. Similarly, whereas an alternation such as *assign–assignation* does require lexical marking for the shallow ORL (since we must simply mark the fact that in the word *assign*, the sequence /aɪn/ is spelled <ign>), there are only six such cases in our list, not an overwhelming amount of lexical marking.

Interestingly, one clear case that requires lexical marking with a deep ORL but *not* with a shallow ORL involves alternations such as *abound–abundance*. The underlying representation of the second vowel in this pair of words is presumably uniformly /ū/, so one would expect a consistent spelling (e.g., <ou>). Yet in this case, the spellings, which alternate in parallel with the phonological vowel alternations, are more consistent with a shallow ORL than with a deep ORL, contrary to what one might expect from SPE.

What do we conclude from all of this? There seems to be some evidence for the English ORL being relatively deep, something that is hardly surprising. However, with the exception of <c> in velar softening cases, the considerations that figured prominently in Chomsky and Halle's discussion of English spelling do not in fact seem to be of such great importance. One further point should be borne in mind: We have considered about 1,100 words, carefully selected to exhibit the kinds of alternations under discussion in SPE. This is hardly a representative sample of the English vocabulary, either in terms of the raw count or in terms of the properties the words exhibit. Indeed, an examination of a larger fragment of the vocabulary would probably make the argument for a deep ORL less convincing since the majority of English words simply do not participate in the kinds of alternations exhibited by the subset considered here.

To reiterate the caveats that we have already presented, one naturally must take the analysis presented here with at least a small grain of salt. In particular if one makes different assumptions about the underlying representations, then one would arrive at different results. Still, I should be surprised if they turned out to be too different, and I would expect the basic conclusion to remain the same: With the exception of the orthographic representation of reduced vowels, which is more elegantly handled if one assumes a relatively deep ORL, the evidence for a deep "morphological" ORL in English is equivocal.

3.3 The Orthographic Representation of Serbo-Croatian Consonant Devoicing

An interesting prima facie counterexample to the Consistency hypothesis is found in Serbo-Croatian and involves the spelling of dental obstruents before /s/ and /š/.[21] According to the standard description of Serbo-Croatian, obstruent clusters agree in voicing, with the voicing of the cluster being determined by the final member of the cluster. Thus alongside *svezati* 'to bind', one finds *sveska* 'notebook'; beside *redak* 'line', one finds the genitive singular form *retka*. This much is in common with other Slavic languages such as Russian. What is unusual about Serbo-Croatian is that these voicing assimilations are reflected in the orthography, so that a /b/ that has become devoiced to a /p/, for instance, is written as <p> rather than <b>. The modern Serbo-Croatian orthography, due to Vuk Karadzic (1787–1864), is often cited as an instance of a "shallow" orthography (see Chapter 5 for some further discussion of this point), and one of the features of this "shallowness" is that it spells words according to their surface phonetic realization. In popular parlance, Serbo-Croatian is written "as it sounds."

If this were the entire story, then Serbo-Croatian would be handleable under the present theory without further comment. The ORL would simply be a level at which voicing assimilation in obstruent clusters had already applied. There is, however, a systematic exception to the spelling principle we have just outlined: Underlying /d/ when followed by /s/ or /š/ retains its spelling as <d>, even though it is described as being voiceless. Note that in other environments (e.g., before /k/ or /p/) devoiced /d/ is spelled as <t>; and other obstruents besides /d/ are spelled as their voiceless counterparts before /s/ or /š/. Thus prefix *od-* before *pad-* "fall" yields *otpad* 'trash'; *srb-* 'Serb' yields *srpski* 'Serbian'. But *grad-* 'city' yields *gradski* 'urban', and *od-* plus *šteta* 'damage' yields *odšteta* 'compensation'.

On the face of it, then, we would appear to have a problem since for most obstruents in most environments the evidence would appear to favor placing the ORL after obstruent voicing assimilation. But just in case we have an underlying /d/ preceding an /s/ or /š/, we seem to need to place the ORL earlier. To maintain Consistency, we would have to resort to one of two possible strategies, neither of which is palatable:

- Assume a late (post–voicing-assimilation) ORL, but mark underlying /d/ before /s/ or /š/ with a diacritic, so that the spelling rules can see the fact that it was /d/, and spell it accordingly.
- Assume an early (pre–voicing-assimiliation) ORL. In this case one has access to the underlying segments, so there is no problem

[21] I am grateful to Wayles Browne for bringing this example to my attention.

spelling underlying /d/ as <d> in *gradski*. Unfortunately, however, in most cases the obstruent is spelled according to its surface phonetic realization, meaning that one would in effect be duplicating, in the orthographic rules, the effects of voicing assimilation that are already handled in the phonology.

The seemingly exceptional spelling of underlying /ds/ and /dš/ sequences is not merely a problem for Consistency, however. It is, in fact, a puzzle more generally. Why did Karadzic fail to spell the voiced stop as its voiceless counterpart in just this one case? Could it be, in fact, that such underlying /d/s sound voiced, despite the standard description? If so, this would suggest, among other things, that obstruent voicing assimilation is not a unitary phenomenon but applies to varying degrees under different conditions.

Support for the nonuniformity of obstruent voicing assimilation is already given by Browne (1993, page 314), who notes that assimilation to a voiced cluster-final obstruent, and assimilation to a voiceless cluster-final obstruent, behave differently with respect to the phonological rule of cluster breaking in nominal genitive plurals. Consonants that have become voiced by voicing assimilation remain voiced after being separated from the consonant that triggered voicing. Thus *primeṯiti* 'to remark', yields *primeḏba* 'comment' (noun); in the genitive plural *primeḏaba*, the acquired voicing on the /d/ is retained. However, the devoiced /z/ in *sves̱ka* 'notebook' shows up again as a /z/ in the genitive plural form *sveẕaka*. Evidently, [+voiced] assimilation is deeper in the phonology than [−voiced] assimilation insofar as a traditional analysis would order the former before cluster breaking, and the latter after.

To explain the orthographic facts, however, we are interested in an even finer-grained question: Is there some reason to believe that [−voice] assimilation is less complete in the sequences /ds/ and /dš/, than it is in other sequences? As a preliminary answer to this question we conducted a pilot study of [−voice] assimilation in the speech of a single Croatian speaker. In this study we addressed the following questions:

1. Are underlying /d/ and /t/ before /s/ phonetically distinct with respect to their voicing profiles, contrary to standard descriptions?
2. Are underlying /b/ and /p/ before /s/ (both spelled <p>) phonetically distinct?
3. How do underlying /d/ and /t/ (both spelled <t>) before a nonsibilant obstruent – /k/ in our data – compare to these stops in the pre-/s/ position?

The study and its results are described in the two sections that follow.

3.3.1 *Methods and Materials*

A list of Croatian words was prepared that covered the environments of interest for the questions above. Specifically these words covered:

1. Underlying /d/ before /s/: *akadski* 'Acadian', *gradski* 'urban'.
2. Underlying /t/ before /s/: *anegdotski* 'anecdotal', *hrvatski* 'Croatian'.
3. Underlying /b/ before /s/: *arapski* 'Arab', *mikropski* 'microbial', *ropski* 'slavish', *srpski* 'Serbian'.
4. Underlying /p/ before /s/: *mikroskopski* 'microscopic'.
5. Underlying /d/ before /k/: *glatka* 'smooth', *lutka* 'doll', *otpatke* 'refuse' (noun), *votka* 'vodka'.

These words were printed, along with filler material, in four iterations, each with a different random order.

The subject of the experiment (a researcher at AT&T Labs) is a male native speaker of a Dalmatian dialect of Croatian. He has lived for over a decade in English-speaking countries, but his Croatian speech is self-described as normal for that dialect, and not affected by his exposure to English. He was not informed of the purpose of the experiment.

The speaker was asked to read the words on the printed list at a normal rate of speed.[22] His speech was recorded to DAT using a Brüel and Kjær Microphone in a quiet room. The data were subsequently uploaded to a Silicon Graphics workstation, and high-pass filtered at 40 Hz to remove low-frequency noise. The speech was then segmented into words using the Entropic Research Laboratories *waves*$^+$ package. Prediction of voicing was computed for each file using the Entropic *get_f0* utility (Talkin, 1995). Note that the voicing profile for a speech file produced by *get_f0* is a time series with two values, namely 1 for voiced and 0 for unvoiced. The individual files were then hand labeled using *waves*$^+$ and the *xmarks* utility for the following features:

- Onset of the pre-/s/ or pre-/k/ stop.
- Offset of the voicing within the stop.
- Onset of the following segment (/s/ or /k/).

The first and third of these were labeled based on visual inspection of the waveform and the spectrogram. The second was labeled based on the voicing profile. A typical waveform and voicing profile for the word *gradski* is shown in Figure 3.1.

[22] The subject was asked to read the first page of the text a second time at the end of the recording session, so that we have five rather than four repetitions of some words.

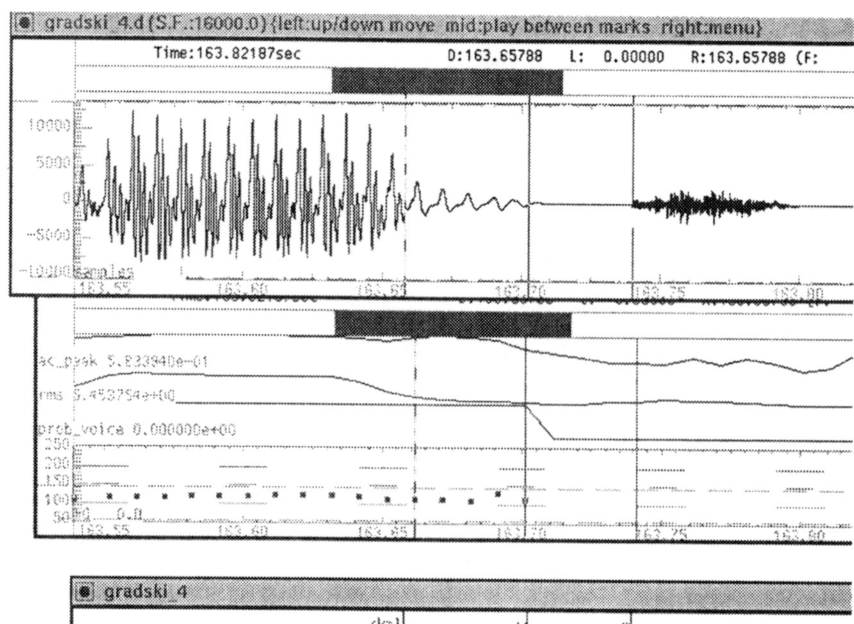

Figure 3.1. Waveform and voicing profile for one utterance of *gradski* 'urban'. The closure for the /d/ is labeled as "dcl", the voicing offset is labeled as "v", and the start of the /s/ is labeled as "s". The voicing profile is the third plot from the top in the second window, labeled as *prob_voice*.

3.3.2 Results

There are at least two plausible measures of the degree of voicing of a stop, given the voicing profile. One measure is the absolute duration of the interval between the onset of the stop and the offset of the voicing; another is the *proportion* or percentage of the stop that is voiced. As it turns out, both measures yield similar results in this study.

Let us deal first with the least surprising result: /d/, written as <t> before /k/, is clearly voiceless, essentially throughout. The mean absolute duration of the voiced region of the stop is 5 msec, and the mean proportion of the voiced region is 0.06. Thus these underlying /d/s really are /t/s, which explains their spelling.

Turning now to the case of /p,b/ before /s/ (both written <p>), the first thing that we note is that voicing is generally found in, on average, the first 25 msec of the stop, which is greater than the amount we observed in the case of /tk/. Between underlying /p/ and /b/ there was no significant difference: For /p/ (4 samples) the average duration of voicing was 24 msec, for /b/ (18 samples) it was 26 msec. A *t*-test showed this small difference to be nonsignificant ($t = 0.20, p = 0.84$). Looking at the proportion of voicing, we do find a mildly significant difference: The mean proportion for underlying /p/ was 0.55 and for underlying /b/ was 0.36 ($t = 1.82, p = 0.08$), but note that the difference is not in the expected direction since the underlying /p/ behaves *more* voiced than underlying /b/ by this measure. This result might at least in part be explained by the fact that the underlying /p/s had shorter durations (mean of 44 msec) compared to underlying /b/s (mean of 72 msec). If there is a tendency to keep a constant duration of voicing, this would result in a larger proportion of voicing for the underlying /p/ cases. All in all though, there seems to be no convincing evidence that underlying /b/ and /p/ before /s/ behave differently with respect to their surface realization.

With /t/ and /d/ before /s/ the story is very different. First, consider absolute duration, which averaged 14 msec for /t/ (10 samples) and 34 msec for /d/ (10 samples). This difference is significant: $t = 3.72, p < 0.005$. The proportion of voicing also shows a significant difference, with a mean of 0.25 for /t/, and 0.46 for /d/: $t = 3.21, p < 0.05$. The proportions of voicing for all samples of /d/ and /t/ are shown in the barplot in Figure 3.2.

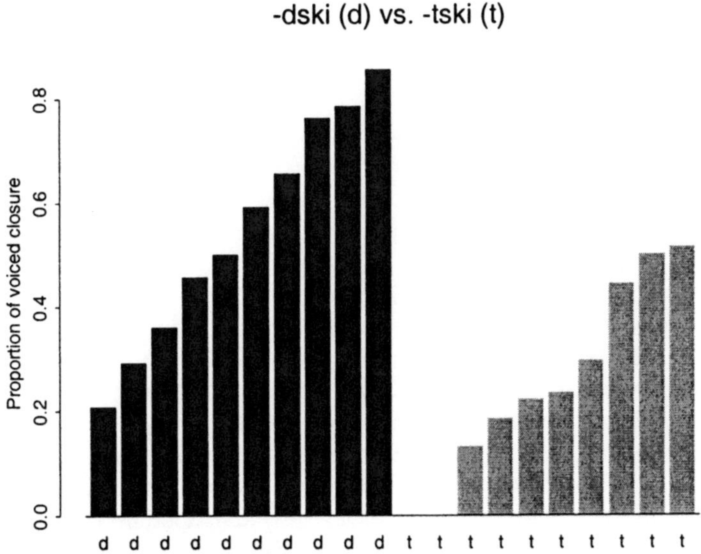

Figure 3.2. Barplot showing the proportions of voicing for all samples of underlying /d/ (black bars) versus /t/ (shaded bars).

Although there is clearly overlap between the two categories, the conclusion seems unequivocal: Contrary to the standard description, /d/ before /s/ in words such as *gradski* or *akadski* has a greater propensity toward being voiced than /t/ in the same position. This is different from the case with /d/ before /k/, which is unequivocally voiceless, and it is different from the case of underlying /p,b/ before /s/, where we found no reliable difference in voicing behavior.

Should /d/ in words *gradski* be considered voiced as opposed to voiceless? This depends upon what one means by "voiced." In Serbo-Croatian, voiced obstruent clusters show clear voicing throughout, whereas /d/ in *gradski* is never voiced throughout. Perhaps for this reason this underlying /d/ should be considered voiceless. But no matter what the correct answer to that question may be, one point seems unequivocal from the data we have presented here: [−voice] assimilation is not a simple across-the-board phenomenon. It happens to different degrees in different environments. Evidently, it applies in the least complete fashion where /d/ precedes /s/, and this fact is reflected in the orthography. Such /d/s sound more voiced and hence are written as <d>s. So, far from being a problem for Consistency, Serbo-Croatian lends rather detailed support to the notion of a uniform ORL.

Needless to say, the results of this preliminary experiment need to be corroborated by a more thorough study of a wider range of speakers. Nonetheless, I believe the burden of proof now lies with those who would stand by the traditional description that presents obstruent cluster devoicing in Serbo-Croatian as a simple across-the-board phenomenon that applies equally in all cases.

One final question needs to be addressed: Is it possible that the speaker in this experiment was influenced by the orthography and was thus producing spelling pronunciations? More generally, might literate Serbo-Croatian speakers be influenced in their application of obstruent devoicing by the very spelling that we are attempting to explain? This would suggest, then, that while in Karadzic's time the voicing assimilation was complete, due to his (once again, peculiar) spelling of underlying /d/ as <d> before /s/, subsequent generations of speakers have been influenced by the spelling and now differentiate the degree of assimilation as we have observed. This is certainly possible, but if it is so, then once again it would appear to support the notion of Consistency. One might invent a writing system that fails to observe Consistency, but there will be a strong tendency on the part of users of that system either to adjust the writing system to make it more Consistent, or else to (unconsciously) adjust their speech to bring it more in line with the orthographic representation. In any case, then, the Consistency hypothesis appears to be supported by the Serbo-Croatian data we have presented in this section.

3.4 Cyclicity in Orthography

Traditional models of Generative Phonology, including classical SPE-style phonology, and later more articulated theories such as Lexical Phonology (Mohanan, 1986), include the familiar mechanism of cyclicity. Phonological rules that apply cyclically do so by applying in tandem with the morphology, so that a set of phonological rules is applied as each affix is attached. Cyclicity is not in favor much in present-day phonological theories.

We are interested here, though, not in cyclicity in phonology but rather in orthography. Perhaps not surprisingly, given the dearth of formal analyses of orthographic systems, very little evidence has been adduced in the literature for cyclicity in orthography. There is however one such potential instance in Dutch, discussed by Nunn (1998, pages 102–103)[23] involving the interaction between Orthographic Consonant Degemination and Orthographic Syllabification. Orthographic Consonant Degemination, roughly speaking, simplifies doubled consonants that occur within the same orthographic syllable. Thus *verbrand+d* (burn+ed) 'burnt' (adjective) is spelled <verbrand>. Orthographic Syllabification is a relatively complex rule in Nunn's analysis, but one result of the rule is to split up intervocalic geminate consonants if the right-hand member of the pair can possibly be syllabified to the right; thus *wasster* 'washerwoman' is syllabified as $[was]_\sigma[ster]_\sigma$. Nunn gives a number of arguments that, despite their similarity to phonological degemination and syllabification, these two processes are in fact orthographically based. I will not repeat her arguments here but refer the reader to her discussion, in particular in Chapters 3 and 5.

As examples such as *wasster* show, Orthographic Syllabification can block Consonant Degemination. Since the two <s>s are separated into two syllables, the rule of Orthographic Consonant Degemination is no longer applicable. In contrast, forms such as *wijste* 'wisest', which is morphologically *wijs+st+e* (wise+Superlative+Inflection), show that in some cases Syllabification seems not to block Degemination: Here one would have expected the syllabification $[wijs]_\sigma[ste]_\sigma$ and the spelling *<wijsste>. Nunn suggests that such examples can be handled if we assume that Syllabification and Degemination apply cyclically. Thus in *wijste*, on the inner cycle we have *wijs+st*. Syllabification has nothing to do here (there being only one orthographic vowel, namely <ij>), and Degemination applies to yield *wijst*. On the next cycle *e* is added, and Syllabification applies to yield $[wij]_\sigma[ste]_\sigma$.

Is cyclic application in orthography a problem for Consistency? It would be if one could show that the orthographic cycles were built in tandem with phonological cycles. In that case, one could no longer speak of a consistent *level* for the ORL; rather there would be multiple levels, one

[23] I thank Anneke Neijt for pointing me to this example.

for each cycle. However, Nunn's evidence does not seem to require this assumption. Precisely because we are dealing here with the cyclic behavior of two *orthographic* rules, we have no evidence for a crucial dependence upon *phonological* cyclicity.

Nunn assumes that her phoneme-to-grapheme rules – the first stage in the mapping from the ORL – map from a somewhat abstract representation of morphologically complex words. Her presumed underlying spelling <wijsste> can only be derived from a phonological representation where one represents both the /s/ of the root and the /s/ of the suffix (*[[[weɪs]st]ə]*) rather than a more surface phonological representation that represents the effects of phonological degemination (/weɪstə/). We could therefore map in one step from a phonological representation including morphological constituency information such as *[[[weɪs]st]ə]* into an orthographic representation *[[[wijs]st]e]*, which also includes morphological constituency information. A cyclic application of orthographic rules could then proceed on this orthographic representation, independently of whatever goes on in the phonology. Thus Nunn's example need not be a problem for Consistency since under this scenario the ORL is indeed a single level of representation (in this case a phonologically abstract one), and the cyclicity of the orthographic rules is entirely internal to the orthography.

It should be stressed that Nunn's case is the only phenomenon that seems to require a cyclic treatment in her analysis of the orthographic system of Dutch, an analysis that includes thirteen autonomous spelling rules (of which these are two) and a couple of hundred phoneme-to-grapheme rules. There may of course be further evidence for cyclicity in orthography in Dutch, or in other writing systems, but at present the evidence is at best sparse, and it is hard therefore to conclude much from it.

3.5 Surface Orthographic Constraints

While many aspects of spelling are best thought of in terms of a mapping from some level of linguistic structure to written form, there are others that seem to be purely orthographic in nature. Venezky (1970, pages 59–62) terms these *graphemic alternations*. Nunn (1998), as we have already noted, distinguishes *phoneme-to-grapheme conversion rules* (our M_{Encode}) from a set of purely orthographic *autonomous spelling rules* (our M_{Spell}). Nunn identifies a number of phenomena in Dutch spelling that she argues are best described in terms of rules that refer only to orthographic information. One such phenomenon involves the orthographic representation of phonologically long vowels. These are generally represented as double vowels in closed syllables, as in *maan* 'moon', but as single vowels in open syllables, as in *manen* 'moons'. Nunn states this generalization as a rule that deletes the second of an identical pair of vowels preceding an orthographic syllable boundary.

Assuming Nunn's analysis of Dutch vowel degemination is correct, we must assume, as indeed we have, that M_{Spell} in general implements a relation, since it includes rewrite rules that change properties of the orthographic representation. However, there is good reason to assume that at least some purely orthographic phenomena are best described as constraints. As we suggested in Section 1.2.3.1, one can then view M_{Spell} as breaking down into two components, one consisting of a regular relation $M_{Spell_{map}}$, and one consisting of a regular language $M_{Spell_{constr}}$. We will have nothing further to say about $M_{Spell_{map}}$ here. (The reader is referred to Nunn (1998) for extensive argumentation for such autonomous spelling rules in Dutch.) Rather we will focus here on a few examples of surface orthographic constraints.

A simple example is afforded by the alternation of <i> and <y> in Malagasy. Both letters represent the vowel /i/, but they are in complementary distribution, with <y> occurring only at the ends of words and <i> only in nonfinal position.[24] For example, from <omby> 'cattle', one can derive the reduplicative form <tsiombiomby> (a children's game in which the children play the role of cattle) (Rajemisa-Raolison, 1971, page 19), where the first copy of the stem *omby* spells the /i/ with <i>, since it is word-internal.

Such a restriction is easily modeled by a surface filter (part of $M_{Spell_{constr}}$) that disallows word-final <i> and non–word-final <y>:

(3.16) $\neg[(\Sigma^* < i > \#) \cup (\Sigma^* < y > \neg\#)]$

where the word boundary is denoted with '#'. Assume now that M_{Encode} contains the following rule, which maps /i/ to either <i> or <y>:

(3.17) $\mathrm{i} \rightarrow$ <i> | <y>

Then the mapping $M_{ORL \rightarrow \Gamma} = M_{Encode} \circ M_{Spell}$ will have the desired property of mapping /i/ to <i> and <y> and restricting these to the appropriate positions.

Another straightforward example of a surface filter involves positional variants of graphemes, which are found in many languages; many writers would term these *allographs*, though Daniels (1991a,b) has argued against this term on theoretical grounds. One example is the f-like "long <s>", which occurred exclusively in non–word-final position in various Roman

[24] It is tempting to think that this purely orthographic restriction may have been borrowed from English, which has the same restriction, at least when you discount words borrowed from Greek, Latin, and other sources; see Venezky's discussion (page 59). This is not an implausible suggestion, since it was British missionaries, invited in 1817 by King Radama I, who introduced the Roman alphabet to Madagascar, replacing the older Arabic-derived orthography.

scripts dating from the Half Uncials of the fourth century (Knight, 1996), as well as later printed forms; the "round <s>" occurred only in word-final position. Clearly this distribution can be modeled in exactly the same way as the distribution of <i> and <y> in Malagasy. The identical distribution is found with Greek *σ* <s> (nonfinal only) and ς (final only). Comparable examples are found in Hebrew; and in Arabic, which has initial, medial, and final forms for most letters.

It is also possible to consider the prohibition on internal **э** <e̲> in Russian to be a surface orthographic constraint. However, the statement of the constraint is certainly more complex than the case we have examined in Malagasy. For one thing the statement would clearly have to restrict **э** <e̲> not to word-initial position, but rather to *syllable*-initial position, since there are numerous cases where one finds word-internal, though syllable-initial **э** <e̲>:

(3.18) **антиэлектрон** <antie̲lektron> 'antielectron'
Аэрофлот <ae̲roflot> 'Aeroflot'
дуэт <due̲t> 'duet'
пируэт <pirue̲t> 'pirouette'

In some cases, as in the case of 'antielectron', the syllable boundary also corresponds to a morpheme boundary, but this is not always the case, as the other examples show. The restriction on the distribution of **э** <e̲> can thus be stated in terms of syllable structure, and more specifically as a prohibition on **э** <e̲> occurring anywhere but right-adjacent to an orthographic syllable boundary.[25] Even so, there are still lexical exceptions that would have to be marked as such and that would have to be able to override this surface constraint. Acronyms, not surprisingly, regularly do so (e.g. НЭП <ne̲p> for *novaja ekonomičeskaja politika* 'New Economic Policy'). There are also a handful of borrowed words that do not obey the principle (e.g. **рэкет** <re̲ket> 'racket'). It might be better therefore to consider this to be not an absolute constraint, but rather a soft constraint, one that could be implemented with a weighted rather than unweighted finite-state acceptor.[26] The constraint would allow noninitial **э** <e̲>, but only at some cost. If a lexical item is marked as having **э** <e̲> in a non–syllable-initial position, then it will be allowed. In all other cases, both noninitial **э** <e̲> and **е** <e> will be allowed, but **э** <e̲> will not be selected since it will be a more costly analysis.

[25] As the reader will not fail to have observed, all of the examples in (3.18) are borrowed words. But this is not surprising, since **э** <e̲> (with the exception of some high-frequency words such as **это** <e̲to> 'this' and its derivatives) is mostly found in borrowed words.

[26] An alternative would be to assume *priority union* (Karttunen, 1998).

3.A English Deep and Shallow ORLs

3.A.1 Lexical Representations

	Deep	Shallow
abound	æ'būnd	ə'baund
abundance	æ'bū$_{<u>}$ndæns	ə'bʌndə$_{<a>}$ns
academe	'ækæˌdēm	'ækə$_{<a>}$ˌdim
academicals	ˌækæ'dēmɪk̲æls	ˌækə$_{<a>}$'dɛmɪkə$_{<a>}$lz
academicism	ˌækæ'dēmɪˌk̲ɪsm	ˌækə$_{<a>}$'dɛmɪˌs$_{<c>}$ɪzəm
academic	ˌækæ'dēmɪk̲	ˌækə$_{<a>}$'dɛmɪk
acetone	'æs$_{<c>}$ɛˌtōn	'æs$_{<c>}$ɪ$_{<e>}$ˌtoun
acetonic	ˌæs$_{<c>}$ɛ'tōnɪk̲	ˌæs$_{<c>}$ɪ$_{<e>}$'tonɪk
acetylene	æ's$_{<c>}$ētɪ$_{<y>}$ˌlēn	ə's$_{<c>}$ɛtə$_{<y>}$ˌlin
acetylenic	æˌs$_{<c>}$ētɪ$_{<y>}$'lēnɪk	əˌs$_{<c>}$ɛtə$_{<y>}$'lɛnɪk
achondrite	ā'k$_{<ch>}$ondrīt	eɪ'k$_{<ch>}$ondraɪt
achondritic	ˌāk$_{<ch>}$on'drītɪk̲	ˌeɪk$_{<ch>}$on'drɪtɪk
acidophile	'æs$_{<c>}$ɪdōˌfīl$_{[+gk]}$	'æs$_{<c>}$ɪdouˌfaɪl$_{[+gk]}$
acidophilic	ˌæs$_{<c>}$ɪdō'fīlɪk$_{[+gk]}$	ˌæs$_{<c>}$ɪdou'fɪlɪk$_{[+gk]}$
aconite	'ækoˌnīt	'ækə$_{<o>}$ˌnaɪt
aconitic	ˌæko'nītɪk	ˌækə$_{<o>}$'nɪtɪk
actinomycete	ˌæktɪnōmi$_{<y>}$'k̲ēt	ˌæktɪnoumaɪ$_{<y>}$'s$_{<c>}$it
actinomycin	ˌæktɪnō'mi$_{<y>}$k̲ɪn	ˌæktɪnou'maɪ$_{<y>}$s$_{<c>}$ɪn
actinomycosis	ˌæktɪnōmi$_{<y>}$'k̲ōsɪs	ˌæktɪnoumaɪ$_{<y>}$'kousɪs
advocation	ˌædvō'kātyon	ˌædvə$_{<o>}$'keɪšən
aeruginous	ɛ$_{<ae>}$'rug̲ɪnos	ɪ$_{<ae>}$'ruǰɪnəs
aerugo	ɛ$_{<ae>}$'rugō	ɪ$_{<ae>}$'rugou
agnosticism	æg'nostɪˌk̲ɪsm	æg'nostɪˌs$_{<c>}$ɪzəm
agnostic	æg'nostɪk̲	æg'nostɪk
albite	'ælbīt	'ælbaɪt
albitic	æl'bītɪk̲	æl'bɪtɪk
alcoholicity	ˌælkoho'lɪk̲ɪti	ˌælkə$_{<o>}$hɔ$_{<o>}$'lɪs$_{<c>}$ɪti
alcoholic	ˌælko'holɪk̲	ˌælkə$_{<o>}$'hɔ$_{<o>}$lɪk
alkaline	'ælk$_{<k>}$æˌlīn	'ælk$_{<k>}$ə$_{<a>}$ˌlaɪn
alkalinity	ˌælk$_{<k>}$æ'lɪnɪti	ˌælk$_{<k>}$ə$_{<a>}$'lɪnɪti
allophone	'æl$_{[+db]}$oˌfōn$_{[+gk]}$	'æl$_{[+db]}$ə$_{<o>}$ˌfoun$_{[+gk]}$
allophonic	ˌ'æl$_{[+db]}$o'f'ōnɪk̲$_{[+gk]}$	ˌæl$_{[+db]}$ə$_{<o>}$'fonɪk$_{[+gk]}$
allotrope	'æl$_{[+db]}$oˌtrōp	'æl$_{[+db]}$ə$_{<o>}$ˌtroup
allotropic	ˌæl$_{[+db]}$o'trōpɪk	ˌæl$_{[+db]}$ə$_{<o>}$'tropɪk
ammonite	'æm$_{[+db]}$oˌnīt	'æm$_{[+db]}$ə$_{<o>}$ˌnaɪt
ammonitic	ˌæm$_{[+db]}$o'nɪtɪk	ˌæm$_{[+db]}$ə$_{<o>}$'nɪtɪk
amortization	ˌæmortī'zātyon	ˌæmə$_{<o>}$rtɪ'zeɪšən
anabolite	æ'næboˌlīt	ə'næbə$_{<o>}$ˌlaɪt

	Deep	**Shallow**
anabolitic	æ,næbo'lītɪk	ə,næbə<o>'lɪtɪk
anecdote	'ænɛk,dōt	'ænɪ<e>k,doʊt
anecdotic	,ænɛk'dōtɪk	,ænɪ<e>k'dotɪk
angelic	ān'gɛlɪk	æn'ǰɛlɪk
angel	'āngɛl	'eɪnǰə<e>l
announce	æ'n[+db]ūns	ə'n[+db]aʊns
annunciate	æ'n[+db]ū<u>ns<c>ɪ,āt	ə'n[+db]ʌns<c>i<i>,eɪt
annunciation	æ,n[+db]ū<u>ns<c>ɪ'ātyon	ə,n[+db]ʌns<c>i<i>'eɪšən
anorthite	æn'orθīt	æn'ɔrθaɪt
anorthitic	,ænor'θītɪk	,ænɔr'θɪtɪk
anthracene	'ænθræ,kēn	'ænθrə<a>,s<c>in
anthracite	'ænθræ,kīt	'ænθrə<a>,s<c>aɪt
anthracitic	,ænθræ'kītɪk	,ænθrə<a>'s<c>ɪtɪk
anthracoid	'ænθræ,koɪd	'ænθrə<a>,koɪd
anticyclone	,æntɪ's<c>i<y>klōn	,ænti<i>'s<c>aɪ<y>kloʊn
anticyclonic	,æntɪs<c>i<y>'klōnɪk	,ænti<i>s<c>aɪ<y>'klonɪk
antique	æn'te<i>k<qu>	æn'ti<i>k<qu>
antiquity	æn'te<i>kwɪti	æn'tɪkwɪti
antitype	'æntɪ,ti<y>p	'ænti<i>,taɪ<y>p
antitypic	,æntɪ'ti<y>pɪk	,ænti<i>'tɪ<y>pɪk
apical	'æpɪkæl	'æpɪkə<a>l
apices	'æpɪk+ēz	'æpɪs<c>+iz
aplite	'æplīt	'æplaɪt
aplitic	æp'lītɪk	æp'lɪtɪk
appeal	æ'p[+db]e<ea>l	ə'p[+db]i<ea>l
appellation	,æp[+db]ɛ'l[+db]ātyon	,æp[+db]ə'l[+db]eɪšən
appendicectomy	æ,p[+db]ɛndɪ'kɛktomɪ	ə,p[+db]ɛndɪ's<c>ɛktə<o>mi
appendicitis	æ,p[+db]ɛndɪ'kītɪs	ə,p[+db]ɛndɪ's<c>aɪtɪs
appendicle	æ'p[+db]ɛndɪkl	ə'p[+db]ɛndɪkə$_{\epsilon}$l<le>
appendix	æ'p[+db]ɛndɪks	ə'p[+db]ɛndɪks
archangelic	,ærk<ch>ān'gɛlɪk	,ɑrk<ch>æn'ǰɛlɪk
archangel	'ærk<ch>,āngɛl	'ɑrk<ch>,eɪnǰə<e>l
arenite	'ærɛ,nīt	'ærə,naɪt
arenitic	,ærɛ'nītɪk	,ærə'nɪtɪk
argillite	'ærgɪ,l[+db]īt	'ɑrǰə<i>,l[+db]aɪt
argillitic	,ærgɪ'l[+db]ītɪk	,ɑrǰə<i>'l[+db]ɪtɪk
asceticism	æ'sϵ<c>ɛtɪ,kɪsm	ə'sϵ<c>ɛtɪ,s<c>ɪzəm
ascetic	æ'sϵ<c>ɛtɪk	ə'sϵ<c>ɛtɪk
asinine	'æsɪ,nīn	'æsə<i>,naɪn
asininity	,æsɪ'nīnɪti	,æsə<i>'nɪnɪti
asparagine	æ'spæræ,ge<i>n	ə'spærə<a>,ǰi<i>n

	Deep	**Shallow**
asparagus	æ'spæræg̲ʊs	ə'spærə<a>gə<u>s
assignation	,æs[+db]īg'nātyon	,æs[+db]ɪg'neɪšən
assign	æ's[+db]īgn	ə's[+db]aɪ<ig>n
asymptote	'æsɪ<y>mɛ<p>,tōt	'æsɪ<y>mɛ<p>,toʊt
asymptotic	,æsɪ<y>mɛ<p>'tōtɪk̲	,æsɪ<y>mɛ<p>'totɪk
athlete	'æθlēt	'æθlit
athletic	æθ'lētɪk̲	æθ'lɛtɪk
atone	æ'tōn	ə'toʊn
atonic	ā'tōnɪk̲	eɪ'tonɪk
atrocious	æ'trōk̲yos	ə'troʊšəs
atrocity	æ'trōk̲ɪti	ə'tros<c>ɪti
audacious	ɔ'dāk̲yos	ɔ'deɪšəs
audacity	ɔ'dāk̲ɪti	ɔ'dæs<c>ɪti
augite	'ɔgīt	'ɔgaɪt
augitic	ɔ'gītɪk̲	ɔ'gɪtɪk
austenite	'ɔstɛ,nīt	'ɔstə,naɪt
austenitic	,ɔstɛ'nītɪk̲	,ɔstə'nɪtɪk
australopithecine	ɔ,strālō'pɪθɛ,k̲e<i>n	ɔ,streɪloʊ'pɪθɪ<e>,s<c>i<i>n
australopithecus	ɔs,trālō'pɪθɛk̲ʊs	ɔs,treɪloʊ'pɪθɪ<e>kə<u>s
authenticity	,ɔθɛn'tɪk̲ɪti	,ɔθɛn'tɪs<c>ɪti
authentic	ɔ'θɛntɪk̲	ɔ'θɛntɪk
authorization	,ɔθorī'zātyon	,ɔθə<o>rɪ'zeɪšən
authorize	'ɔθo,rīz	'ɔθə<o>,raɪz
automate	'ɔto,māt	'ɔtə<o>,meɪt
automatic	,ɔto'mætɪk̲	,ɔtə<o>'mætɪk
autophyte	'ɔto,fi<y>t[+gk]	'ɔtə<o>,faɪ<y>t[+gk]
autophytic	,ɔto'fi<y>tɪk̲[+gk]	,ɔtə<o>'fɪ<y>tɪk[+gk]
autotype	'ɔto,ti<y>p	'ɔtə<o>,taɪ<y>p
autotypic	,ɔto'ti<y>pɪk̲	,ɔtə<o>'tɪ<y>pɪk
avocation	,ævō'kātyon	,ævə<o>'keɪšən
azeotrope	æ'zɪ<e>o,trōp	ə'ziə<o>,troʊp
azeotropic	,āzɪ<e>o'trōpɪk̲	,eɪziə<o>'tropɪk
bacteriophage	bæk'tɛrɪo,fāg̲[+gk]	bæk'tɪ<e>r̩i<i>ə<o>,feɪǰ[+gk]
bacteriophagic	bæk,tɛrɪo'fāg̲ɪk̲[+gk]	bæk,tɪ<e>r̩i<i>ə<o>'fæǰɪk[+gk]
balance	'bælæns	'bælə<a>ns
bale	'bāl	'beɪl
baroscope	'bæro,skōp	'bærə<o>,skoʊp
baroscopic	,bæro'skōpɪk̲	,bærə<o>'skopɪk
basicity	bā'sɪk̲ɪti	beɪ'sɪs<c>ɪti
basic	'bāsɪk̲	'beɪsɪk
beneficence	bɛ'nɛfɪk̲ɛns	bə'nɛfɪs<c>əns

	Deep	Shallow
beneficent	bɛ'nɛfɪk̲ɛnt	bə'nɛfɪs<c>ənt
benefic	bɛ'nɛfɪk̲	bə'nɛfɪk
biconcave	bī'konkāv	baɪ'konkeɪv
biconcavity	ˌbīkon'kāvɪti	ˌbaɪkon'kævɪti
biophysicist	ˌbīō'fɪ<y>z<s>ɪk̲ɪst[+gk]	ˌbaɪoʊ'fɪ<y>z<s>ɪs<c>ɪst[+gk]
biophysics	ˌbīō'fɪ<y>z<s>ɪk̲+s[+gk]	ˌbaɪoʊ'fɪ<y>z<s>ɪk+s[+gk]
biotite	'bīoˌtīt	'baɪə<o>ˌtaɪt
biotitic	ˌbīo'tītɪk̲	ˌbaɪə<o>'tɪtɪk
biotype	'bīoˌti<y>p	'baɪə<o>ˌtaɪ<y>p
biotypic	ˌbīo'ti<y>pɪk	ˌbaɪə<o>'tɪ<y>pɪk
biquadrate	bī'kwædrāt	baɪ'kwodreɪt
biquadratic	ˌbīkwæ'drātɪk̲	ˌbaɪkwo'drætɪk
breve	'brēv	'briv
brevity	'brēvɪti	'brɛvɪti
bromide	'brōmīd	'broʊmaɪd
bromidic	brō'mīdɪk̲	broʊ'mɪdɪk
bronchoscope	'bronk<ch>oˌskōp	'broŋk<ch>ə<o>ˌskoʊp
bronchoscopic	ˌbronk<ch>o'skōpɪk̲	ˌbroŋk<ch>ə<o>'skopɪk
bryophyte	'bri<y>oˌfi<y>t[+gk]	'braɪ<y>ə<o>ˌfaɪ<y>t[+gk]
bryophytic	ˌbri<y>o'fi<y>tɪk̲[+gk]	ˌbraɪ<y>ə<o>'fɪ<y>tɪk[+gk]
calcination	ˌkælk̲ɪ'nātyon	ˌkæls<c>ɪ'neɪšən
calcine	'kælk̲īn	'kæls<c>aɪn
calcite	'kælˌk̲īt	'kælˌs<c>aɪt
calcitic	kæl'k̲ɪtɪk̲	kæl's<c>ɪtɪk
calices	'kælɪˌk̲+ēz	'kælɪˌs<c>+iz
calicle	'kælɪk̲l	'kælɪkəl
calyces	'kælɪ<y>ˌk̲+ēz	'kælɪ<y>ˌs<c>+iz
calycine	'kælɪ<y>k̲ɪnϵ<e>	'kælɪ<y>s<c>ɪnϵ<e>
calycle	'kælɪ<y>kl	'kælɪ<y>kəl
capacious	kæ'pāk̲yos	kə<a>'peɪšəs
capacity	kæ'pāk̲ɪti	kə<a>'pæs<c>ɪti
capitalization	ˌkæpɪtælī'zātyon	ˌkæpɪtə<a>lɪ'zeɪšən
capitalize	'kæpɪtæˌlīz	'kæpɪtə<a>ˌlaɪz
capitation	ˌkæpɪ'tātyon	ˌkæpɪ'teɪšən
caput	'kāpʊt	'keɪpə<u>t
carbonization	ˌkærbonī'zātyon	ˌkɑrbə<o>nɪ'zeɪšən
carbonize	'kærboˌnīz	'kɑrbə<o>ˌnaɪz
cathode	'kæθōd	'kæθoʊd
cathodic	kæ'θōdɪk̲	kæ'θodɪk
catholicity	ˌkæθo'lɪk̲ɪti	ˌkæθə<o>'lɪs<c>ɪti
catholic	'kæθolɪk	'kæθə<o>lɪk

	Deep	**Shallow**
causticity	kɔ'stɪk̲ɪti	kɔ'stɪs<c>ɪti
caustic	'kɔstɪk̲	'kɔstɪk
cave	'kāv	'keɪv
cavity	'kāvɪti	'kævɪti
cease	's<c>e<ea>s	's<c>i<ea>s
cenobite	's<c>ēno,bīt	's<c>inə<o>,baɪt
cenobitic	,s<c>ēno'bītɪk̲	,s<c>inə<o>'bɪtɪk
cenocyte	's<c>ēno,s<c>i<y>t	's<c>inə<o>,s<c>aɪ<y>t
cenocytic	,s<c>ēno's<c>i<y>tɪk̲	,s<c>inə<o>'s<c>ɪ<y>tɪk
centricity	s<c>ɛn'trɪk̲ɪti	s<c>ɛn'trɪs<c>ɪti
centric	's<c>ɛntrɪk̲	's<c>ɛntrɪk
centrosome	's<c>ɛntro,sōm	's<c>ɛntrə<o>,soʊm
centrosomic	,s<c>ɛntro'sōmɪk̲	,s<c>ɛntrə<o>'somɪk
cercopithecid	,s<c>ɛrkōpɪ'θēk̲ɪd	,s<c>r̩koupɪ'θis<c>ɪd
cercopithecoid	,s<c>ɛrkōpɪ'θēk̲oɪd	,s<c>r̩koupɪ'θikoɪd
cervical	's<c>ɛrvɪk̲æl	's<c>r̩vɪkə<a>l
cervicitis	,s<c>ɛrvɪ'k̲ītɪs	,s<c>r̩vɪ's<c>aɪtɪs
cervix	's<c>ɛrvɪk̲s	's<c>r̩vɪks
cessation	s<c>ē's[+db]ātyon	s<c>ɛ's[+db]eɪšən
characterization	,k<ch>ærækterī'zātyon	,k<ch>ærɪ<a>ktr̩ɪ'zeɪšən
characterize	'k<ch>ærækte,rīz	'k<ch>ærɪ<a>ktə,raɪz
chaste	'čāst	'čeɪst
chastity	'čāstɪti	'čæstɪti
chondrite	'k<ch>ondrīt	'k<ch>ondraɪt
chondritic	k<ch>on'drītɪk̲	k<ch>on'drɪtɪk
chromate	'k<ch>rōmāt	'k<ch>roʊmeɪt
chromaticism	k<ch>rō'mātɪ,k̲ɪsm	k<ch>roʊ'mætɪ,s<c>ɪzəm
chromatic	k<ch>rō'mātɪk̲	k<ch>roʊ'mætɪk
chronicity	k<ch>ro'nɪk̲ɪti	k<ch>ro'nɪs<c>ɪti
chronic	'k<ch>ronɪk̲	'k<ch>ronɪk
chronoscope	'k<ch>rono,skōp	'k<ch>ronə<o>,skoʊp
chronoscopic	,k<ch>rono'skōpɪk̲	,k<ch>ronə<o>'skopɪk
chrysolite	'k<ch>rɪ<y>so,līt	'k<ch>rɪ<y>sə<o>,laɪt
chrysolitic	,k<ch>rɪ<y>so'lītɪk̲	,k<ch>rɪ<y>sə<o>'lɪtɪk
civilization	,s<c>ɪvɪlī'zātyon	,s<c>ɪvə<i>lɪ'zeɪšən
civilize	's<c>ɪvɪ,līz	's<c>ɪvə<i>,laɪz
classicism	'klæs[+db]ɪ,k̲ɪsm	'klæs[+db]ɪ,s<c>ɪzəm
classicist	'klæs[+db]ɪk̲ɪst	'klæs[+db]ɪs<c>ɪst
classic	'klæs[+db]ɪk̲	'klæs[+db]ɪk
clone	'klōn	'kloʊn
clonic	'klōnɪk̲	'klonɪk

	Deep	**Shallow**
cognizance	ˈkognīzæns	ˈkognɪzə<a>ns
cognize	ˈkognīz	ˈkognaɪz
coincidence	kōˈɪns<c>īdɛns	koʊˈɪns<c>ɪdəns
coincide	ˌkōɪnˈs<c>īd	ˌkoʊɪnˈs<c>aɪd
colic	ˈkōlɪk	ˈkolɪk
collotype	ˈkol[+db]oˌti<y>p	ˈkol[+db]ə<o>ˌtaɪ<y>p
collotypic	ˌkol[+db]oˈti<y>pɪk̲	ˌkol[+db]ə<o>ˈtɪ<y>pɪk
colonic	kōˈlonɪk̲	koʊˈlonɪk
colonization	ˌkolonīˈzātyon	ˌkolə<o>nɪˈzeɪšən
colonize	ˈkoloˌnīz	ˈkolə<o>ˌnaɪz
colon	ˈkōlon	ˈkoʊlə<o>n
combination	ˌkombɪˈnātyon	ˌkombə<i>ˈneɪšən
combine	komˈbīn	kə<o>mˈbaɪn
commode	koˈm[+db]ōd	kə<o>ˈm[+db]oʊd
commodity	koˈm[+db]ōdɪti	kə<o>ˈm[+db]odɪti
compilation	ˌkompīˈlātyon	ˌkompə<i>ˈleɪšən
compile	komˈpīl	kə<o>mˈpaɪl
concave	konˈkāv	konˈkeɪv
concavity	konˈkāvɪti	konˈkævɪti
conceal	konˈs<c>e<ea>l	kə<o>nˈs<c>i<ea>l
cone	ˈkōn	ˈkoʊn
confidence	ˈkonfīdɛns	ˈkonfɪdəns
confide	konˈfīd	kə<o>nˈfaɪd
congeal	konˈg̲e<ea>l	kə<o>nˈǰi<ea>l
congelation	ˌkong̲ēˈlātyon	ˌkonǰəˈleɪšən
conic	ˈkōnɪk̲	ˈkonɪk
consignation	ˌkonsīgˈnātyon	ˌkonsɪgˈneɪšən
consign	konˈsīgn	kə<o>nˈsaɪ<ig>n
consolation	ˌkonsoˈlātyon	ˌkonsə<o>ˈleɪšən
contravene	ˌkontræˈvēn	ˌkontrə<a>ˈvin
contravention	ˌkontræˈvɛntyon	ˌkontrə<a>ˈvɛnčən
convene	konˈvēn	kə<o>nˈvin
convention	konˈvɛntyon	kə<o>nˈvɛnčən
convocation	ˌkonvōˈkātyon	ˌkonvə<o>ˈkeɪšən
convoke	konˈvōk	kə<o>nˈvoʊk
cormophyte	ˈkormoˌfi<y>t[+gk]	ˈkɔrmə<o>ˌfaɪ<y>t[+gk]
cormophytic	ˌkormoˈfi<y>tɪk̲[+gk]	ˌkɔrmə<o>ˈfɪ<y>tɪk[+gk]
creophagous	krɪ<e>ˈofāg̲os[+gk]	kriˈofə<a>gəs[+gk]
creophagy	krɪ<e>ˈofāg̲ɪ[+gk]	kriˈofə<a>ǰi[+gk]
creosote	ˈkrɪ<e>oˌsōt	ˈkriə<o>ˌsout
creosotic	ˌkrɪ<e>oˈsōtɪk̲	ˌkriə<o>ˈsotɪk

	Deep	Shallow
criticism	ˈkrɪtɪˌk̲ɪsm	ˈkrɪtɪˌs<c>ɪzəm
criticize	ˈkrɪtɪˌk̲īz	ˈkrɪtɪˌs<c>aɪz
critic	ˈkrɪtɪk̲	ˈkrɪtɪk
crocein	ˈkrōk̲ēɪn	ˈkroʊs<c>iɪn
crocus	ˈkrōk̲ʊs	ˈkroʊkə<u>s
cryoscope	ˈkri<y>oˌskōp	ˈkraɪ<y>ə<o>ˌskoʊp
cryoscopic	ˌkri<y>oˈskōpɪk̲	ˌkraɪ<y>ə<o>ˈskopɪk
crystallite	ˈkrɪ<y>stæˌl[+db]īt	ˈkrɪ<y>stə<a>ˌl[+db]aɪt
crystallitic	ˌkrɪ<y>stæˈl[+db]ītɪk̲	ˌkrɪ<y>stə<a>ˈl[+db]ɪtɪk
cyanite	ˈs<c>i<y>æˌnīt	ˈs<c>aɪ<y>ə<a>ˌnaɪt
cyanitic	ˌs<c>i<y>æˈnītɪk̲	ˌs<c>aɪ<y>ə<a>ˈnɪtɪk
cyclone	ˈs<c>i<y>klōn	ˈs<c>aɪ<y>kloʊn
cyclonic	s<c>i<y>ˈklōnɪk	s<c>aɪ<y>ˈklonɪkˈ
cynicism	ˈs<c>ɪ<y>nɪˌk̲ɪsm	ˈs<c>ɪ<y>nɪˌs<c>ɪzəm
cynic	ˈs<c>ɪ<y>nɪk̲	ˈs<c>ɪ<y>nɪk
cystoscope	ˈs<c>ɪ<y>stoˌskōp	ˈs<c>ɪ<y>stə<o>ˌskoʊp
cystoscopic	ˌs<c>ɪ<y>stoˈskōpɪk̲	ˌs<c>ɪ<y>stə<o>ˈskopɪk
declination	ˌdɛklīˈnātyon	ˌdɛklə<i>ˈneɪšən
decline	dɛˈklīn	dɪˈklaɪn
dendrite	ˈdɛndrīt	ˈdɛndraɪt
dendritic	dɛnˈdrītɪk̲	dɛnˈdrɪtɪk
denounce	dɛˈnūns	dɪˈnaʊns
denunciate	dɛˈnū<u>ns<c>ɪˌāt	dɪˈnʌns<c>i<i>ˌeɪt
denunciation	dɛˌnū<u>ns<c>ɪˈātyon	dɪˌnʌns<c>i<i>ˈeɪšən
deprave	dɛˈprāv	dɪˈpreɪv
depravity	dɛˈprāvɪti	dɪˈprævɪti
deprivation	ˌdɛprīˈvātyon	ˌdɛprə<i>ˈveɪšən
deprive	dɛˈprīv	dɪˈpraɪv
derivation	ˌdɛrīˈvātyon	ˌdɛrə<i>ˈveɪšən
derive	dɛˈrīv	dɪˈraɪv
dermatome	ˈdɛrmˌætōm	ˈdṛmə<a>ˌtoʊm
dermatomic	ˌdɛrmæˈtōmɪk̲	ˌdṛmə<a>ˈtomɪk
dermatophyte	ˈdɛrmætˌofi<y>t[+gk]	ˈdṛmə<a>tə<o>ˌfaɪ<y>t[+gk]
dermatophytic	ˌdɛrmætoˈfi<y>tɪk̲[+gk]	ˌdṛmə<a>tə<o>ˈfɪ<y>tɪk[+gk]
desensitization	dēˌsɛnsɪtɪˈzātyon	diˌsɛnsɪtɪˈzeɪšən
desensitize	dēˈsɛnsɪˌtīz	diˈsɛnsɪˌtaɪz
designation	ˌdɛsīgˈnātyon	ˌdɛz<s>ɪgˈneɪšən
design	dɛˈsīgn	dɪˈz<s>aɪ<ig>n
deuteranope	ˈdu<eu>tɛræˌnōp	ˈdu<eu>tṛə<a>ˌnoʊp
deuteranopic	ˌdu<eu>tɛræˈnōpɪk̲	ˌdu<eu>tṛə<a>ˈnopɪk
diaphone	ˈdīæˌfōn[+gk]	ˈdaɪə<a>ˌfoʊn[+gk]

	Deep	**Shallow**
diaphonic	ˌdīæˈfōnık̲$_{[+gk]}$	ˌdaıə$_{\text{<a>}}$ˈfonık$_{[+gk]}$
dibasicity	ˌdībāˈsık̲ıti	ˌdaıbeıˈsıs$_{\text{<c>}}$ıti
dibasic	dīˈbāsık̲	daıˈbeısık
dichroite	ˈdīk$_{\text{<ch>}}$rōˌīt	ˈdaık$_{\text{<ch>}}$rouˌaıt
dichroitic	ˌdīk$_{\text{<ch>}}$rōˈītık̲	ˌdaık$_{\text{<ch>}}$rouˈıtık
dichromate	dīˈk$_{\text{<ch>}}$rōmāt	daıˈk$_{\text{<ch>}}$roumeıt
dichromaticism	ˌdīk$_{\text{<ch>}}$rōˈmātıˌk̲ısm	ˌdaık$_{\text{<ch>}}$rouˈmætıˌs$_{\text{<c>}}$ızəm
dichromatic	ˌdīk$_{\text{<ch>}}$rōˈmātık̲	ˌdaık$_{\text{<ch>}}$rouˈmætık
dichroscope	ˈdīk$_{\text{<ch>}}$roˌskōp	ˈdaık$_{\text{<ch>}}$rə$_{\text{<o>}}$ˌskoup
dichroscopic	ˌdīk$_{\text{<ch>}}$roˈskōpık̲	ˌdaık$_{\text{<ch>}}$rə$_{\text{<o>}}$ˈskopık
diorite	ˈdīoˌrīt	ˈdaıə$_{\text{<o>}}$ˌraıt
dioritic	ˌdīoˈrıtık̲	ˌdaıə$_{\text{<o>}}$ˈrıtık
discommode	ˌdıskoˈm$_{[+db]}$ōd	ˌdıskə$_{\text{<o>}}$ˈm$_{[+db]}$oud
discommodity	ˌdıskoˈm$_{[+db]}$ōdıti	ˌdıskə$_{\text{<o>}}$ˈm$_{[+db]}$odıti
disinclination	ˌdısınklīˈnātyon	ˌdısınklıˈneıšən
disincline	ˌdısınˈklīn	ˌdısınˈklaın
divination	ˌdıvīˈnātyon	ˌdıvə$_{\text{<i>}}$ˈneıšən
divine	dıˈvīn	dı$_{\text{<i>}}$ˈvaın
divinity	dıˈvīnıti	dı$_{\text{<i>}}$ˈvınıti
dolerite	ˈdolɛˌrīt	ˈdoləˌraıt
doleritic	ˌdolɛˈrītık̲	ˌdoləˈrıtık
dramatization	ˌdræmætīˈzātyon	ˌdræmə$_{\text{<a>}}$tıˈzeıšən
dramatize	ˈdræmæˌtīz	ˈdræmə$_{\text{<a>}}$ˌtaız
dynamite	ˈdi$_{\text{<y>}}$næˌmīt	ˈdaı$_{\text{<y>}}$nə$_{\text{<a>}}$ˌmaıt
dynamitic	ˌdi$_{\text{<y>}}$næˈmītık̲	ˌdaı$_{\text{<y>}}$nə$_{\text{<a>}}$ˈmıtık
ecclesiastical	ɛˌk$_{[+db]}$lēz$_{\text{<s>}}$ıˈæstık̲æl	ı$_{\text{<e>}}$ˌk$_{[+db]}$liz$_{\text{<s>}}$i$_{\text{<i>}}$ˈæstıkə$_{\text{<a>}}$l
ecclesiasticism	ɛˌk$_{[+db]}$lēz$_{\text{<s>}}$ıˈæstıˌk̲ısm	ı$_{\text{<e>}}$ˌk$_{[+db]}$liz$_{\text{<s>}}$i$_{\text{<i>}}$ˈæstıˌs$_{\text{<c>}}$ızəm
ecclesiastic	ɛˌk$_{[+db]}$lēz$_{\text{<s>}}$ıˈæstık̲	ı$_{\text{<e>}}$ˌk$_{[+db]}$liz$_{\text{<s>}}$i$_{\text{<i>}}$ˈæstık
eclecticism	ɛˈklɛktıˌk̲ısm	ı$_{\text{<e>}}$ˈklɛktıˌs$_{\text{<c>}}$ızəm
eclectic	ɛˈklɛktık̲	ı$_{\text{<e>}}$ˈklɛktık
ecotype	ˈɛkoˌti$_{\text{<y>}}$p	ˈɛkə$_{\text{<o>}}$ˌtaı$_{\text{<y>}}$p
ecotypic	ˌɛkoˈti$_{\text{<y>}}$pık̲	ˌɛkə$_{\text{<o>}}$ˈtı$_{\text{<y>}}$pık
ectoparasite	ˌɛktōˈpæræˌsīt	ˌɛktouˈpærə$_{\text{<a>}}$ˌsaıt
ectoparasitic	ˌɛktōˌpæræˈsītık̲	ˌɛktouˌpærə$_{\text{<a>}}$ˈsıtık
edacious	ɛˈdāk̲yos	ı$_{\text{<e>}}$ˈdeıšəs
edacity	ɛˈdāk̲ıti	ı$_{\text{<e>}}$ˈdæs$_{\text{<c>}}$ıti
elasticity	ɛlæˈstık̲ıti	ı$_{\text{<e>}}$læˈstıs$_{\text{<c>}}$ıti
elasticize	ɛˈlæstıˌk̲īz	ı$_{\text{<e>}}$ˈlæstıˌs$_{\text{<c>}}$aız
elastic	ɛˈlæstık̲	ı$_{\text{<e>}}$ˈlæstık
electrical	ɛˈlɛktrık̲æl	ı$_{\text{<e>}}$ˈlɛktrıkə$_{\text{<a>}}$l
electricity	ɛlɛkˈtrık̲ıti	ı$_{\text{<e>}}$lɛkˈtrıs$_{\text{<c>}}$ıti

	Deep	**Shallow**
electric	ɛ'lɛktrɪk̲	ɪ$_{<e>}$'lɛktrɪk
electrolyte	ɛ'lɛktroˌli$_{<y>}$t	ɪ$_{<e>}$'lɛktrə$_{<o>}$ˌlaɪ$_{<y>}$t
electrolytic	ɛˌlɛktro'li$_{<y>}$tɪk̲	ɪ$_{<e>}$ˌlɛktrə$_{<o>}$'lɪ$_{<y>}$tɪk
electrophone	ɛ'lɛktroˌfōn$_{[+gk]}$	ɪ$_{<e>}$'lɛktrə$_{<o>}$ˌfoʊn$_{[+gk]}$
electrophonic	ɛˌlɛktro'fōnɪk̲$_{[+gk]}$	ɪ$_{<e>}$ˌlɛktrə$_{<o>}$'fonɪk$_{[+gk]}$
electroscope	ɛ'lɛktroˌskōp	ɪ$_{<e>}$'lɛktrə$_{<o>}$ˌskoʊp
electroscopic	ɛˌlɛktro'skōpɪk̲	ɪ$_{<e>}$ˌlɛktrə$_{<o>}$'skopɪk
elliptical	ɛ'l$_{[+db]}$ɪptɪkæl	ɪ$_{<e>}$'l$_{[+db]}$ɪptɪkə$_{<a>}$l
ellipticity	ɛl$_{[+db]}$ɪp'tɪk̲ɪti	ɪ$_{<e>}$l$_{[+db]}$ɪp'tɪs$_{<c>}$ɪti
empiricism	ɛm'pɪrɪˌk̲ɪsm	ɛm'pɪrɪˌs$_{<c>}$ɪzəm
empiric	ɛm'pɪrɪk̲	ɛm'pɪrɪk
endoparasite	ˌɛndō'pæræˌsīt	ˌɛndoʊ'pærə$_{<a>}$ˌsaɪt
endoparasitic	ˌɛndōˌpæræ'sītɪk̲	ˌɛndoʊˌpærə$_{<a>}$'sɪtɪk
endophyte	'ɛndoˌfi$_{<y>}$t$_{[+gk]}$	'ɛndə$_{<o>}$ˌfaɪ$_{<y>}$t$_{[+gk]}$
endophytic	ˌɛndo'fi$_{<y>}$tɪk̲$_{[+gk]}$	ˌɛndə$_{<o>}$'fɪ$_{<y>}$tɪk$_{[+gk]}$
endoscope	'ɛndoˌskōp	'ɛndə$_{<o>}$ˌskoʊp
endoscopic	ˌɛndo'skōpɪk̲	ˌɛndə$_{<o>}$'skopɪk
enounce	ɛ'nūns	ɪ$_{<e>}$'naʊns
entophyte	'ɛntoˌfi$_{<y>}$t$_{[+gk]}$	'ɛntə$_{<o>}$ˌfaɪ$_{<y>}$t$_{[+gk]}$
entophytic	ˌɛnto'fi$_{<y>}$tɪk̲$_{[+gk]}$	ˌɛntə$_{<o>}$'fɪ$_{<y>}$tɪk$_{[+gk]}$
enunciable	ɛ'nū$_{<u>}$ns$_{<c>}$ɪæbɪl	ɪ$_{<e>}$'nʌns$_{<c>}$i$_{<i>}$ə$_{<a>}$bəl
enunciate	ɛ'nū$_{<u>}$ns$_{<c>}$ɪˌāt	ɪ$_{<e>}$'nʌns$_{<c>}$i$_{<i>}$ˌeɪt
enunciation	ɛˌnū$_{<u>}$ns$_{<c>}$ɪ'ātyon	ɪ$_{<e>}$ˌnʌns$_{<c>}$i$_{<i>}$'eɪšən
epidote	'ɛpɪˌdōt	'ɛpɪˌdoʊt
epidotic	ˌɛpɪ'dōtɪk̲	ˌɛpɪ'dotɪk
epiphyte	'ɛpɪˌfi$_{<y>}$t$_{[+gk]}$	'ɛpə$_{<i>}$ˌfaɪ$_{<y>}$t$_{[+gk]}$
epiphytic	ˌɛpɪ'fi$_{<y>}$tɪk̲$_{[+gk]}$	ˌɛpə$_{<i>}$'fɪ$_{<y>}$tɪk$_{[+gk]}$
episode	'ɛpɪˌsōd	'ɛpə$_{<i>}$ˌsoʊd
episodic	ˌɛpɪ'sōdɪk̲	ˌɛpə$_{<i>}$'sodɪk
equivocation	ɛˌkwɪvō'kātyon	ɪ$_{<e>}$ˌkwɪvə$_{<o>}$'keɪšən
equivoke	'ɛkwɪˌvōk	'ɛkwə$_{<i>}$ˌvoʊk
eremite	'ɛrɛˌmīt	'ɛrəˌmaɪt
eremitic	ˌɛrɛ'mītɪk̲	ˌɛrə'mɪtɪk
eroticism	ɛ'rotɪˌk̲ɪsm	ə$_{<e>}$'rotɪˌs$_{<c>}$ɪzəm
erotic	ɛ'rotɪk̲	ə$_{<e>}$'rotɪk
erythrocyte	ɛ'rɪ$_{<y>}$θroˌs$_{<c>}$i$_{<y>}$t	ɪ$_{<e>}$'rɪ$_{<y>}$θrə$_{<o>}$ˌs$_{<c>}$aɪ$_{<y>}$t
erythrocytic	ɛˌrɪ$_{<y>}$θro's$_{<c>}$i$_{<y>}$tɪk̲	ɪ$_{<e>}$ˌrɪ$_{<y>}$θrə$_{<o>}$'s$_{<c>}$ɪ$_{<y>}$tɪk
esophageal	ɛˌsofā'g̲ɪ$_{<e>}$æl$_{[+gk]}$	ɪ$_{<e>}$ˌsofə$_{<a>}$'ǰiə$_{<a>}$l$_{[+gk]}$
esophagus	ɛ'sofāg̲us$_{[+gk]}$	ɪ$_{<e>}$'sofə$_{<a>}$gə$_{<u>}$s$_{[+gk]}$
esthete	'ɛsθēt	'ɛsθit
estheticism	ɛs'θētɪˌk̲ɪsm	ɛs'θɛtɪˌs$_{<c>}$ɪzəm

	Deep	Shallow
esthetic	ɛsˈθētɪk̲	ɛsˈθɛtɪk
ethicize	ˈɛθɪˌk̲īz	ˈɛθɪˌs$_{<c>}$aɪz
ethic	ˈɛθɪk̲	ˈɛθɪk
evocation	ˌɛvōˈkātyon	ˌɛvə$_{<o>}$ˈkeɪšən
evoke	ɛˈvōk	ɪ$_{<e>}$ˈvoʊk
exegete	ˈɛksɛˌg̲ēt	ˈɛksɪ$_{<e>}$ˌǰit
exegetic	ˌɛksɛˈg̲ētɪk̲	ˌɛksɪ$_{<e>}$ˈǰɛtɪk
exile	ˈɛgzīl	ˈɛgzaɪl
exilic	ɛˈgzīlɪk̲	ɛˈgzɪlɪk
extreme	ɛˈkstrēm	ɪ$_{<e>}$ˈkstrim
extremity	ɛˈkstrēmɪti	ɪ$_{<e>}$ˈkstrɛmɪti
falciform	ˈfælk̲ɪˌform	ˈfæls$_{<c>}$ə$_{<i>}$ˌfɔrm
falcon	ˈfælk̲on	ˈfælkə$_{<o>}$n
fanaticism	fæˈnætɪˌk̲ɪsm	fə$_{<a>}$ˈnætɪˌs$_{<c>}$ɪzəm
fanaticize	fæˈnætɪˌk̲īz	fə$_{<a>}$ˈnætɪˌs$_{<c>}$aɪz
fanatic	fæˈnætɪk̲	fə$_{<a>}$ˈnætɪk
fasciation	ˌfāsϵ$_{<c>}$ɪˈātyon	ˌfæš$_{<sc>}$i$_{<i>}$ˈeɪšən
fascia	ˈfāsϵ$_{<c>}$ɪæ	ˈfeɪš$_{<sc>}$i$_{<i>}$ə$_{<a>}$
fascination	ˌfæsϵ$_{<c>}$ɪˈnātyon	ˌfæsϵ$_{<c>}$ə$_{<i>}$ˈneɪšən
fascine	fæˈsϵ$_{<c>}$e$_{<i>}$n	fæˈsϵ$_{<c>}$i$_{<i>}$n
federalization	ˌfɛdɛrælˈɪzātyon	ˌfɛdr$_{<er>}$ə$_{<a>}$lə$_{<i>}$ˈzeɪšən
federalize	ˈfɛdɛrˌælīz	ˈfɛdr$_{<er>}$ə$_{<a>}$ˌlaɪz
felsite	ˈfɛlsīt	ˈfɛlsaɪt
felsitic	fɛlˈsītɪk̲	fɛlˈsɪtɪk
ferocious	fɛˈrōk̲yos	fəˈroʊšəs
ferocity	fɛˈrōk̲ɪti	fəˈros$_{<c>}$ɪti
ferroelectricity	ˌfɛr$_{[+db]}$ōɛlɛkˈtrɪk̲ɪti	ˌfɛr$_{[+db]}$oʊɪ$_{<e>}$lɛkˈtrɪs$_{<c>}$ɪti
ferroelectric	ˌfɛr$_{[+db]}$ōɛˈlɛktrɪk̲	ˌfɛr$_{[+db]}$oʊɪ$_{<e>}$ˈlɛktrɪk
fertilization	ˌfɛrtɪlīˈzātyon	ˌfr̩tə$_{<i>}$lɪˈzeɪšən
fertilize	ˈfɛrtˌɪlīz	ˈfr̩tə$_{<i>}$ˌlaɪz
finance	fɪˈnæns	fɪˈnæns
finance	ˈfīˌnæns	ˈfaɪˌnæns
fluoroscope	ˈflu$_{<uo>}$roˌskōp	ˈflu$_{<uo>}$r̩ə$_{<o>}$ˌskoʊp
fluoroscopic	ˌflu$_{<uo>}$roˈskōpɪk̲	ˌflu$_{<uo>}$r̩ə$_{<o>}$ˈskopɪk
fugacious	fugˈāk̲yos	fyuˈgeɪšəs
fugacity	fugˈāk̲ɪti	fyuˈgæs$_{<c>}$ɪti
fumarole	ˈfumærˌōl	ˈfyumə$_{<a>}$ˌroʊl
fumarolic	ˌfumærˈōlɪk̲	ˌfyumə$_{<a>}$ˈrolɪk
fungicide	ˈfʌng̲ɪˌk̲īd	ˈfʌnǰɪˌs$_{<c>}$aɪd
fungic	ˈfʌng̲ɪk̲	ˈfʌnǰɪk
galvanoscope	ˈgælvænoˌskōp	ˈgælvə$_{<a>}$nə$_{<o>}$ˌskoʊp

	Deep	Shallow
galvanoscopic	ˌgælvænoˈskōpɪk̲	ˌgælvə<a>nə<o>ˈskopɪk
gastronome	ˈgæstroˌnōm	ˈgæstrə<o>ˌnoʊm
gastronomic	ˌgæstroˈnōmɪk̲	ˌgæstrə<o>ˈnomɪk
gastroscope	ˈgæstroˌskōp	ˈgæstrə<o>ˌskoʊp
gastroscopic	ˌgæstroˈskōpɪk̲	ˌgæstrə<o>ˈskopɪk
generalization	ˌǰɛnɛrælˈīzātyon	ˌǰɛnr<er>ə<a>lə<i>ˈzeɪšən
generalize	ˈǰɛnɛrˌælīz	ˈǰɛnr<er>ə<a>ˌlaɪz
geneticist	ǰēˈnɛtɪk̲ɪst	ǰəˈnɛtɪs<c>ɪst
genetic	ǰēˈnɛtɪk̲	ǰəˈnɛtɪk
gene	ˈǰēn	ˈǰin
genic	ˈǰēnɪk̲	ˈǰɛnɪk
genotype	ˈǰēnoˌti<y>p	ˈǰɛnə<o>ˌtaɪ<y>p
genotypicity	ˌǰēnoti<y>ˈpɪk̲ɪti	ˌǰɛnə<o>tɪ<y>ˈpɪs<c>ɪti
genotypic	ˌǰēnoˈti<y>pɪk̲	ˌǰɛnə<o>ˈtɪ<y>pɪk
geode	ˈǰēōd	ˈǰioʊd
geodic	ǰēˈōdɪk̲	ǰiˈodɪk
geophagism	ǰēˈofāˌg̲ɪsm[+gk]	ǰiˈofə<a>ˌǰɪzəm[+gk]
geophagous	ǰēˈofāg̲os[+gk]	ǰiˈofə<a>gəs[+gk]
geophagy	ǰēˈofāg̲ɪ[+gk]	ǰiˈofə<a>ǰi[+gk]
geophyte	ˈǰēoˌfi<y>t[+gk]	ˈǰiə<o>ˌfaɪ<y>t[+gk]
geophytic	ˌǰēoˈfi<y>tɪk̲[+gk]	ˌǰiə<o>ˈfɪ<y>tɪk[+gk]
gibbose	ˈgɪb[+db]ōs	ˈgɪb[+db]oʊs
gibbosity	gɪˈb[+db]ōsɪti	gɪˈb[+db]osɪti
glauconite	ˈglɔkoˌnīt	ˈglɔkə<o>ˌnaɪt
glauconitic	ˌglɔkoˈnītɪk̲	ˌglɔkə<o>ˈnɪtɪk
globose	ˈglōˌbōs	ˈgloʊˌboʊs
globosity	glōˈbōsɪti	gloʊˈbosɪti
glucose	ˈglukōs	ˈglukoʊs
glucosic	gluˈkōsɪk̲	gluˈkosɪk
glucoside	ˈglukōˌsīd	ˈglukə<o>ˌsaɪd
glucosidic	ˌglukōˈsīdɪk̲	ˌglukə<o>ˈsɪdɪk
glycine	ˈgli<y>k̲e<i>n	ˈglaɪ<y>s<c>i<i>n
glycoside	ˈgli<y>koˌsīd	ˈglaɪ<y>kə<o>ˌsaɪd
glycosidic	ˌgli<y>koˈsīdɪk̲	ˌglaɪ<y>kə<o>ˈsɪdɪk
grandiose	ˈgrændɪˌōs	ˈgrændi<i>ˌoʊs
grandiosity	ˌgrændɪˈōsɪti	ˌgrændi<i>ˈosɪti
granulite	ˈgrænʊlˌīt	ˈgrænyəˌlaɪt
granulitic	ˌgrænʊlˈītɪk̲	ˌgrænyəˈlɪtɪk
granulocyte	ˈgrænʊlōs<c>ˌi<y>t	ˈgrænyəloʊˌs<c>aɪ<y>t
granulocytic	ˌgrænʊlōˈs<c>i<y>tɪk̲	ˌgrænyəloʊˈs<c>ɪ<y>tɪk
grave	ˈgrāv	ˈgreɪv

	Deep	**Shallow**
gravity	'grāvɪti	'grævɪti
gyroscope	'ǰi<y>ro,skōp	'ǰaɪ<y>rə<o>,skoʊp
gyroscopic	,ǰi<y>ro'skōpɪk̲	,ǰaɪ<y>rə<o>'skopɪk
hagioscope	'hægɪo,skōp	'hægi<i>ə<o>,skoʊp
hagioscopic	,hægɪo'skōpɪk̲	,hægi<i>ə<o>'skopɪk
halophyte	'hælo,fi<y>t[+gk]	'hælə<o>,faɪ<y>t[+gk]
halophytic	,hælo'fi<y>tɪk̲[+gk]	,hælə<o>'fɪ<y>tɪk[+gk]
haplite	'hæplīt	'hæplaɪt
haplitic	hæp'lītɪk̲	hæp'lɪtɪk
helical	'hɛlɪk̲æl	'hɛlɪkə<a>l
helices	'hɛlɪ,k̲+ēz	'hɛlɪ,s<c>+iz
heliocentricism	,hēlɪo's<c>ɛntrɪ,k̲ɪsm	,hili<i>oʊ's<c>ɛntrɪ,s<c>ɪzəm
heliocentricity	,hēlɪos<c>ɛn'trɪk̲ɪti	,hili<i>oʊs<c>ɛn'trɪs<c>ɪti
heliocentric	,hēlɪo's<c>ɛntrɪk̲	,hili<i>oʊ's<c>ɛntrɪk
heliotrope	'hēlɪo,trōp	'hili<i>ə<o>,troʊp
heliotropic	,hēlɪo'trōpɪk̲	,hili<i>ə<o>'tropɪk
heliotype	'hēlɪo,ti<y>p	'hili<i>ə<o>,taɪ<y>p
heliotypic	,hēlɪo'ti<y>pɪk̲	,hili<i>ə<o>'tɪ<y>pɪk
hematite	'hɛmæ,tīt	'hɛmə<a>,taɪt
hematitic	,hɛmæ'tītɪk̲	,hɛmə<a>'tɪtɪk
hemitrope	'hɛmɪ,trōp	'hɛmɪ,troʊp
hemitropic	,hɛmɪ'trōpɪk̲	,hɛmɪ'tropɪk
hemophile	'hēmo,fīl[+gk]	'himə<o>,faɪl[+gk]
hemophilic	,hēmo'fīlɪk̲[+gk]	,himə<o>'fɪlɪk[+gk]
heteroclite	'hɛtɛro,klīt	'hɛtr̩ə<o>,klaɪt
heteroclitic	,hɛtɛro'klītɪk̲	,hɛtr̩ə<o>'klɪtɪk
histiocyte	'hɪstɪo,s<c>i<y>t	'hɪsti<i>ə<o>,s<c>aɪ<y>t
histiocytic	,hɪstɪo's<c>i<y>tɪk̲	,hɪsti<i>ə<o>'s<c>ɪ<y>tɪk
historicism	hɪ'storɪ,k̲ɪsm	hɪ'stɔrɪ,s<c>ɪzəm
historic	hɪ'storɪk̲	hɪ'stɔrɪk
holophyte	'holo,fi<y>t[+gk]	'holə<o>,faɪ<y>t[+gk]
holophytic	,holo'fi<y>tɪk̲[+gk]	,holə<o>'fɪ<y>tɪk[+gk]
holotype	'holo,ti<y>p	'holə<o>,taɪ<y>p
holotypic	,holo'ti<y>pɪk̲	,holə<o>'tɪ<y>pɪk
homologize	ho'molo,g̲īz	hə<o>'molə<o>,ǰaɪz
homologous	ho'molog̲os	hə<o>'molə<o>gəs
homology	ho'molog̲ɪ	hə<o>'molə<o>ǰi
homophile	'hōmo,fīl[+gk]	'hoʊmə<o>,faɪl[+gk]
homophone	'homo,fōn[+gk]	'homə<o>,foʊn[+gk]
homophonic	,homo'fōnɪk̲[+gk]	,homə<o>'fonɪk[+gk]
homophyllic	,hōmo'fɪ<y>l[+db]ɪk̲[+gk]	,hoʊmə<o>'fɪ<y>l[+db]ɪk[+gk]

	Deep	**Shallow**
homozygote	ˌhōmoˈzi<y>gōt	ˌhoʊmə<o>ˈzaɪ<y>goʊt
homozygotic	ˌhōmozi<y>ˈgōtɪk̲	ˌhoʊmə<o>zaɪ<y>ˈgotɪk
hoplite	ˈhoplīt	ˈhoplaɪt
hoplitic	hopˈlītɪk̲	hopˈlɪtɪk
horoscope	ˈhoroˌskōp	ˈhɔrə<o>ˌskoʊp
horoscopic	ˌhoroˈskōpɪk̲	ˌhɔrə<o>ˈskopɪk
hospitalization	ˌhospɪtælīˈzātyon	ˌhospɪtə<a>lɪˈzeɪšən
hospitalize	ˈhospɪtæˌlīz	ˈhospɪtə<a>ˌlaɪz
humane	humˈān	hyuˈmeɪn
humanity	humˈænɪti	hyuˈmænɪti
hydroelectricity	ˌhi<y>droɛlɛkˈtrɪk̲ɪti	ˌhaɪ<y>droʊɪ<e>lɛkˈtrɪs<c>ɪti
hydroelectric	ˌhi<y>droɛˈlɛktrɪk̲	ˌhaɪ<y>droʊɪ<e>ˈlɛktrɪk
hydrolyte	ˈhi<y>droˌli<y>t	ˈhaɪ<y>drə<o>ˌlaɪ<y>t
hydrolytic	hi<y>droˈli<y>tɪk̲	haɪ<y>drə<o>ˈlɪ<y>tɪk
hydrophyte	ˈhi<y>droˌfi<y>t[+gk]	ˈhaɪ<y>drə<o>ˌfaɪ<y>t[+gk]
hydrophytic	ˌhi<y>droˈfi<y>tɪk̲[+gk]	ˌhaɪ<y>drə<o>ˈfɪ<y>tɪk[+gk]
hydroscope	ˈhi<y>droˌskōp	ˈhaɪ<y>drə<o>ˌskoʊp
hydroscopic	ˌhi<y>droˈskōpɪk̲	ˌhaɪ<y>drə<o>ˈskopɪk
hygroscope	ˈhi<y>groˌskōp	ˈhaɪ<y>grə<o>ˌskoʊp
hygroscopic	ˌhi<y>groˈskōpɪk̲	ˌhaɪ<y>grə<o>ˈskopɪk
hypersthene	ˈhi<y>pɛrˌsθēn	ˈhaɪ<y>pr̩ˌsθin
hypersthenic	ˌhi<y>pɛrˈsθēnɪk̲	ˌhaɪ<y>pr̩ˈsθɛnɪk
hypogene	ˈhi<y>poˌǰēn	ˈhaɪ<y>pə<o>ˌǰin
hypogenic	ˌhi<y>poˈǰēnɪk̲	ˌhaɪ<y>pə<o>ˈǰɛnɪk
ichthyolite	ˈɪk<ch>θɪ<y>oˌlīt	ˈɪk<ch>θi<y>ə<o>ˌlaɪt
ichthyolitic	ˌɪk<ch>θɪ<y>oˈlītɪk̲	ˌɪk<ch>θi<y>ə<o>ˈlɪtɪk
ichthyophagous	ˌɪk<ch>θɪ<y>ˈofāg̲os[+gk]	ˌɪk<ch>θi<y>ˈofə<a>gəs[+gk]
ichthyophagy	ˌɪk<ch>θɪ<y>ˈofāg̲ɪ[+gk]	ˌɪk<ch>θi<y>ˈofə<a>ǰi[+gk]
iconomaticism	īˌkonoˈmætɪˌk̲ɪsm	aɪˌkonə<o>ˈmætɪˌs<c>ɪzəm
iconomatic	īˌkonoˈmætɪk̲	aɪˌkonə<o>ˈmætɪk
idiophone	ˈɪdɪoˌfōn[+gk]	ˈɪdi<i>ə<o>ˌfoʊn[+gk]
idiophonic	ˌɪdɪoˈfōnɪk̲[+gk]	ˌɪdi<i>ə<o>ˈfonɪk[+gk]
imide	ˈɪmīd	ˈɪmaɪd
imidic	ɪˈmīdɪk̲	ɪˈmɪdɪk
impastation	ˌɪmpāsˈtātyon	ˌɪmpæsˈteɪšən
impaste	ɪmˈpāst	ɪmˈpeɪst
impolite	ˌɪmpoˈlīt	ˌɪmpə<o>ˈlaɪt
impolitic	ɪmˈpolītɪk̲	ɪmˈpolɪtɪk
inane	ɪˈnān	ɪˈneɪn
inanity	ɪˈnānɪti	ɪˈnænɪti
inclination	ˌɪnklɪˈnātyon	ˌɪnklə<i>ˈneɪšən

	Deep	Shallow
incline	ɪnˈklīn	ɪnˈklaɪn
incommode	ˌɪnkoˈm[+db]ōd	ˌɪnkə<o>ˈm[+db]oud
incommodity	ˌɪnkoˈm[+db]ōdɪti	ˌɪnkə<o>ˈm[+db]odɪti
indigene	ˈɪndɪˌǰēn	ˈɪndɪˌǰin
indigenity	ˌɪndɪˈǰēnɪti	ˌɪndɪˈǰɛnɪti
indignation	ˌɪndīgˈnātyon	ˌɪndɪgˈneɪšən
indignity	ɪnˈdīgnɪti	ɪnˈdɪgnɪti
indign	ɪnˈdīgn	ɪnˈdaɪ<ig>n
inefficacious	ˌɪnɛf[+db]ɪˈkāk̲yos	ˌɪnɛf[+db]ə<i>ˈkeɪšəs
inefficacity	ˌɪnɛf[+db]ɪˈkāk̲ɪti	ˌɪnɛf[+db]ə<i>ˈkæs<c>ɪti
inelasticity	ˌɪnɛlæsˈtɪk̲ɪti	ˌɪnɪ<e>læsˈtɪs<c>ɪti
inelastic	ˌɪnɛˈlæstɪk̲	ˌɪnɪ<e>ˈlæstɪk
iniquity	ɪˈnɪkwɪti	ɪˈnɪkwɪti
insane	ɪnˈsān	ɪnˈseɪn
insanity	ɪnˈsānɪti	ɪnˈsænɪti
intervene	ˌɪntɛrˈvēn	ˌɪntr̩ˈvin
intervention	ˌɪntɛrˈvɛntyon	ˌɪntr̩ˈvɛnčən
inurbane	ˌɪnurˈbān	ˌɪnr̩<ur>ˈbeɪn
inurbanity	ˌɪnurˈbænɪti	ˌɪnr̩<ur>ˈbænɪti
invitation	ˌɪnvīˈtātyon	ˌɪnvɪˈteɪšən
invite	ɪnˈvīt	ɪnˈvaɪt
invocation	ˌɪnvōˈkātyon	ˌɪnvə<o>ˈkeɪšən
invoke	ɪnˈvōk	ɪnˈvouk
ionization	ˌīonīˈzātyon	ˌaɪə<o>nə<i>ˈzeɪšən
ionize	ˈīoˌnīz	ˈaɪə<o>ˌnaɪz
isocline	ˈīsoˌklīn	ˈaɪsə<o>ˌklaɪn
isoclinic	ˌīsoˈklīnɪk̲	ˌaɪsə<o>ˈklɪnɪk
isotone	ˈīsoˌtōn	ˈaɪsə<o>ˌtoun
isotonic	ˌīsoˈtōnɪk	ˌaɪsə<o>ˈtonɪk
isotope	ˈīsoˌtōp	ˈaɪsə<o>ˌtoup
isotopic	ˌīsoˈtōpɪk	ˌaɪsə<o>ˈtopɪk
kaleidoscope	k<k>æˈli<ei>doˌskōp	k<k>ə<a>ˈlaɪ<ei>də<o>ˌskoup
kaleidoscopic	k<k>æˌli<ei>doˈskōpɪk̲	k<k>ə<a>ˌlaɪ<ei>də<o>ˈskopɪk
karyotype	ˈk<k>ærɪ<y>oˌti<y>p	ˈk<k>æri<y>ə<o>ˌtaɪ<y>p
karyotypic	ˌk<k>ærɪ<y>oˈti<y>pɪk̲	ˌk<k>æri<y>ə<o>ˈtɪ<y>pɪk
kyanite	ˈk<k>i<y>æˌnīt	ˈk<k>aɪ<y>ə<a>ˌnaɪt
kyanitic	ˌk<k>i<y>æˈnītɪk̲	ˌk<k>aɪ<y>ə<a>ˈnɪtɪk
laccolite	ˈlæk[+db]oˌlīt	ˈlæk[+db]ə<o>ˌlaɪt
laccolitic	ˌlæk[+db]oˈlɪtɪk̲	ˌlæk[+db]ə<o>ˈlɪtɪk
lachrymose	ˈlæk<ch>rɪ<y>ˌmōs	ˈlæk<ch>rə<y>ˌmous
lachrymosity	ˌlæk<ch>rɪ<y>ˈmōsɪti	ˌlæk<ch>rə<y>ˈmosɪti

	Deep	**Shallow**
lactone	ˈlæktōn	ˈlæktoʊn
lactonic	lækˈtōnı$\underline{k}$	lækˈtonık
lanose	ˈlānōs	ˈleınoʊs
lanosity	lāˈnōsıti	leıˈnosıti
lanuginous	læˈnu$\underline{g}$ınos	lə<a>ˈnuǰə<i>nəs
lanugo	læˈnugo	lə<a>ˈnugoʊ
laryngoscope	læˈrı<y>ngoˌskōp	lə<a>ˈrı<y>ŋgə<o>ˌskoʊp
laryngoscopic	læˌrı<y>ngoˈskōpı$\underline{k}$	lə<a>ˌrı<y>ŋgə<o>ˈskopık
laterite	ˈlætɛˌrīt	ˈlætəˌraıt
lateritic	ˌlætɛˈrītı$\underline{k}$	ˌlætəˈrıtık
lavation	læˈvātyon	læˈveıšən
lenticellate	ˌlɛntıˈ$\underline{k}$ɛl[+db]āt	ˌlɛntıˈs<c>ɛl[+db]ı<a>tɛ<e>
lenticel	ˈlɛntıˌ$\underline{k}$ɛl	ˈlɛntıˌs<c>ɛl
lentic	ˈlɛntı$\underline{k}$	ˈlɛntık
leucite	ˈlu<eu>$\underline{k}$īt	ˈlu<eu>s<c>aıt
leucitic	lu<eu>ˈ$\underline{k}$ītı$\underline{k}$	lu<eu>ˈs<c>ıtık
leukocyte	ˈlu<eu>$\underline{k}$<k>oˌs<c>i<y>t	ˈlu<eu>k<k>ə<o>ˌs<c>aı<y>t
leukocytic	ˌlu<eu>$\underline{k}$<k>oˈs<c>i<y>tı$\underline{k}$	ˌlu<eu>k<k>ə<o>ˈs<c>ı<y>tık
lignite	ˈlıgnīt	ˈlıgnaıt
lignitic	lıgˈnītı$\underline{k}$	lıgˈnıtık
limonite	ˈlīmoˌnīt	ˈlaımə<o>ˌnaıt
limonitic	ˌlīmoˈnītı$\underline{k}$	ˌlaımə<o>ˈnıtık
lithophyte	ˈlıθoˌfi<y>t[+gk]	ˈlıθə<o>ˌfaı<y>t[+gk]
lithophytic	ˌlıθoˈfi<y>tı$\underline{k}$[+gk]	ˌlıθə<o>ˈfı<y>tık[+gk]
logicism	ˈlo$\underline{g}$ıˌ$\underline{k}$ısm	ˈloǰıˌs<c>ızəm
logic	ˈlo$\underline{g}$ı$\underline{k}$	ˈloǰık
loquacious	lōˈkwā$\underline{k}$yos	loʊˈkweıšəs
loquacity	lōˈkwæ$\underline{k}$ıti	loʊˈkwæs<c>ıti
lycanthrope	ˈli<y>kænˌθrōp	ˈlaı<y>kə<a>nˌθroʊp
lycanthropic	ˌli<y>kænˈθrōpı$\underline{k}$	ˌlaı<y>kə<a>nˈθropık
lymphocyte	ˈlı<y>mfoˌs<c>i<y>t[+gk]	ˈlı<y>mfə<o>ˌs<c>aı<y>t[+gk]
lymphocytic	ˌlı<y>mfoˈs<c>i<y>tı$\underline{k}$[+gk]	ˌlı<y>mfə<o>ˈs<c>ı<y>tık[+gk]
lyricism	ˈlı<y>rıˌ$\underline{k}$ısm	ˈlı<y>rıˌs<c>ızəm
lyricist	ˈlı<y>rı$\underline{k}$ıst	ˈlı<y>rıs<c>ıst
lyric	ˈlı<y>rı$\underline{k}$	ˈlı<y>rık
macrocyte	ˈmækroˌs<c>i<y>t	ˈmækrə<o>ˌs<c>aı<y>t
macrocytic	ˌmækroˈs<c>i<y>tı$\underline{k}$	ˌmækrə<o>ˈs<c>ı<y>tık
macrophage	ˈmækroˌfā$\underline{g}$[+gk]	ˈmækrə<o>ˌfeıǰ[+gk]
macrophagic	ˌmækroˈfā$\underline{g}$ı$\underline{k}$[+gk]	ˌmækrə<o>ˈfæǰık[+gk]
magnetite	ˈmægnɛˌtīt	ˈmægnı<e>ˌtaıt
magnetitic	ˌmægnɛˈtītı$\underline{k}$	ˌmægnı<e>ˈtıtık

	Deep	**Shallow**
magnificence	mægˈnıfık̲ɛns	mægˈnıfıs<c>əns
magnificent	mægˈnıfık̲ɛnt	mægˈnıfıs<c>ənt
magnific	mægˈnıfık̲	mægˈnıfık
malignity	mæˈlīgnıti	mə<a>ˈlıgnıti
malign	mæˈlīgn	mə<a>ˈlaı<ig>n
martensite	ˈmærtɛnˌz<s>īt	ˈmɑrtɛnˌz<s>aıt
martensitic	ˌmærtɛnˈz<s>ītık̲	ˌmɑrtɛnˈz<s>ıtık
matrices	ˈmātrıˌk̲+ēz	ˈmeıtrıˌs<c>+iz
matrix	ˈmātrık̲s	ˈmeıtrıks
medicine	ˈmɛdık̲ınϵ<e>	ˈmɛdıs<c>ınϵ<e>
medic	ˈmɛdık̲	ˈmɛdık
megaphone	ˈmɛgæˌfōn[+gk]	ˈmɛgə<a>ˌfoun[+gk]
megaphonic	ˌmɛgæˈfōnık̲[+gk]	ˌmɛgə<a>ˈfonık[+gk]
mendacious	mɛnˈdāk̲yos	mɛnˈdeıšəs
mendacity	mɛnˈdāk̲ıti	mɛnˈdæs<c>ıti
mesophyte	ˈmɛz<s>oˌfi<y>t[+gk]	ˈmɛz<s>ə<o>ˌfaı<y>t[+gk]
mesophytic	ˌmɛz<s>oˈfi<y>tık̲[+gk]	ˌmɛz<s>ə<o>ˈfı<y>tık[+gk]
mesothoracic	ˌmɛz<s>oθoˈræk̲ık̲	ˌmɛz<s>ə<o>θɔˈræs<c>ık
mesothorax	ˌmɛz<s>oˈθoræk̲s	ˌmɛz<s>ə<o>ˈθɔræks
metaphysicist	ˌmɛtæˈfı<y>z<s>ık̲ıst[+gk]	ˌmɛtə<a>ˈfı<y>z<s>ıs<c>ıst[+gk]
metaphysic	ˌmɛtæˈfı<y>z<s>ık̲[+gk]	ˌmɛtə<a>ˈfı<y>z<s>ık[+gk]
metathoracic	ˌmɛtæθoˈræk̲ık	ˌmɛtə<a>θɔˈræs<c>ık
metathorax	ˌmɛtæˈθoræk̲s	ˌmɛtə<a>ˈθɔræks
meteorite	ˈmētēoˌrīt	ˈmitiə<o>ˌraıt
meteoritic	ˌmētēoˈrītık̲	ˌmitiə<o>ˈrıtık
metronome	ˈmɛtroˌnōm	ˈmɛtrə<o>ˌnoum
metronomic	ˌmɛtroˈnomık̲	ˌmɛtrə<o>ˈnomık
microcyte	ˈmīkroˌs<c>i<y>t	ˈmaıkrə<o>ˌs<c>aı<y>t
microcytic	ˌmīkroˈs<c>i<y>tık̲	ˌmaıkrə<o>ˈs<c>ı<y>tık
microparasite	ˌmīkrōˈpæræˌsīt	ˌmaıkrouˈpærə<a>ˌsaıt
microparasitic	ˌmīkrōˌpæræˈsītık̲	ˌmaıkrouˌpærə<a>ˈsıtık
microphone	ˈmīkroˌfōn[+gk]	ˈmaıkrə<o>ˌfoun[+gk]
microphonic	ˌmīkroˈfōnık̲[+gk]	ˌmaıkrə<o>ˈfonık[+gk]
microphyte	ˈmīkroˌfi<y>t[+gk]	ˈmaıkrə<o>ˌfaı<y>t[+gk]
microphytic	ˌmīkroˈfi<y>tık̲[+gk]	ˌmaıkrə<o>ˈfı<y>tık[+gk]
microscope	ˈmīkroˌskōp	ˈmaıkrə<o>ˌskoup
microscopic	ˌmīkroˈskōpık̲	ˌmaıkrə<o>ˈskopık
microtome	ˈmīkroˌtōm	ˈmaıkrə<o>ˌtoum
microtomic	ˌmīkroˈtōmık̲	ˌmaıkrə<o>ˈtomık
mime	ˈmīm	ˈmaım
mimic	ˈmīmık̲	ˈmımık

	Deep	**Shallow**
misanthrope	'mɪsæn,θrōp	'mɪsə$_{<a>}$n,θroʊp
misanthropic	,mɪsæn'θrōpɪk̲	,mɪsə$_{<a>}$n'θropɪk
mispronounce	,mɪspro'nūns	,mɪsprə$_{<o>}$'naʊns
mispronunciation	,mɪspro,nū$_{<u>}$ns$_{<c>}$ɪ'ātyon	,mɪsprə$_{<o>}$,nʌns$_{<c>}$i$_{<i>}$'eɪšən
mithridate	'mɪθrɪ,dāt	'mɪθrə$_{<i>}$,deɪt
mithridatic	,mɪθrɪ'dātɪk̲	,mɪθrɪ'dætɪk
monasticism	mo'næstɪ,k̲ɪsm	mə$_{<o>}$'næstɪ,s$_{<c>}$ɪzəm
monastic	mo'næstɪk̲	mə$_{<o>}$'næstɪk
monochromate	,mono'k$_{<ch>}$rōmāt	,monə$_{<o>}$'k$_{<ch>}$roʊmeɪt
monochromatic	,monok$_{<ch>}$rō'mātɪk̲	,monə$_{<o>}$k$_{<ch>}$roʊ'mætɪk
monocline	'mono,klīn	'monə$_{<o>}$,klaɪn
monoclinic	,mono'klīnɪk̲	,monə$_{<o>}$'klɪnɪk
monocyte	'mono,s$_{<c>}$i$_{<y>}$t	'monə$_{<o>}$,s$_{<c>}$aɪ$_{<y>}$t
monocytic	,mono's$_{<c>}$i$_{<y>}$tɪk̲	,monə$_{<o>}$'s$_{<c>}$ɪ$_{<y>}$tɪk
monotype	'mono,ti$_{<y>}$p	'monə$_{<o>}$,taɪ$_{<y>}$p
monotypic	,mono'ti$_{<y>}$pɪk̲	,monə$_{<o>}$'tɪ$_{<y>}$pɪk
monzonite	'monzo,nīt	'monzə$_{<o>}$,naɪt
monzonitic	,monzo'nītɪk̲	,monzə$_{<o>}$'nɪtɪk
mordacious	mor'dāk̲yos	mɔr'deɪšəs
mordacity	mor'dāk̲ɪti	mɔr'dæs$_{<c>}$ɪti
mucose	'mukōs	'myukoʊs
mucosity	muk'ōsɪti	myu'kosɪti
myope	'mi$_{<y>}$ōp	'maɪ$_{<y>}$oʊp
myopic	mi$_{<y>}$'ōpɪk̲	maɪ$_{<y>}$'opɪk
mysticism	'mɪ$_{<y>}$stɪ,k̲ɪsm	'mɪ$_{<y>}$stɪ,s$_{<c>}$ɪzəm
mystic	'mɪ$_{<y>}$stɪk̲	'mɪ$_{<y>}$stɪk
neoclassicism	,nēō'klæs$_{[+db]}$ɪ,k̲ɪsm	,nioʊ'klæs$_{[+db]}$ɪ,s$_{<c>}$ɪzəm
neoclassic	,nēō'klæs$_{[+db]}$ɪk̲	,nioʊ'klæs$_{[+db]}$ɪk
neophyte	'nēo,fi$_{<y>}$t$_{[+gk]}$	'niə$_{<o>}$,faɪ$_{<y>}$t$_{[+gk]}$
neophytic	,nēo'fi$_{<y>}$tɪk̲$_{[+gk]}$	,niə$_{<o>}$'fɪ$_{<y>}$tɪk$_{[+gk]}$
neuroticism	nu$_{<eu>}$'rotɪ,k̲ɪsm	nu$_{<eu>}$'rotɪ,s$_{<c>}$ɪzəm
neurotic	nu$_{<eu>}$'rotɪk̲	nu$_{<eu>}$'rotɪk
noctiluca	,noktɪ'luk̲æ	,noktə$_{<i>}$'lukə
noctilucent	,noktɪ'luk̲ɛnt	,noktə$_{<i>}$'lus$_{<c>}$ənt
nodose	'nō,dōs	'noʊ,doʊs
nodosity	nō'dōsɪti	noʊ'dosɪti
nummulite	'nʌm$_{[+db]}$ul,īt	'nʌm$_{[+db]}$yə,laɪt
nummulitic	,nʌm$_{[+db]}$u'lītɪk̲	,nʌm$_{[+db]}$yə'lɪtɪk
obligee	,oblɪ'g̲ē	,oblə$_{<i>}$'ǰi
obligor	,oblɪ'g̲or	,oblə$_{<i>}$'gɔr
oblique	o'ble$_{<i>}$k$_{<qu>}$	ə$_{<o>}$'bli$_{<i>}$k$_{<qu>}$

	Deep	**Shallow**
obliquity	o'ble<i>kwɪti	ə<o>'blɪkwɪti
obscene	ob'sɛ<c>ēn	ə<o>b'sɛ<c>in
obscenity	ob'sɛ<c>ēnɪti	ə<o>b'sɛ<c>ɛnɪti
omnificent	om'nɪfɪk̲ɛnt	om'nɪfɪs<c>ənt
omnific	om'nɪfɪk̲	om'nɪfɪk
omophagous	ō'mofāg̲os[+gk]	oʊ'mofə<a>gəs[+gk]
omophagy	ō'mofæg̲ɪ[+gk]	oʊ'mofə<a>ǰi[+gk]
oolite	'ōo,līt	'oʊə<o>,laɪt
oolitic	,ōo'lītɪk̲	,oʊə<o>'lɪtɪk
oophyte	'ōo,fi<y>t[+gk]	'oʊə<o>,faɪ<y>t[+gk]
oophytic	,ōo'fi<y>tɪk̲[+gk]	,oʊə<o>'fɪ<y>tɪk[+gk]
opacity	ō'pāk̲ɪti	oʊ'pæs<c>ɪti
opaque	ō'pāk̲<qu>	oʊ'peɪk<qu>
operate	'opɛ,rāt	'opə,reɪt
operatic	,opɛ'rātɪk̲	,opə'rætɪk
ophthalmoscope	of'θælmo,skōp[+gk]	of'θælmə<o>,skoʊp[+gk]
ophthalmoscopic	of,θælmo'skōpɪk̲[+gk]	of,θælmə<o>'skopɪk[+gk]
organicism	or'gænɪ,k̲ɪsm	ɔr'gænɪ,s<c>ɪzəm
organic	or'gænɪk̲	ɔr'gænɪk
organization	,orgænɪ'zātyon	,ɔrgə<a>nɪ'zeɪšən
organize	'orgæ,nīz	'ɔrgə<a>,naɪz
orthoscope	'orθo,skōp	'ɔrθə<o>,skoʊp
orthoscopic	,orθo'skōpɪk̲	,ɔrθə<o>'skopɪk
osteophyte	'ostēo,fi<y>t[+gk]	'ostiə<o>,faɪ<y>t[+gk]
osteophytic	,ostēo'fi<y>tɪk̲[+gk]	,ostiə<o>'fɪ<y>tɪk[+gk]
otiose	'ōtɪ,ōs	'oʊš<t>i<i>,oʊs
otiosity	,ōtɪ'ōsɪti	,oʊš<t>i<i>'osɪti
otoscope	'ōto,skōp	'oʊtə<o>,skoʊp
otoscopic	,ōto'skōpɪk̲	,oʊtə<o>'skopɪk
oxidase	'oksī,dās	'oksɪ,deɪs
oxidasic	,oksɪ'dāsɪk̲	,oksɪ'dæsɪk
oxidation	,oksī'dātyon	,oksɪ'deɪšən
oxide	'oksīd	'oksaɪd
ozone	'ōzōn	'oʊzoʊn
ozonic	ō'zōnɪk̲	oʊ'zonɪk
palindrome	'pælɪn,drōm	'pælɪn,droʊm
palindromic	,pælɪn'drōmɪk̲	,pælɪn'dromɪk
pantomime	'pænto,mīm	'pæntə<o>,maɪm
pantomimic	,pænto'mīmɪk̲	,pæntə<o>'mɪmɪk
parasite	'pæræ,sīt	'pærə<a>,saɪt
parasiticide	,pæræ'sītɪ,s<c>īd	,pærə<a>'sɪtɪ,s<c>aɪd

	Deep	Shallow
parasitic	ˌpæræˈsītɪk̲	ˌpærə$_{<a>}$ˈsɪtɪk
paroxytone	pæˈroksɪ$_{<y>}$ˌtōn	pə$_{<a>}$ˈroksɪ$_{<y>}$ˌtoun
paroxytonic	ˌpæroksɪ$_{<y>}$ˈtōnɪk̲	ˌpæroksɪ$_{<y>}$ˈtonɪk
pasteurization	ˌpæsty$_{<e>}$urˈɪzātyon	ˌpæsč$_{<t>}$ə$_{<eu>}$rɪˈzeɪšən
pasteurize	ˈpæsty$_{<e>}$ˌurīz	ˈpæsč$_{<t>}$ə$_{<eu>}$ˌraɪz
pathogene	ˈpæθoˌǰēn	ˈpæθə$_{<o>}$ˌǰin
pathogenic	ˌpæθoˈǰēnɪk̲	ˌpæθə$_{<o>}$ˈǰɛnɪk
pearlite	ˈpɛ$_{<ea>}$rlīt	ˈpr̩$_{<ear>}$laɪt
pearlitic	pɛ$_{<ea>}$rˈlītɪk̲	pr̩$_{<ear>}$ˈlɪtɪk
pedicel	ˈpɛdɪk̲ɛl	ˈpɛdɪs$_{<c>}$ə$_{<e>}$l
pedicle	ˈpɛdɪk̲l	ˈpɛdɪkəl
pegmatite	ˈpɛgmæˌtīt	ˈpɛgmə$_{<a>}$ˌtaɪt
pegmatitic	ˌpɛgmæˈtītɪk̲	ˌpɛgmə$_{<a>}$ˈtɪtɪk
peptone	ˈpɛptōn	ˈpɛptoun
peptonic	pɛpˈtōnɪk̲	pɛpˈtonɪk
peridotite	ˌpɛrɪˈdōtīt	ˌpɛrɪˈdoutaɪt
peridotitic	ˌpɛrɪdōˈtītɪk̲	ˌpɛrɪdouˈtɪtɪk
periscope	ˈpɛrɪˌskōp	ˈpɛrɪˌskoup
periscopic	ˌpɛrɪˈskōpɪk̲	ˌpɛrɪˈskopɪk
perlite	ˈpɛrlīt	ˈpr̩laɪt
perlitic	pɛrˈlītɪk̲	pr̩ˈlɪtɪk
perspicacious	ˌpɛrspɪˈkāk̲yos	ˌpr̩spə$_{<i>}$ˈkeɪšəs
perspicacity	ˌpɛrspɪˈkāk̲ɪti	ˌpr̩spə$_{<i>}$ˈkæs$_{<c>}$ɪti
pertinacious	ˌpɛrtɪˈnāk̲yos	ˌpr̩tə$_{<i>}$ˈneɪšəs
pertinacity	ˌpɛrtɪˈnāk̲ɪti	ˌpr̩tə$_{<i>}$ˈnæs$_{<c>}$ɪti
phagocyte	ˈfægoˌs$_{<c>}$i$_{<y>}$t$_{[+gk]}$	ˈfægə$_{<o>}$ˌs$_{<c>}$aɪ$_{<y>}$t$_{[+gk]}$
phagocytic	ˌfægoˈs$_{<c>}$i$_{<y>}$tɪk̲$_{[+gk]}$	ˌfægə$_{<o>}$ˈs$_{<c>}$ɪ$_{<y>}$tɪk$_{[+gk]}$
phallicism	ˈfæl$_{[+db]}$ɪˌk̲ɪsm$_{[+gk]}$	ˈfæl$_{[+db]}$ɪˌs$_{<c>}$ɪzəm$_{[+gk]}$
phallic	ˈfæl$_{[+db]}$ɪk̲$_{[+gk]}$	ˈfæl$_{[+db]}$ɪk$_{[+gk]}$
pharmacal	ˈfærmæk̲æl$_{[+gk]}$	ˈfɑrmə$_{<a>}$kə$_{<a>}$l$_{[+gk]}$
pharmacist	ˈfærmæk̲ɪst$_{[+gk]}$	ˈfɑrmə$_{<a>}$s$_{<c>}$ɪst$_{[+gk]}$
pharmacy	ˈfærmæk̲ɪ$_{[+gk]}$	ˈfɑrmə$_{<a>}$s$_{<c>}$i$_{[+gk]}$
pharyngoscope	fæˈrɪ$_{<y>}$ngoˌskōp$_{[+gk]}$	fə$_{<a>}$ˈrɪ$_{<y>}$ŋgə$_{<o>}$ˌskoup$_{[+gk]}$
pharyngoscopic	fæˌrɪ$_{<y>}$ngoˈskōpɪk̲$_{[+gk]}$	fə$_{<a>}$ˌrɪ$_{<y>}$ŋgə$_{<o>}$ˈskopɪk$_{[+gk]}$
phenotype	ˈfēnoˌti$_{<y>}$p$_{[+gk]}$	ˈfinə$_{<o>}$ˌtaɪ$_{<y>}$p$_{[+gk]}$
phenotypic	ˌfēnoˈti$_{<y>}$pɪk̲$_{[+gk]}$	ˌfinə$_{<o>}$ˈtɪ$_{<y>}$pɪk$_{[+gk]}$
philhellene	fɪlˈhɛl$_{[+db]}$ēn$_{[+gk]}$	fɪlˈhɛl$_{[+db]}$in$_{[+gk]}$
philhellenic	ˌfɪlhɛˈl$_{[+db]}$ēnɪk̲$_{[+gk]}$	ˌfɪlhɛˈl$_{[+db]}$ɛnɪk$_{[+gk]}$
phonolite	ˈfōnoˌlīt$_{[+gk]}$	ˈfounə$_{<o>}$ˌlaɪt$_{[+gk]}$
phonolitic	ˌfōnoˈlītɪk̲$_{[+gk]}$	ˌfounə$_{<o>}$ˈlɪtɪk$_{[+gk]}$
phonotype	ˈfōnoˌti$_{<y>}$p$_{[+gk]}$	ˈfounə$_{<o>}$ˌtaɪ$_{<y>}$p$_{[+gk]}$

	Deep	**Shallow**
phonotypic	ˌfōnoˈti$_{<y>}$pɪk̲$_{[+gk]}$	ˌfoʊnə$_{<o>}$ˈtɪ$_{<y>}$pɪk$_{[+gk]}$
phosphate	ˈfosfāt$_{[+gk]}$	ˈfosfeɪt$_{[+gk]}$
phosphatic	fosˈfātɪk̲$_{[+gk]}$	fosˈfætɪk$_{[+gk]}$
phosphorite	ˈfosfoˌrīt$_{[+gk]}$	ˈfosfə$_{<o>}$ˌraɪt$_{[+gk]}$
phosphoritic	ˌfosfoˈrītɪk̲$_{[+gk]}$	ˌfosfə$_{<o>}$ˈrɪtɪk$_{[+gk]}$
photoelectricity	ˌfōtōɛlɛkˈtrɪk̲ɪtɪ$_{[+gk]}$	ˌfoʊtoʊɪ$_{<e>}$lɛkˈtrɪs$_{<c>}$ɪti$_{[+gk]}$
photoelectric	ˌfōtōɛˈlɛktrɪk̲$_{[+gk]}$	ˌfoʊtoʊɪ$_{<e>}$ˈlɛktrɪk$_{[+gk]}$
photogene	ˈfōtoˌǰēn$_{[+gk]}$	ˈfoʊtə$_{<o>}$ˌǰin$_{[+gk]}$
photogenic	ˌfōtoˈǰēnɪk̲$_{[+gk]}$	ˌfoʊtə$_{<o>}$ˈǰɛnɪk$_{[+gk]}$
phototype	ˈfōtoˌti$_{<y>}$p$_{[+gk]}$	ˈfoʊtə$_{<o>}$ˌtaɪ$_{<y>}$p$_{[+gk]}$
phototypic	ˌfōtoˈti$_{<y>}$pɪk̲$_{[+gk]}$	ˌfoʊtə$_{<o>}$ˈtɪ$_{<y>}$pɪk$_{[+gk]}$
phyllite	ˈfɪ$_{<y>}$l$_{[+db]}$īt$_{[+gk]}$	ˈfɪ$_{<y>}$l$_{[+db]}$aɪt$_{[+gk]}$
phyllitic	fɪ$_{<y>}$ˈl$_{[+db]}$ītɪk̲$_{[+gk]}$	fɪ$_{<y>}$ˈl$_{[+db]}$ɪtɪk$_{[+gk]}$
phyllome	ˈfɪ$_{<y>}$l$_{[+db]}$ōm$_{[+gk]}$	ˈfɪ$_{<y>}$l$_{[+db]}$oʊm$_{[+gk]}$
phyllomic	fɪ$_{<y>}$ˈl$_{[+db]}$ōmɪk̲$_{[+gk]}$	fɪ$_{<y>}$ˈl$_{[+db]}$omɪk$_{[+gk]}$
phylogenesis	ˌfi$_{<y>}$loˈǰēnɛsɪs$_{[+gk]}$	ˌfaɪ$_{<y>}$lə$_{<o>}$ˈǰɛnɪ$_{<e>}$sɪs$_{[+gk]}$
phylogenic	ˌfi$_{<y>}$loˈǰēnɪk̲$_{[+gk]}$	ˌfaɪ$_{<y>}$lə$_{<o>}$ˈǰɛnɪk$_{[+gk]}$
physical	ˈfɪ$_{<y>}$z$_{<s>}$ɪk̲æl$_{[+gk]}$	ˈfɪ$_{<y>}$z$_{<s>}$ɪkə$_{<a>}$l$_{[+gk]}$
physicist	ˈfɪ$_{<y>}$z$_{<s>}$ɪk̲ɪst$_{[+gk]}$	ˈfɪ$_{<y>}$z$_{<s>}$ɪs$_{<c>}$ɪst$_{[+gk]}$
physics	ˈfɪ$_{<y>}$z$_{<s>}$ɪk̲+s$_{[+gk]}$	ˈfɪ$_{<y>}$z$_{<s>}$ɪk+s$_{[+gk]}$
physic	ˈfɪ$_{<y>}$z$_{<s>}$ɪk̲$_{[+gk]}$	ˈfɪ$_{<y>}$z$_{<s>}$ɪk$_{[+gk]}$
phytophagous	fi$_{<y>}$ˈtofāg̲os$_{[+gk]}$	faɪ$_{<y>}$ˈtofə$_{<a>}$gəs$_{[+gk]}$
phytophagy	fi$_{<y>}$ˈtofāǰɪ$_{[+gk]}$	faɪ$_{<y>}$ˈtofə$_{<a>}$ǰi$_{[+gk]}$
pilose	ˈpīlōs	ˈpaɪloʊs
pilosity	pīˈlōsɪti	paɪˈlosɪti
pisolite	ˈpīsoˌlīt	ˈpaɪsə$_{<o>}$ˌlaɪt
pisolitic	ˌpīsoˈlītɪk̲	ˌpaɪsə$_{<o>}$ˈlɪtɪk
plasmagene	ˈplæz$_{<s>}$mæˌǰēn	ˈplæz$_{<s>}$mə$_{<a>}$ˌǰin
plasmagenic	ˌplæz$_{<s>}$mæˈǰēnɪk̲	ˌplæz$_{<s>}$mə$_{<a>}$ˈǰɛnɪk
plasticity	plæˈstɪk̲ɪti	plæˈstɪs$_{<c>}$ɪti
plasticize	ˈplæstɪˌk̲īz	ˈplæstɪˌs$_{<c>}$aɪz
plastic	ˈplæstɪk̲	ˈplæstɪk
pleasance	ˈple$_{<ea>}$z$_{<s>}$æns	ˈplɛ$_{<ea>}$z$_{<s>}$ə$_{<a>}$ns
please	ˈple$_{<ea>}$z$_{<s>}$	ˈpli$_{<ea>}$z$_{<s>}$
plumose	ˈplumōs	ˈplumoʊs
plumosity	pluˈmōsɪti	pluˈmosɪti
podsolization	ˌpodsolīˈzātyon	ˌpodsə$_{<o>}$lɪˈzeɪšən
podsolize	ˈpodsoˌlīz	ˈpodsə$_{<o>}$ˌlaɪz
podzolization	ˌpodzolīˈzātyon	ˌpodzə$_{<o>}$lɪˈzeɪšən
podzolize	ˈpodzoˌlīz	ˈpodzə$_{<o>}$ˌlaɪz
poeticize	pōˈɛtɪˌk̲īz	poʊˈɛtɪˌs$_{<c>}$aɪz

	Deep	Shallow
poetic	pō'ɛtɪk	poʊ'ɛtɪk
polarization	ˌpōlærɪ'zātyon	ˌpoʊlə<a>rɪ'zeɪšən
polarize	'pōlæˌrīz	'poʊlə<a>ˌraɪz
polemicist	po'lɛmɪk̲ɪst	pə<o>'lɛmɪs<c>ɪst
polemic	po'lɛmɪk̲	pə<o>'lɛmɪk
polite	po'līt	pə<o>'laɪt
political	po'lītɪk̲æl	pə<o>'lɪtɪkə<a>l
politicize	po'lītɪˌk̲īz	pə<o>'lɪtɪˌs<c>aɪz
politic	'polītɪk̲	'polɪtɪk
polyphone	'polɪ<y>ˌfōn[+gk]	'poli<y>ˌfoʊn[+gk]
polyphonic	ˌpolɪ<y>'fōnɪk̲[+gk]	ˌpoli<y>'fonɪk[+gk]
porcine	'pork̲īn	'pɔrs<c>aɪn
pork	'pork̲<k>	'pɔrk<k>
posterity	po'stɛrɪti	po'stɛrɪti
poster	'pōstr	'poʊstr̩
precocious	prɛ'kōk̲yos	prɪ<e>'koʊšəs
precocity	prɛ'kōk̲ɪti	prɪ'kos<c>ɪti
predaceous	prɛ'dāk̲y<e>os	prɪ'deɪš<ce>əs
predacious	prɛ'dāk̲yos	prɪ'deɪšəs
predacity	prɛ'dæk̲ɪti	prɪ'dæs<c>ɪti
prevocational	ˌprēvō'kātyonæl	ˌprivoʊ'keɪšənə<a>l
proctoscope	'proktoˌskōp	'proktə<o>ˌskoʊp
proctoscopic	ˌprokto'skōpɪk̲	ˌproktə<o>'skopɪk
prodigal	'prodɪg̲æl	'prodə<i>gə<a>l
prodigy	'prodɪg̲ɪ	'prodə<i>ǰi
prodrome	'prōdrōm	'proʊdroʊm
prodromic	prō'drōmɪk̲	proʊ'dromɪk
profane	pro'fān	prə<o>'feɪn
profanity	pro'fānɪti	prə<o>'fænɪti
profound	pro'fūnd	prə<o>'faʊnd
profundity	pro'fū<u>ndɪti	prə<o>'fʌndɪti
pronounce	pro'nūns	prə<o>'naʊns
pronunciation	proˌnū<u>ns<c>ɪ'ātyon	prə<o>ˌnʌns<c>i<i>'eɪšən
prosaicism	prō'z<s>āɪˌk̲ɪsm	proʊ'z<s>eɪɪˌs<c>ɪzəm
prosaic	prō'z<s>āɪk̲	proʊ'z<s>eɪɪk
prototype	'prōtoˌti<y>p	'proʊtə<o>ˌtaɪ<y>p
prototypic	ˌprōto'ti<y>pɪk̲	ˌproʊtə<o>'tɪ<y>pɪk
providence	'provɪdɛns	'provɪdəns
provide	pro'vīd	prə<o>'vaɪd
provocation	ˌprovō'kātyon	ˌprovə<o>'keɪšən
provoke	pro'vōk	prə<o>'voʊk

	Deep	**Shallow**
psammite	'ϵ<p>sæm[+db]īt	'ϵ<p>sæm[+db]aɪt
psammitic	ϵ<p>sæ'm[+db]ītɪk̲	ϵ<p>sæ'm[+db]ɪtɪk
psephite	'ϵ<p>sēfīt[+gk]	'ϵ<p>sifaɪt[+gk]
psephitic	ϵ<p>sē'fītɪk̲[+gk]	ϵ<p>si'fɪtɪk[+gk]
pteridophyte	ϵ<p>tɛ'rɪdo,fi<y>t[+gk]	ϵ<p>tə'rɪdə<o>,faɪ<y>t[+gk]
pteridophytic	ϵ<p>tɛ,rɪdo'fi<y>tɪk̲[+gk]	ϵ<p>tə,rɪdə<o>'fɪ<y>tɪk[+gk]
publicist	'pʌblɪk̲ɪst	'pʌblɪs<c>ɪst
publicity	pʌ'blɪk̲ɪti	pʌ'blɪs<c>ɪti
publicize	'pʌblɪ,k̲īz	'pʌblɪ,s<c>aɪz
public	'pʌblɪk̲	'pʌblɪk
pugnacious	pʌg'nāk̲yos	pʌg'neɪšəs
pugnacity	pʌg'nāk̲ɪti	pʌg'næs<c>ɪti
pyrite	'pi<y>rīt	'paɪ<y>raɪt
pyritic	pi<y>'rītɪk̲	paɪ<y>'rɪtɪk
pyroelectricity	,pi<y>rōɛlɛk'trɪk̲ɪti	,paɪ<y>roʊɪ<e>lɛk'trɪs<c>ɪti
pyroelectric	,pi<y>rōɛ'lɛktrɪk̲	,paɪ<y>roʊɪ<e>'lɛktrɪk
pyrrole	'pɪ<y>r[+db]ōl	'pɪ<y>r[+db]oʊl
pyrrolic	pɪ<y>'r[+db]ōlɪk̲	pɪ<y>'r[+db]olɪk
radioisotope	,rādɪō'īsotōp	,reɪdi<i>oʊ'aɪsə<o>toʊp
radioisotopic	,rādɪō,īso'tōpɪk̲	,reɪdi<i>oʊ,aɪsə<o>'topɪk
radiopacity	,rādɪō'pāk̲ɪti	,reɪdi<i>oʊ'pæs<c>ɪti
radiopaque	,rādɪō'pāk̲<qu>	,reɪdi<i>oʊ'peɪk<qu>
radiophone	'rādɪō[−gk],fōn[+gk]	'reɪdi<i>oʊ[−gk],foʊn[+gk]
radiophonic	,rādɪō[−gk]'fōnɪk̲[+gk]	,reɪdi<i>oʊ[−gk]'fonɪk[+gk]
radioscope	'rādɪō,skōp	'reɪdi<i>oʊ,skoʊp
radioscopic	,rādɪō'skōpɪk̲	,reɪdi<i>oʊ'skopɪk
radiotelephone	,rādɪō[−gk]'tɛlɛ,fōn[+gk]	,reɪdi<i>oʊ[−gk]'tɛlə,foʊn[+gk]
radiotelephonic	,rādɪō[−gk],tɛlɛ'fōnɪk̲[+gk]	,reɪdi<i>oʊ[−gk],tɛlə'fonɪk[+gk]
rapacious	ræ'pāk̲yos	rə<a>'peɪšəs
rapacity	ræ'pæk̲ɪti	rə<a>'pæs<c>ɪti
realization	,rēælɪ'zātyon	,riə<a>lɪ'zeɪšən
realize	'rēæ,līz	'riə<a>,laɪz
recitation	,rɛs<c>ī'tātyon	,rɛs<c>ɪ'teɪšən
recite	rɛ's<c>īt	rɪ's<c>aɪt
reclination	,rɛklī'nātyon	,rɛklə<i>'neɪšən
recline	rɛ'klīn	rɪ'klaɪn
regale	rɛ'gāl	rɪ'geɪl
regality	rɛ'gālɪti	rɪ'gælɪti
renounce	rɛ'nūns	rɪ'naʊns
renunciation	rɛ,nū<u>ns<c>ɪ'ātyon	rɪ,nʌns<c>i<i>'eɪšən
reorganization	,rēorgænɪ'zātyon	,riɔrgə<a>nɪ'zeɪšən

	Deep	**Shallow**
reorganize	rē'orgæ,nīz	ri'ɔrgə$_{<a>}$,naɪz
residence	'rɛz$_{<s>}$īdɛns	'rɛz$_{<s>}$ɪdəns
reside	rɛ'z$_{<s>}$īd	rɪ'z$_{<s>}$aɪd
resignation	,rɛsīg'nātyon	,rɛz$_{<s>}$ɪg'neɪšən
resign	rɛ'sīgn	rɪ'z$_{<s>}$aɪ$_{<ig>}$n
reveal	rɛ've$_{<ea>}$l	rɪ'vi$_{<ea>}$l
revelation	,rɛvē'lātyon	,rɛvə'leɪšən
revile	rɛ'vīl	rɪ'vaɪl
revocation	,rɛvō'kātyon	,rɛvə$_{<o>}$'keɪšən
revoke	rɛ'vōk	rɪ'voʊk
rhetoric	'rētorɪk̲$_{[+gk]}$	'rɛtə$_{<o>}$rɪk$_{[+gk]}$
rhetor	'rētor$_{[+gk]}$	'ritə$_{<o>}$r$_{[+gk]}$
rhyolite	'ri$_{<y>}$o,līt$_{[+gk]}$	'raɪ$_{<y>}$ə$_{<o>}$,laɪt$_{[+gk]}$
rhyolitic	,ri$_{<y>}$o'lītɪk̲$_{[+gk]}$	,raɪ$_{<y>}$ə$_{<o>}$'lɪtɪk$_{[+gk]}$
rhythmicity	rɪ$_{<y>}$ð'mɪk̲ɪtɪ$_{[+gk]}$	rɪ$_{<y>}$ð'mɪs$_{<c>}$ɪti$_{[+gk]}$
rhythmics	'rɪ$_{<y>}$ðmɪk̲+s$_{[+gk]}$	'rɪ$_{<y>}$ðmɪk+s$_{[+gk]}$
rimose	'rīmōs	'raɪmoʊs
rimosity	rī'mōsɪti	raɪ'mosɪti
romanticism	rō'mæntɪ,k̲ɪsm	roʊ'mæntɪ,s$_{<c>}$ɪzəm
romanticist	rō'mæntɪk̲ɪst	roʊ'mæntɪs$_{<c>}$ɪst
romanticize	rō'mæntɪ,k̲īz	roʊ'mæntɪ,s$_{<c>}$aɪz
romantic	rō'mæntɪk̲	roʊ'mæntɪk
rugose	'rugōs	'rugoʊs
rugosity	ru'gōsɪti	ru'gosɪti
rusticity	rʌ'stɪk̲ɪti	rʌ'stɪs$_{<c>}$ɪti
rustic	'rʌstɪk̲	'rʌstɪk
sabulose	'sæbʊl,ōs	'sæbyə,loʊs
sabulosity	,sæbʊ'lōsɪti	,sæbyə'losɪti
sagacious	sæ'gāk̲yos	sə$_{<a>}$'geɪšəs
sagacity	sæ'gāk̲ɪti	sə$_{<a>}$'gæs$_{<c>}$ɪti
salacious	sæ'lāk̲yos	sə$_{<a>}$'leɪšəs
salacity	sæ'lāk̲ɪti	sə$_{<a>}$'læs$_{<c>}$ɪti
salicine	'sælɪk̲ɪnϵ$_{<e>}$	'sælɪs$_{<c>}$ɪnϵ$_{<e>}$
salicin	'sælɪk̲ɪn	'sælɪs$_{<c>}$ɪn
salic	'sælɪk̲	'sælɪk
sane	'sān	'seɪn
sanity	'sānɪti	'sænɪti
saprolite	'sæpro,līt	'sæprə$_{<o>}$,laɪt
saprolitic	,sæpro'lītɪk̲	,sæprə$_{<o>}$'lɪtɪk
saprophyte	'sæpro,fi$_{<y>}$t$_{[+gk]}$	'sæprə$_{<o>}$,faɪ$_{<y>}$t$_{[+gk]}$
saprophytic	,sæpro'fi$_{<y>}$tɪk̲$_{[+gk]}$	,sæprə$_{<o>}$'fɪ$_{<y>}$tɪk$_{[+gk]}$

	Deep	**Shallow**
satellite	ˈsætɛˌl[+db]īt	ˈsætəˌl[+db]aɪt
satellitic	ˌsætɛˈl[+db]ītɪk̲	ˌsætəˈl[+db]ɪtɪk
saturnine	ˈsæturˌnīn	ˈsætə<u>rˌnaɪn
saturninity	ˈsæturˌnīnɪti	ˈsætə<u>rˌnɪnɪti
saxophone	ˈsæksoˌfōn[+gk]	ˈsæksə<o>ˌfoʊn[+gk]
saxophonic	ˌsæksoˈfōnɪk̲[+gk]	ˌsæksə<o>ˈfonɪk[+gk]
schizomycete	ˌsk<ch>ɪzōmi<y>ˈk̲ēt	ˌsk<ch>ɪzoʊmaɪ<y>ˈs<c>it
schizomycetic	ˌsk<ch>ɪzōmi<y>ˈk̲ētɪk̲	ˌsk<ch>ɪzoʊmaɪ<y>ˈs<c>ɛtɪk
schizophyte	ˈsk<ch>ɪzoˌfi<y>t[+gk]	ˈsk<ch>ɪzə<o>ˌfaɪ<y>t[+gk]
schizophytic	ˌsk<ch>ɪzoˈfi<y>tɪk̲[+gk]	ˌsk<ch>ɪzə<o>ˈfɪ<y>tɪk[+gk]
scholasticism	sk<ch>oˈlæstɪˌk̲ɪsm	sk<ch>ə<o>ˈlæstɪˌs<c>ɪzəm
scholastic	sk<ch>oˈlæstɪk̲	sk<ch>ə<o>ˈlæstɪk
seismoscope	ˈsi<ei>z<s>moˌskōp	ˈsaɪ<ei>z<s>mə<o>ˌskoʊp
seismoscopic	ˌsi<ei>z<s>moˈskōpɪk̲	ˌsaɪ<ei>z<s>mə<o>ˈskopɪk
semen	ˈsēmɛn	ˈsimən
semination	ˌsēmɛ<i>ˈnātyon	ˌsɛmə<i>ˈneɪšən
semiparasite	ˌsɛmɪˈpæræˌsīt	ˌsɛmi<i>ˈpærə<a>ˌsaɪt
semiparasitic	ˌsɛmɪˌpæræˈsītɪk̲	ˌsɛmi<i>ˌpærə<a>ˈsɪtɪk
septicemia	ˌsɛptɪˈk̲ēmɪæ	ˌsɛptɪˈs<c>imi<i>ə
septicidal	ˌsɛptɪˈk̲īdæl	ˌsɛptɪˈs<c>aɪdə<a>l
septicity	sɛpˈtɪk̲ɪti	sɛpˈtɪs<c>ɪti
septic	ˈsɛptɪk̲	ˈsɛptɪk
sequacious	sɛˈkwāk̲yos	sɪ<e>ˈkweɪšəs
sequacity	sɛˈkwāk̲ɪti	sɪ<e>ˈkwæs<c>ɪti
serene	sɛˈrēn	səˈrin
serenity	sɛˈrēnɪti	səˈrɛnɪti
siderite	ˈsɪdɛˌrīt	ˈsɪdəˌraɪt
sideritic	ˌsɪdɛˈrītɪk̲	ˌsɪdəˈrɪtɪk
sigmoidoscope	sɪgˈmoɪdoˌskōp	sɪgˈmoɪdə<o>ˌskoʊp
sigmoidoscopic	sɪgˌmoɪdoˈskōpɪk̲	sɪgˌmoɪdə<o>ˈskopɪk
silicic	sɪˈlɪk̲ɪk̲	sɪˈlɪs<c>ɪk
silicide	ˈsɪlɪˌk̲īd	ˈsɪlɪˌs<c>aɪd
siliciferous	ˌsɪlɪˈk̲ɪfɛros	ˌsɪlɪˈs<c>ɪfṛəs
silicify	sɪˈlɪk̲ɪˌfī	sɪˈlɪs<c>ə<i>ˌfaɪ
silicon	ˈsɪlɪk̲on	ˈsɪlɪkə<o>n
somite	ˈsōmīt	ˈsoʊmaɪt
somitic	sōˈmītɪk̲	soʊˈmɪtɪk
sone	ˈsōn	ˈsoʊn
sonic	ˈsōnɪk̲	ˈsonɪk
specifiable	ˈspɛs<c>ɪˌfīæbɪl	ˈspɛs<c>ə<i>ˌfaɪə<a>bəl
specification	ˌspɛs<c>ɪfɪˈkātyon	ˌspɛs<c>ə<i>fə<i>ˈkeɪšən

	Deep	**Shallow**
specificative	ˈspɛs<c>ɪfɪˌkātɪvϵ<e>	ˈspɛs<c>ə<i>fə<i>ˌkeɪtɪvϵ<e>
specificity	ˌspɛs<c>ɪˈfīk̲ɪti	ˌspɛs<c>ə<i>ˈfɪs<c>ɪti
specify	ˈspɛs<c>ɪˌfī	ˈspɛs<c>ə<i>ˌfaɪ
specimen	ˈspɛs<c>ɪmɛn	ˈspɛs<c>ə<i>mən
spectrohelioscope	ˌspɛktroˈhēlɪoˌskōp	ˌspɛktrə<o>ˈhili<i>ə<o>ˌskoʊp
spectrohelioscopic	ˌspɛktroˌhēlɪoˈskōpɪk̲	ˌspɛktrə<o>ˌhili<i>ə<o>ˈskopɪk
spectroscope	ˈspɛktroˌskōp	ˈspɛktrə<o>ˌskoʊp
spectroscopic	ˌspɛktroˈskōpɪk̲	ˌspɛktrə<o>ˈskopɪk
sphericity	sfēˈrɪk̲ɪtɪ[+gk]	sfɛˈrɪs<c>ɪti[+gk]
spherics	ˈsfērɪk+s[+gk]	ˈsfɛrɪk+s[+gk]
spinose	ˈspīˌnōs	ˈspaɪˌnoʊs
spinosity	spīˈnōsɪti	spaɪˈnosɪti
sporophyte	ˈsporoˌfi<y>t[+gk]	ˈspɔrə<o>ˌfaɪ<y>t[+gk]
sporophytic	ˌsporoˈfi<y>tɪk̲[+gk]	ˌspɔrə<o>ˈfɪ<y>tɪk[+gk]
state	ˈstāt	ˈsteɪt
static	ˈstātɪk̲	ˈstætɪk
staurolite	ˈstɔroˌlīt	ˈstɔ<au>rə<o>ˌlaɪt
staurolitic	ˌstɔroˈlītɪk̲	ˌstɔ<au>rə<o>ˈlɪtɪk
stauroscope	ˈstɔroˌskōp	ˈstɔ<au>rə<o>ˌskoʊp
stauroscopic	ˌstɔroˈskōpɪk̲	ˌstɔ<au>rə<o>ˈskopɪk
steatite	ˈstēæˌtīt	ˈstiə<a>ˌtaɪt
steatitic	ˌstēæˈtītɪk̲	ˌstiə<a>ˈtɪtɪk
steatopyga	ˌstēætōˈpi<y>g̲æ	ˌstiə<a>toʊˈpaɪ<y>gə
steatopygia	ˌstēætōˈpi<y>g̲ɪæ	ˌstiə<a>toʊˈpaɪ<y>ǰi<i>ə
steatopygous	ˌstēætōˈpi<y>g̲os	ˌstiə<a>toʊˈpaɪ<y>gəs
stenotype	ˈstɛnoˌti<y>p	ˈstɛnə<o>ˌtaɪ<y>p
stenotypic	ˌstɛnoˈti<y>pɪk̲	ˌstɛnə<o>ˈtɪ<y>pɪk
stereoscope	ˈstɛrēoˌskōp	ˈstɛriə<o>ˌskoʊp
stereoscopic	ˌstɛrēoˈskōpɪk̲	ˌstɛriə<o>ˈskopɪk
stereotype	ˈstɛrēoˌti<y>p	ˈstɛriə<o>ˌtaɪ<y>p
stereotypic	ˌstɛrēoˈti<y>pɪk̲	ˌstɛriə<o>ˈtɪ<y>pɪk
sterilization	ˌstɛrɪlɪˈzātyon	ˌstɛrə<i>lɪˈzeɪšən
sterilize	ˈstɛrɪˌlīz	ˈstɛrə<i>ˌlaɪz
stethoscope	ˈstɛθoˌskōp	ˈstɛθə<o>ˌskoʊp
stethoscopic	ˌstɛθoˈskōpɪk̲	ˌstɛθə<o>ˈskopɪk
stoicism	ˈstōɪˌk̲ɪsm	ˈstoʊɪˌs<c>ɪzəm
stoic	ˈstōɪk̲	ˈstoʊɪk
strobilation	ˌstrōbɪˈlātyon	ˌstroʊbə<i>ˈleɪšən
strobila	strōˈbīlæ	stroʊˈbaɪlə
stroboscope	ˈstrōboˌskōp	ˈstroʊbə<o>ˌskoʊp
stroboscopic	ˌstrōboˈskōpɪk̲	ˌstroʊbə<o>ˈskopɪk

	Deep	Shallow
stromatolite	strō'mæto,līt	strou'mætə<o>,laɪt
stromatolitic	strō,mæto'lītɪk̲	strou,mætə<o>'lɪtɪk
stylite	'sti<y>līt	'staɪ<y>laɪt
stylitic	sti<y>'lītɪk̲	staɪ<y>'lɪtɪk
stylolite	'sti<y>lo,līt	'staɪ<y>lə<o>,laɪt
stylolitic	,sti<y>lo'lītɪk̲	,staɪ<y>lə<o>'lɪtɪk
stypticity	stɪ<y>p'tɪk̲ɪti	stɪ<y>p'tɪs<c>ɪti
styptic	'stɪ<y>ptɪk̲	'stɪ<y>ptɪk
sublime	sᴜ'blīm	sə<u>'blaɪm
sublimity	sᴜ'blɪmɪti	sə<u>'blɪmɪti
subvene	sᴜb'vēn	sə<u>b'vin
subvention	sᴜb'vēntyon	sə<u>b'vɛnčən
sulfite	'sʌlfīt	'sʌlfaɪt
sulfitic	sʌl'fītɪk̲	sʌl'fɪtɪk
supervene	,supɛr'vēn	,supr̩'vin
supervention	,supɛr'vēntyon	,supr̩'vɛnčən
sybarite	'sɪ<y>bæ,rīt	'sɪ<y>bə<a>,raɪt
sybaritic	,sɪ<y>bæ'rītɪk̲	,sɪ<y>bə<a>'rɪtɪk
syenite	'si<y>ɛ,nīt	'saɪ<y>ə,naɪt
syenitic	,si<y>ɛ'nītɪk̲	,saɪ<y>ə'nɪtɪk
synagogical	,sɪ<y>næ'gog̲ɪkæl	,sɪ<y>nə<a>'goǰɪkə<a>l
synagogue	'sɪ<y>næ,gog̲ϵ<u>ϵ<e>	'sɪ<y>nə<a>,gogϵ<u>ϵ<e>
syndrome	'sɪ<y>ndrōm	'sɪ<y>ndroʊm
syndromic	sɪ<y>n'drōmɪk̲	sɪ<y>n'dromɪk
tachistoscope	tæ'k<ch>ɪsto,skōp	tə<a>'k<ch>ɪstə<o>,skoʊp
tachistoscopic	tæ,k<ch>ɪsto'skōpɪk̲	tə<a>,k<ch>ɪstə<o>'skopɪk
tachylite	'tæk<ch>ɪ<y>,līt	'tæk<ch>ə<y>,laɪt
tachylyte	'tæk<ch>ɪ<y>,li<y>t	'tæk<ch>ə<y>,laɪ<y>t
tachylytic	,tæk<ch>ɪ<y>'li<y>tɪk̲	,tæk<ch>ə<y>'lɪ<y>tɪk
telescope	'tɛlɛ,skōp	'tɛlə,skoʊp
telescopic	,tɛlɛ'skōpɪk̲	,tɛlɪ<e>'skopɪk
tenacious	tɛ'nāk̲yos	tə'neɪšəs
tenacity	tɛ'næk̲ɪti	tə'næs<c>ɪti
tephrite	'tɛfrīt[+gk]	'tɛfraɪt[+gk]
tephritic	tɛf'rītɪk̲[+gk]	tɛf'rɪtɪk[+gk]
tetrabasicity	,tɛtræbā'sɪk̲ɪti	,tɛtrə<a>beɪ'sɪs<c>ɪti
tetrabasic	,tɛtræ'bāsɪk̲	,tɛtrə<a>'beɪsɪk
thallophyte	'θæl[+db]o,fi<y>t[+gk]	'θæl[+db]ə<o>,faɪ<y>t[+gk]
thallophytic	,θæl[+db]o'fi<y>tɪk̲[+gk]	,θæl[+db]ə<o>'fɪ<y>tɪk[+gk]
theodolite	θē'odo,līt	θi'odə<o>,laɪt
theodolitic	θē,odo'lītɪk̲	θi,odə<o>'lɪtɪk

	Deep	**Shallow**
thermoelectricity	ˌθɛrmōɛlɛkˈtrɪk̲ɪti	ˌθr̩moʊɪ<e>lɛkˈtrɪs<c>ɪti
thermoelectric	ˌθɛrmōɛˈlɛktrɪk̲	ˌθr̩moʊɪ<e>ˈlɛktrɪk
thermoplasticity	ˌθɛrmoplæˈstɪk̲ɪti	ˌθr̩mə<o>plæˈstɪs<c>ɪti
thermoplastic	ˌθɛrmoˈplæstɪk̲	ˌθr̩mə<o>ˈplæstɪk
thermoscope	ˈθɛrmˌoskōp	ˈθr̩mə<o>ˌskoʊp
thermoscopic	ˌθɛrmoˈskōpɪk̲	ˌθr̩mə<o>ˈskopɪk
thoracic	θoˈræk̲ɪk̲	θɔˈræs<c>ɪk
thorax	ˈθoræk̲s	ˈθɔræks
thrombocyte	ˈθromboˌs<c>i<y>t	ˈθrombə<o>ˌs<c>aɪ<y>t
thrombocytic	ˌθromboˈs<c>i<y>tɪk̲	ˌθrombə<o>ˈs<c>ɪ<y>tɪk
tone	ˈtōn	ˈtoʊn
tonic	ˈtōnɪk̲	ˈtonɪk
tope	ˈtōp	ˈtoʊp
topic	ˈtōpɪk̲	ˈtopɪk
torose	ˈtorōs	ˈtɔroʊs
torosity	toˈrōsɪti	tɔˈrosɪti
toxicity	toˈksɪk̲ɪti	toˈksɪs<c>ɪti
toxic	ˈtoksɪk̲	ˈtoksɪk
toxophilite	toˈksofɪˌlīt[+gk]	toˈksofə<i>ˌlaɪt[+gk]
toxophilitic	toˌksofɪˈlītɪk̲[+gk]	toˌksofə<i>ˈlɪtɪk[+gk]
trephination	ˌtrɛfīˈnātyon[+gk]	ˌtrɛfə<i>ˈneɪšən[+gk]
trephine	trɛˈfīn[+gk]	trɪ<e>ˈfaɪn[+gk]
triazole	ˈtrīæˌzōl	ˈtraɪə<a>ˌzoʊl
triazolic	ˌtrīæˈzōlɪk̲	ˌtraɪə<a>ˈzolɪk
trichite	ˈtrɪk<ch>īt	ˈtrɪk<ch>aɪt
trichitic	trɪˈk<ch>ītɪk̲	trɪˈk<ch>ɪtɪk
trilobite	ˈtrīloˌbīt	ˈtraɪlə<o>ˌbaɪt
trilobitic	ˌtrīloˈbītɪk̲	ˌtraɪlə<o>ˈbɪtɪk
troglodyte	ˈtrogloˌdi<y>t	ˈtroglə<o>ˌdaɪ<y>t
troglodytic	ˌtrogloˈdi<y>tɪk̲	ˌtroglə<o>ˈdɪ<y>tɪk
trope	ˈtrōp	ˈtroʊp
tropic	ˈtrōpɪk̲	ˈtropɪk
tropophyte	ˈtropoˌfi<y>t[+gk]	ˈtropə<o>ˌfaɪ<y>t[+gk]
tropophytic	ˌtropoˈfi<y>tɪk̲[+gk]	ˌtropə<o>ˈfɪ<y>tɪk[+gk]
trypanosome	ˈtrɪ<y>pænoˌsōm	ˈtrɪ<y>pə<a>nə<o>ˌsoʊm
trypanosomic	ˌtrɪ<y>pænoˈsōmɪk̲	ˌtrɪ<y>pə<a>nə<o>ˈsomɪk
tuberose	ˈtubɛˌrōs	ˈtubəˌroʊs
tuberosity	ˌtubɛˈrōsɪti	ˌtubəˈrosɪti
ultramicroscope	ˌʌltræˈmīkroˌskōp	ˌʌltrə<a>ˈmaɪkrə<o>ˌskoʊp
ultramicroscopic	ˌʌltræˌmīkroˈskōpɪk̲	ˌʌltrə<a>ˌmaɪkrə<o>ˈskopɪk
unchaste	ˌʌnˈčāst	ˌʌnˈčeɪst

	Deep	**Shallow**
unchastity	ˌʌnˈčāstɪti	ˌʌnˈčæstɪti
uralite	ˈyʊræˌlīt	ˈyʊr̩ə$_{<a>}$ˌlaɪt
uralitic	ˌyʊræˈlītɪk̲	ˌyʊr̩ə$_{<a>}$ˈlɪtɪk
uranite	ˈyʊrāˌnīt	ˈyʊr̩ə$_{<a>}$ˌnaɪt
uranitic	ˌyʊrāˈnītɪk̲	ˌyʊr̩ə$_{<a>}$ˈnɪtɪk
urbane	ʊrˈbān	r̩$_{<ur>}$ˈbeɪn
urbanity	ʊrˈbānɪti	r̩$_{<ur>}$ˈbænɪti
urbanization	ˌʊrbænīˈzātyon	ˌr̩$_{<ur>}$bə$_{<a>}$nɪˈzeɪšən
urbanize	ˈʊrbˌænīz	ˈr̩$_{<ur>}$bə$_{<a>}$ˌnaɪz
vaccination	ˌvæk$_{<c>}$s$_{<c>}$ɪˈnātyon	ˌvæk$_{<c>}$s$_{<c>}$ə$_{<i>}$ˈneɪšən
vaccine	væˈk$_{<c>}$s$_{<c>}$e$_{<i>}$n	væˈk$_{<c>}$s$_{<c>}$i$_{<i>}$n
vaporization	ˌvāporīˈzātyon	ˌveɪpə$_{<o>}$rɪˈzeɪšən
vaporize	ˈvāpoˌrīz	ˈveɪpə$_{<o>}$ˌraɪz
varicose	ˈværɪˌkōs	ˈværə$_{<i>}$ˌkoʊs
varicosity	ˌværɪˈkōsɪti	ˌværə$_{<i>}$ˈkosɪti
variolite	ˈværɪoˌlīt	ˈvɛ$_{<a>}$r̩i$_{<i>}$ə$_{<o>}$ˌlaɪt
variolitic	ˌværɪoˈlītɪk̲	ˌvɛ$_{<a>}$r̩i$_{<i>}$ə$_{<o>}$ˈlɪtɪk
vaticination	ˌvætɪk̲ɪˈnātyon	ˌvætɪs$_{<c>}$ɪˈneɪšən
vatic	ˈvætɪk̲	ˈvætɪk
ventricose	ˈvɛntrɪˌkōs	ˈvɛntrə$_{<i>}$ˌkoʊs
ventricosity	ˌvɛntrɪˈkōsɪti	ˌvɛntrə$_{<i>}$ˈkosɪti
veracious	vɛˈrāk̲yos	vəˈreɪšəs
veracity	vɛˈrāk̲ɪti	vəˈræs$_{<c>}$ɪti
verbose	vɛrˈbōs	vr̩ˈboʊs
verbosity	vɛrˈbōsɪti	vr̩ˈbosɪti
verrucose	ˈvɛr$_{[+db]}$ʊˌkōs	ˈvɛr$_{[+db]}$ə$_{<u>}$ˌkoʊs
verrucosity	ˌvɛr$_{[+db]}$ʊˈkōsɪti	ˌvɛr$_{[+db]}$ə$_{<u>}$ˈkosɪti
vertical	ˈvɛrtɪk̲æl	ˈvr̩tɪkə$_{<a>}$l
vertices	ˈvɛrtˌɪk̲+ēz	ˈvr̩tɪˌs$_{<c>}$+iz
videophone	ˈvɪdēoˌfōn$_{[+gk]}$	ˈvɪdiə$_{<o>}$ˌfoʊn$_{[+gk]}$
videophonic	ˌvɪdēoˈfōnɪk̲$_{[+gk]}$	ˌvɪdiə$_{<o>}$ˈfonɪk$_{[+gk]}$
vinosity	vɪˈnosɪti	vɪˈnosɪti
vinous	ˈvīnos	ˈvaɪnəs
viscose	ˈvɪskōs	ˈvɪskoʊs
viscosity	vɪsˈkōsɪti	vɪsˈkosɪti
vivacious	vɪˈvāk̲yos	vɪˈveɪšəs
vivacity	vɪˈvæk̲ɪti	vɪˈvæs$_{<c>}$ɪti
vocational	vōˈkātyonæl	voʊˈkeɪšənə$_{<a>}$l
vocation	vōˈkātyon	voʊˈkeɪšən
voracious	voˈrāk̲yos	vɔˈreɪšəs
voracity	voˈrāk̲ɪti	vɔˈræs$_{<c>}$ɪti

	Deep	**Shallow**
vortical	ˈvortıkæl	ˈvɔrtıkə$_{<a>}$l
vortices	ˈvortıˌk̲+ēz	ˈvɔrtıˌs$_{<c>}$+iz
vorticism	ˈvortıˌk̲ısm	ˈvɔrtıˌs$_{<c>}$ızəm
xerophyte	ˈz$_{<x>}$ɛroˌfi$_{<y>}$t$_{[+gk]}$	ˈz$_{<x>}$ɪ$_{<e>}$r̩ə$_{<o>}$ˌfaı$_{<y>}$t$_{[+gk]}$
xerophytic	ˌz$_{<x>}$ɛroˈfi$_{<y>}$tık̲$_{[+gk]}$	ˌz$_{<x>}$ɪ$_{<e>}$r̩ə$_{<o>}$ˈfı$_{<y>}$tık$_{[+gk]}$
xylophone	ˈz$_{<x>}$i$_{<y>}$loˌfōn$_{[+gk]}$	ˈz$_{<x>}$aı$_{<y>}$lə$_{<o>}$ˌfoʊn$_{[+gk]}$
xylophonic	ˌz$_{<x>}$i$_{<y>}$loˈfōnık̲$_{[+gk]}$	ˌz$_{<x>}$aı$_{<y>}$lə$_{<o>}$ˈfonık$_{[+gk]}$
zeolite	ˈzēoˌlīt	ˈziə$_{<o>}$ˌlaıt
zeolitic	ˌzēoˈlītık̲	ˌziə$_{<o>}$ˈlıtık
zoophile	ˈzōoˌfīl$_{[+gk]}$	ˈzoʊə$_{<o>}$ˌfaıl$_{[+gk]}$
zoophilic	ˌzōoˈfīlık̲$_{[+gk]}$	ˌzoʊə$_{<o>}$ˈfılık$_{[+gk]}$
zoophyte	ˈzōoˌfi$_{<y>}$t$_{[+gk]}$	ˈzoʊə$_{<o>}$ˌfaı$_{<y>}$t$_{[+gk]}$
zoophytic	ˌzōoˈfi$_{<y>}$tık̲$_{[+gk]}$	ˌzoʊə$_{<o>}$ˈfı$_{<y>}$tık$_{[+gk]}$
zygote	ˈzi$_{<y>}$gōt	ˈzaı$_{<y>}$goʊt
zygotic	zi$_{<y>}$ˈgōtık̲	zaı$_{<y>}$ˈgotık

3.A.2 *Rules for the Deep ORL*

The next two subappendices give the rules needed for the two different ORLs. Also indicated are rules needed for the deep ORL but not the shallow ORL, and vice versa, with the symbol "†". Deciding which rules are shared is not as completely trivial as it might seem since, for instance, a rule that converts an underlying /ū/ into <ou> is really equivalent to a rule that converts surface /aʊ/ into <ou>, because the latter phonological representation is supposed to be derived from the former. Such cases are counted as matching.

1	ɔ	→	<au>	
2	tyon	→	<tion>	
3	k̲yos	→	<cious>	/__ #
4	os	→	ous	/ __ #
5	(k|k̲)s	→	x	
6	kw	→	<qu>	
7	gz	→	<x>	
†8	īz	→	<es>	/ + __ # *(plural /iz/ spelled <es>)*
†9	il	→	<le>	/ (a|i)b __ #
10	r	→	<er>	/ C __ #

11	ϵ	→	<e>	/ [+tense] C^{+} __ #
			(Add a "silent" <e> after tense vowels)	
12	e	→	ϵ	/ īgn __ #
13	e	→	ϵ	/ ī$_{\langle ea\rangle}$ ¬[+cor,+cont] __ #
(<ea> requires no "silent" <e> except with intervening <s>)				
14	l	→	<le>	/ C __ #
15	ī	→	<ee>	/ 'C* __ #
16	č	→	<ch>	
17	ð	→	<th>	
†18	$\underline{g}$	→	<g>	
19	θ	→	<th>	
20	b	→	<b>	
†21	$\underline{k}$	→	<c>	
22	d	→	<d>	
23	f	→	<ph>	/ __ . . . [+gk]
24	r	→	<rh>	/ # __ . . . [+gk]
25	f	→	<f>	
26	g	→	<g>	
27	h	→	<h>	
28	l	→	<l>	
29	m	→	<m>	
30	n	→	<n>	
31	p	→	<p>	
32	r	→	<r>	
33	t	→	<t>	
34	v	→	<v>	
35	w	→	<w>	
36	yu	→	<u>	/ # __
37	y	→	<y>	
38	z	→	<z>	
39	s	→	<ce>	/ n __ #
40	s	→	<s>	
41	ū	→	<ou>	
42	oɪ	→	<oi>	
43	ʌ	→	<u>	
44	a	→	<a>	
45	ā	→	<a>	
46	ē	→	<e>	
47	ī	→	<i>	
48	ō	→	<o>	
49	u	→	<u>	
50	u	→	<u>	
51	o	→	<o>	
52	ɪ	→	<i>	
53	e	→	<e>	
54	ǰ	→	<g>	/ __ (< i > | < e > | < y >)
55	ǰ	→	<j>	

56 k → <k> / __ (< i > | < e > | < y >)
57 k → <c>
58 i → <y> / __ #

(this of course could be modeled as a surface constraint – Section 3.5)

3.A.3 Rules for the Shallow ORL

†1 ɔ → <o> / __ r
2 ɔ → <au>
3 (č|š)ən → <tion> / __ (əl)? #
4 šəs → <cious> / __ #
†5 o → <a> / w __
6 ks → <x>
7 gz → <x>
8 kw → <qu>
†9 ɪ → <e> / # pr | r | d __
†10 aɪz → <ize> / __ #
†11 z → <s> / __ #
12 r → <er> / C __ #
†13 zəm → <sm> / __ #
14 əs → <ous> / __ #
15 əl → <le> / __ #
16 ϵ → <e> / [+tense] C^+ __ #
17 e → ϵ / $\bar{\imath}_{<ea>}$ ¬[+cor,+cont] __ #
18 l → <le> / C __ #
19 i → <ee> / 'C* __ #
20 č → <ch>
21 ð → <th>
22 θ → <th>
23 b → <b>
24 d → <d>
25 f → <ph> / __ . . . [+gk]
26 r → <rh> / # __ . . . [+gk]
27 f → <f>
28 g → <g>
29 h → <h>
30 l → <l>
31 m → <m>
32 n → <n>
33 p → <p>
34 r → <r>
35 t → <t>
36 v → <v>
37 w → <w>
38 yu → <u> / # __
†39 yə → <u>

†40 yʊ → <u>
41 y → <y>
42 z → <z>
43 s → <ce> / n __ #
44 s → <s>
†45 aʊ → <ou>
46 ɔɪ → <oi>
47 ʌ → <u>
48 æ → <a>
49 eɪ → <a>
50 i → <y> / __ #
51 i → <e>
52 aɪ → <i>
53 oʊ → <o>
54 u → <u>
55 ʊ → <u>
56 o → <o>
57 ɪ → <i>
58 e → <e>
†59 ṛ → <r> / V __
60 ṛ → <er>
†61 ɑ → <a>
†62 ŋ → <n> / __ [+velar]
†63 ə → <a> / # __
†64 ə → <a> / __ #
†65 ə → <e>
66 ǰ → <g> / __ (< i > | < e > | < y >)
67 ǰ → <j>
68 k → <k> / __ (< i > | < e > | < y >)
69 k → <c>

4 Linguistic Elements

Un petit d'un petit
S'étonne aux Halles
Un petit d'un petit
Ah! degrés te fallent
Indolent qui ne sort cesse
Indolent qui ne se mène
Qu'importe un petit d'un petit
Tout Gai de Reguennes.
van Rooten, Luis d'Antin. 1967. *Mots d'Heures: Gousses, Rames. The d'Antin Manuscript*, page I. Penguin Books, New York.

In Section 1.2 we made a number of specific assumptions about what kinds of linguistic elements written symbols represent. More specifically and more formally we assumed that both phonological and semantic portions of an AVM representing a morpheme or word can in principle license graphical elements. This assumption naturally begs the question of the range of linguistic elements that can be represented by written symbols in the world's writing systems. This question is the topic of this chapter. The question of what kinds of linguistic elements written symbols represent is the single most investigated issue in the study of writing systems. Gelb (1963) is normally credited with being the first to systematically investigate the matter, and every extensive discussion of the topic since has presented a classification of writing systems based on which linguistic elements the writing system supposedly represents.

We start the discussion (Section 4.1) with a review of some of the more influential taxonomies of writing systems. As we shall see, these taxonomies are mostly arboreal. We will end the section with a proposal for a nonarboreal two-dimensional taxonomy that takes as one dimension the *type* of phonography encoded by the writing system and as another dimension the *degree* of *logography* of the system.

Chinese writing was introduced in Chapter 1 as a mixed system that generally involves both phonographic and semantic – or logographic – elements, a position argued most forcefully by DeFrancis (1984, 1989). We further justify this assumption here in Section 4.2. Also as we have previously argued, the phonographic and semantic elements represented graphically in a Chinese character are in a relation of overlap. This formal property, along with Axiom 1.3, makes an interesting and correct prediction about the written representation of *disyllabic* morphemes in Chinese.

We turn in Section 4.3 to a discussion of Japanese writing, in particular with respect to its use of Chinese characters. Japanese is surely the most complex modern writing system, and the hardest to force into any taxonomic mold. The properties of the Chinese script as it is used in the Chinese writing system contrast rather dramatically with the use of the same basic writing system – *kanji* – in Japanese, a point that Sampson (1985, 1994) shows convincingly in his discussion of this topic. As we shall argue, Japanese use of kanji is logographic to a greater degree than is use of the superficially similar set of symbols in Chinese. Characterizing the Japanese writing system *as a whole* is a rather different matter, however. The best characterization would appear to be that it is basically a phonographic system, but with significant amounts of logography.

We end the chapter (Section 4.4) with a discussion of a few esoteric graphical devices used in some writing systems, and we present an analysis of each within the present framework.

4.1 Taxonomies of Writing Systems: A Brief Overview

Our purpose here is not to be exhaustive but rather to present a small sample of some of the more influential taxonomies of writing systems; a more balanced review can be found in Coulmas (1994); see also DeFrancis (1989, pages 56–64).

4.1.1 Gelb

Gelb's taxonomy of writing systems is generally viewed as the starting point for all subsequent taxonomies. Gelb's purpose in his classification was largely teleological: He viewed the segmental phonographic alphabet as the evolutionary high point of writing systems, and all other writing systems could be viewed as falling on a continuum from pictographic nonwriting to alphabetic writing. Thus a linear presentation seems most appropriate for Gelb's taxonomy, and this is what is presented in Figure 4.1. Note that Gelb classified Mayan writing among his "limited-systems" subcategory of the *forerunners of writing*; of course, this is now known to be false, since Mayan writing is a full writing system containing both logographic and phonographic elements; see Macri (1996) inter alia. There is also general disagreement with Gelb's classification of the consonantal Semitic writing systems as syllabic.

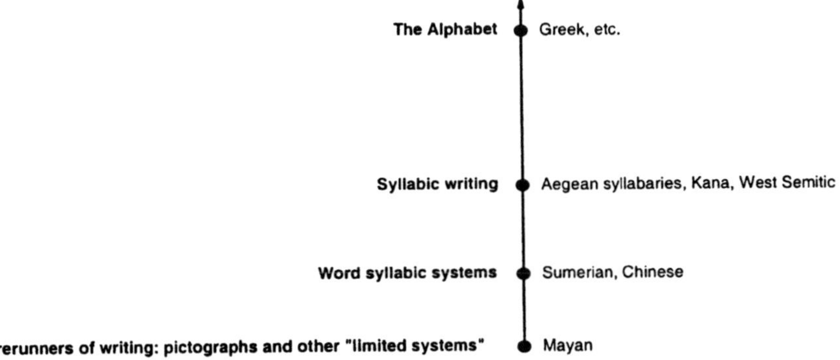

Figure 4.1. The taxonomy of Gelb (1963), along with examples of writing systems that belong to each case.

4.1.2 *Sampson*

A less teleological view of writing is presented in Sampson (1985); see Figure 4.2. One important innovation of Sampson's system is the primary division between "glottographic" writing, where the symbols represent linguistic elements, and "semasiographic" writing, where the symbols represent concepts but provide no specification of a linguistic form to express those concepts. Sampson (pages 28–29) tentatively presents as an example of

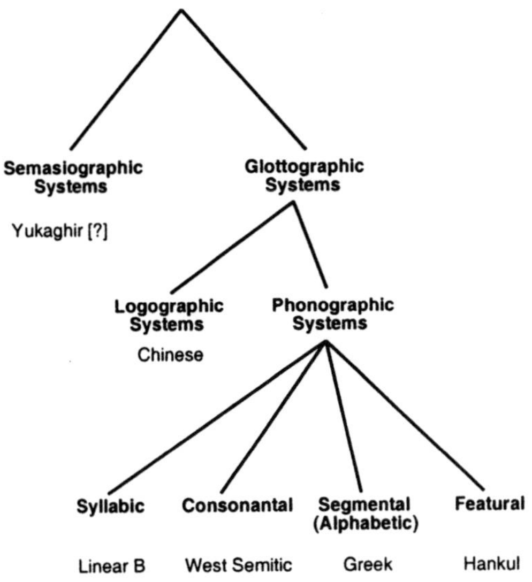

Figure 4.2. The taxonomy of Sampson (1985).

semasiographic writing a Yukaghir "love letter"; he gives a few other instances as well – for example a set of pictographic instructions for starting a Ford car (page 30). But on the whole, the evidence for semasiography as a viable category of writing systems is tenuous. Indeed, Sampson's primary interest appears to be to suggest merely that a fully communicative system of semasiography might in principle be possible, rather than to argue that such a system has ever existed.

Among glottographic systems Sampson takes the relatively traditional view that Chinese writing is logographic. This is because, in his view, Chinese characters do not encode phonological information: Rather, he claims, Chinese characters directly represent morphemes, so that the Chinese reader must simply learn which character goes with which morpheme, and ultimately with which pronunciation. This is of course a fairly standard definition of logography.[1] It differs from the view that we are assuming here (see Section 1.2.2 and the discussion below in Section 4.2) *in that we view any component of a writing system as having a logographic function if it formally encodes a portion of nonphonological linguistic structure*, whether it be a whole morpheme or merely some semantic portion of that morpheme. The latter kind of encoding might perhaps be called "semasiographic," but for various reasons I prefer to avoid that term.

In addition to adopting the common view of Chinese writing, Sampson also takes the more innovative (and controversial) position that Korean Hankul is featural, an issue that we will return to below.

4.1.3 DeFrancis

DeFrancis (1989) takes issue with a number of Sampson's claims.

4.1.3.1 No Full Writing System Is Semasiographic

First, and most importantly, DeFrancis argues against the existence or even the possibility of semasiographic writing. His major attack consists of demonstrating that the Yukaghir "love letter" cited by Sampson was not an instance of a system of written communication at all; rather it was a prop in a kind of "party game" that was never intended to be understood by a reader but rather was interpreted for others by the author (pages 24–35). Still, as Sampson (1994) correctly observes, the argument is not really fair. Even though the Yukaghir "letter" turns out not to be an instance of semasiographic writing, DeFrancis ignores the other instances

[1] Note that the basic division among glottographic systems between logographic systems and phonographic systems corresponds exactly to what Haas (1983) terms *pleremic* and *cenemic*, respectively. See also Coulmas (1989).

of semasiographic writing (e.g., the iconic Ford instruction manual) that Sampson (1985) had previously discussed. Indeed DeFrancis cannot deny the existence of iconic symbology that communicates ideas without recourse to representing any specifically linguistic information. However, DeFrancis is correct in observing that such systems are always limited in what they are capable of expressing. Nobody has shown the existence of a writing system that is entirely semasiographic, relying on no linguistic basis to communicate ideas, and which allows people to write to one another on any topic they choose. It seems fair to say that the burden of proof is on those who would claim that semasiographic writing is possible to demonstrate the existence of such a system. For DeFrancis, then, all full writing is glottographic.

4.1.3.2 All Full Writing Is Phonographic

But DeFrancis makes an even stronger claim: All full writing is largely phonographic. A purely logographic system is, according to him, impossible. Thus Sampson's classification of Chinese writing as logographic is incorrect. DeFrancis's basic argument is simple: The vast majority of Chinese characters that have been created throughout history are so-called semantic–phonetic compounds, such as the character 蟬 <INSECT+CHÁN> *chán* 'cicada' discussed in Section 1.2.2, where one element in the character gives a hint of the meaning, and the other element gives a hint at the pronunciation. The exact percentage depends upon the size of the character set being considered. For the 9,353 characters that had been developed up to the second century A.D., about 82% of the characters were semantic–phonetic compounds; for the entire set of 48,641 characters that were recorded by the eighteenth century, 97% were semantic–phonetic compounds (DeFrancis, 1989, page 99), meaning that essentially all of the characters created between the second and eighteenth centuries were of the semantic–phonetic type. No explicit estimate is given for the percentage of such compounds in the written vocabulary of the average Chinese reader (who can be expected to know between 5,000 and 7,000 characters), but there is no question that it will be the vast majority. Thus, for DeFrancis, Chinese writing is not primarily logographic at all, but what he terms *morphosyllabic*: It is basically a phonographic writing system, with additional logographic information encoded.

4.1.3.3 Hankul Is Not Featural

Finally, DeFrancis argues that although Korean Hankul clearly has some featural aspects that went into its design, it is basically segmental (pages 186–200); note that this is also the position of King (1996). The major reason that DeFrancis gives (and this is also echoed in Coulmas (1994)) is that Korean children learning to read typically memorize the syllable-sized groupings of elements as wholes and that Korean readers are certainly unaware of the featural relationships between the symbols. This argument, it seems to me, is rather shaky: What readers are taught or explicitly aware of in their writing system is often at odds with what a careful analysis tells us is true of that system. For example Flesch (1981) cites several instances of American readers of English taught reading by the so-called whole-word method, who were unaware that English writing is basically segmental with particular letters or combinations representing particular sounds.

Nevertheless, DeFrancis is probably correct in asserting that Hankul is basically segmental, rather than featural. To see this, it is worth considering a truly featural script, namely Bell's "Visible Speech" (Bell, 1867, MacMahon, 1996), which was developed for use as a universal phonetic alphabet. The construction of the individual glyphs in the system encodes articulatory features in a *consistent* iconic fashion. For instance consonant place of articulation is indicated by orientation of the basic consonant glyph (a C-shaped symbol for *consonant*). Thus C is /x/ with the bowl of the glyph pointing leftwards, indicating a constriction at the back of the mouth; and Ɔ is /ϕ/, with the rightward-pointing bowl representing a bilabial constriction. Stops (closures) are indicated by closing off the open part of the glyph. Thus Ɑ is /k/ and D is /p/. Voicing is indicated by a bar that is iconic for the near closure of the glottis during voicing. Thus Є is /g/ and ϶ is /b/. Nasality is indicated by turning half of the closure bar into a wavy line, which indicates the lowered soft palate (MacMahon, 1996, page 838). Thus Ɛ is /ŋ/ and Ʒ is /m/. Other features are similarly indicated in a *consistent* fashion.

In contrast, Hankul is not by any means as consistent in its representation of features. While some features *are* represented consistently by properties of the script, others are only inconsistently represented, and still others not at all. Consider the basic Hankul segmental elements presented in Sampson (1985, page 124) and shown here in Figure 4.3. As we have noted, certain phonological features do have a consistent representation in the elements of the Hankul script. Thus, for instance, the feature (bundle) [+tense,−aspirated] (fifth row of Hankul symbols) is represented by a doubling of the basic symbol used for the corresponding (in terms of place of articulation) lax stop. Similarly, the sibilants (third column) have in common the basic symbol ㅅ <s>, which represents a tooth (Sampson, 1985, page 125) or in other words is an indication of the place of articulation of the consonants in question. However, labiality is not consistently represented: /m/, /b/, and /p/ share a common shape (the square representing a mouth), but $/p^h/$ is different. And some features are not represented at all. Thus there is no representation of the feature nasal: /m/, /n/, and /s/ appear

Consonants

	bilabial	apical	sibilant	velar	laryngal
lax continuant	ㅁ m	ㄴ n	ㅅ s		ㅇ
lax stop	ㅂ b	ㄷ d	ㅈ ɟ	ㄱ g	
tense aspirated stop	ㅍ p^h	ㅌ t^h	ㅊ c^h	ㅋ k^h	ㅎ h
tense continuant			ㅆ s^*		
tense unaspirated stop	ㅃ p^*	ㄸ t^*	ㅉ c^*	ㄲ k^*	
liquid		ㄹ l			

Vowels

	front		back	
	spread	rounded	spread	rounded
close	i ㅣ		ɯ ㅡ	u ㅜ
mid	e ㅔ	ø ㅚ	ɤ ㅓ	o ㅗ
open	æ ㅐ		a ㅏ	

Figure 4.3. Featural representation of Korean Hankul, from Sampson (1985, page 124, Figure 19). (Presented with permission of Geoffrey Sampson.)

to be on a par, involving the "basic" glyphs for each place of articulation. There is similarly no consistent representation of the feature [voiced] (lax, in Sampson's classification) for stops. The apical and sibilant voiced elements have an overbar, but in the case of /b/ we find not an overbar, but an extension of the two vertical sides of the square of /m/; the overbar for /g/, according to Sampson, represents the roof of the mouth touching the palate, and thus it is presumably not the same as the overbar for the apical and sibilant glyphs. Finally, there is no consistent representation of aspiration. In some symbols (/c^h/, /h/) it seems to be represented as a dot over the basic glyph (third row), and in other cases (/t^h/, /k^h/) it appears as a horizontal bar inside the basic glyph.

None of this should be interpreted as denigrating the Hankul script for it is probably the most scientific script in common use today. There is no question that the basic design of Hankul is phonetically motivated to a highly sophisticated degree. After all, many of the shapes *are* depictions

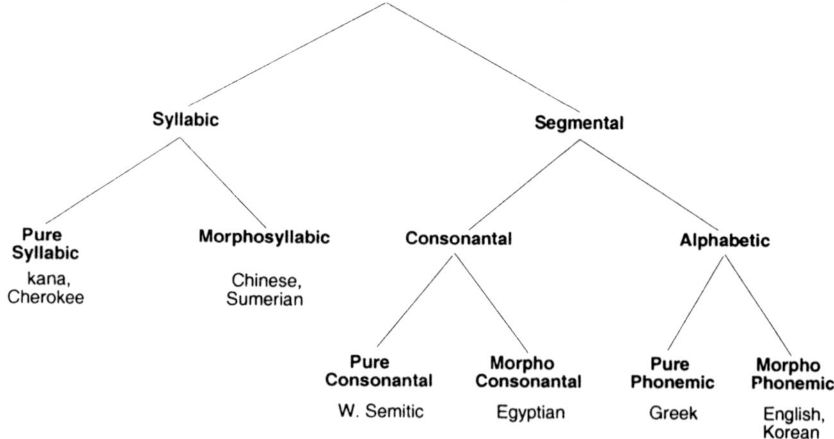

Figure 4.4. DeFrancis's classification of writing systems.

of modes of articulation and are iconic in a way similar to Bell's Visible Speech. But it falls short of being a featural script in the way that Visible Speech is; rather, it is better viewed as an intelligently constructed segmental alphabet. This conclusion should not be surprising for even in unequivocally segmental systems, one still finds symbols that seem to encode individual features. So in Russian, for instance, the soft sign ь <'> marks palatalized consonants and thus might be viewed as encoding the feature [+high] for consonants. Clearly Hankul has more featural aspects than Russian orthography, yet it is probably more a matter of degree than of kind.

The three views we have just discussed, taken together, lead DeFrancis to propose a classification of true writing systems as depicted in Figure 4.4.

Some comments are in order. DeFrancis's basic division is according to the type of phonological unit represented: syllabic versus segmental, and within the latter consonantal (representing mostly or only consonants) versus alphabetic (representing all segments). Within each category he assumes two variants, namely a pure variant, where only phonological information is represented in the system, and a morpho variant, where, additionally, morphological information is represented. This is obvious enough for Chinese, Sumerian, and Egyptian, where each of these writing systems has semantic elements that represent meaning-related properties of morphemes. English and Korean Hankul are similarly classified since in both cases the writing systems fail to be fully phonemic. We shall argue in the next subsection that this classification represents a category error: English and Hankul are not on a par with Chinese or Egyptian.

4.1.4 A New Proposal

While I accept several basic assumptions of DeFrancis's classification scheme, there are nonetheless several areas where I feel his scheme is deficient. These are enumerated below:

1. Despite the prominent position given to syllabaries in DeFrancis's taxonomy (as well as most other schemes), it is important to realize that full syllabaries – that is, systems where all syllables of the language are represented by (one or more) single symbols – are actually very rare. Though scholars of writing systems have undoubtedly been aware of this point for a long while, it was to my knowledge first made explicitly by Bill Poser in a presentation at the Linguistic Society of America in 1992. Poser's basic point was simple. In the majority of systems that are called "syllabic" – among them, Japanese Kana, Linear B, the phonological component of Sumerian writing, and the phonological component of Mayan writing – one does not find a symbol for every full syllable of the language. Instead, what one finds are symbols for simple "core" (C)V syllables, possibly augmented to include onglides (CGV); more complex syllables are represented in writing by combining the core syllable symbols with symbols either representing single phonemes or other symbols representing core syllables. A few examples will serve to illustrate the point.
   - Kana symbols represent V, CV, or CGV. To represent a CVV syllable, one must combine a basic CV symbol with a V symbol. Thus a syllable /nai/ would be represented as <na><i>. Japanese orthography might therefore be described as *moraic* (cf. Horodeck (1987, page 33)).
   - In Linear B (Miller, 1994; Bennett, 1996), symbols represent (C)V, CGV, or in a few cases CCV. More complex syllables are (partially) represented using combinations of these basic units. Thus the (disyllabic) word /ksenwion/ was represented as <ke><se><ni><wi><jo> (with no representation of the final /n/), and the (tetrasyllabic) word /mnāsiwergos/ was represented <ma><na><si><we><ko> (with no orthographic representation of the /r/ and final /s/) (Miller, 1994, pages 18–22).
   - In Sumerian, complex syllables were often represented by "syllable telescoping" (DeFrancis, 1989, pages 81–82), whereby a CV graphemic unit and a VC graphemic unit were combined to represent a CVC phonological syllable. Thus <ki>+<ir> would represent /kir/.

In one sense, of course, such systems *are* syllabaries since the phonological units represented by the simple glyphs are generally well-formed syllables of the language. But this is misleading. When one speaks of alphabetic symbols it is taken for granted that there are symbols available to represent every phonemic segment of the language. So, the term syllabary ought to similarly imply that every syllable of the language has a graphemic symbol associated with it. Most so-called syllabaries do not meet that requirement.[2] For lack of a better term, I will henceforth term such systems *core syllabaries*.[3]

Still, full syllabaries certainly do occur: Chinese is one such example, though of course it is not a pure phonological system. Another example seems to be the Yi syllabary (DeFrancis, 1989; Shi, 1996), which in its classic form was a morphosyllabic system like Chinese (and may have been influenced by Chinese writing), but in its modern form – at least the popular standardized form that is recommended by the government (Shi, 1996, 241) – it is a purely phonographic syllabary. Yi syllable-structure is exceedingly simple, with basically only CV syllables (including some diphthongs) allowed. However, there are 44 consonants (including the empty onset), 10 vowels, and 3 lexical tones, resulting in a syllabary of 819 characters once all legal C+V+Tone combinations are considered. Of course the complexity of the syllable structure represented by Yi syllabograms is no more complex than those represented by typical core syllabaries, but in Yi each distinct full syllable is represented by a separate glyph, unlike, for example, the case in Japanese.

Note that to say that true syllabaries are rarer than usually supposed is not, of course, to deny the importance of the syllable as an organizational unit in a great many writing systems; we have noted (as have others) the importance of syllables in Hankul, Devanagari, and Pahawh Hmong, and many other systems could be cited. We even argued for the importance of syllables in the Russian writing system (Section 3.5).

2. "Morphophonemic" systems such as English or Korean are parallel in DeFrancis's taxonomy to morphosyllabic systems such as Chinese

[2] Of course, this argument is not entirely fair, since in many alphabetic systems certain phonemes are only represented by combinations of basic symbols, such as digraphs. Hence /č/ in Spanish is only representable by <ch>, and /θ/ and /ð/ in English are only representable by <th>. But polygraphs are typically the minority in alphabetic systems, and there are many segmental systems that do not have polygraphs. In contrast, polygraphic representation of complex syllables in so-called syllabaries appears to be the norm.

[3] Fischer (1997a,b) terms them "open syllabaries," but this term is suboptimal: CVV syllables are after all "open," though they tend not to be represented with single symbols in core syllabaries.

or Sumerian and morphoconsonantal systems such as Egyptian. This is a category error.

What makes Korean and English less than fully "phonemic" relates not to *what* is represented, by the basic symbols of the script, but to the phonological depth of what is represented and the amount of lexical marking one must assume. In other words it relates to the depth of the ORL and other issues discussed in Chapter 3. This issue was explicitly discussed for English in that chapter; relevant discussion on Korean can be found in Sampson (1985, pages 135ff.), who describes a set of rules to predict the actual surface pronunciation of a string of Korean Hankul, given regular (morpho)phonological processes of the language. As was also discussed in Section 3.2, it is particularly a mistake to equate the lexical orthographic marking of English (e.g., the marked spelling of /n/ in *knit*) with the logographic components of Chinese writing, an equation that is implicit in DeFrancis's classification.

3. Calling Egyptian "consonantal" and thus equating it with Semitic writing systems obscures one unique property of Egyptian, namely the existence of bi- and triliterals, standing for two and three consonants respectively (Ritner, 1996). In fact these make up the majority of the system: There are only 25 "uniliteral" symbols but 80 biliterals and 70 triliterals. Egyptian writing might therefore better be described as "polyconsonantal."
4. While I accept DeFrancis's basic hypothesis that one cannot construct a full writing system on completely logographic principles without recourse to phonography, logography is nonetheless an important aspect of many writing systems, a point that no scholar would presumably deny.[4]

   However, as DeFrancis has argued, for a writing system to be extensible it must have a robust phonographic component for one cannot efficiently develop written representations for neologisms if one is restricted to purely logographic means.[5] Thus no matter how large the amount of logography a particular writing system has,

[4] Indeed, as Sampson (1994, page 122) cogently points out, logography is in no way anomalous once one observes that "any natural language has units at many levels, and in particular that all human languages exhibit a 'double articulation' into units carrying meaning, on the one hand, and phonological units ... on the other. ... It is at least logically possible, therefore, that a glottographic script might assign distinctive symbols to elements of the first rather than of the second articulation."

[5] As we shall see in our discussion of Japanese below, *kokuji* – Japanese-invented Chinese characters – are instances of purely logographic constructions invented to represent words that did not previously have a written representation. But there are no more than a couple of hundred of these, whereas the number of new words that have representations in the *kana* core syllabary number in the thousands.

Type of Phonography

Amount of Logography ↓	Consonantal	Polyconsonantal	Alphabetic	Core Syllabic	Syllabic
	W. Semitic		English, Greek, Korean, Devanagari Pahawh Hmong	Linear B	Modern Yi
	Perso–Aramaic				
					Chinese
		Egyptian		Sumerian, Mayan, Japanese	

Figure 4.5. A nonarboreal classification of writing systems. On Perso-Aramaic, see Section 6.1.

logography is clearly not on a par with phonography and should therefore not be represented as part of the same arboreal taxonomy as it is, for example, in Sampson's system.

The last point motivates us to abandon the traditional arboreal classification of writing systems in favor of a two-dimensional arrangement where the type of phonography used represents the primary dimension and *amount* of logography used represents the second. This scheme is represented in Figure 4.5. Naturally the degree of logography is tricky to estimate (though I believe it can be estimated) and the arrangement of particular writing systems in this second dimension is largely impressionistic. But it is important to realize that *all* writing systems probably have some degree of logography. So written English contains numerous symbols and letter sequences that can only be construed logographically: <&>, <lb>, and <$> are just three examples. In the taxonomy, alphasyllabaries such as Devanagari (Section 2.3.2) are classified as alphabets. The status of "onset-rime" scripts such as Pahawh Hmong (Section 2.3.3) is unclear: They are *almost* segmental, but symbols for rimes such as /ɔŋ/ show them not to be completely so. One might consider setting up a special category for such scripts; in the current scheme I classify Pahawh Hmong as falling somewhere between alphabets and core syllabaries.

There is of course no reason to stop at two dimensions, though it is more convenient to do so for simplicity of presentation. An additional dimension would relate to the depth of the ORL and other topics discussed in Chapter 3; in this dimension, English and Korean would pattern differently from, say, Greek. This is of course the sense in which DeFrancis meant that English and Korean are "morphophonemic," unlike Greek, but the dimension on which they differ is orthogonal to the dimension on which, say, Chinese and Modern Yi differ.

Yet another dimension would be the degree to which complex planar arrangements have a significant function in a writing system, the topic of Chapter 2. Korean and Devanagari would pattern differently from English on this dimension (Faber, 1992).

4.1.5 Summary

We have suggested a view of writing systems where logography – defined as the graphical encoding of nonphonological linguistic information – is an orthogonal dimension from phonography. Writing systems can thus be classified minimally in a two-dimensional space according to what types of phonological elements are encoded, and to how much logography they have. Encoded phonological elements represent a range of possibilities, as is well known, but normally the maximum size of such elements is a core-syllabic CV or VC unit. In particular rarely does one find a purely phonographic system that represents each possible syllable of the language with a distinct element. Egyptian represents an apparently unique polyconsonantal system.

The orthogonality of logography and phonography is entirely in keeping with the formal model we presented in Section 1.2.2: Assuming that logographic elements represent information related to the SYNSEM attribute, then as we previously observed, the linguistic information encoded by logographic elements is not in a hierarchical relationship with information encoded by phonographic elements. Therefore it should in principle be possible for writing systems to select different mixes of logographic and phonographic encodings and to exhibit both in the same system. For different types of phonography this ability to mix is less natural. Syllables dominate segment-sized units, and so if a system is core-syllabic it is natural for it to choose most or all of its elements at that level of the hierarchy; mixes could happen, but one in fact rarely if ever finds systems that have both a large collection of graphemes that denote core syllables and another collection of graphemes that denote segments. Systems tend to choose one phonological level to encode.

DeFrancis's main thesis is that Chinese is a writing system that is basically phonographic (as he claims are all writing systems), but with a large logographic component. The conclusion of the preceding paragraph that such systems are expected given the formal apparatus of Section 1.2.2 is of course consistent with this thesis. But the formal model of Chinese semantic–phonetic characters presented there still begs the question of whether there is compelling evidence that Chinese writing really behaves that way: Does it actually buy you anything to assume that the <INSECT> portion of *chán* 'cicada' encodes a portion of the SYNSEM field, whereas the putatively phonographic portion <CHÁN> encodes phonological information? We will argue that it does, both in the next section, and in Chapter 5 where we address psycholinguistic evidence for readers' online processing of characters. In the next section, in particular, we will argue not only that the phonographic portion of Chinese characters plays an important role in encoding phonological information but that the formal model presented earlier makes an interesting prediction about the encoding of disyllabic morphemes in Chinese.

4.2 Chinese Writing

The traditional Chinese classification of characters divides them into six groups, the so-called *liù shū*, or Six Categories of Characters. Of these, four relate to the structural properties of the characters and two to their usage (Wieger, 1965, page 10). It is the structural properties that will concern us here; the four categories of interest are:

- Pictographs (*xiàngxíng*): e.g., 人 <PERSON> *rén* 'person', 龜 <TURTLE> *guī* 'turtle'.
- Indicative symbols (*zhǐshì*): e.g., 下 <DOWN> *xià* 'downwards', 上 <UP> *shàng* 'upwards'.
- Semantic–semantic compounds (*huìyì*): e.g., 好 <FEMALE+CHILD> *hǎo* 'good', 苗 <GRASS+FIELD> *miáo* 'sprout'.
- Semantic–phonetic compounds (*xíng shēng*): e.g., 蟬 <INSECT+CHÁN> *chán* 'cicada', 橡 <TREE+XIÀNG> *xiàng* 'oak'.

The first three cases are reasonably uncontroversial. There is no question that these three groups of signs, which in total number no more than about 1,500 in the largest dictionary (DeFrancis, 1989, page 99), are logographs, without any representation of phonetic information. Of course, as Coulmas (1989, page 50) notes, logographic symbols, which theoretically should map directly to a nonphonological portion of the morphological level of representation, do, in the minds of skilled readers, also map directly to phonological representation. A skilled English reader, for example, will unconsciously map <lb> to /paʊnd/, and equivalent facts hold for Chinese.[6] The controversial characters are of course those in the fourth

[6] This is presumably the basis of the use of characters purely for their pronunciation, a practice that has been followed for centuries to transliterate foreign words, whether they be Sanskrit terms from Buddhist tracts, or present-day foreign names such as 克林頓 *kèlíndùn* 'Clinton'. In Modern Chinese, the particular characters that are used for this kind of "phonetic transcription" are a more-or-less closed class; see Sproat et al. (1996) for some discussion. See also Section 4.3 for a discussion of the equivalent Japanese *ateji*.

category, the semantic–phonetic group, the category that DeFrancis insists is basically phonetic, whereas Sampson has argued (and many others have merely assumed) that it is logographic.

The problem with the categorization of the semantic–phonetic category revolves around the fact that the phonological information provided by the phonetic component is sometimes perfect, frequently only partial, and in some cases completely useless. An example of each case is given below:

Char.	Analysis	Phon. Component	Actual Pron.	Gloss
橡	<TREE+XIÀNG>	象 *xiàng* ('elephant')	*xiàng*	'oak'
鴨	<BIRD+JIǍ>	甲 *jiǎ* ('cuirass')	*yā*	'duck'
猜	<DOG+QĪNG>	青 *qīng* ('green')	*cāi*	'guess'

The distribution of these three types is quite skewed: There are a small number of the first category (perfect match), a few of the last category (completely useless), with most falling into the second category (somewhat helpful). Some phonetic components are in general more useful than others. For example all characters having 皇 *huáng* ('emperor') as a phonetic component have the pronunciation *huáng*, matching the base character down to the level of the tone; see DeFrancis (1989, e.g., pages 102–103) for a range of other examples.[7]

Now, if the phonetic component were always a perfect indicator of the pronunciation of the character, then there would presumably be no contention: Everyone would agree that most Chinese characters are basically phonetic symbols, with additional logographic information (the semantic component). But because of the imperfections in the representation of the phonological information, most authors have assumed that the system is no longer phonographic. Although the comparison with English is not

7 What is the reason for inexact matches? In some cases it is historical sound change. For example, many characters with the phonetic component 行 *xíng/háng* are pronounced *xing* or *hang* (Wieger, 1965, page 443) (as is the base character). These two syllables are the result of a historical split in Mandarin. There is no question that the phonetic components were more useful in the past than they are in Modern Mandarin (and may be more useful even today in other Chinese languages, such as Cantonese, though I have not seen an investigation of this topic). Even Sampson (1994) admits that the Chinese system may have been a much more phonographic system at one time. See Baxter (1992) for a comprehensive discussion of the phonology of early Chinese and its relationship with the phonetic components.

In other cases, the historical argument is less convincing: 衍 <WATER+XÍNG> 'overflow' is pronounced *yǎn*, which presumably was never historically derivable from *xíng/háng*: presumably this way of writing the character was chosen since the phonetic component was deemed similar enough to the intended reading, and since 行 in its reading *xíng* means 'go', it may have also contributed some semantic information to the composite character.

entirely fair (English orthography is never as irregular as Chinese), it is interesting to note that precisely the same assumptions have been popularly made about English. Indeed, the misguided assumption that English is *not* basically a phonetic but rather a logographic writing system has had a significant impact on the teaching of reading in the United States, as lamented and attacked in Bloomfield and Barnhart (1961) and in Flesch (1981); this assumption stems in large measure from the fact that English spelling is not optimal for cuing the reader to the pronunciation of the word, meaning that the spelling and pronunciation of some words must simply be learned.[8]

DeFrancis's argument, however, is not that Chinese writing is a good phonographic system – indeed, he stresses that it is a lousy one. However, it is much more useful to view it as an imperfect phonographic system with additional logographic attributes, than it is to view it as a wholly logographic system. Apart from the distributional reasons that DeFrancis discusses, there are other reasons for assuming that Chinese is largely phonographic and that, in particular, the phonographic information resides in the phonetic component, when that is present. Among these reasons are:

- The evidence for the psychological reality of the phonetic component, as discussed in the next chapter.
- The common-sense observation that Chinese readers, when encountering an unfamiliar character, will attempt to guess its pronunciation from the phonetic component. Indeed, with a completely unfamiliar character, they have no choice but to adopt this strategy. An instance of this is the character 鱈 <FISH+XUĚ> *xuě* 'cod'. Apparently this character was a Japanese invention, a *kokuji* (Section 4.3), where the second element 雪 was used not for its pronunciation *xuě* but for its meaning 'snow' (the flesh of cooked cod being snowy white). Thus the correct analysis for Japanese would be <FISH+SNOW>, a typical semantic–semantic construction common in kokuji. When this character was borrowed back into Chinese, Chinese readers interpreted the 雪 component as a phonetic component, thus assigning the character the pronunciation *xuě*.
- The development of some simplified characters in the Mainland involving the substitution of a different phonetic component for the one used in the traditional script. The main motivation in character

[8] Sampson (1985), as we have noted elsewhere, makes a similar assumption about English spelling, though it should be stressed that he cannot be accused of the same kind of naiveté as American educators who have subscribed to this view.

simplification was the reduction of the number of strokes needed to write the character, with the goal of making Chinese writing easier to learn; see (DeFrancis, 1984) inter alia. The majority of simplifications involved stroke reductions in components of characters, without actually changing the components used. However, a small percentage involved actually substituting an easier-to-write component – usually a phonetic component – for a more complex traditional component. In such cases, a substituted phonetic component was more often that not a *closer* phonetic match to the pronunciation of the whole character than the traditional component it replaced. For instance, a count of phonetic-component substitutions from the list of simplified/traditional character pairs in one dictionary (Nanyang Siang Pau, 1984) revealed 74 characters (64%) where the pronunciation of the substituted phonetic component is a closer match to the pronunciation of the whole character than that of the traditional component, and 42 (36%) where the substituted component is actually a worse match. Thus, 進 <GOING+ZHUĪ> *jìn* 'enter' has been replaced in the simplified script by 进 <GOING+JǏNG>.[9] Similarly, traditional 塊 <EARTH+GUǏ> *kuài* 'lump' has been replaced by 块 <EARTH+GUÀI>. An instance where the pronunciation of the substituted component is worse is 動 <FORCE+ZHÒNG> *dòng* 'move', where the (left-hand) phonetic component 重 *zhòng* is replaced to form 动 <FORCE+YÚN>.

Given these observations, it makes sense to assume as we have that the phonetic component is licensed by the phonological information of the syllable that it encodes. What then of the semantic component, which we have assumed is licensed separately by a portion of the SEM attribute's value? For 蟬 <INSECT+CHÁN> *chán* 'cicada', we had assumed an AVM as in (1.8), repeated here as (4.1), and an annotation graph as in (1.10), repeated here as (4.2):

(4.1)

$$\begin{bmatrix} \text{PHON} & \begin{bmatrix} \text{SYL} & \begin{bmatrix} \text{SEG} & \left\langle \begin{bmatrix}\text{ONS } ch\end{bmatrix}\begin{bmatrix}\text{RIME } an\end{bmatrix}\right\rangle \\ \text{TONE} & 2 \end{bmatrix}\end{bmatrix}_{1*} \\ \text{SYNSEM} & \begin{bmatrix}\text{CAT } noun \\ \text{SEM } cicada_{2*}\end{bmatrix} \\ \text{ORTH} & \{\text{虫}_2, \text{單}_1\} \end{bmatrix}$$

[9] Note that the syllables *jin* and *jing* are homophonous for many Mandarin speakers.

(4.2)

SEM:	___ *cicada* : 虫___	
TONE:	______ 2 ______	
SYL:	_____ σ : 單_____	
ONS-RIME:	___*ch*___	___*an*___

The two licensing components in (4.2) overlap, and Axiom 1.3 tells us that they must catenate with each other. The specific catenation operator chosen is (in this case) predictable by rule, following the discussion in Section 2.3.4.

Note, however, that since most Chinese morphemes are monosyllabic (DeFrancis, 1984), it would seem hard to distinguish between the somewhat elaborate theory presented here and the seemingly simpler theory that states that the phonetic component 單 <CHÁN> is indeed licensed by the syllable, but that the semantic component 虫 <INSECT> is simply some excess baggage that happens to be associated with the syllable for this particular word. In other words we would like to distinguish our proposal from the alternative theory that states that the so-called semantic component is *not* licensed by the semantic portion of the AVM at all.

Crucial evidence comes from the orthographic representation of disyllabic morphemes. Some well-known examples of disyllabic morphemes include *húdié* 'butterfly', *pútáo* 'grape', and *bīnláng* 'betel': As far as historical records allow us to determine these words do not derive from morphologically complex forms and there is certainly no synchronic evidence of morphological complexity. While various sources discuss disyllabic morphemes, one rarely gets a clear sense of how many of these morphemes there are DeFrancis (1984; 1989), for instance, only discusses a few such cases, and such cursory treatment is the norm.[10] In fact disyllabic morphemes probably number around a hundred. Seventy-four are listed in Tables 4.1 and 4.2, and this by no means a complete list.

Before we consider those lists, however, let us see what the theory predicts about the orthographic represention. Consider *bīnláng* 'betelnut' which is written using the <TREE> radical 木 and phonetic components 賓 and 郎 representing, respectively, the two syllables *bīn* and *láng* and thus could be transcribed as <TREE+BĪNLÁNG>. The two phonetic symbols are obviously

[10] Plausibly, the reason for the relative neglect of disyllabic morphemes comes from the fact that traditional Chinese dictionaries are organized around monosyllabic characters, not around words or morphemes. Since meanings are traditionally listed in the dictionary as entries for these characters, this obscures the fact that many characters are in fact meaningless unless combined with a specific second character.

Table 4.1. *Disyllabic morphemes collected from the ROCLING corpus (10 million characters) and 10 million characters of the United Informatics corpus. This set consists of pairs of characters occurring at least twice, and where each member of the pair only co-occurs with the other*

Orthography	Analysis	Pronunciation	Gloss
囹圄	<SURROUND+LÌNGWÚ>	*língyú*	'imprisoned'
囫圇	<SURROUND+WÙLÚN>	*húlún*	'swallow whole'
轇轕	<CART+LIÀOGĚ>	*jiūgé*	'entwined'
窈窕	<CAVE+YÒUTIAO$_{15/34\ p.438}$>	*yǎotiǎo*	'graceful'
魍魎	<DEMON+WĂNGLIĂNG>	*wǎngliǎng*	'roaming ghost'
妯娌	<FEMALE+ZHOU$_{8/22\ p.436}$LǏ>	*zhóulǐ*	'sister in laws'
餛飩	<FOOD+KŪNTÚN>	*húntún*	'wonton'
蹉跎	<FOOT+CUŌTUŌ>	*cuōtuó*	'procrastinate'
踉蹌	<FOOT+LÁNG$_{13/25\ p.460}$QIANG$_{7/19\ p.516}$>	*lángqiāng*	'hobble'
蹂躪	<FOOT+RÓULÌN>	*róulìn*	'trample'
躊躇	<FOOT+CHÓU$_{6/16\ p.555}$ZHÙ>	*chóuchú*	'hesitate'
躑躅	<FOOT+ZHÌ$_{2/3\ p.582}$SHŬ>	*zhízhú*	'hesitate'
氤氳	<GAS+YĪNYUN$_{8/17\ p.517}$>	*yīnyūn*	'misty atmosphere'
邂逅	<GOING+XIÈHÒU>	*xièhòu*	'encounter'
迤邐	<GOING+YÍLÌ>	*yǐlǐ*	'trailing'
荸薺	<GRASS+BÓQÍ>	*bíqí*	'water chestnut'
萵苣	<GRASS+GUĂJÙ>	*wōjù*	'lettuce'
菡萏	<GRASS+HÁNXIÀN>	*hàndàn*	'lotus'
蒹葭	<GRASS+JIĀNJIĂ>	*jiānjiā*	'type of reed'
苜蓿	<GRASS+MÙSÙ>	*mùsù*	'clover'
揶揄	<HAND+YĒYÚ>	*yéyú*	'tease'
顢頇	<HEAD+MĂNHAN$_{14/32\ p.401}$>	*mánhān*	'muddleheaded'
慫恿	<HEART+CÓNGYǑNG>	*sǒngyǒng*	'egg on'
忸怩	<HEART+NIU$_{8/9\ p.408}$NÍ>	*niǔní*	'coy'
慇懃	<HEART+YĪNQÍN>	*yīnqín*	'attentively'
蝙蝠	<INSECT+BIĂNFÙ>	*biānfú*	'bat'
蜉蝣	<INSECT+FÚYÓU>	*fúyóu*	'mayfly'
蚯蚓	<INSECT+QIŪYǏN>	*qiūyǐn*	'earthworm'
璀璨	<JADE+CUĪCÀN>	*cuǐcàn*	'brilliant'
玳瑁	<JADE+DÀIMÀO>	*dàimào*	'tortoise shell'
鞦韆	<LEATHER+QIŪQIĀN>	*qiūqiān*	'swing'
耄耋	<OLD+MÁOZHÌ>	*màodié*	'old people'
旖旎	<OVERHANGING+YI$_{9/26\ p.469}$NÍ>	*yǐnǐ*	'fluttering'
倥傯	<PERSON+KŌNGZǑNG$_{5/9\ pp.531–532}$>	*kǒngzǒng*	'busy'
疙瘩	<SICKNESS+GE$_{9/22\ p.400}$DÁ>	*gēdā*	'cyst, boil'
徬徨	<STEP+PÁNGHUÁNG>	*pánghuáng*	'roam aimlessly'
徜徉	<STEP+SHÀNGYÁNG>	*chángyáng*	'roam leisurely'
齟齬	<TEETH+JŪWÚ>	*jǔyǔ*	'bickering'
枇杷	<TREE+PI$_{14/22\ pp.413–414}$BĀ>	*pípá*	'loquat'
檸檬	<TREE+NÍNGMÉNG>	*níngméng*	'lemon'
酩酊	<WINE+MÍNGDĪNG>	*míngdǐng*	'drunk'
醍醐	<WINE+TÍ$_{9/19\ p.498}$HÚ>	*tíhú*	'clear wine, butterfat'
匍匐	<WRAP+PU$_{15/22\ pp.456–457}$FÙ>	*púfú*	'crawl'

Table 4.2. *Further disyllabic morphemes collected from the ROCLING corpus (10 million characters) and 10 million characters of the United Informatics corpus. This set consists of other pairs of characters that do not exclusively occur with each other, but where there is nonetheless a high mutual information for the pair. Note that* LV *(†) indicates that the phonetic component in question occurs 9 out of 38 times in characters pronounced with initial /l/ followed by some vowel*

Orthography	Analysis	Pronunciation	Gloss
鴛鴦	<BIRD+YUĀNYĀNG>	*yuānyāng*	'mandarin duck'
狡猾	<DOG+JIĀOHUA$_{4/9\ p.542}$>	*jiǎohuā*	'cunning'
蕃薯	<GRASS+FĀNSHÙ>	*fānshǔ*	'yam'
葫蘆	<GRASS+HÚLÚ>	*húlú*	'gourd'
蘿蔔	<GRASS+LUÓFÙ>	*luóbō*	'daikon'
葡萄	<GRASS+PÚTÁO>	*pútáo*	'grape'
恍惚	<HEART+GUĀNGHŪ>	*huǎnghū*	'illusionarily'
慷慨	<HEART+KĀNGJÌ>	*kāngkǎi*	'generous'
蝴蝶	<INSECT+HÚDIE$_{15/25\ p.502}$>	*húdié*	'butterfly'
螞蟻	<INSECT+MǍYÌ>	*mǎyǐ*	'ant'
螃蟹	<INSECT+PÁNGXIÈ>	*pángxiè*	'crab'
蟑螂	<INSECT+ZHĀNGLÁNG>	*zhānglǎng*	'cockroach'
琥珀	<JADE+HÚBÓ>	*hǔpò*	'amber'
琳瑯	<JADE+LÍNLÁNG>	*línláng*	'kind of jade'
玻璃	<JADE+PÍLÍ>	*bōlí*	'glass'
尷尬	<LAME+JIĀNJIÈ>	*gāngà*	'awkward'
咆哮	<MOUTH+PAO$_{16/30\ pp.430\text{–}431}$XIÀO>	*páoxiào*	'roar'
喉嚨	<MOUTH+HÓULÓNG>	*hóulóng*	'throat'
咳嗽	<MOUTH+HÀISÙ>	*késòu*	'cough'
咀嚼	<MOUTH+JŪJUÉ>	*jǔjué*	'chew'
咖啡	<MOUTH+JIĀFĒI>	*kāfēi*	'coffee'
喇叭	<MOUTH+LÀBĀ>	*lǎbā*	'trumpet, speaker'
唏噓	<MOUTH+XĪXŪ>	*xīxū*	'sniffling'
傀儡	<PERSON+GUǏLÉI>	*kuílěi*	'puppet'
伉儷	<PERSON+KÀNGLÌ>	*kànglì*	'couple'
宇宙	<ROOF+YÚZHOU$_{8/22\ p.436}$>	*yǔzhòu*	'universe'
賄賂	<SHELL+YǑULV$_{9/38\ p.446}$>†	*huìluò*	'bribe'
徘徊	<STEP+FĒIHUÍ>	*páihuí*	'going to and fro'
檳榔	<TREE+BĪNLÁNG>	*bīnláng*	'betelnut'
橄欖	<TREE+GǍNLǍN>	*gǎnlǎn*	'olive'
醞釀	<WINE+YUN$_{8/17\ p.517}$XIĀNG>	*yùnniàng*	'brewing (i.e. trouble . . .)'

licensed by the individual syllables. Given that the SYNSEM attribute is associated with the entire *morpheme* rather than with the individual syllables, the theory states that the <TREE> radical is associated with the whole morpheme rather than with the individual syllables. The AVM for this morpheme would be as in (4.3) and the annotation graph as in (4.4):

(4.3)

$$\begin{bmatrix} \text{PHON} & \begin{bmatrix} \text{SYLS} \left\langle \begin{bmatrix} \text{SEG} & \left\langle \begin{bmatrix}\text{ONS } b\end{bmatrix} \begin{bmatrix}\text{RIME } in\end{bmatrix} \right\rangle \\ \text{TONE } 1 & \end{bmatrix}_{1^*}, \begin{bmatrix} \text{SEG} & \left\langle \begin{bmatrix}\text{ONS } l\end{bmatrix} \begin{bmatrix}\text{RIME } ang\end{bmatrix} \right\rangle \\ \text{TONE } 2 & \end{bmatrix}_{2^*} \right\rangle \end{bmatrix} \\ \text{SYNSEM} & \begin{bmatrix} \text{CAT } noun \\ \text{SEM } betel_{3^*} \end{bmatrix} \\ \text{ORTH} & \{\text{木}_3, \{\text{賓}_1\ \text{郎}_2\}\} \end{bmatrix}$$

(4.4)

SEM:	*betel* : 木			
TONE:	*1*		*2*	
SYL:	σ : 賓		σ : 郎	
ONS-RIME:	*b*	*in*	*l*	*ang*

Given the representation in (4.4), how are the semantic and phonetic components to be realized relative to one another? First observe that both the following overlap statements are true, where σ_1 and σ_2 are the first and second syllables:

1. $betel \bigcirc \sigma_1$.
2. $betel \bigcirc \sigma_2$.

From Axiom 1.3 we would then expect that $\gamma(betel)$ must catenate with $\gamma(\sigma_1)$ and that $\gamma(betel)$ must also catenate with $\gamma(\sigma_2)$; in other words, the semantic radical must show up on both components of the written representation of the morpheme. This prediction is correct: The written form is **檳榔**, with the <TREE> component 木 on both components.

Of course in addition to overlapping with the individual syllables, it is also true that the semantic information *betel* overlaps with the whole phonological word *bīnláng*. In that case we would say that $betel \bigcirc b\bar{\imath}nl\acute{a}ng$ and we might then expect to find a written form such as *檳郎, with the <TREE> component catenated to the left of the pair of syllables – thus in effect showing up on the first component. Note that this obeys the catenation formula $\gamma(betel) \cdot \gamma(b\bar{\imath}nl\acute{a}ng)$, which can be derived from $betel \bigcirc b\bar{\imath}nl\acute{a}ng$ from Axiom 1.3. However, recall that the combination of semantic and phonetic radicals in Chinese frequently involves a different catenation operator from the macroscopic operator. In general a formula such as $\gamma(betel) \cdot \gamma(b\bar{\imath}nl\acute{a}ng)$ would require choosing a different operator from the macroscopic operator at the *word* level. This in turn violates the constraint that the SLU is the syllable in Chinese; see Section 2.3.4. Therefore the only option given the theory and the writing-system particular constraints is to duplicate the semantic element across both syllables. This duplication has been noted elsewhere in the literature (e.g. in DeFrancis (1989), Law and Caramazza (1995), among others) but never to my knowledge explained.

The duplication of semantic radicals across both components of a disyllabic morpheme predicted by the theory holds quite generally. One problem, of course, is to define what one means by a disyllabic morpheme. One cannot in general rely on dictionaries, since standard Chinese dictionaries are arranged by character, and under the multicharacter subentries they rarely distinguish "compounds" of two or more compounds that are morphologically simplex from compounds that are morphologically complex. One can however collect disyllabic morphemes from corpora, if we make the reasonable assumption that a disyllabic morpheme should consist of two elements that are statistically highly associated with each other, but not with anything else. Two such lists are presented here, based on 20 million characters of Chinese text.[11] The first list, presented in Table 4.1, consists of pairs of characters that occur at least twice and only co-occur with each other (i.e., the token count of the pair is identical to the token counts of the individual characters). The second list, Table 4.2, consists of other pairs of characters not in the first list, which have high *mutual information* (Fano, 1961).[12] In this second table, at least one of the component characters can occur elsewhere. In some cases this is purely an orthographic fact. For instance, the 咖 *kā* of 咖啡 *kāfēi* 'coffee' is also used to write 咖哩 *gālǐ* 'curry'. In other cases, as with the 蝶 *dié* of 蝴蝶 *húdié*, what was originally part of a disyllabic morpheme has taken on a "life of its own" and can be used nowadays in new derivatives (as well as in personal names); see Sproat and Shih (1995) for some discussion. But what is clear about all these cases is that both on the basis of distributional evidence, and on the basis of native-speaker judgments, these pairs of characters all seem to form single indivisible units. The most striking feature of these lists, of

[11] This in turn consists of the 10-million character ROCLING (R.O.C. Computational Linguistics Society) corpus, plus ten million characters of another corpus from United Informatics, Inc.

[12] Mutual information is defined for two events c_1 and c_2, and their co-occurrence c_1c_2, as follows:

$$I \equiv \log_2\left(\frac{\text{prob}(c_1c_2)}{\text{prob}(c_1)\text{prob}(c_2)}\right).$$

Here we estimate the probabilities by the maximum likelihood estimate, $p(c) = f(c)/N$, where $f(c)$ is the frequency of c and N is the size of the corpus. Mutual information has been used in many computational linguistic applications for computing the strength of association between lexical items; see, e.g. Church and Hanks (1989) and also Sproat and Shih (1990) for an application to Chinese word segmentation.

course, is the predicted duplication of the semantic radicals in each of the cases.

Beyond distributional evidence, such examples reflect what is in fact a very strong intuition of Chinese readers that characters that belong to such relatively inseparable constructions must be written with the same radical. Indeed, it is possible to trace the history of some of these cases, and show that the semantic radical shared by both characters was added in accordance with this "same-radical constraint." For instance, 徜徉 <STEP+SHÀNGYÁNG> *chángyáng* 'roam leisurely' has in the past been written in various ways, including 常羊 (*chángyáng*, the literal interpretation of 'everyday sheep' being irrelevant) (Ci Hai, 1979). Over time, the same-radical constraint forced the word into its present shape.

It is worth noting at this juncture that one also finds a few pairs of disyllabic morphemes with identical pronunciations and phonetic components, differing only in the semantic components. The meaning differences may be subtle, or stark, but in any case there is a strong sense that one is dealing with different senses of the same word, with different spellings for the different senses. One pair where the semantic difference is rather stark is 枇杷 <TREE+$\text{PI}_{14/22\ pp.413\text{–}414}\text{BĀ}$> *pípá* 'loquat' and 琵琶 <MUSIC+$\text{PI}_{14/22\ pp.413\text{–}414}\text{BĀ}$> *pípá* 'Chinese lute'. But despite the difference in meaning, the words are clearly related: The Chinese lute (or "pipa") is a loquat-shaped instrument. A more subtle pair is 崎嶇 <MOUNTAIN+QÍQŪ> *qíqū* and 踦𨅮 <FOOT+QÍQŪ> *qíqū*, both with the sense of 'rugged', though with the former seeming to emphasize the terrain, and the latter the journey or path over a rugged terrain. A crucial point about such cases is that although there is some freedom to choose the semantic radical, mixing the semantic radicals across the two characters results in an ill-formed result: *踦嶇 <FOOT+QÍ MOUNTAIN+JŪ> is not a possible way to write this word. Clearly these examples are consistent with a model where the semantic radical is a property of the morpheme. It is both independent of the phonetic component in that there is some freedom to choose alternative radicals while keeping the phonetics constant, while at the same time the same radical must be used for both characters used to write the syllables of the morpheme.

Although the appropriate representation of *xíng shēng* characters thus seems clear, we need to say something about the representation of the other classes – pictographs, indicative symbols, and semantic-semantic compounds – that formally lack a semantic or phonetic component. Taking as our example the pictograph 人 *rén* 'person', we will assume a representation such as that in (4.5) where the grapheme is licensed by the SEM entry. From a purely formal point of view 人 *rén* is a logograph for it does not strictly speaking encode phonological information. Nonetheless, as we have observed above, even in such cases of formal logography, skilled readers phonologically "recode" the symbol (Coulmas, 1989), which in turn suggests a second licensing from the phonological portion of the AVM. Both these licensings are indicated here:

(4.5)

$$\begin{bmatrix} \text{PHON} & \begin{bmatrix} \text{SYL} & \begin{bmatrix} \text{SEG} & \left\langle \begin{bmatrix}\text{ONS } r\end{bmatrix} \begin{bmatrix}\text{RIME } en\end{bmatrix} \right\rangle \\ \text{TONE } 2 & \end{bmatrix} \end{bmatrix}_{1*} \\ \text{SYNSEM} & \begin{bmatrix} \text{CAT } noun \\ \text{SEM } person_{2*} \end{bmatrix} \\ \text{ORTH} & \{\text{人}_{1,2}\} \end{bmatrix}$$

4.3 Japanese Writing

Treatments of writing systems need to say something about Japanese writing, widely considered to be the most complex writing system in use today. I therefore briefly treat Japanese writing here and in Section 5.2.2. This section provides an informal treatment of the degree to which Japanese writing is logographic, a sizeable bone of contention among scholars of writing systems. Section 5.2.2 discusses psycholinguistic evidence that, no matter how *formally* logographic Japanese may be, Japanese readers and writers seem to treat it as a phonographic system. That is, the kind of phonological recoding suggested by Coulmas (1989) does indeed seem to occur in Japanese (and also in Chinese as we will argue in Section 5.2.1).

Japanese apparently exhibits the most most extensive use of logography of any modern writing system. The reasons for this are well documented elsewhere and will only be briefly sketched here; see Sampson (1985), DeFrancis (1989), Sampson (1994), among others. When the Japanese adapted Chinese writing for representing their own language, they experimented with various ways of using Chinese characters (*kanji*) to represent Japanese words. One way was to use Chinese characters to represent Japanese words with roughly the same meaning but (of course) with quite different pronunciations. Thus 人 'person' would be used to represent *hito* 'person' (Mandarin *rén*) and 魚 'fish' would be used to represent *sakana* 'fish' (Mandarin *yú*). Characters used in this way to represent native Japanese words are said to have their *kun* ('instruction') reading. In some cases a *sequence* of characters with the appropriate interpretation would be used to represent a *monomorphemic* Japanese word. Thus 何時 for *itsu* 'when' (Mandarin *héshí*), or 貴方 *anata* 'you' (Mandarin *guìfāng*). In these cases – termed *jukujikun* – the character sequence behaves in effect as a single complex character.

Right from the start, Chinese characters were also used phonetically to represent Japanese syllables, and in this usage the characters took on pronunciations corresponding (roughly) to their pronunciation in Chinese. Thus, 乃 (Mandarin *nǎi*) would be used to represent the Japanese syllable *no* (Sampson, 1985, page 175). Over time, a conventional set of these *manyō'gana*, reduced in form, evolved into the two modern *kana* core syllabaries. But in early Japanese texts one found admixtures of Chinese characters functioning as phonetic elements along with characters to be read with a kun pronunciation.

To add to the complexity, Japanese borrowed not only Chinese writing, but also a large number of Chinese vocabulary items. Naturally these were written as they would be in Chinese, and they were also pronounced approximately as in Chinese. Significantly, such Sino-Japanese readings are called *on* meaning 'sound' (Chinese 音 *yīn*); the inherent 'sound' of a character is its Chinese pronunciation, and this is consistent with the use of the Chinese pronunciation in manyō'gana. As is well documented in Sampson's (1985) discussion, further complications arose because Chinese vocabulary was borrowed into Japanese at different times and from different parts of China, resulting in various "Chinese" pronunciations for many characters. It is not unusual for a character to have, in addition to a kun pronunciation, three or four distinct *on* pronunciations. Typically these different pronunciations are restricted to different words. Thus 定 'definite' is pronounced *tei* in 定価 *teika* 'fixed price' (Mandarin *dìngjià*), but as *jō* in 定連 *jōren* 'regular customer' (which would be *dìnglián* in Mandarin if this were a Chinese word). Such facts guarantee that for most Chinese characters, the Japanese reader has little choice other than to memorize the association between lexical entries and their written form, with little or no useful recourse to phonological information: In other words these characters are logographic.

The logographic nature of Chinese characters, as they are used in Japanese, is underscored in a different way by *kokuji* (literally 'domestic characters'), Chinese characters that were invented in Japan to represent Japanese words (Lehman and Faust, 1951; Coulmas, 1989; Daniels and Bright, 1996). A sample of these is given in Table 4.3. The most striking feature of kokuji is the overwhelming prevalence of semantic–semantic constructions and the relatively small number of semantic–phonetic constructs; particularly rare are semantic–phonetic constructs involving native kun pronunciations. Alexander's compilation of kokuji (reported in Lehman and Faust (1951)) includes 249 examples for which approximately 184 have a clear etymology and are not simply contractions of multicharacter expressions. (For instance 俥 *jinrikisha* 'rickshaw' is clearly derived from the character sequence 人力車 *jin riki sha* (human power car).) Of these, 72% are semantic–semantic constructs. The remainder are semantic–phonetic compounds, with 20% based on an *on* pronunciation, and the remaining

Table 4.3. *A sample of Japanese kokuji (second column), with their componential analysis (third column). The first column is the entry number in Alexander's list (Lehman and Faust, 1951). The fourth column lists the phonetic, if any. The fifth column lists the kun pronunciation, and the sixth column the* on *pronunciation, if any: in one case –* goza *– there is no kun pronunciation. The last three kokuji shown are formed as semantic–phonetic constructs, with the last two being based on the kun pronunciation: Note that the phonetic component of* masa *also means 'straight', so it is possible that this one is also a semantic–semantic construct*

Alex. #	Kokuji	Analysis	(Phonetic)	Kun	(*on*)	Gloss
10	働	<PERSON+MOVE>		*hataraki*	*dō*	'effort'
12	凪	<WIND+STOP>		*nagi*		'lull, calm'
33	峠	<MOUNTAIN+UP+DOWN>		*touge*		'mountain pass'
37	怺	<HEART+FOREVER>		*kore*		'endure'
74	毟	<FEW+HAIR>		*mushi*		'pluck'
124	聢	<EAR+CERTAIN>		*shika*		'clearly'
160	躾	<BODY+BEAUTIFUL>		*shitsuke*		'upbringing'
198	颪	<DOWN+WIND>		*oroshi*		'mountain wind'
240	鴫	<FIELD+BIRD>		*shigi*		'snipe'
249	嬶	<FEMALE+NOSE>		*kakā*		'wife'
138	蓙	<GRASS+ZA>	座 *za* (*on*)		*goza*	'matting'
51	柾	<TREE+MASA>	正 *masa* (*kun*)	*masa*		'straight grain'
147	裄	<CLOTHING+YUKI>	行 *yuki* (*kun*)	*yuki*		'sleeve length'

8% on a kun pronunciation. Some examples of each of these categories can be seen in Table 4.3.[13] The prevalence of semantic–semantic formations among Japanese character innovations is striking in that it so strongly contrasts with the situation in Chinese. There, as we have already noted, semantic–phonetic constructs were overwhelmingly the preferred means of forming new characters. The Japanese situation also contrasted with another Chinese-based script, namely the *Chū' Nôm* writing system of Vietnam. Exclusively Vietnamese character innovations were found in *Chū' Nôm*, but these were apparently *all* semantic–phonetic constructions (Nguyen, 1959).

A couple of factors might seem to explain the low percentage of semantic–phonetic constructs in kokuji. Both of these explanations depend upon the

[13] Note that the semantic elements used in kokuji do *not* always correspond to traditional semantic elements in Chinese. Thus, for instance, 定 'definite' is not a traditional semantic element, though it is used as such in the character for *shika* 'clearly', in Table 4.3.

observation that many of the kokuji were invented to write words that have only a kun pronunciation. However, as we shall see, neither of these explanations really work.

The first idea is that the most obvious source of the phonetic component for kun-only characters would be a character with the same or similar kun pronunciation as the intended target. But since the "sound" (*on*) of a Chinese character is its Sino-Japanese pronunciation (or pronunciations), using a kun pronunciation in this way might have been disfavored. However, as we have noted, 8% of the kokuji *were* formed in this way, so there cannot have been an absolute prohibition on using kun pronunciations in phonetic components. Furthermore, such a prohibition would not have ruled out the more widespread use of *on* pronunciations to represent both *on* (20% of the cases) as well as kun pronunciations. Indeed, some instances of the latter type do occur, as in 鱚 <FISH+KI> *kisu* (kun) 'sillago' (Alexander's entry 230), where the phonetic component 喜 *ki* is an *on* reading.

The second potential explanation relates to the length of kun pronunciations. In Chinese, and also in Vietnamese, characters almost exclusively represent single syllables. Given the relatively simple syllable structures of these languages, there is a high degree of homophony. Thus in inventing a new character to represent a morpheme with a given pronunciation, there are usually many identically or similarly pronounced characters to choose from to act as a phonetic component. Kun pronunciations in Japanese, in contrast, are often polysyllabic (three-syllable native morphemes are not unusual), and therefore the degree of potential homophony is reduced. Again there may be a grain of truth to this explanation, but it cannot represent more than a tendency. Polysyllabic homophones do exist in Japanese, and this fact is apparently made use of in forming some of the kokuji; see, for instance, 裄 <CLOTHING+YUKI> *yuki* 'sleeve length' in Table 4.3, which is homophonous with (among other things) *yuki* 'go' (written 行), and this is taken advantage of in forming this character. Secondly, there seems to be no requirement in general that the homophony be particularly close. Thus the 214th entry in Alexander's list (see Lehman and Faust (1951)) is 鯐 <FISH+HASHI> *subashiri* 'young of grey mullet', which is apparently derived using 走 *hashi* 'run' as a phonetic; here the target is quite different in pronunciation (even allowing for the well-known /h/↔/b/ alternation in Japanese) from that of the phonetic component.

The only reasonable guess as to the high incidence of semantic–semantic kokuji, in my view, is that there was simply a preference among the users of the Japanese writing system for creating these kinds of "visual puns." This may in part be due to the fact that throughout much of history writing was an elite skill in Japan (as in much of the rest of the world) (Sampson, 1985) and the people who possessed that skill had time for what may be viewed as practically oriented language games. But the spread of literacy has by no means killed this kind of creativity. Alexander explicitly excludes from discussion more recent widely known formations such as 𡚴 <FEMALE+UP+DOWN> *erebētā gāru* 'elevator girl' precisely because they are puns and are not seriously considered part of the writing system. But the difference in kind between this example and the genuine kokuji 峠 <MOUNTAIN+UP+DOWN> *touge* 'mountain pass' is in fact minimal.

As a logographic system – or more properly, a logographic *subset* of a writing system – semantic–semantic kokuji exemplify the creative limits of logography. But what do they tell us about the nature of Japanese writing? And secondly what do they tell us about the possibility of developing an entire writing system based on logography – something that Sampson (1985), it will be recalled, claims exists already in the case of Chinese?

In answer to the first question, as we noted in the introduction to this section, the amount of logography that Japanese readers must face is large, more than in any other modern writing system. But it is also clear that this percentage has been on the decline within the past century, as the use of the system moved out of the circle of literati into the general population; as Smith (1996, page 210) notes, the use of kanji in a wide variety of functions has declined steadily throughout the twentieth century. With the decrease in the use of kanji, there has been necessarily a concomitant increase in the use of the phonologically based kana scripts. Japanese writing has always involved a mixture of logographic and phonetic elements; it is, and always has been, a "mixed script," as Sampson (1985) terms it, one where there is a large logographic core, but where phonologically based devices are available and are widely and productively used. The mix has simply shifted more and more to the phonologically based methods.

Over and above this one must make a clear distinction between the purely formal characterization of the script and how the script is actually used by fluent readers of Japanese. Large numbers of logographic elements clearly exist in Japanese, but recall that even logographic elements can be recoded so as to represent phonological elements directly, as we discussed in Section 4.2. Thus we would assume that the kokuji 鱈 *tara* 'cod' has a representation like that of Chinese 人 *rén* 'person' in (4.5), given in (4.6) below:

(4.6)
$$\begin{bmatrix} \text{PHON} & \langle tara \rangle_{1*} \\ \text{SYNSEM} & \begin{bmatrix} \text{CAT } noun \\ \text{SEM } cod_{2*} \end{bmatrix} \\ \text{ORTH} & \{\text{鱈}_{1,2}\} \end{bmatrix}$$

There are two kinds of evidence that this has happened in Japanese. First, there is psycholinguistic evidence from Horodeck (1987) and Matsunaga (1994) demonstrating that readers of Japanese access *phonological* representations when they read kanji; this evidence will be discussed in Section 5.2. Secondly, kanji (like characters in Chinese) may be used purely for their phonological value, ignoring their semantic value: In this usage they are called *ateji.* (Of course this is precisely the way in which they were used in early Japanese manyō'gana.) An example is 珈琲 *kōhī* 'coffee' (Smith, 1996, page 210), where the component characters 珈 *kō* ('ornamental hatpin') and 琲 *hī* ('string of many pearls') are used purely for phonological reasons, with the independent meanings of the characters being irrelevant. Thus we may assume a purely phonographic analysis for 珈琲, as in (4.7):

(4.7)
$$\left[\begin{array}{ll} \text{PHON} & \left[\text{SYLS}\langle \text{kō}_{1*}\ \text{hī}_{2*}\rangle\right] \\ \text{SYNSEM} & \left[\begin{array}{l}\text{CAT } \textit{noun}\\ \text{SEM } \textit{coffee}\end{array}\right] \\ \text{ORTH} & \{\text{珈}_1, \text{琲}_2\}\end{array}\right]$$

Ateji really involve exactly the same process by which one can write the English sentence *I see you forgot that* as <i c u 4got that>; the difference is that specific ateji are an accepted standard part of Japanese writing.

On the second question, semantic–semantic characters in Japanese (and in Chinese also) certainly give some indication of what a purely logographic system might look like. Now, in their reply to Sampson (1994), DeFrancis and Unger (1994) argue against the possibility of a learnable purely logographic system by citing the case of military codes. In such codes (as distinct from *ciphers*), words are randomly substituted for each other, so that *battleship* might be transmitted as *grapefruit* and *attack* might be transmitted as *fallacious.* Such systems are indeed unlearnable (nobody, presumably, has sufficient memory), but the example is not entirely fair either: The system has no structure, which is of course why it is so effective for its intended purpose. Semantic–semantic characters provide what seems like a more reasonable model. There would be a limited set of primitives – in the case of Chinese and Japanese writing, the components of the characters – and there would be a calculus that defines how they are to be combined. Of course there would be no phonological cues to the learner; rather, the learner would need to learn to associate collections of purely semantic information with intended words or morphemes. It seems fair to guess that such a system would be extremely difficult to design, which is presumably part of the reason such a system never has been designed. And it seems fair to guess that such a system would also be difficult to learn, though presumably not as difficult as a military code. For the latter reason alone such a system would not serve the needs of a society in which reading is taken as a basic skill to be mastered as rapidly as possible by a large number of people since most people in a society have little time for complex linguistic games. To serve those needs a writing system must have a significant phonographic component.

4.4 Some Further Examples

In this chapter we have given an overview of some of the kinds of linguistic information that may be encoded by orthographic elements. We have proposed a taxonomy of writing systems based on the kind of phonographic elements used in the system and the amount of logography present in the system. However, unequivocally phonographic elements, and the kinds of semantically motivated logographic elements that we have considered, by no means exhaust the possible functions of orthographic devices. We close this chapter with three mildly esoteric kinds of functions: an orthographic plural marker in Syriac; reduplication markers; and cancellation signs. In each case we give a formal description in terms of our model.

4.4.1 Syriac Syame

The Syriac *syame* is a pair of dots that marks plurality in nouns and adjectives in Syriac and some other Aramaic dialects (Daniels, 1996a, page 507). For example, the plural of ܡܠܟܐ ← <mlkʔ> /malkā/ 'king' is written ܡܠܟ̈ܐ ← <mlk"ʔ> /malke/ (with *syame* transliterated as "̲"). In unvocalized text, the *syame* are often the only mark of plurality, so one can plausibly analyze this device as logographic, in this case being licensed by the SYNSEM feature [+PL]. A representation for /malke/ 'kings' is given in (4.8):

(4.8)
$$\begin{bmatrix} \text{PHON} & \langle m_{1*}\, al_{2*}\, k_{3*}\, e\rangle \\ \text{ORTH} & \{\{< m >_1, < l >_2, < k >_3, <ʔ>\}, \{< \underline{''} >_4\}\} \\ \text{SYNSEM} & \begin{bmatrix} \text{CAT } noun \\ \text{PL } +_{4*} \end{bmatrix} \end{bmatrix}$$

(Ultimately, the *syame* will catenate with the orthographic expression of the word as a whole; therefore the letters in the word are grouped here (using '{}') separately from the *syame*.) Since the PL attribute overlaps with the phonological information in the word, the *syame*, as the orthographic representation of [+PL], catenate – more specifically downwards catenate – with the orthographic representation of the phonological information in the word, in this case the letters <m>, <l>, <k>, and <ʔ>.

The exact placement of the *syame* above the word depends upon the particular letters in the word. If ܪ <r> is present, the *syame* are attracted to it and are written as a second dot over the <r>: ܪ̈. Otherwise the *syame* are written preferably near the end of the word, avoiding the letters <l> and <ʔ>, which have long ascenders.

The categorical requirements that the *syame* appear above the word; that they must appear above <r> if there is one are captured by the rules in (4.9) and (4.10). The first places the syame as the graphical expression of [+pl] above the graphical expression of the noun or adjective w. The second reassociates the *syame* to the position of the <r> in the word, if there is one; note that if more than one <r> is present, the *syame* can occur on either one. Other details of *syame*-placement we assume to be stylistic.

(4.9) $\gamma(w \cdot [+\mathrm{pl}]) = \mathit{syame} \overset{\downarrow}{\cdot} \gamma(w).$

(4.10) Let $\gamma(w)_{1...i-1}$ denote the first $i-1$ letters of $\gamma(w)$, $\gamma(w)_i$ the ith letter, and $\gamma(w)_{i+1...n}$ the remaining letters. If $\gamma(w)_i$ is <r>, then:
$\mathit{syame} \overset{\downarrow}{\cdot} \gamma(w) \rightarrow \gamma(w)_{1...i-1} \overset{\rightarrow}{\cdot} [\mathit{syame} \overset{\downarrow}{\cdot} \gamma(w)_i] \overset{\rightarrow}{\cdot} \gamma(w)_{i+1...n}.$

Note that we would say that in Syriac the SLU is the word.

4.4.2 Reduplication Markers

A number of writing systems, including earlier forms of Malay and Bahasa Indonesia as well as Khmer, have markers that indicate repetition of preceding material. Khmer, for instance, has a sign that marks the repetition of the preceding word or word group (Schiller, 1996, page 472). (In Malay and Bahasa Indonesia a raised '2' was used.) Such signs might appear to constitute a counterexample to regularity. To identify where such signs can be written, the mapping $M_{ORL \rightarrow \Gamma}$ would have to identify copied stretches of linguistic material, something that cannot be handled by finite-state devices for unbounded copy lengths. However, as far as I have been able to ascertain, these devices are not used to mark arbitrary copies of surface strings, but rather only copies that arise from some form of morphological reduplication. We can reasonably assume that the lexical representation of a reduplicated form indicates that a given stretch of linguistic material has been copied. For example, standard autosegmental analyses of reduplication (Marantz, 1982, and much subsequent work) assume that the base that is copied is affixed or compounded with a morpheme that is lexically phonologically empty, but which derives its surface phonological material by copying from the base. Clearly such reduplicating morphemes must be marked as such in the lexical representation of constructs that contain them, and we only need assume that this information is indicated as part of the representation at the ORL.

For example, let's say that we have a form like *oraŋoraŋ*, where we will assume for the sake of argument that the first portion is the base and the second is the copy. The information about which is the base and which the copy is known to the morphology and presumably could be lexically marked as such. For instance, one might imagine a representation such as that in (4.11), where the copy is marked with labeled brackets:

(4.11) $ora\eta[_{copy}ora\eta]_{copy}$

Assume that the writing system in question marks reduplicated constituents using the symbol '²'. Then one can write a rule that simply states that the image under $M_{ORL \to \Gamma}$ of any span w bracketed by $[_{copy}$ and $]_{copy}$ is '²':

(4.12) $\gamma([_{copy}w]_{copy}) = \ ^2$

Thus if we assume a spelling of <orang> for the base, the spelling of $ora\eta[_{copy}ora\eta]_{copy}$ would become <orang² >.

4.4.3 Cancellation Signs

A number of scripts have cancellation signs, used to mark symbols that are not pronounced. For example, Syriac marks letters that are not pronounced in some dialects with a diagonal bar (called *mbaṭlānā*) under the letter (George Kiraz, personal communication). Similarly, Thai (Diller, 1996) uses a cancellation sign to indicate letters that are not to be pronounced, mostly in words derived from Sanskrit, which are spelled etymologically in Modern Thai orthography.

Cancellation signs thus mark graphemes that are not licensed by any linguistic material. More formally, they mark graphemes α where the image of α under the *inverse* of $M_{ORL \to \Gamma}$ (which we will denote here as γ^{-1}) is empty: $\gamma^{-1}(\alpha) = \emptyset$. Thus, given a cancellation sign κ, we want to rewrite α as $\kappa \cdot \alpha$ just in case $\gamma^{-1}(\alpha) = \emptyset$:

(4.13) For an orthographic symbol α and cancellation sign κ if $\gamma^{-1}(\alpha) = \emptyset$ then $\alpha \to \kappa \cdot \alpha$.

5 Psycholinguistic Evidence

There is to date a large literature on the psycholinguistics of reading and writing, which deals in the question of how humans extract linguistic information from written text, and how they compose written text given a mental linguistic representation. Some useful general collections include Frost and Katz (1992), de Gelder and Morais (1995), Perfetti, Rieben, and Fayol (1997), and Balota, Flores d'Arcais, and Rayner (1990); there has also been a large amount of work on reading and writing Chinese script, including the papers collected in Chen and Tzeng (1992) and Wang, Inhoff, and Chen (1999).

Since we are proposing a computational model of writing systems and their relation to linguistic structure, it makes sense to ask what "psychological reality" there is in the model that we have proposed. It is not my intention here to review the various psycholinguistic models (many of them mutually inconsistent) that have been proposed. Rather the approach that will be taken will be to examine the model and see if there is any support in the psycholinguistic literature for some of the properties of the model.

Clearly such an approach requires caution. What do we mean by "psychologically realistic"? This is a term that unfortunately has been much abused in the history of linguistics and computational linguistics. In the context of the present discussion we need to be rather precise about the level of granularity at which we would want to investigate the psychological reality of our model of writing systems. For example, there are specific computational devices – finite-state transducers in particular – that have been proposed as plausible computational mechanisms for mapping between written form and linguistic representation. It seems unlikely that these specific devices are plausible models of what goes on inside a reader's (or writer's) head.

However, there are more macroscopic properties of the model that do make sense to compare with the results of psycholinguistic research. I will focus on two such properties here:

- **Architectural Uniformity**: The same model of the relation between orthography and linguistic form is proposed for all writing systems.
- **Dual Routes**: The model makes a distinction between *spelling rules* and the *lexical specifications*, possibly including marked

orthographic information, that these rules operate on. It is assumed that in normal reading orthographic representations are mapped to lexical elements (i.e., the ORLs of morphemes, words, and phrases), and thence to pronunciations. However, in most writing systems, for most words, only partial lexical orthographic specifications are required, with the bulk of the spelling being predictable by spelling rules. Inverted, these spelling rules can serve as rules for inferring an ORL representation from spelling; if one then *composes* these inverted spelling rules with whatever rules or principles of the language predict the actual pronunciation from the ORL, one can derive pronunciations for spelled words without actually "consulting" the lexicon. Thus we have an additional rule-based path to pronunciation that bypasses the lexicon.

One of the main topics in the literature on reading has been the question of the number of routes by which a reader can get from a written word into a phonological representation. As we describe in more detail below, the most common assumption in the literature is that there are at least two such routes; these may be characterized broadly as via the lexicon or via "grapheme-to-phoneme correspondences."

Within this framework, one question that has received a great deal of attention is whether writing systems differ in which of these two routes is taken. The *Orthographic Depth Hypothesis* (henceforth ODH) claims, in its strongest form, that some languages – the orthographically "deep" languages, of which English is an oft-cited example – require readers to go via the lexicon; whereas orthographically "shallow" languages – Serbo-Croatian is supposedly such a case – only make use of the grapheme-to-phoneme route. One might be tempted to equate this notion of orthographic depth with the notion of the depth of the ORL, discussed in Chapter 3. But there is a crucial difference: We claim that languages differ in the depth of their orthography, and in the regularity of their "grapheme-phoneme" correspondences, but *not* in the *manner* in which one maps from orthography to linguistic representation, or ultimately to pronunciation.

It seems that one can draw two conclusions from the literature (though it would be disingenuous to suggest that there is anything like a consensus on these points). Both of these conclusions are consistent with the properties of the model that we outlined above:

- Multiple routes from written form to pronunciation are available.
- The ODH, at least in its strongest form, is incorrect: All writing systems can be shown to make use of both a lexical and a phonological (i.e, rule-based) route.

The remainder of this chapter is organized as follows. In Section 5.1, we will outline the evidence for multiple routes, and we will discuss the ODH and give some of the evidence that has been presented, both in support of and against this hypothesis. Section 5.2 continues this discussion with some evidence from Chinese and Japanese – two writing systems that would appear on the face of it to be unequivocally "deep" – showing that even there one finds evidence of "shallow" processing. Finally, not all psycholinguists support the hypothesis of multiple routes, and the most vocal advocates of an alternative single-route approach have been the connectionists. A somewhat dated, though still influential work in this mold is Seidenberg and McClelland (1989). Section 5.3 gives a brief critique of this work.

5.1 Multiple Routes and the Orthographic Depth Hypothesis

Two kinds of experiments figure prominently in the psycholinguistic work on reading. One involves *lexical decision*, and the other *naming*.

In a lexical decision paradigm, subjects are presented with a written stimulus (usually on a CRT screen) and are asked to answer (e.g., by pressing a button on a keyboard) whether or not the stimulus in question is a word of their language. Their reaction time is measured, as is the correctness of their responses.

In the naming paradigm, subjects are again presented with a written stimulus, but this time they are asked to pronounce the stimulus aloud – to "name" the word that is on the screen. In this case what is normally measured is the time between the presentation of the stimulus and the onset of vocalization.

The ODH has implications both for naming and for lexical decision, but it is perhaps easiest to illustrate the idea behind the hypothesis in the context of a model of naming. One such model is presented schematically in Figure 5.1; this model is adapted, with simplifications, from Besner and Smith (1992, Figure 1), and the presentation of the ODH hypothesis draws heavily on their discussion of this topic.

The model in Figure 5.1 allows for three routes to naming. The simplest is labeled 'A' in the figure and involves the application of "grapheme-to-phoneme" rules. In that scheme, input text is fed into a block of rules, and a phonological representation is derived solely via that block of rules. Crucially, there is no lexical access involved. To take an example, the string <peat> in English can be pronounced by applying the rules <p>→ /p/, <ea>→ /i/, and <t>→ /t/, deriving the pronunciation /pit/. Since this route involves assembling a phonological representation on the fly, it is often termed the *assembled* route.

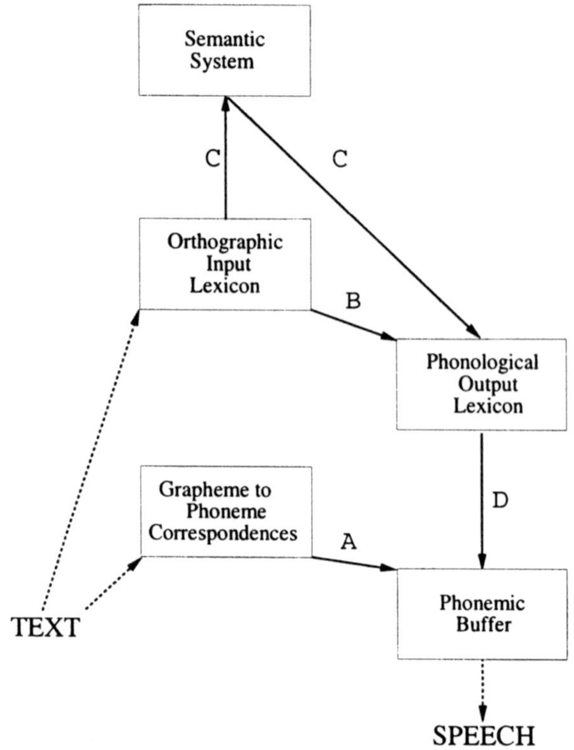

Figure 5.1. A model of reading a word aloud, simplified from Besner and Smith (1992).

The second and third routes do involve lexical access, to varying degrees. The route labeled 'B–D' involves the *orthographic input lexicon*, which stores words in their orthographic forms, presumably with associated phonological information; it corresponds pretty much exactly to the orthographic lexical entry in the ORL in our model. Naming via route 'B–D' thus involves lexical access, but of a fairly shallow kind, in that only the formal properties of the word are addressed. Under this scheme <peat> would be pronounced by matching the string <p>, <e>, <a>, <t> against the lexical entry for *peat* in the orthographic input lexicon, and retrieving the stored pronunciation /pit/.

The third route, 'C–D,' is the deepest. It too involves the orthographic input lexicon, but it also involves accessing the meaning of the word. In this case, semantic attributes of the lexical entry of *peat* would be accessed, and from there one would derive a pronunciation for the word associated with that set of attributes.[1] In normal readers under normal conditions accessing the semantics should not in principle yield a different result from the 'B–D' route. Different results may be obtained, however, in neurologically impaired patients, as we shall see momentarily. Routes involving lexical access derive pronunciations for written words by addressing a lexical representation and hence are often termed *addressed* routes.

As Besner and Smith note (page 47) there is evidence for the existence of each of these routes in readers of *deep* orthographies, like that of English. Some of the most compelling evidence comes from patients with various kinds of brain lesions that impair their ability to read aloud in various ways. Specifically:

- One class of patients finds it easier to name words whose spellings are "more regular" given their pronunciations. For example *cave* follows the rules of English spelling better than *have* does, and such patients find it easier to correctly name *cave* than *have*. Plausibly, such patients have been damaged in such a way that the grapheme-to-phoneme rule path A is the only one left open to them.
- At the other extreme, some patients make semantic errors when asked to name: For <tulip> they may answer *crocus*, for example. A reasonable explanation is that for these patients the semantic access route C–D has become favored (and this only imperfectly).
- In the middle are patients who have no particular problems naming ordinary words (either *have* or *cave*), and who don't tend to make semantic errors. Yet they are impaired in that they are unable to read nonwords. This suggests that they are using neither a grapheme-to-phoneme strategy (route A) nor do they seem to be using a semantic strategy (route C–D). Rather they are forced by their impairment into route B–D. This correctly predicts that they will be able to read words that are in the lexicon already, but not novel words.

We turn now to the ODH. Two flavors of this hypothesis have been proposed in the literature, the *strong* form and the *weak* form. The strong ODH can be stated as follows:

[1] This third, semantic, route is the one that has no direct correspondent in our model, although it would of course be easy enough to add an additional layer of semantic processing whereby lexical entries at the ORL map to a semantic representation, and thence back to phonological entries.

(5.1) *Orthographic depth hypothesis (strong form)*:
Readers of languages that have completely regular grapheme-phoneme correspondences lack an orthographic input lexicon.

In other words, route A is the only route available to such readers. In the literature on the ODH, the most often cited instance of a shallow orthography is probably Serbo-Croatian.[2]

A (significantly) weaker version of the hypothesis – one supported, for example, by Katz and Frost (1992) – states that all written languages allow for both a grapheme-to-phoneme correspondence route (route A) and for a lexical access route (routes B–D, or perhaps C–D): But the cost of each route directly relates to the type of orthography (deep or shallow) involved. In shallow orthographies, the grapheme-to-phoneme route is usually cheaper in naming, though there may be instances in which lexical access is involved. Contrariwise, in a deep orthography, lexical access will typically be cheaper to use in naming, though there will be instances where the grapheme-to-phoneme route might be used.

Insofar as it makes a far stronger claim about the mental process of reading, the strong ODH is more interesting than the weak ODH. We shall therefore start by outlining the evidence that has been marshalled, both for and against this version of the hypothesis. Our conclusion will be that the evidence against the strong ODH seems on the whole more compelling than the evidence for it, and that therefore there seems to be no reason to accept that readers of different orthographies have fundamentally different mental architectures. Rather the evidence seems more consistent with a model (possibly like the weak ODH) where readers of all orthographies use fundamentally the same model, though of course differences among orthographies will inevitably lead to differences in how the mental resources are allocated.

5.1.1 Evidence for the Orthographic Depth Hypothesis

According to the strong ODH, the processing of shallow orthographies in naming involves pathway A in Figure 5.1. Thus, it bypasses both of the lexical pathways B–D and C–D. This would appear to make the rather clear prediction that readers of shallow orthographies should fail to show effects

[2] Note however that Serbo-Croatian orthography does not mark lexical accent, which is determined by (unwritten) lexical properties of the word much as in the case of Russian stress (Section 1.2.1; Seidenberg, 1990, pages 50–51; Wayles Browne, personal communication). This is the case whether we are talking about Croatian (written in the Roman alphabet) or Serbian (written in the Cyrillic alphabet). Thus it is by no means possible to predict every aspect of the pronunciation of a word in Serbo-Croatian. This differs from the case of Spanish where almost without exception one can predict the pronunciation of a written form without consideration of what lexical form it may represent.

of lexical access in naming tasks. In contrast, readers of deep orthographies should show such effects since in general pathway A is not sufficient to correctly name written forms, and one of the lexical routes must be used.

Two widely reported lexical effects are the effect of word frequency and lexical priming. The *lexical frequency* effect relates the frequency of particular lexical items with the speed with which they can be retrieved from the lexicon: Other things being equal more frequent words are retrieved more quickly. The lexical *priming* effect relates the speed with which a word will be retrieved, to the presence of a semantically related word. For instance, if the word *couch* has been used in a previous context, semantically related *sofa* will be retrieved faster than if a semantically related word had not been used. The speed of lexical retrieval is often measured using a lexical decision paradigm, and in this paradigm, both priming and lexical frequency effects have been demonstrated both in languages that have deep orthographies and in shallow orthographies (Besner and Smith, 1992, page 50).

Given these observations, it would appear to be strong confirmation of the ODH that priming and word frequency effects were *not* observed in naming tasks for Serbo-Croatian, a language with a supposedly shallow orthography (Katz and Feldman, 1983; Frost, Katz, and Bentin, 1987). In these experiments, subjects were asked to name both real words and plausible nonwords; the expected priming and frequency effects did not obtain for the real word stimuli. In contrast, readers of deep orthographies, like that of English, do show these lexical access effects in similarly constructed naming tasks (Besner and Smith, 1992).

Still, Besner and Smith observe (page 50):

> ... in contrast to the large number of papers showing priming and frequency effects in deep orthographies, the attempt to prove the null hypothesis of no priming and no frequency effects in the oral reading of shallow orthographies rests upon a very narrow data base. There have been only *two* reports that a related context does not facilitate naming relative to an unrelated contexts (Frost, Katz & Bentin, 1987; Katz & Feldman, 1983), and only *one* report that word frequency does not affect naming (Frost et al., 1987)

As Besner and Smith note, one critical design feature of both the Frost et al. and Katz and Feldman experiments is that, as we have already described, they used both words and nonwords as stimuli. Presumably nonwords can *only* be pronounced via the assembled route since they have, after all, no lexical representations. Could this then not simply bias subjects to *always* use the assembled route? After all, in a shallow orthography this will nearly always work. So what these experiments report may be indicative not of what readers of shallow orthographies do in reading normal text (where the majority of words will be known), but rather simply be the result of a strategy that subjects have adopted under the conditions of this experiment.

5.1.2 Evidence against the Orthographic Depth Hypothesis

Besner and Smith discuss several pieces of evidence that would appear to undermine the conclusions reached in the Katz and Feldman and Frost et al. papers, including data from Serbo-Croatian, Persian (Farsi), and Japanese written in kana. For Serbo-Croatian, experiments were performed where only real words were presented to subjects. In this case, both lexical frequency and priming effects were found.

The Persian results were originally reported in Baluch and Besner (1991). Persian orthography is an Arabic-derived abjad (Kaye, 1996) (and see Section 6.1 for an explanation of the term *abjad*): For many words the phonological information provided by the written form is incomplete, in particular information about the vowels. However, as in Arabic, the consonant letters <w>, <y>, and <'> (*alif*) can function as vowels (/u/, /i/, and /a/, respectively), and some words written with these symbols happen to be complete in their phonological specifications. Thus Persian provides both cases where lexical access is necessary to name a written form and cases where lexical access is in principle not necessary. The ODH would predict lexical access effects – word frequency and priming effects – for those words that are relatively "deep" and no such effects for "shallow" words. Baluch and Besner's data support this expectation, but *only when a significant portion of nonwords were included among the stimuli.* When such nonword stimuli were not presented, lexical access effects were obtained for both "shallow" and "deep" words. This, then, supports the contention that the reported lack of such lexical access effects in previous work on Serbo-Croatian may be due to a strategy adopted by subjects when given a task where the assembled route is often required. When nonwords are removed, the assembled route is no longer automatically adopted, and subjects behave as if they are uniformly using an addressed route.

The experiment on reading of Japanese kana reported in Besner and Hildebrandt (1987) leads to a similar conclusion. Japanese has an even more extreme case of a mixed orthography than Persian, using both Chinese characters (kanji), many of which function logographically as we have seen (Section 4.3, though see Section 5.2.2 below), as well two kana core syllabarics – hiragana and katakana, which are fairly phonemic in their representation.[3] Besner and Hildebrandt presented subjects with stimuli written in katakana, which is normally used to write foreign loan words. The stimuli were of two types: words normally written in katakana and words that would normally be written in kanji. The latter group were thus written in an unfamiliar way, whereas the former group was orthographically familiar. However, if the ODH were correct, this familiarity should

[3] Note however, that pitch accent, which is lexically distinctive in Japanese, is not marked in the kana scripts.

have no effect on naming speed since katakana is in any event a shallow orthography. Registering a form as "familiar" or "unfamiliar" presumes that one is matching a written form against a lexical entry, yet if one assumes, following the ODH, that kana is read using only pathway A from Figure 5.1, then no matching against lexical entries can be involved. In fact, Besner and Hildebrandt's results show definite effects of familiarity, with words that are not normally written in katakana (unfamiliar orthographic forms) taking significantly longer to name than words that are normally written in katakana (familiar orthographic forms). This suggests that lexical access must be involved in reading katakana, contrary to the expectations of the ODH.

5.2 "Shallow" Processing in "Deep" Orthographies

The previous section has examined some of the psycholinguistic evidence surrounding the ODH, which in its strong form claims that readers of shallow orthographies largely bypass lexical access when reading aloud. The bulk of the evidence does not seem to support that radical conclusion. Rather there seems to be evidence that readers of both shallow and deep orthographies do perform lexical access when naming, except under experimental conditions that favor adopting a uniform assembled route.

Yet surely there is a sense that "deep" orthographies, such as English or Chinese, typically require lexical access that is "deeper" than one would expect for a shallow orthography? For example, while naming a Spanish form such as *cocer* 'to cook' may after all usually involve lexical access, presumably the whole lexical entry doesn't need to be retrieved, but rather just the phonological information, which corresponds fairly straightforwardly to the orthographic form. In contrast, to read a Chinese word such as 馬 *mǎ* 'horse', where there seems to be no indication of the pronunciation in the orthographic form, presumably one has to retrieve the whole lexical entry. Indeed, as we have noted elsewhere, it has often been supposed that Chinese writing is primarily logographic in that each character represents not a phonological unit at all, but rather a word or morpheme. In this section we discuss evidence that in Chinese and Japanese – two canonical examples of deep orthographies – rapid access to the phonology, without (complete) lexical access, is possible. This then provides evidence of a complementary nature to what was presented in the previous section: A "deep" orthography can nonetheless show shallow processing effects.

5.2.1 Phonological Access in Chinese

In an experiment reported by Tzeng (1994), Chinese readers were presented with a series of Chinese characters presented in rapid succession, possibly containing some intervening character-like nonsense material.[4] The task for the subjects was simply to write down the characters that they were presented with. The stimuli were presented with an interval of between 90 and 110 milliseconds, fast enough to result in an effect of *repetition blindness* under appropriate conditions. Repetition blindness, first reported in Kanwisher (1987), denotes a situation where two tokens of a particular type are presented in rapid succession, and where subjects fail to note that more than one token was presented. In the context of Tzeng's experiment, presentation of two identical characters (e.g., two instances of 勝 *shèng* 'win') resulted in a mean accuracy rate in subjects' performance of about 51%. In contrast, presentation of a control sequence of two distinct and *nonhomophonous* characters (e.g., 勝 *shèng* and 迪 *dí*) resulted in a higher accuracy (around 61%). Crucially, presentation of two graphically dissimilar but homographic characters (e.g., 勝 *shèng* and 聖 *shèng* 'holy') resulted in a mean error rate of 52%, or the same as the rate for identical characters.[5]

The critical factor in this experiment is that the homographic pairs chosen were graphically distinct, so it is not plausible that the subjects were simply confusing the characters at a visual level. Neither is it possible that the subjects were doing full lexical access and confusing the two instances at a lexical level. Putting aside the implausibility of doing lexical access in as little time as 90–110 milliseconds (most experiments are more consistent with lexical access requiring on the order of a few hundred milliseconds, especially for lower frequency items), full lexical access could not be involved, since the characters in question correspond to different morphemes: 勝 *shèng* 'win' and 聖 *shèng* 'holy' certainly must have different lexical entries, and if the subjects were doing lexical access then they surely would have registered the fact that they were dealing with a succession of distinct characters. The only solution, it seems, is to conclude that Chinese characters map, in the initial stages of processing, to a level of representation that is basically phonological. Put in another way, while Chinese characters certainly contain nonphonological information, it is nonetheless the case that skilled Chinese readers have learned an association between characters and their corresponding syllables that allows for very rapid access to the phonological form, in effect bypassing the rest of lexical access.

Tzeng's results are consistent with other more recent findings. For example Perfetti and Tan (1998) report results of a priming experiment where

[4] The "nonsense" material used was Korean Hankul syllable glyphs, which are of course meaningless to Chinese readers who do not know Korean but have the useful property that they look somewhat like Chinese characters.

[5] The behavior for high and low frequency characters was different, with high frequency homophonic pairs showing a higher accuracy than repeated characters, though a lower accuracy than different and nonhomophonic pairs; for low frequency characters the performance for homophonic pairs was actually significantly *worse* than the performance for repeated identical character pairs.

subjects were presented with a character prime followed immediately by a target, which the subjects were then asked to read aloud as quickly and accurately as possible. The time difference between the start of the prime and start of the target – the *Stimulus Onset Asynchrony* or SOA – was varied, as was the nature of the prime: The prime could either be graphically similar, homophonous, semantically related (either vaguely or "precisely"), or an unrelated control. A stronger priming effect resulted in a shorter and generally more accurate naming of the target. With the shortest SOAs (43 msec) the strongest priming was obtained from graphically similar characters, but as the SOA increased to 57 msec, the graphic similarity effect attenuated. Across the longer SOA conditions, homophonous primes consistently had a stronger effect than semantically similar primes. In other words, the naming of target characters is facilitated more by a prime that sounds the same, than with a prime that has a related meaning.

In the context of the computational model, a sensible interpretation of this class of results would appear to be that skilled readers of Chinese, in addition to knowing which characters represent which lexical entries, have also learned a set of "grapheme-to-phoneme" correspondences by which they know, for example, that 勝 maps to *shèng*. In terms of the discussion in Section 4.2, this amounts to saying that the relation between the syllable *shèng* and the entire character 勝 implicit in the representation has been extracted as a rule by the skilled Chinese reader; we return to this point in Section 5.2.4.

5.2.2 Phonological Access in Japanese

Tzeng's results for Chinese are mirrored by the results obtained for Japanese kanji by two studies, Horodeck (1987) and Matsunaga (1994).

Horodeck's goal was to refute the widespread view that Chinese characters are *ideographic* in the sense that they directly represent ideas in the mind of the reader; this view has of course been heavily attacked by others, most notably DeFrancis (1984, 1989). To this end, Horodeck conducted two studies, one involving writing and the other reading. In the writing study, spontaneously written short essays from 2,410 Japanese speakers with a variety of occupations and educational backgrounds were studied for spelling errors involving kanji. Horodeck classified the errors along three dimensions:

- whether the errorful character had the right sound (i.e., was a homophone of the correct character);
- whether the errorful character had the right form (i.e., shared a major structural component with the correct character); and
- whether the errorful character had the right meaning (i.e., was similar enough in its sense to the correct character).

For the purposes of Horodeck's intentions, the most useful kinds of errors were errors involving either characters with the right sound, but wrong form and wrong meaning, or characters with the wrong sound, wrong form, but right meaning. All other categories of error are either ambiguous or could be explained purely on the basis of formal similarities between the error and the target. In Horodeck's corpus there were 136 right-sound/wrong-form/wrong-meaning errors; among these errors 127 involved *on* (Sino-Japanese) readings and 9 involved kun (native) readings. In contrast, there were a total of 14 wrong-sound/wrong-form/right-meaning errors. Thus, in spontaneous writing one is much more likely to make an error on the basis of sound than on the basis of meaning.

Horodeck's second experiment involved a reading test where kanji with inappropriate meanings were inserted in a text, and where the object was to measure how often these errors were detected. All of the errors in this portion of the study involved multicharacter compounds with *on* readings. Kanji occur much more frequently in these constructions than they do either with kun readings or as single characters with *on* readings ("*on*-isolates"), and it was therefore easier to construct stimuli using multicharacter *on* constructions. For the stimulus texts, newspaper headlines were chosen since these have a higher density of kanji than normal running prose. The error stimuli used were of two types: right-sound/right-form/wrong-meaning and wrong-sound/right-form/wrong-meaning. Readers on average detected only 40.5% of the former kind of stimulus, as opposed to 54.3% of the latter kind of stimulus. This difference was statistically significant and demonstrated that errors homophonous with their targets are harder to detect than errors that are nonhomophonous.

Matsunaga's (1994) experiment, like Horodeck's second experiment, involved homophonous and nonhomophonous kanji errors. However, rather than asking readers to mark errors in newspaper headlines, she instead measured readers' eye movements as they read full sentences containing such errors. The assumption here is that errors, when detected, will disrupt the reader's reading and will translate into fixations on the location of the error, which in turn will show up in the eye-tracking data. Matsunaga found that the rate of fixations per error was significantly higher in the case of nonhomophonic errors than in the case of homophonic errors. In other words, nonhomophonic errors were easier to detect, a result that replicates Horodeck's second study.

The studies of Horodeck and Matsunaga thus lead to the same conclusion for Japanese reading of kanji as does Tzeng's study of Chinese. Users of both writing systems more readily miss errors that are homophonous with their targets, and they more readily miss repeated characters if they are homophonous with a previously presented character. All of these studies therefore support the idea that Chinese characters map directly to phonological representations in the minds of fluent readers.

5.2.3 *Evidence for the Function of Phonetic Components in Chinese*

Psycholinguistic evidence for low-level phonological processing of Chinese, of the kind discussed in Section 5.2.1, seems on the face of it to be direct confirmation of the claim of DeFrancis (1984, 1989), also discussed in Chapter 4, that Chinese writing is essentially phonographic in design, though obviously imperfectly so. Recall that the most powerful evidence for this claim is the large number of semantic–phonetic characters, where the pronunciation is indicated, to a greater or lesser degree, by a phonetic radical. The importance of phonetic information in the development of the Chinese writing system is unequivocal, and it is even plausible to suppose that the phonological information provided by the phonetic component is an aid to learning the writing system. What Tzeng's experiments show is that skilled Chinese readers have internalized the written symbols as a kind of alphabet, so that they can retrieve pronunciations for each of the symbols in the absence of any further lexical information. But one must be careful about drawing a connection between the results of this experiment and the evidence adduced by DeFrancis. To see this, consider the following thought experiment. Suppose that the Chinese writing system were, counterfactually, completely arbitrary in its mapping between orthographic symbols and their pronunciation; that is, there would be no equivalent to a "phonetic" component, and therefore no way to look at a novel character and guess its pronunciation. Suppose furthermore that someone had mastered this writing system as well as literate Chinese readers master the real Chinese writing system. One might expect that the results of Tzeng's experiments on this pseudo-Chinese would be identical to what she demonstrated with real Chinese. If that turned out to be the case, then one would have to conclude that a skilled reader of any writing system is likely to "phonologically recode" the system in that they would be able to map between written symbols and pronunciation without performing full lexical access.[6]

So Tzeng's experiment might not relate directly to DeFrancis's results at all. We must then ask what the evidence is that readers of Chinese actually make use of the phonetic information provided in the majority of Chinese characters.

In fact, there is such evidence; one relevant experiment is that of Hung, Tzeng, and Tzeng (1992). In that experiment a Stroop picture-word interference paradigm was used to test subjects' abilities to name a picture when a single-character word of varying degrees of congruence to the picture was simultaneously presented. For example, suppose a picture of a basket is presented. A completely congruent word would be the word 籃 *lán* 'basket'; following Hung et al.'s terminology, we will call this word/character *CC*

[6] Coulmas (1989, page 50) makes exactly this point when he notes that a skilled reader of Chinese can equally well map between a character such as 筆 and its phonological (*bǐ*) and lexical ('pen') values.

for "completely congruent." An example of a completely incongruent (CI) word would be 釘 *dīng* 'nail'. Partially congruent words were:

- A homophonous (but semantically distinct) character having the same phonetic component as CC, or having CC as a phonetic component, for example 藍 *lán* 'blue'. (SGSS: similar graph, same sound.)
- A homophonous and structurally distinct character: 蘭 *lán* 'orchid'. (DGSS: different graph, same sound.)
- A nonhomophonous character sharing a component with CC: 監 *jiān* 'jail'. (SGDS: similar graph, different sound.)
- A pseudocharacter (PC), where the CC served as the phonetic component of a nonexistent character: 䍀.

Subjects were asked to name the pictures, and their reaction times were recorded, along with their error rates. Not surprisingly, the CC and CI conditions showed the fastest and slowest reaction times, respectively, as well as the best and worst error rates. The other conditions listed above were arranged as follows, ordered from fastest/lowest error to slowest/highest error: PC < SGSS < SGDS < DGSS. As Hung et al. argue, there are two independent effects, one of graphic similarity to the target (CC) character, and one of phonological similarity. Taken together, these results support the later work of Tzeng (1994) in underscoring the importance of phonological information in Chinese, and they also show that the phonetic component is both accessible and used by Chinese readers, since the two non-CC conditions (PC, SGSS) where the phonetic component is the same as that of CC were the ones where subjects performed the best.[7]

5.2.4 Summary

There appears to be evidence that phonological information is both available to and used by readers of Chinese and Japanese. Furthermore, at least for readers of Chinese, information in the phonetic component of the character, when present, is used. When a useful phonetic component does not exist, we assume, as we did in the previous chapter, that the orthographic entry for the

[7] The importance of the phonetic component is further underscored by several studies cited in Hung, Tzeng, and Tzeng (1992, page 127), where it was shown that the phonological consistency of a phonetic component was negatively correlated with the naming latency for characters having that phonetic component.

One might also suppose that Japanese readers make use of the phonetic component when it is both present and useful. Clearly the phonetic component will not generally be useful for kun readings, but for *on* readings, the phonetic component would in many cases have approximately the same utility as it would for the same character in Chinese. One study that seems to support the utility of the phonetic component in Japanese *on* readings is Flores d'Arcais, Saito, and Kawakami (1995).

morpheme is linked simultaneously to both the semantic and phonological entries and that the character thus serves as its own "phonetic component." In the discussion in the previous chapter, we assumed a static representation whereby the orthographic symbol is simply listed as part of the lexical entry of the morpheme, with indices indicating which portions of the symbol correspond to the semantic and phonological fields. What the experimental evidence presented in this section suggests is that skilled Chinese readers have advanced one step further than this static knowledge. So rather than merely representing (Chinese) 鴨 <BIRD+JIĂ> *yā* 'duck' as in (5.2), they have formulated a spelling rule as in (5.3), which would be lexically marked to apply only to this morpheme.

(5.2)

$$\left[\begin{array}{ll} \text{PHON} & \left[\text{SYL}\left[\begin{array}{l}\text{SEG}\left\langle[\text{ONS } y][\text{RIME } a]\right\rangle\\ \text{TONE } 1\end{array}\right]\right]_{1*} \\ \text{SYNSEM} & \left[\begin{array}{l}\text{CAT } noun\\ \text{SEM } duck_{2*}\end{array}\right]\\ \text{ORTH} & \{\text{鳥}_2,\text{甲}_1\}\end{array}\right]$$

(5.3) *yā* → 鳥 <BIRD> $\overset{\leftarrow}{\cdot}$ 甲 <JIĂ> (= 鴨)

(5.4) (鴨 =) 鳥 $\overset{\leftarrow}{\cdot}$ 甲 → *yā*

Inverted, as in (5.4), this rule will map directly between 鴨 and *yā*. The presence of the phonetic component 甲 <JIĂ> on the left-hand side of several such inverted rules will, given the phonological similarity (though certainly not identity in this case), tend to reinforce the salience of the phonetic contribution of that component to the pronunciations of the characters containing it as a phonetic element. And the existence of such inverted rules yields the result that it is possible to map directly between a character and its pronunciation, without lexical access.

The situation in Chinese is really no different in kind from the lexically marked spellings in English. For the word *light*, for example, one must mark the spelling <igh> in the lexicon, since there is no way to predict that spelling from general principles. However, one can certainly extract from the set of words spelled with <igh> the useful generalization that this grapheme sequence is generally pronounced /aɪ/.[8] Imputing a rule that maps 鴨 to *yā* from a lexical representation that states that 'duck' is written

[8] Or, if one prefers to assume a deep ORL for English (see Section 3.2), that it maps to /ī/, which subsequently changes to /aI/ by phonological rule. Note that sets of such inverted rules serve as the basis for linguistically informed approaches to the teaching of reading such as that of Bloomfield and Barnhart (1961).

with the <BIRD> radical and a phonetic component <JIĂ> is merely an instance of the same phenomenon.

5.3 Connectionist Models: The Seidenberg-McClelland Model

As we discussed above, most studies of reading have assumed a dual or multiple route model. By definition such models presume a strict distinction between stored lexical information on the one hand and rules on the other. In separating rules from static lexical information, such psychological models are of course taking a fairly traditional stance, one that is in accord with traditional linguistic models.

As is well known, since the mid-1980s, an alternative view of language has emerged that eschews a formal distinction between rules and lexicon. This is the connectionist view, so called because the belief is that complex systems of behavior can be modeled using large numbers of simple, but massively interconnected units (sometimes called "neurons"). Phenomena that have been termed "rules" or "lexical entries" are merely emergent properties of such interconnected networks. Probably the most famous application of this idea to a problem in natural language is Rumelhart and McClelland's (1986) oft-cited simulation of the learning of the English past tense. Their basic claim was that there was no difference between English regular past tense verbs, which add some variant of /-d/, and irregular (mostly historically "strong" verbs), which involve a change of the stem vowel (along with other changes in some cases): Both types of verbs are learned by their network in the same way, and the network is – to some extent – able to generalize what it has "learned" to new cases. Thus there is no need to posit a formal distinction between rules and stored lexical items, as both "kinds" of knowledge are "learned" by the network in the same way. An effective rebuttal to this paper can be found in Pinker and Prince (1988).

The classic connectionist approach to reading is the system of Seidenberg and McClelland (1989). Naturally, one of the main claims of their theory is that dual-route models are not necessary. In particular, regularly spelled words, such as *ate*, which could in principle be pronounced without reference to lexical information, are learned in the same way as irregularly spelled words (*plaid*), where lexical access seems to be required. Indeed, in subsequent work (Seidenberg, 1990) the model is presented as providing an alternative to the traditional "dual route" model (though see Seidenberg (1992) for a slightly modified position). The work is also cited (Seidenberg, 1997) as a viable alternative to symbolic rule/principle-based approaches of the kind familiar from generative linguistics. There are more recent and arguably more sophisticated connectionist approaches to reading – see, for example, the work of Van Orden and colleagues (Van Orden, Pennington, and Stone, 1990; Stone and Van Orden, 1994) – but Seidenberg and McClelland's paper seems to present the most detailed discussion of a

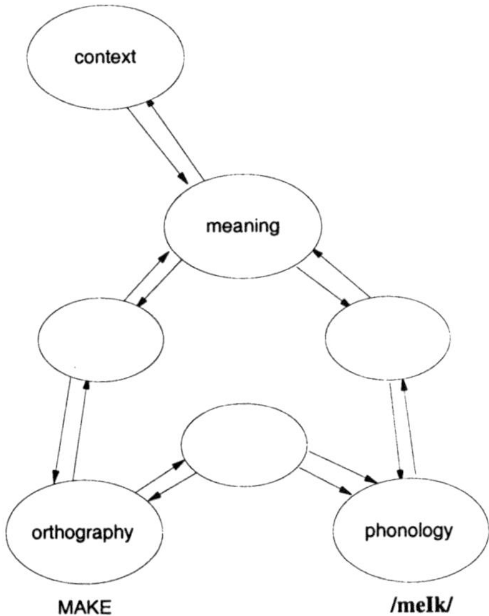

Figure 5.2. The Seidenberg and McClelland model of lexical processing Seidenberg and McClelland, 1989, page 526, Figure 1). Used with permission of the American Psychological Association, Inc.

computational simulation of a connectionist model of reading, as well as the most detailed discussion comparing that model's behavior to experiments on human subjects.

It is not our purpose here to give an extensive review of Seidenberg and McClelland's model. Rather, a very brief summary will be given, and a few of the weaknesses of the approach will be pointed out. The main conclusion will be that Seidenberg and McClelland have failed to provide convincing evidence that their model has learned the task that it is claimed to have learned; thus there is little reason to accept their conclusion that more traditional kinds of models have been superseded.

5.3.1 *Outline of the Model*

Seidenberg and McClelland have in mind a complete model of lexical processing relating orthographic, semantic, phonological, and contextual information. Their model is diagrammed in Figure 5.2.[9] The portion of the model that is actually implemented in the 1989 paper is depicted in

[9] Oddly, morphological information, so crucial for the correct pronunciation of words in many languages, is missing from their conception of the lexical processing system. It is unclear, for instance, where the morphologically determined stress information in Russian (Section 1.2.1) that is crucial for correct vowel pronunciation would fit into the model. Would it be part of "phonology" or "meaning"?

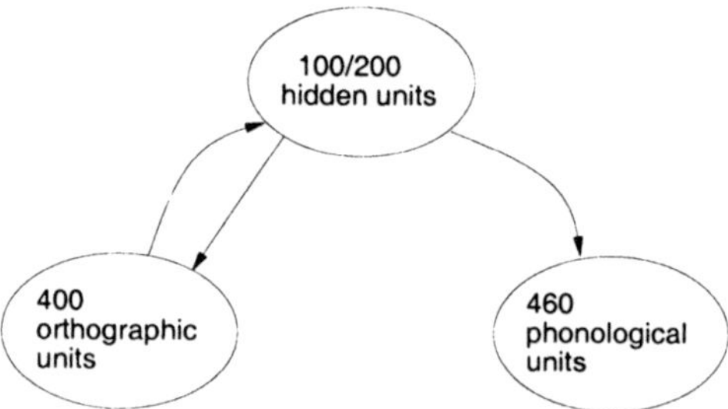

Figure 5.3. The implemented portion of Seidenberg and McClelland's model of lexical processing (Seidenberg and McClelland, 1989, page 527, Figure 2). Used with permission of American Psychological Association, Inc.

Figure 5.3. This system was trained on a set of 2,884 word-pronunciation pairs consisting of all minimally three-letter monosyllables from the Kucera and Francis (1967) wordlist of English, from which they removed "proper nouns, words we judged to be foreign, abbreviations, and morphologically complex words that were formed from the addition of a final *-s* or *-ed* inflection" (page 530). The training was divided into epochs, and words were presented to the system in each epoch with a probability proportional to their occurrence in the Kucera/Francis database. Input (orthography) and output (pronunciation) was coded using a "Wickelgren triple" letter/phoneme trigram scheme similar to that used in Rumelhart and McClelland (1986). Thus <cat> would be coded as {_ca, cat, at_} (where '_' is the boundary symbol). Each input and output unit is sensitive to exactly one of these triples.

The testing methodology is described by Seidenberg and McClelland as follows (page 532):

> The phonological output computed for each word was compared to all of the target patterns that could be created by replacing a single phoneme with some other phoneme. For the word HOT, for example, the computed output was compared to the correct code, /hot/, and to all of the strings in the set formed by /Xot/, /hXt/, and /hoX/, where X was any phoneme. We then determined the number of cases for which the best fit (smallest error score) was provided by the correct code or one of the alternatives.

The system was tested on the training set, and the error rate of the trained system on this set was 2.7%. Among the errors reported, some are plausible regularization errors (e.g., /bruč/ for <brooch>); others are less plausible (e.g., /hɔrs/ for <hearth>).

The remainder of the paper is devoted mostly to demonstrating equivalences between experimental data on human subjects and the behavior of the model on the kind of data reported in the experiments. The typical comparison made is between humans' *naming latencies* – the amount of time it takes for a human to start to pronounce a given word aloud – and the phonological error score of the model (computed as described above) for the correct pronunciation of the given word. For example, in a study reported in Taraban and McClelland (1987), subjects showed slower naming latencies in low-frequency words than in high-frequency words; they also showed slower naming latencies for exceptionally spelled words over regularly spelled words, but this difference was only significant among low-frequency words. This pattern of behavior is apparently replicated in the phonological error rates of the model: Low-frequency words show higher phonological error rates than high-frequency words; and among the low-frequency words, exceptionally spelled words showed significantly higher error rates than regularly spelled words.

5.3.2 What Is Wrong with the Model?

The Seidenberg–McClelland model is not the first connectionist model that was applied to the problem of reading aloud. It was predated by several years by the NETtalk system of Sejnowski and Rosenberg (eventually reported in a journal article in Sejnowski and Rosenberg (1987)). Sejnowski and Rosenberg were only marginally interested in psychology, being concerned instead in an engineering problem: How could one design a computational device that "learns" to correctly pronounce words given a training corpus consisting of text with aligned orthography and pronunciation? Rather than restrict themselves to a few thousand monosyllables, Sejnowski and Rosenberg's system was exposed to English words of various structures, aligned with their pronunciations, taken from running text. The results of Sejnowski and Rosenberg's experiment were clearly not acceptable for a real application (reported error rates were about 8% *by phoneme*) but were promising enough to spawn a great deal of subsequent research in self-organizing methods for learning word pronunciations (see Section 6.6).

Compared with Sejnowski and Rosenberg's system, the Seidenberg–McClelland system seems rather weak, even if the results do on the face of it appear to be backed up by experimental evidence. Consider that the model has been trained and tested only on a few thousand monosyllables (and further tested on possibly a few hundred more examples in the various replications of experiments). Restricting oneself to monosyllables one naturally avoids one of the most difficult problems in learning to read English, namely predicting where the stress is placed. Linguistically motivated models of pronunciation, such as those typically used in good text-to-speech systems, model stress placement by some combination of lexical marking and phonological rules that are sensitive to morphological structure.

Seidenberg and McClelland's model provides no answer to how the learner learns to appropriately stress words when reading aloud.[10]

As we noted previously, some of the errors produced by the system are bizarre, at least if one is considering the system to be a model of a normal mature reader of English. Some errors that fall into this category are given in (5.5):

(5.5)	chew	čw
	frappe	frlp
	lewd	lid
	mow	ml
	ouch	eɪč
	plume	plom
	swarm	swlrm
	angst	ondst
	breadth	brebθ
	czar	var
	feud	flud
	garb	garg
	nerse	mers
	nymph	mimf
	sphinx	spinks
	taps	tats
	tsar	tar
	zip	vip

As Pinker and Prince (1988) observe about a similar set of errors in the Rumelhart–McClelland (1986) model, this does not appear to be the behavior of a mature system.

What, then, of the replications of the various psycholinguistic experiments that Seidenberg and McClelland discuss? Several of these depend upon analogizing between subjects' naming latencies and the error rate of the model. Whether this is a meaningful comparison is unclear, though one might accept it if enough examples show parallel behaviors between these two measures. The problem is, however, that some of the supposed parallels are highly misleading. The best example of this is shown in Seidenberg and McClelland's Figure 19, reproduced here in Figure 5.4. This is a replication of a study reported in Seidenberg, McRae, and Jared (1988), which compared naming latencies for regularly pronounced English words to regularly pronounced English words that belong to an inconsistently pronounced class (*Reg Inc* in the figure). For example *hone* is regularly pronounced

[10] Similarly, by avoiding names, the model avoids another complex area that mature readers of English learn to deal with. Because names – personal names in particular – often come from languages other than English, the pronunciation of names does not always follow the general conventions of English words.

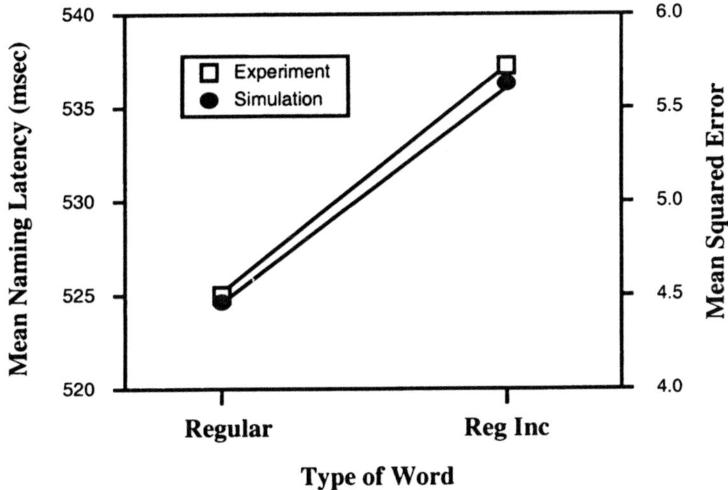

Figure 5.4. Replication of the Seidenberg, McRae, and Jared (1988) experiment, from Seidenberg and McClelland (1989, page 545, Figure 19). Used with permission of American Psychological Association, Inc.

(/hon/), but there are (frequent) words sharing the letter sequence <one>, that have pronunciations for that sequence that are inconsistent with the pronunciation in *hone*: *gone*, *done*. The experimental results demonstrated a 13 millisecond naming latency difference between the regular and regular inconsistent classes, as shown in Figure 5.4. Also shown in that figure are the mean squared phonological error scores for the model on the same stimuli, which according to Seidenberg and McClelland "also provide a good fit to the latency data." But this can hardly be described as an honest comparison. Note that there is no prescribed formula for mapping between latency differences and (mean-squared) phonological error scores of the model. In other words, given a line representing latency differences for human subjects, there is no prescribed formula that, given that line, allows one to derive the slope and intersect of the expected phonological error scores of the model. Thus, with only two data points, Seidenberg and McClelland could have chosen to give the line corresponding to the model's performance *any* slope and intersect. In particular, they could have matched the line exactly to the experimental data; but this would have looked too good and would have emphasized the point that the comparison is meaningless. Instead they presented an *almost* exact match, a tactic that is incredibly effective, unless one is paying close attention.

In summary, Seidenberg and McClelland present their model as an alternative to standard psychological theories of reading. But it is hard to accept that conclusion. What we are presented with is a toy system, one that is shown to perform well (and even then with bizarre exceptions) only on a very small portion of the problem. The comparisons offered with real experimental data range from the plausible to the highly misleading.

In the fields of computational linguistics or speech technology, nobody would accept that a model provided a useful alternative solution to a problem if that model had only been tested on a small and carefully selected subset of the relevant examples. Neither should one believe similar claims in psychology.

5.4 Summary

The computational model of orthography that we have presented implicitly assumes a "dual route" for mapping between written forms and their pronunciation. On the one hand we have the mapping to the ORL, the level of lexical representation relevant for orthographic encoding; on the other, the mapping between the ORL and the orthography – $M_{ORL \rightarrow \Gamma}$ – is a set of spelling rules, which, inverted and composed with the map between the ORL and the pronunciation, serve also as a set of "letter-to-sound" rules.

The model also has *Architectural Uniformity* in that it assumes the same architecture for all writing systems, that is, that one reads Chinese or Japanese by the same mechanisms as one reads English or Serbo-Croatian.

These two properties are well supported by the psycholinguistic literature on reading. Connectionist proposals notwithstanding, there is evidence for dual (or multiple) routes during reading. And the same mechanisms appear to be available to readers of a variety of scripts. In particular there is evidence both for "deep" (lexical) processing in supposedly shallow orthographies and also for "shallow" processing in supposedly deep orthographies. Of course different experimental conditions may favor certain strategies with certain scripts. For instance presenting nonsense words to readers of a relatively shallow orthography will certainly favor an "assembled" route. But on the whole, whether one finds evidence for deep or shallow processing depends, it seems, more upon the task being examined than on the orthographic system one is studying.

So, while I would not go so far as to claim "psychological reality" for the computational model, we can state with some confidence that the overall architecture is at least not at odds with what we know about human orthographic processing.

6 Further Issues

Needless to say, there are many problems in the analysis of writing systems that are left unresolved by this discussion. This chapter will address four of these issues.

First, in Section 6.1, we examine the adaptation of writing systems and ask what it means to adapt an orthography to a new language.

In Section 6.2 we consider spelling reforms, and in particular the 1995 reform of Dutch spelling. As we shall see in this case, contrary to popular notions of what spelling reforms should be like, extant examples of spelling reforms (as in the Dutch case) often are more concerned with "morphological faithfulness" than with making the writing system more "phonetic," though they may not be particularly successful in either goal.

Throughout most of this book we have considered what one might term "core writing," that is, the ordinary spelling of words in the normal orthography for a language. Largely left out of this discussion have been a large number of types of symbols that are rampant in written language – abbreviations, special symbols (%, &, etc.), and numerical symbols among them. How do such things fit into the general model that we have developed here? This question is addressed, at least in a preliminary fashion, in Section 6.3 with an examination of written numerals and their relation to number names, and in Section 6.4 with a short discussion of abbreviatory devices.

Finally, implicit in the approach adopted here has been the Bloomfieldian (Bloomfield, 1933, page 21) maxim that written language is "merely a way of recording language by means of visible marks." This view, while assumed in much of the work on writing systems, is by no means a universally popular one, and there is a long tradition that takes the view that written language is on a par with spoken language and that there are a number of features of the former that are not best understood by appealing to the latter. In fact, I believe that there is no fundamental incompatibility between the two views, and I will argue this point in Section 6.5.

6.1 Adaptation of Writing Systems: The Case of Manx Gaelic

Almost all of the literate cultures in the world today originally borrowed their script from another culture. The only clear exceptions to this generalization are the very few cultures whose writing systems were developed totally indigenously. Chinese is the most obvious example of this, but others might include Semitic (depending upon one's views of the origins of Semitic scripts – see O'Connor (1996)) and of course writing systems, such as Pahawh Hmong, that were developed in recent times by inspired individuals in previously illiterate cultures.

It is worth making a distinction (one not often made) between the adaptation of *scripts* and the adaptation of *writing systems*. The distinction can be illustrated perfectly by the various adaptations of Semitic scripts, notably Hebrew and Arabic (Hary, 1996; Aronson, 1996; Kaye, 1996). As is well known, the most notable feature of Semitic writing systems is their systematic lack of representation of short vowels and their imperfect representation for long vowels.[1] Also systematically lacking are representations of certain consonantal properties such as gemination in Standard Arabic. Daniels (1996b) terms this kind of writing system an *abjad*. As is also well known, Semitic languages have a characteristic "root-and-pattern" morphology, where morphologically related words share a common consonantal root, differing mainly in the pattern of vowels and gemination (in Arabic) or spirantization (in Hebrew) of root consonants. The Semitic writing systems are often claimed to be well adapted to Semitic languages since, by omitting symbols for vowels and alterations of root consonants, the root is rendered more transparent across whole sets of derivationally related forms.

Whatever the merits of this argument, it is noteworthy that when Semitic writing systems have been adapted to other languages two rather divergent courses have been taken. One course is simply to *borrow the entire writing system*. That is, the symbol set is borrowed (with possible augmentations), the symbols are used to denote (roughly) the same phonemes, and the way in which the script is used to represent linguistic form is more or less identical to the original. This was the course taken by the Arabic-based abjads for Persian and Urdu, and by the Hebrew-based abjad of Judeo-Arabic. In these cases, the resulting system is the same as the original writing system in that, for instance, short vowels tend not to be orthographically expressed. There are other senses in which a writing system can be borrowed, and we return to these momentarily.

The second way in which Semitic scripts have been adapted is for the borrowing language *to borrow the script, but not the way in which it is used*. That is, the symbol set is borrowed (again with possible augmentation), the symbols are (again) used to represent (roughly) the same phonemes, but the resulting system is not an abjad. Examples are the Arabic-based Kurdish

[1] Vowel symbols are of course available in the form of "points" written above or below the consonant symbols, but such symbols are generally reserved for pedagogical uses to ensure that the learner pronounces the vowels correctly, and for religious texts for the same reason.

and Uyghur alphabets and the Hebrew-based alphabets for Yiddish and Judezmo (Ladino). Indeed, in these cases more than just the symbol set and the grapheme-to-phoneme correspondences were borrowed: One also finds positional preferences for certain symbols reflecting certain sounds borrowed into the new system. For instance, in Judezmo (Bunis, 1975) the Hebrew consonant א <'> is used to represent /a/ in initial and medial position; however, in final position ה <h> is used since Hebrew words ending in /a/ are most frequently spelled with final ה. Thus *kada* 'each' is spelled קאדה ← <q'dh>. Similarly, א <'> doubles as a "support" for syllable-initial vowels besides /a/, so that *i* 'and' is written אי ← <'y>, and *es* 'is' is written איס ← <'ys>; note also that י <y> is used for both /i/ and /e/. Again, this follows Hebrew practice since א <'>, etymologically /ʔ/, is one way of representing an empty syllable onset in Hebrew, and י <y> may represent either (long) /e/ or /i/. But despite this inheritance, the system used in Judezmo is clearly an alphabet, not an abjad, since all vowels are represented in the orthography.

Let us now return to the notion of borrowing a writing system, rather than merely a script. What does this notion entail? Clearly the interpretation of this concept hinges crucially upon one's understanding of what specific kinds of linguistic information are represented by a given writing system, and how they are represented. For example, we have noted earlier (Section 3.2, Footnote 17) that there is a tension between "phonological faithfulness" and "morphological faithfulness": Writing systems often face a choice between representing a word in a form that is representative of its (surface) pronunciation and representing the morphemes of a word in a fashion consistent with their spelling in other related words. Semitic writing systems have addressed this tension in a rather interesting fashion. Owing to their peculiar properties, they are able, to a large extent, to consistently represent morphological roots, abstracting away from a variety of surface pronunciations of those roots; but at the same time, precisely because vowels and certain other features are not generally represented, Semitic writing systems represent words in a manner consistent with, if not particularly informative of, the actual pronunciation. (In other words, Semitic writing systems have incomplete coverage; see Section 1.2.1.) For a Semitic written form such as <mlk> 'king', one could interpret this as either representing a particular surface pronunciation (e.g., /malik/ in Arabic) or else a particular root morpheme.

Carried one step further, one might imagine "forgetting" the phonetic basis of a string of graphemes such as <mlk> and taking this to be a logographic representation of the morpheme 'king'. For a particular word derived from 'king', one might consider any additional graphemes to be phonetic cues as to the particular derivative of 'king' in question. This abstraction would appear to be the source of the *heterograms* found in adaptations of Aramaic writing systems to Persian languages (Skjærvø, 1996). Heterograms are words or morphemes that are spelled exactly as they would be spelled in their Aramaic source language but are intended to be read as a Persian word. Often the word, in addition to its Aramaic core, has additional graphemic material to reflect, for example, Persian inflectional endings, and these are spelled according to Persian, not Aramaic, pronunciation. To give an example from Middle Persian (Skjærvø, 1996, page 523), a word spelled <YHWWNd> consisted of an Aramaic core <YHWWN> 'be, become' (the Aramaic stem being /yhwwn/) and the final <d> representing a Persian inflectional ending. The word was to be pronounced /bawānd/, with the pronunciation /bawān/ 'become' corresponding to the heterogram <YHWWN>. One could cast this as a reinterpretation of the mapping M_{Spell} for a given written sign: Rather than mapping from the value of PHON attribute to spelling, it is reinterpreted as being a mapping from a value of the SYNSEM attribute. Aramaic heterograms thus have a strong family resemblance to the adaptation of Chinese script to the writing of native words in Japanese (Section 4.3), where the phonographic basis of the Chinese character was lost.

Turning to another case, consider how a writing system might look if it were an adaptation of the English writing system. Consider first what particular properties are essential features of English writing. Two important properties come to mind:

- a particular association between phonological structure and grapheme sequences (M_{Spell}),
- a large amount of lexical marking of orthographic features (see Section 3.2).

One writing system that is adapted from that of English and that seems to have adopted the above-mentioned two features is that of Manx Gaelic. Unlike Irish and Scots Gaelic, which preserved a written tradition dating back to the seventh century (see McManus (1996) for a concise outline of the history of Gaelic orthography), the Gaelic speakers on the Isle of Man completely lost touch with that literary tradition. So when Bishop Phillips, the Welsh Bishop of Sodor and Man, undertook to translate the Anglican Book of Common Prayer into Manx sometime between 1605 and 1610 (Thomson, 1969), he was forced to invent an orthography for the language. This he did, with a system that represented the consonants as in English and the vowels (apparently) at least in part based on Welsh. This first attempt to introduce an orthography for Manx was not very successful, however. In the early eighteenth century the first printed book in Manx appeared, a bilingual version of Bishop Thomas Wilson's *Principles and Duties of Christianity*, and it was the orthographic scheme used here that, with some minor changes, became the standard orthography for Manx Gaelic.

This later orthography, unlike Phillips's, was based almost wholly on that of English. This much is generally accepted as being clearly borrowed:

- The values of the vowels. Thus, for instance, <ee> represented /i/ and <oo> represented /u/.
- The use of 'silent' <e> to mark vowel length. Thus *lane* /lɛːn/ 'full'.
- Doubled consonants marking short vowels. Thus *moddey* */mɔdə/[2] and *balley* /bælʲə/ 'town, farm'.
- <gh> is used to represent /x/ (word internally), as it was in various dialects of English at the time.

To be sure, some choices for spelling certain sounds do not make a great deal of sense given an English model. So <y> generally represents /ə/, something that might perhaps be a holdover from Phillips's earlier orthography, since <y> is used to represent /ə/ in Welsh. Equally puzzling from an English (or a Welsh) point of view is the use of <ey> to represent /ə/, particularly in final position: *ushtey* /uščə/ 'water', *carrey* /kærə/ 'friend'.[3] Also not apparently from English (though very reminiscent of traditional Gaelic spelling) was the sporadic use of <i> before a consonant to represent palatalization of that consonant. But on the whole, the English provenance of most features of Manx spelling is quite clear.

Not only did Manx borrow a large number of its spelling-sound correspondences from English, but it also apparently borrowed the propensity of English for irregular spelling; in more technical terms, it adopted the

[2] The pronunciation here does not reflect the pronunciation of Late Spoken Manx (Broderick, 1984b), which would be */mɔːðə/ for this word. Between the time that the orthography was invented, and the early twentieth century, several innovations had taken place in the Manx sound system including the lenition of intervocalic stops, and a process of lengthening of /a/ and /ɔ/ in stressed open syllables of disyllabic words.

[3] One possible explanation of this particular puzzle is that the <ey> spelling was motivated by a final reduced vowel other than /ə/, namely /ɪ/. At least some of the words spelled with final <ey> and pronounced with /ə/ in Late Spoken Manx may have had an /ɪ/-like vowel in eighteenth century Manx, as evidenced by the quasi-phonetic transcriptions collected in Edward Lhuyd's *Geiriau Manaweg* ('Manx Words') (Ifans and Thomson, 1979). Thus we find: *wystèe* for *ushtey* 'water'; *ylèe* for *eoylley* 'mud'; *maji* for *maidjey* 'wood'; *lomyr yn kyrri* for *loamrey'n cheyrrey* 'fleece'; *fàni* for *fahney* 'wart'. For at least some of these there is etymological evidence in that cognates in Irish or Scots Gaelic have a palatalized consonant before the final reduced vowel, which could plausibly result in a higher /ɪ/-like reduced vowel. Thus (palatalized consonants underlined): (Irish) *uis̲c̲e* 'water' (= *ushtey*), *maid̲e* 'stick' (= *maidjey*), and (Scots Gaelic) *foin̲n̲e* 'wart' (= *fahney*); note that in Gaelic spelling, palatalization of consonants is indicated by <e> or <i> adjacent to the consonant cluster (and if possible on both sides). Given that <y> was at least sometimes used to represent /ə/ in other positions, the use of <ey> to represent this /ɪ/ would have been reasonable, especially since the pronunciation of final /i/ (as in *chimney*) was most likely /ɪ/ in nearby (Lancashire) dialects of English. (Indeed, Geoffrey Sampson (personal communication) notes that such final high vowels are lax in present-day Received Pronunciation; see also Wells (1982, page 119).) It is conceivable that <ey> was then generalized to represent all final reduced vowels.

tendency of English for lexical marking of orthographic features. One interesting instance is the use of <h> after initial consonants, which, with only four exceptions, would appear to correlate with no phonological distinction. The four exceptions are <gh> (representing /ɣ/), <ch> (representing both /x/ and /č/), <ph> (representing /f/), and <sh> (representing /š/).[4]

But <h> can also occur after initial <b>, <d>, <f>, <k>, <l>, <m>, <n>, <r>, and <t>,[5] and in none of these cases does the spelling with <h> apparently correspond to a different phonological form from the spelling without it.[6] Consider, for example, what Cregeen in his classic dictionary (1835, page vi) states concerning <lh> – the only <h> spelling that he explicitly comments on:

> L. Some say that this letter admits of no aspiration, and is pronounced as *l* (in English) in *law, live, love*; as LAUE, LIOAR, LANE; but I think there is a distinction between *lie* or *ly* in English, and LHIE in Manks; and had the words LOO, LOOR, etc. been spelled or written LHOO and LHOOR, they would have answered the Manks pronunciation better; for without the *h* the sound is too narrow, except to those who know that they require that sound.

Though it is hard to say what Cregeen is describing here, it is evident that, at least in the Manx of the early nineteenth century when his dictionary was compiled, the pronunciation of /l/ in Manx was distinct from that of English /l/, and the spelling with <h> was intended to answer this difference.[7] However, as is also evident from Cregeen's comments, other words that were spelled with plain <l> also had this non-English /l/, so that the <h>, if indeed it served the function of marking the consonant as distinct from the English pronunciation, at least did not do so consistently.[8]

[4] Note that in Phillips's earlier orthography <ch> was not ambiguous as it represented only /č/. In that system /x/ was represented as <gh> in all positions.

[5] One also finds <vh> to represent initial lenition of words spelled with <bh> or <mh>.

[6] Of course, <bh>, <mh>, <fh>, <th>, and <dh> have an overt similarity to Gaelic spellings for lenited /b/ (/v/ or /w/), /m/ (/v/ or /w/), /f/ (/∅/), /t/ (/h/), and /d/ (/ɣ/). But it seems unlikely that traditional Gaelic orthography is the source of these spellings, since there is no evidence that the developers of the orthography were aware of Gaelic orthographic traditions, so there would have been little opportunity for them to attempt to give Manx a superficial similarity to Gaelic. Besides, a Gaelic source could not directly explain the most common <h> spelling, <lh>, nor could it explain <kh>, <nh>, or <rh>, since none of these sequences occur initially in Gaelic spelling.

[7] Robert Thomson (personal communication) suggests that Cregeen may have heard a dark /l/ in Manx in contrast to the light /l/ one would expect to get in English in initial position.

[8] One might be tempted to suppose that <lh> represents palatal ("slender") /l/, since for a number of words spelled with <lh>, the corresponding Irish or Scots Gaelic forms have palatalized /l/: thus *lhaih* 'read' corresponding to Scots Gaelic *leugh* (where the <e> serves to mark a palatalized /l/). However, palatalized /l/ is also marked in other ways, especially by <i>: *lioar* 'book' (Irish *leabhar*). And there are many instances of words spelled with <lh> that are not palatalized in Gaelic, for instance *lhag* 'weak' (Irish *lag*). This is also confirmed by late spoken Manx pronunciations as catalogued by Broderick (1984a). Thus for example the word *lhon* (Irish *lon*) 'blackbird' has attested pronunciations /lɑːn/ or /lɔn/, neither of them with palatalized /l/.

Table 6.1. *Total counts in Cregeen's dictionary of words spelled with initial <C h>, where C denotes a consonant, and the number and percentages of those words that are minimal pairs with homophonic or close-homophonic words spelled without the <h>*

Spelling	Total number	Homophones	Percentage
<bh>	14	1	7%
<dh>	32	1	3%
<fh>	2	0	0%
<kh>	6	2	33%
<lh>	186	8	4%
<mh>	24	3	13%
<nh>	3	0	0%
<rh>	23	0	0%
<th>	90	5	6%

Did <h> serve to distinguish homophones or close homophones? It clearly did at least partly serve this function, as the following close minimal pairs (from Cregeen's dictionary) show:

beill	'mouths'	*bheill*	'grind'
leih	'forgiveness'	*lheih*	'place'
lott	'lot'	*lhott*	'wound'
meeley	'soft'	*mheeley*	'mile'
taal	'flow'	*thaal*	'adze'
tie	'the ill'	*thie*	'house'

Indeed, in one case Cregeen himself explicitly notes this function. Commenting on the word *mhill* 'spoil' and on the alternative spelling *mill*, he notes (page 126) that "for the better sound's sake and a difference from *Mill* (honey), the *h* is inserted."[9] However, providing a means of orthographically distinguishing homophones seems only to have been a minor function of postconsonantal <h>. Table 6.1. shows the total counts in Cregeen's dictionary of words spelled with initial <*C*h> (for *C* a consonant) and the number of those words that are minimal pairs with homophonic or close-homophonic words spelled without the <h>. (In these calculations, I discounted derived compounds; thus *thie* 'house' is counted, but not *thie lhionney* 'alehouse'.)

About the only consistent function that <h> in these spellings seems to have is that it serves to make Manx spelling irregular: That is, one must

[9] It is unclear what he means by "the better sound's sake."

simply list for a word such as *bheill* 'grind', the fact that there is an <h> in the orthography. Thus we might assume a representation along the lines of (6.1), where the <bh> spelling is (irregularly) licensed by /b/:

(6.1)
$$\begin{bmatrix} \text{PHON}\langle b_{1*}\, e_{2*}\, l_{3*} \rangle \\ \text{ORTH}\{bh_1, ei_2, ll_3\} \end{bmatrix}$$

This is, needless to say, highly reminiscent of English, where large amounts of such lexical marking are necessary. The particular use of <h> is of course not apparently borrowed from English. It is distinctively Manx. However, the property of irregularity itself plausibly *is* borrowed. One can imagine the original developers of the Manx writing system, being intimately familiar with English orthography, consciously or unconsciously importing the property that words may have orthographically marked lexical entries. Occasionally this irregularity would be used to distinguish homophones (as in English *road/rode*), but more often it would be used as a lexical marking with no apparent other function. Put in another way, the developers of Manx orthography, given their experience with English, were not particularly motivated to provide a consistent spelling system for Manx.[10]

What does it mean to borrow a writing system? Apparently it can mean much more than merely adapting the mapping M_{Spell} to a new language. In some cases, as in Perso-Aramaic heterograms, it can involve a reinterpretation of what M_{Spell} is mapping between. In the case of Manx, what was borrowed (apart from the particular "letter-to-sound" correspondences) is the property of having rampant lexical marking of orthographic properties.

6.2 Orthographic Reforms: The Case of Dutch

English is one of the few major languages that has been blessed *not* to have had any large-scale formally sanctioned spelling reforms during its history, this despite the numerous attempts on the part of various individuals for the past three hundred years. Not surprisingly, the major intention of all spelling reforms proposed for English is to render English spelling "more phonetic," or in other words to make it more phonologically faithful. An Anglocentric viewpoint would thus assume that spelling reforms in general should aim for phonological faithfulness. In fact, this is not usually the case, and morphological faithfulness – a property that English orthography already has to some extent (see Section 3.2) – can often play a role in the

[10] As Robert Thomson (personal communication) notes besides the idiosyncratic use of postconsonantal <h>, there are many other instances of idiosyncratic spellings in Manx. For instance, the words *leigh* 'law', *leih* 'forgive', *lheiy* 'calf', and *lhiy* 'colt' are homophones or near homophones, which are kept distinct in somewhat arbitrary ways in spelling.

redesign of spelling systems. We examine here the case of the 1995 spelling reform for Dutch, which illustrates this point.

In 1995 a new revision of Dutch spelling was formulated (Instituut voor Nederlandse Lexicologie, 1995); this new spelling became official in the fall of 1996 in the Netherlands and Belgium. Various changes proposed in the 1995 spelling system have been the source of much linguistic debate; see Neijt and Nunn (1997) for a comprehensive review of this and previous spelling changes for Dutch.

In this discussion we will concern ourselves with only one issue, namely the spelling of two of the so-called linking morphemes in nominal compounds, those that are spelled <e> or <en>, both of which are pronounced /ə/. Some examples, using the conventions of the pre-1995 (1954) spelling, are shown below, with the linking morpheme in question underlined.

(6.2) (a) slangebeet (snake+LM+bite) 'snakebite'
paardebloem (horse+LM+flower) 'dandelion'
kattevel (cat+LM+skin) 'catskin'
forellevangst (trout+LM+catch) 'trout catch'

(b) bessenjam (berry+LM+jam) 'berry jam'
boekenkast (book+LM+case) 'bookcase'
paardenvolk (horse+LM+people) 'cavalry'
kreeftenvangst (crab+LM+catch) 'crab catch'

(Here we have glossed the linking morpheme as "LM.")[11]

6.2.1 The 1954 Spelling Rules

Under the 1954 spelling conventions, the decision on which form to use was based largely on whether the left-hand member is interpreted as plural. A common plural suffix for Dutch nouns is written <en> – and pronounced /ə/. If the left-hand member of the compound has a plural in <en> (not all nouns do), and if the interpretation of the left-hand member in the compound in question is plausibly plural, spell the linking morpheme as <en>; otherwise spell it as <e>. Thus, in principle one should write *bessenjam* for 'berry jam' because the word for berry (*bes*) has a plural in <en>, and because one normally makes jam out of multiple berries. In contrast, one writes *slangebeet* for 'snakebite', because even though the plural of *slange* is *slangen*, a snakebite typically only involves one snake. As Neijt

[11] The *-e* and *en* forms are only two of the five possible ways of linking elements of nominal compounds in Dutch. Of the other three ways, the most common is simply to have no linking morpheme: *rundvlees* (ox+meat) 'beef'. Less common is *-s* (*lamsvlees* (lamb+S+meat) 'lamb (meat)'), and even rarer is *-er* (*rundergehakt* (ox+ER+chopped) 'ground beef'). As Schreuder et al. (1998) note (from whom these particular examples were taken), all of the nonzero linking morphemes are relics of an obsolete medieval Dutch nominal inflection system.

and Nunn (1997, pages 11–12) note, and as one might expect, things were by no means uniformly so simple. So, sometimes the principles were applied rather arbitrarily: Why is it *kreeftenvangst* 'crab catch', implying the catch of more than one crab, but *forellevangst* 'trout catch', implying the catch of just one trout?[12] Furthermore, some portions of the vocabulary apparently licensed categorical overrides of the general principle. For instance, if the left-hand term denoted a person or persons, *en* was always used, even if a singular interpretation might be plausible: *weduwenpensioen* 'widow's pension'.[13] However, if a particular individual is intended, then <e> is written: *koninginnedag* (queen+LM+day) 'Queen's day'.

But ignoring these (somewhat large) nits in the system, and working under the assumption that the 1954 spelling conventions were more-or-less consistent, what is the best analysis of the mapping between linguistic representation and orthography in terms of the theory under development here? The spelling conventions stated that one should write <en> if the linking morpheme was pronounced /ə/, if the intended interpretation of the left-hand member was plural, and if the noun in question had a plural in *-en*. They did not actually make the linguistic claim that in such instances the linking morpheme *is* the plural morpheme. However, several linguists (e.g., Booij (1996) and Schreuder and colleagues (1998) who provide experimental data supporting Booij's claim) have made precisely this argument, and indeed it seems to result in the most succinct description if we make this assumption. If this is the case, then we can assume that nouns that have a plural in *-en* select the linking morpheme (spelled <en>, and marked [+PL]) in (6.3a), which is in fact just the *-en* plural morpheme; and in all other cases the form in (6.3b) (which is unspecified for plurality) is selected:

(6.3) (a)
$$\begin{bmatrix} \text{SYNSEM}\langle[+PL]\rangle \\ \text{PHON} \quad \langle ə_{1*} \rangle \\ \text{ORTH} \quad \{en_1\} \end{bmatrix}$$

(b)
$$\begin{bmatrix} \text{SYNSEM}\langle\rangle \\ \text{PHON} \quad \langle ə_{1*} \rangle \\ \text{ORTH} \quad \{e_1\} \end{bmatrix}$$

12 As a reviewer has pointed out to me, the answer might be that "crabs are typically caught in numbers, while trout are caught individually on a line." However, a trout fisherman may capture multiple trout on a single fishing trip, and yet under the old spelling system, this would still have to be written *forellevangst*.

13 Note that the English translation has a singular form *widow's*, corresponding to the Dutch plural form *weduwen*.

6.2.2 The 1995 Spelling Rules

For all of their relative consistency, the 1954 conventions suffer from one major problem that makes them ideal fodder for spelling reformers. Deciding whether to write <en> or <e> requires one to judge whether a left-hand member of a compound is plausibly plural in interpretation. Since this may differ from compound instance to compound instance, the 1954 conventions had the disadvantage that one could not guarantee a consistent spelling of a given compound, or a given class of similar compounds since in some instances a plural interpretation might seem appropriate, in others a singular interpretation. Thus from the point of view of those who prefer a superficially consistent spelling system, the 1954 design is rather poor.

Under the 1995 conventions, one is no longer required to decide upon whether a plural meaning is more appropriate to a given context. Rather the rule for using <en> and <e> depends, at least in its simplest form, on what the plural form of the left-hand noun is (Instituut voor Nederlandse Lexicologie, 1995, page 25, my translation):

> Write an *-n-* when the first part of the compound is an independent noun which has a plural exclusively in *-(e)n*.[14]

The connection between the <en> form of the linking morpheme and the plural is thus also drawn in the 1995 conventions as in the 1954 conventions, but here the semantics of the compound do not enter into the decision. On the face of it, then, the 1995 conventions would appear to be a simplification over the earlier conventions.

However, there are some exceptions to the main rule, which significantly complicate the new spelling principle. Among these are cases in which:

1. the first part denotes a person or thing that in the given context is a unique type: *zonneschijn* 'sunshine';
2. the first part is an animal name, and the second part is a botanical term: *paardebloem* (horse+LM+flower) 'dandelion';
3. the first part denotes a body part, and the whole compound is a fossilized construction: *kakebeen* (jaw+LM+bone[?]) 'jawbone', *ruggespraak* (back+LM+speech) 'consultation'.

The first of these exceptions is of course almost identical to the stipulation of the 1954 conventions relating to compounds with left-hand members denoting persons, and for this class of cases the writer is still forced to judge whether the left-hand member is appropriately interpreted as unique given the context. The "flora-fauna rule" is apparently a concession to the

[14] Besides the exceptions to the rule to be discussed below, there are a couple of additional amendments. For example, if the singular of the left-hand noun does *not* end in /ə/ and can form a plural both in /s/ and /en/, then the linking morpheme should also be spelled with <en>.

fact that most such compounds had previously been spelled with <e>, and there was a desire to minimize the number of spelling changes required by the new conventions (Neijt and Nunn, 1997, page 22). The third seems perhaps the most difficult to apply since it requires one to determine whether the construction in question is "fossilized" (the Dutch term used here is *versteende samenstelling* 'petrified compound'), presumably meaning that it is semantically opaque. *Ruggespraak* 'consultation' clearly counts as opaque, but *kakebeen* 'jawbone' is much less obviously so, and only after some rather circuitous reasoning does it become clear that one should probably consider it to be opaque after all: *Been* means either 'bone' or 'leg'; the plural for 'bone' is *beenderen*, for 'leg' *benen*; the plural of *kakebeen* is *kakebenen*, suggesting that the *been* here has, etymological considerations aside, the 'leg' reading. On that reasoning, then certainly *kakebeen* should be considered opaque.

What is an appropriate formal analysis for the 1995 convention on <e> versus <en>? Since the basic rule is no longer based on the semantics of the situation, but rather on a morphological property of the left-hand noun (whether or not it has a plural in *-en*), it no longer makes any sense to assume a linking-morpheme entry with a [+PL] semantic specification (as in (6.3a). Simpler would be to assume a single linking morpheme that is unspecified for orthographic and semantic information:

(6.4) $$\begin{bmatrix}\text{PHON}\langle \text{ə} \rangle \\ \text{ORTH}\{\}\end{bmatrix}$$

To predict the appropriate spelling, we need to assume a morphological feature [+en], which marks nouns that have a plural exclusively in /en/. Then we can write spelling rules as in (6.5), to capture the basic rule of the 1995 conventions, and fill in value for the ORTH attribute in (6.4):

(6.5) /ə/ → <en> / [+en] ___
/ə/ → <e>

For the exceptional classes there are two possible routes. Firstly, one could prespecify the exceptional <e> spelling in the orthographic field of the compounds fitting the terms of the exception. This seems perhaps the most reasonable route in the third class of exceptions given above. Secondly, one could assume an additional rule introducing <e> in certain semantically specified contexts. The flora–fauna exception could be handled by the rule in (6.6), which would apply so as to bleed the first of the rules in (6.5):

(6.6) /ə/ → <e> / [+flora] ___ [+fauna]

But, however the exceptions are to be treated, clearly the system proposed in 1995 is more complex than the conventions it supplants.

What would have been a more reasonable approach for the 1995 proposal to have taken with regard to the linking morpheme? One approach would have simply been to leave it unchanged from the 1954 conventions. This is more or less what Booij (1996) suggests. Of course, this does leave some ambiguity in some cases. For example, depending upon what one means one could have either *schapevlees* or *schapenvlees* (sheep+LM+meat) for 'mutton'. But, as Booij rightly asks (page 133): "what is wrong with that?"

A second approach would have achieved *complete* consistency and would at the same time have been much simpler to state: Since the linking morpheme is invariably pronounced /ə/ no matter how it is spelled, one could simply *always* write it <e>, and eliminate the <en> spelling entirely. Alternatively, one could have chosen to spell the linking morpheme exclusively with <en> (eliminating <e> entirely); in the latter case, the pronunciation of <en> as /ə/ would be consistent with the pronunciation of the plural suffix <en>, whose spelling has not been changed under the 1995 reform. Either of these reforms, had they been adopted, would have made Dutch spelling slightly more "phonologically faithful." Instead what has been adopted is a system that attempts to be as "morphologically faithful" as the 1954 conventions but at the same time drains the morphological faithfulness of any semantic sense. Rather than depending upon the semantics of the situation, the 1995 conventions require that one consider a purely formal property of the left-hand noun (whether it exclusively forms its plural in *-en*). In principle this could of course guarantee more consistent spellings than the 1954 conventions since the writer would merely have to reflect on the morphological properties of the base noun and would not have to determine possibly subtle semantic nuances. Needless to say, whatever benefit might have been gained by this new convention has been effectively eliminated by the additional stipulated exceptions.

6.3 Other Forms of Notation: Numerical Notation and Its Relation to Number Names

In our discussion of writing systems we have thus far focused exclusively on what might be termed the core of writing systems, where written symbols clearly represent some sort of linguistic object, be it phonological or lexical. But written language contains many forms that cannot be so described; the most prominent and widespread of these is numerical notation. Here we will concern ourselves mostly with the Hindu-Arabic numeral system, which has become practically universal.

There have of course been numerous written representations of numbers developed throughout history by various cultures speaking various languages; for an overview see Pettersson (1996). In some cases, the system, in addition to serving as a representation for numerals, also served as a reasonable written representation of the associated number names. Such is the case with traditional Chinese numerals. Thus a numeral representation such as 三千六百八十四 *sān qiān liù bǎi bā shísì* '3 10^3 6 10^2 8 10^1 4' serves simultaneously as a representation for the number '3,684' and as a specification of how the number is actually read; indeed there is no other way to represent the number name for '3,684' in Chinese than by the string of characters given.[15] And numerical representation schemes developed by a particular culture tend, not surprisingly, to have properties that are influenced by the linguistic facts of the language spoken by that culture. Thus Ancient Mayan numerical representation is basically vigesimal, reflecting the vigesimal system used in number name construction in Mayan languages.

Thus some numerical representation schemes are at least partly glottographic in design, in that they reflect at least some aspects of the structure of the linguistic system of number names of the language spoken by the designers of the system. In contrast, the Hindu-Arabic system is decidedly nonglottographic in design even for the speakers of the South Asian languages (whichever they may have been) who developed it around 600 A.D. from an earlier more glottographic system (Pettersson, 1996, page 804). Rather it is a purely mathematically motivated "positional" representation (Harris, 1995; Pettersson, 1996) where powers of the base (10) are represented by the position of digits in a grid starting from the rightmost position, and the digits themselves represent multipliers of the power of the base. Thus a number such as <3,684> represents straightforwardly (omitting 10^0):

(6.7) $3 \times 10^3 + 6 \times 10^2 + 8 \times 10^1 + 4$

The Hindu-Arabic system is now used to represent numbers in the written representation of nearly all languages, and the systems of number names in the languages cover a wide spectrum of possibilities. A sample of the range of possibilities for the example '3,684' is given below in (6.8).

(6.8) (a) three thousand six hundred eighty four

(b) dreitausendsechshundertvierundachtzig
(three+thousand+six+hundred+four+and+eighty)
$3 \times 10^3 + 6 \times 10^2 + 4 + 8 \times 10^1$

[15] Business and accounting variants of the standard number name characters do exist. Thus 貳 *èr* instead of 二 èr for '2'. But these are merely contextually determined graphical variants of the standard forms.

For serious mathematical calculations, standard Chinese numerals are not very convenient, and other numerical representations were invented for such purposes; see Needham (1959) and Pettersson (1996).

(c) efatra amby valopolo sy eninjato sy telo arivo
(four and eight+ten and six+hundred and three thousand)
$4 + 8 \times 10^1 + 6 \times 10^2 + 3 \times 10^3$

(d) hiru mila seirehunda laurogeita lau
(three thousand six+hundred four+score four)
$3 \times 10^3 + 6 \times 10^2 + 4 \times 20^1 + 4$

English (6.8a) is a fairly straightforward decimal system where there is a close one-to-one mapping of the words in the number name to the multipliers and multiplicands in the factorized representation in (6.7). German (6.8b) is similarly straightforward with the exception that, as in most other Germanic languages (Modern English being the notable exception), the digits and tens are presented in the reverse of their "logical" order. In Malagasy (6.8c) (Rajemisa-Raolison, 1971), the entire number name is presented in the reverse of its "logical" order. Finally, in the case of Basque (6.8d) we find a partially decimal-vigesimal system where numbers below 100 are regularly represented in terms of sums of products of powers of 20 followed by units or 'ten' plus a unit.[16]

The relationship between the blatantly nonglottographic Hindu-Arabic numeral system and the number name systems of the various languages in which it is used would be of largely academic interest were it not for the fact that converting between the two representations is something that literate speakers do routinely – and something that automatic text-to-speech conversion systems must also be capable of. This immediately raises the question of what kind of mapping such speakers perform and how the model of this mapping relates to the theory of writing systems that we have been developing.

On first consideration, our model of writing systems would appear to have little to say about this mapping, since the two most prominent assumptions that one must make seem to directly contradict what we know to be true of the Hindu-Arabic numeral system, and what is claimed to be true of number name systems:

- A numerical representation such as '3,684' maps directly to a *linguistic* level of representation, in this case the lexical representation of the number name itself.[17]
- The mapping between the two levels is regular.

The first assumption patently contradicts the mathematical design of the system, which was clearly nonglottographic. The second assumption is also

16 See Hurford (1975) and Stampe (1976) for surveys and linguistic models of number name systems and Brandt Corstius (1968) for some early grammatical models of number names.

17 We take it for granted that numerical representations do not generally represent phonological information.

clearly false in general since the "alphabet" of powers of ten is infinite and by definition one cannot have a regular relation that involves an infinite alphabet.[18]

But these two points are misleading. First of all, the original design of a written representation system should not confuse the issue of how the system is actually used by readers of a language that uses that system. There is no reason why the Hindu-Arabic numeral system as used, say, in English could not have a dual function, namely as a mathematically motivated representation of the number, but also as a crude logographic representation of the number names of the language. Secondly, the observation that the alphabet of powers of ten is nonfinite misses the important point that there is a limit to the length of a digit string that will be read by a human reader *as a number name* (as opposed to merely a string of digits). The limit of course varies from reader to reader, and presumably depends upon the level of literacy and mathematical acumen of the person involved. But such a limit clearly exists: While most readers of American English would have no problem reading '1,000,000' as *one million*, fewer would be so confident about *one quadrillion* for '1,000,000,000,000,000'; and presumably none would be able to translate (without the aid of pencil and paper, and possibly a dictionary) a number such as '1,000,000,000,000,000,000,000,000,000'. In practical situations, such numbers are typically either represented in scientific notation (10^{27}), which has a totally different mode of reading aloud, or else (at least with smaller numbers) partly in words (e.g., American English *1 trillion* for '1,000,000,000,000'). Given these observations, we can proceed to develop a finite-state model for the conversion of Hindu-Arabic numerals into number names for a given language; this model is the one used in the Bell Labs multilingual TTS system, as described in Sproat (1997a,b).

The problem is best understood by factoring it into two components. The first component, which we shall term *factorization*, is a mechanism for expanding a Hindu-Arabic numeral sequence into a representation in terms of sums of products of powers of ten. The second component maps from this factorized representation into the sequence of words that make up the number name corresponding to the particular numeral sequence; let us term this latter component the *number name generator*. Both of these operations can be handled using finite-state transducers. For example, a simple transducer that factors numerals up to multiples of 10^2 is shown in Figure 6.1. Generating a number name from a numeral string then consists of composing the string with the factorization transducer, composing the result with the number name generator, and then computing the projection

[18] Number-name systems themselves have been argued to be mildly context sensitive, hence not regular; see Radzinski (1991).

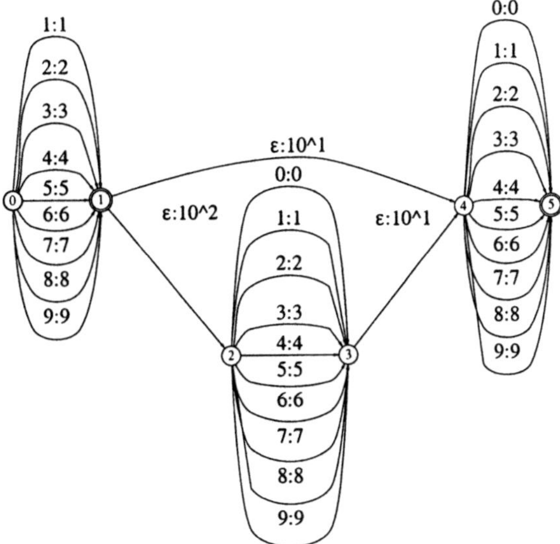

Figure 6.1. A numeral factorization transducer for numbers up to 999.

of the output, or formally:

number name = π_2[numeral ∘ [factorization] ∘ [number name generator]]

The number name generator is obviously language specific, since not only are the lexical items involved specific to a given language, but also various aspects of their combination. It is a language-specific fact of English, for example that one may (in some dialects *must*) use the word *and* between *hundred* and following material in the number name, but one does not use it after *thousand*, *million*, etc; similarly in Russian complex case and gender agreement is required between elements of the number name (Wade, 1992).[19]

The factorization transducer is also language specific – or one might better say, language-area specific. This is in part because languages differ in the way they logically factorize a long number name. Most (decimal) number name systems have distinct words for 10^1, 10^2, and 10^3, but differ significantly on higher powers. The first five powers of ten for which there are separate lexical items in American English, Chinese (along with several other East Asian languages), and Hindi (along with most South Asian languages) are given in (6.9):[20]

19 In a working system, such as the Bell Labs TTS system, such linguistic facts can be handled in part by rewrite rules compiled into finite-state transducers.

20 The system for American English differs, of course, from that used traditionally in British English and currently in other Western European languages.

(6.9) English $10^1, 10^2, 10^3, 10^6, 10^9$
Chinese $10^1, 10^2, 10^3, 10^4, 10^8$
Hindi $10^1, 10^2, 10^3, 10^5, 10^7$

For the "missing" powers, languages revert to an *analytic* strategy, so that 1×10^4 in English is expressed as *ten thousand* and $1 \times 10^5 + 1 \times 10^4$ is expressed as *a hundred and ten thousand*. Thus a number such as '12345678' would be factored differently in these three languages. Here, the analytic blocks are underlined:

(6.10)

English $\underline{[1 \times 10^1 + 2] \times 10^6} + \underline{[3 \times 10^2 + 4 \times 10^1 + 5] \times 10^3} + \underline{6 \times 10^2 + 7 \times 10^1 + 8}$

Chinese $\underline{[1 \times 10^3 + 2 \times 10^2 + 3 \times 10^1 + 4] \times 10^4} + \underline{5 \times 10^3 + 6 \times 10^2 + 7 \times 10^1 + 8}$

Hindi $\underline{1 \times 10^7} + \underline{[2 \times 10^1 + 3] \times 10^5} + \underline{[4 \times 10^1 + 5] \times 10^3} + \underline{6 \times 10^2 + 7 \times 10^1 + 8}$

One point that is not often noted in discussions of numerical representations and their relation to number names relates to the positioning of commas or other aids to interpretation that are typically inserted into long numerals.[21] Where one finds a comma written depends exactly upon which powers of ten the language has distinct words for. For English, the comma is written in positions corresponding to the end of the first and second underlined blocks in (6.10): Thus one writes <12,345,678>. In Chinese, the comma is also written after the first underlined block, this time resulting in <1234,5678>. Finally, in Hindi, one writes the comma after the first second and third underlined blocks, resulting in <1,23,45,678>.[22] Thus the placement of the comma corresponds exactly to the (right) edge of analytic number name constructions. It is hard to interpret the comma in any other way than as an aid for the reader in the mapping between the numerical representation and the number name. In other words, the numerical representation is being treated in the writing system as a representation not only of mathematical objects, but simultaneously as an orthographic representation of linguistic objects.

For some languages, additional mechanisms are required in the factorization step. In German, for example, digits and decades occur in the number name in the reverse of their 'logical' order, as noted in (6.8b) This "decade flop" can be handled by a finite-state transducer, but only at some cost, since transducers can only perform string reversals (for a finite set of strings) by enumerating all strings paired with their reversed form. (This is exactly what is done in the German version of the Bell Labs TTS system; see

[21] The symbol is ',' in English, Chinese, and Hindi, as it happens. In many European languages besides English one uses either '.' or simply a space; the ',' is used to represent what is represented with a decimal point in English.

[22] The surface *form* of the numerals in Hindi and other Indian languages (and also Arabic) is different from that used in English or Chinese, but the system otherwise works exactly the same.

Sproat (1997b).) So the mapping between numerals and their associated factorizations is still regular, but not elegantly so. It is perhaps not surprising that speakers of German and Dutch (which has an equivalent number name system) have some difficulty in reading number names from their numerical representation.[23]

For Malagasy, which has a complete reversal of the logical order (6.8c), it makes more sense to assume that readers, when faced with a number, shift their attention to the end of the numeral string and read (within that string) from right to left, temporarily overriding the normal left-to-right order of reading. Thus, a simple regular mapping between numeral and number name can be maintained, with the only added assumption being the additional low-level processing strategy just described. A similar strategy must in any case be assumed for Hebrew and Arabic, where the script runs from right to left, but Hindu-Arabic numerals run from *left to right* as they do in other languages.[24]

Turning to vigesimal systems we note that there are two possible strategies for dealing the mapping between decimal-based Hindu-Arabic numerals and number names. The first would be to insert into the factorization step a step that performs the base conversion between 10 and 20. For numerical representations of a finite size, this can be handled by a regular relation. Once this factorization into powers of 20 is accomplished, the number name generator would work in a vigesimal system precisely as in a decimal system. As a practical matter however there seem to be relatively few extant vigesimal systems that have distinct words for anything above a small power of 20. In Basque for example, the system becomes decimal above 10^2. Merrifield (1968) reports on the Macro-Mayan language Ch'ol, which has words for 20^1, 20^2, and 20^3, thus reflecting an old Mayan purely vigesimal system; but he also notes that the system for the larger numbers has essentially given way to the decimal system of Spanish. Furthermore there are no data on Ch'ol speakers reading numbers from a Hindu-Arabic decimal representation (assuming it would be possible for them to do this). So for the point at hand, namely the conversion of decimal Hindu-Arabic numerals into vigesimal number names, we cannot deduce anything from the existence of such a system of number names. For simpler (one might even say semifossilized) decimal-vigesimal systems such as

[23] Harald Baayen, personal communication. The evidence is currently only anectodal, and this claim certainly needs to be supported by experimental evidence.

[24] It is interesting to note that when Malagasy was written in the Arabic script (before the early nineteenth century), this low-level processing step need not have been assumed. The script ran from right to left, of course, but numerals would have been represented, as in Arabic or in present day Malagasy, from left to right. Thus a reader of Arabic-script-based Malagasy could maintain a right-to-left reading order throughout both the ordinary text and (as in modern Malagasy) the number.

Basque, it is a relatively straightforward matter to list the vigesimal-based words in the number lexicon, associating them with *decimal* rather than vigesimal factorizations. The solution is not entirely elegant, but it is not totally unreasonable either, especially since, as was noted above, Basque number names are decimal above 10^2; numbers under 10^2 are thus lexical exceptions to the general pattern of the number name system of Modern Basque.

It should be stressed, if it is not already clear, that what I have presented is *not* a linguistic theory of number names, but rather a model of the mapping between a numerical representation – the Hindu-Arabic system – and the number name systems of various languages. Number name systems themselves can be quite complex. Stampe, for example, gives an example of an exotic system employed in Sora, a Munda language of India (Stampe, 1976, page 601):

> Most Munda languages have decimal-vigesimal counting: They count 10, 20, 20 + 10, 2 × 20, (2 × 20) + 10. Sora changed from a decimal to a duodecimal (12) base within this vigesimal structure. Soras therefore add units to 12 to reach 19 *miggəl-gulji* (12 + 7); then count 20 *bɔ-koṛi* (1 × 20) and add units to reach 32 *bɔ-koṛi-miggəl* ((1 × 20) + 12), to which are added units to reach 39 *bɔ-koṛi-miggəl-gulji* ((1 × 20) + 12 + 7); 40 is *ba-koṛi* (2 × 20), and so on, in a Stravinskian alternation of twelves and eights unparalleled in any known language.

The current theory would be able to provide a model for the reading of Sora number names from a Hindu-Arabic decimal representation. But of course it would not really account for the form of the number names themselves, a topic that falls rather under the domain of a linguistic theory of number names.

In summary, it is indisputable that the primary representational function of the Hindu-Arabic numeral system is mathematical, not linguistic. Indeed Hindu-Arabic numerals are often held up as an archetypal example of a patently nonlinguistically motivated written representation. However, the mapping between numerals and their associated number names in a large variety of languages can, somewhat surprisingly, be handled by a model that is consistent with the more general model of writing systems that has been developed in the remainder of this book.

6.4 Abbreviatory Devices

The literature on writing and writing systems contains very little discussion of abbreviations, acronyms, and other shortening devices falling under the general rubric of "initialisms." This is perhaps unsurprising given the heavy focus in that literature on what linguistic objects written symbols represent, and how they represent them in the spelling of "ordinary words." Yet it is at the same time somewhat of an oversight since abbreviatory devices of various kinds have a history as old as that of writing itself (Cannon, 1989; Römer, 1994).

Abbreviations, as defined below, are of particular practical importance in the development of TTS systems since the system must decide on how to read them, given that they typically do not obey the normal "pronunciation rules" of the language. For standardized cases such as <Blvd> for *Boulevard*, this is less of a problem since such cases can be catalogued. (There is, however, the problem that many abbreviations can conventionally stand for more than one thing, as in <St> (*Street*, *Saint*) or <Dr> (*Drive*, *Doctor*, *drachma*), or are confusable with ordinary words as in <Ave> (*Avenue*, or *ave* as in *ave maria.*) These issues are amenable to *sense disambiguation* techniques, such as those of Yarowsky (1996).) But creatively coined abbreviations are not at all uncommon, and in certain genres, such as real estate advertisements, they are rife. Consider the example in (6.11) taken from the *New York Times* real estate ads for January 12, 1999:

(6.11) 2400' REALLY! HI CEILS, 18' KIT,
MBR/Riv vu, mds, clsts galore! $915K.

Here we find <CEILS> (*ceilings*), <KIT> *kitchen*, <MBR> *master bedroom*, <Riv vu> *river view*, <mds> *maids (room)* (?), and <clsts> *closets*, none of which are standard abbreviations, at least not in general written English. While human readers (usually) have no problem reconstructing the intended words, these are a serious problem for TTS systems, which generally will fail to correctly expand the abbreviation in such cases. Clearly, abbreviation is a productive process that must be modeled in any theory of the relation between language and writing.

The purpose of this section is to propose how abbreviatory devices might fit into the theory that we have developed. Before we proceed, however, it is necessary to define some of our terminology, since terms such as *abbreviation, acronym*, and so forth are used in different ways by different people; see Cannon (1989) for a discussion of some of this terminological quagmire.

For the purposes of the present discussion, we will distinguish three categories. The first category, *abbreviations*, constitute all cases where the normal spelling of a construction – typically, though by no means always, a single word – is shortened either by deleting letters (e.g., <St.>, <Dr.>, <kg>, <CEILS>, or <clsts>) or by substituting a shorter string of symbols that is synchronically unrelated to the target word; the latter cases include <lb> for *pound*, <%> for *percent*, <&> for *and*, and <$> for *dollar*. Note that my use of the term *abbreviation* differs from Cannon's (see next paragraph). What all of these cases have in common, and what sets them apart from the other two categories to be discussed momentarily, is that they all involve shortened forms *where it is nonetheless intended that one read the full form of the word.* Thus, when encountering the abbreviation <lb>, one would normally read *pound* or *pounds*, but not *l. b.*.

The second category, which we shall term *letter sequences*, behave differently. In this case the intention is that one read them as sequences of letters, irrespective of what they stand for. Thus <CIA>, <USA>, and <ACL> are to be read as sequences of letters, despite the fact that they stand for (among other things) *Central Intelligence Agency*, *United States of America*, and *Association for Computational Linguistics.* Note that Cannon includes cases such as these under the rubric of *abbreviation*, though these really differ in kind from what I have termed abbreviations above, since letter sequences are not generally to be expanded into a word or set of words. However, what I term letter sequences are often popularly called *acronyms*, which is more properly used to name the third category (described in the next paragraph). To avoid these potential confusions, then, I suggest the term *letter sequence.* Typically a letter sequence is formed from the initial letters of the words of the phrase being abbreviated, though function words are often omitted in this computation (as in <USA>). Periods may be used within the letter sequence though these seem never to be required; see Cannon (1989) for further details.

The third category are *acronyms*, which can be thought of as letter sequences that are to be read as words. Well-known examples are <NATO>, <UNESCO>, and <AIDS>. The formation principles of acronyms are similar to those of initial letter sequences, but there are differences. Acronyms are more likely than letter sequences to have additional letters added beyond the initial letters of the constituent nonfunction words; Cannon (page 114) cites examples such as <APEX> from *advance purchase excursion.* And acronyms can be longer than letter sequences; the initial letter sequences in Cannon's corpus had maximally five letters, whereas acronyms could have as many as eight letters (pages 110–113). Unlike abbreviations, both letter sequences and acronyms are derived most often from multiword phrases.

How are these various classes of initialisms accounted for within the current model? Let us start with abbreviations, which are the easiest to describe. For standardized abbreviations it makes sense simply to assume that they are listed as an alternative orthographic entry for the word, or words, with which they are associated. This would yield a representation such as the one in (6.12) for <Dr> representing *Doctor*:

$$(6.12) \quad \begin{bmatrix} \text{PHON}\langle d_{1*}\, akt\partial r_{2*} \rangle \\ \text{ORTH}\{D_1, r_2\} \end{bmatrix}$$

Note that there are some words for which there is no standard non-abbreviated form. In English these include *Mrs* (*missus* is a possible full spelling, but this is in fact hardly ever used) and *Ms*. In these cases one assumes there is simply no full orthographic entry.

For novel abbreviations – cases such as <clsts> in (6.11) above – we must assume a device whereby the abbreviation may be derived productively from the normal spelling of the word. But what the constraints on abbreviation formation are is not entirely clear. In English vowels are particularly prone to being deleted, and there seems to be a tendency to delete noninitial consonants too, but beyond this it is hard to pin down exactly what distinguishes a good from an unacceptable abbreviation. However, it seems likely that whatever the constraints are, they can be described in terms of regular relations. This being so, we can model productively formed abbreviations by composing an additional abbreviation transducer A onto the output of $M_{ORL \rightarrow \Gamma}$: $M_{ORL \rightarrow \Gamma} \circ A$. This predicts that abbreviations, as we have defined them, can be formed purely on the basis of the orthographic form. It must therefore be possible to recast apparent phonological influences on abbreviation (if any) in purely orthographic terms. Whether this is true or not remains to be seen.

For acronyms and letter sequences the model must be different. Acronyms such as <NATO> and letter sequences such as <CIA> certainly represent, respectively, *North Atlantic Treaty Organization* and *Central Intelligence Agency* (or *Culinary Institute of America*). But they are not generally *to be read* as such. Rather <NATO>, for instance, is the orthographic rendition of a lexical item that happens to denote the same as *North Atlantic Treaty Organization* but is pronounced /neɪto/:

(6.13) $$\begin{bmatrix} \text{PHON}\langle n_{1*}\, eɪ_{2*}\, t_{3*}\, o_{4*} \rangle \\ \text{ORTH}\{N_1, A_2, T_3, O_4\} \end{bmatrix}$$

A similar analysis would be given for <CIA>, where here the syllables /si aɪ eɪ/ are represented orthographically by the letters with the corresonding names:

(6.14) $$\begin{bmatrix} \text{PHON}\langle si_{1*}\, aɪ_{2*}\, eɪ_{3*} \rangle \\ \text{ORTH}\{C_1, I_2, A_3\} \end{bmatrix}$$

Thus, whereas abbreviations merely constitute shorter ways of writing existing lexical items, acronyms and initial letter sequences correspond to new lexical items. The creation of acronyms and initial letter sequences is thus a type of word formation (Aronoff, 1976; Cannon, 1989), applying to the orthographic representation of the word, rather than (as would normally be the case) to the phonological representation. Once one has the new orthographic form, the pronunciation can be derived in one of two ways. In the case of acronyms the relation that maps between phonology and orthographic form ("spelling rules") can be inverted ("grapheme-to-phoneme rules") to produce a phonological representation. In the case of initial letter sequences the phonological representation is formed out of the normal names of the letters; note here, though, that other devices such as descriptions of the letter sequence involved (*Triple A* for <AAA>) are possible.

While the range of abbreviatory devices possible for English seems to be widely available for many written languages, the distribution of the varying types seems to differ from language to language. (I am not aware of any cross-linguistic surveys of the distributions of types of abbreviatory devices.) In some languages, indeed, certain types seem to be essentially lacking. For example, Chinese seems to have very few abbreviations in the sense that I have used this term, and it will be instructive to digress for a moment and consider the case of Chinese, since it offers an interesting example of how different properties of the writing system can result in different possibilities for abbreviatory devices.

In Chinese, acronyms – termed *suoxie* 'shrunken writing' – abound. Thus one finds many standard examples such as 北大 *bĕi dà* for 北京大學 *bĕijīng dàxué* 'Beijing University'; 鄧選 *dèng xuăn* for 鄧小平文選 *dèng xiăopíng wénxuăn* (Deng Xiaoping selected-works) 'the selected works of Deng Xiaoping'; and 文革 *wén gé* for 文化大革命 *wénhuà dàgémìng* 'Cultural Revolution' (Wang, 1996). An examination of the examples given will reveal that the pieces selected for the *suoxie* construction need not come from the initial of the corresponding constituent, unlike what one would almost invariably find in English. Nonetheless, Chinese *suoxie* are like English acronyms in that they are shortened forms of longer constructions, which, crucially, are read in their shortened form, not expanded into the construction from which they were derived. Now, as the astute reader will have already noted, the nature of the Chinese writing system makes it impossible to determine whether *suoxie* is more correctly equated with acronyms, as we have heretofore assumed, or with letter sequences. The key distinction is in how these two kinds of constructions are read: Acronyms are pronounced by applying pronunciation rules to the sequence of symbols; initial letter sequences are pronounced by naming the letters in sequence. In Chinese, these two routes yield the same result since the pronunciation of a character is also the name of that character.

As we noted, Chinese basically lacks abbreviations in the sense that we have defined. With the exception of special symbols such as '%' and '$', which are expanded into the corresponding expressions for 'percent', 'dollar', etc., there are essentially no other cases where a shortened form is expanded during reading. This even applies to borrowed forms, such as <kg> or <cm>, which are obligatorily treated as abbreviations in English, but which Chinese readers spell out as sequences of letters; thus <kg> is read literally as *k. g.* (Chilin Shih, personal communication). The apparent avoidance of treating borrowed graphical elements as abbreviations to be expanded when reading could be explained by the fact that Chinese has historically lacked abbreviations. But why did it lack abbreviations?

I believe the explanation may be due to a conspiracy among properties of Chinese morphology, the nature of the Chinese script, and the function of abbreviations. First, Chinese words are typically short; one- and two-syllable words make up the overwhelming majority. (This is with the notable exception of nominal compounds, which can be quite long.) In the earliest forms of Chinese, it is commonly conjectured that words were largely monosyllabic (see various chapters in Packard (1998) for discussion), and even in later Classical Chinese, which was the written standard up until the early part of this century, monosyllabic words made up a larger proportion of words in a typical text than they would in present-day spoken Mandarin. Second, Chinese characters phonologically almost always represent single syllables. Third, as we observed above, abbreviations are most commonly used to abbreviate single words (though abbreviations of phrases certainly do occur). In Chinese, then, all one could hope to gain in most cases would be the shortening of a word that would be written with two characters (a two-syllable word) into a one-character abbreviation, something that would not have afforded much of a savings. There was therefore little to be gained by introducing graphical shortening devices in the form of abbreviations.[25]

Abbreviations, as we have defined them, are a purely graphical device intended to shorten the form of written words. Acronyms and initial letter sequences are somewhat more complex than this, but they too depend upon the written form of words. As such, all of these forms of "initialisms" have a place in a complete model of writing systems. In this section we have made some tentative steps toward fitting these devices into the proposed model.

6.5 Non-Bloomfieldian Views on Writing

It has often been noted that scholars of language have been divided in their attitudes about writing along two partly independent dimensions. The primary dimension relates to whether the study of writing is even interesting. Bloomfield is generally cited as the source of the view that writing itself is not interesting (since written language is merely at best a crude approximation of spoken language, the true object of study), and this view has to a large

[25] Note that other graphical shortening devices were employed, such as a special symbol to indicate reduplicated characters similar in function to the reduplication markers discussed in Section 4.4.2.

extent survived in modern generative linguistics.[26] The second dimension, assuming one at least accepts that writing systems might be interesting, is how written language relates to language. Specifically, is it in Bloomfield's terms a "way of recording [spoken] language by means of visible marks," or is it indeed a separate form of communication that need not relate to spoken language at all?[27]

The Praguians, most notably Vachek (e.g. Vachek (1973)) have been among the most staunch defenders of the view that written language should be treated separately from spoken language, but a number of British linguists, including Sampson (1985) and Harris (1995), have challenged the essentially "glottocentric" Bloomfieldian view. For example, as we discussed earlier, Sampson distinguishes between glottographic writing systems, where the written symbols represent some aspect of specifically linguistic information, and "semasiographic" writing systems, where the written symbols directly represent the "meaning" of the intended message, giving no information about how one would actually express this meaning linguistically. Crucially, for Sampson both of these kinds of systems count as writing, and this view is echoed by Harris (1995).

Perhaps the clearest instance of the opposing view is offered by DeFrancis (1989), who defines "writing system" as synonymous with "glottographic writing system."[28] One central reason is that if one insists that writing systems are exactly those graphical systems of communication wherein one can express any message expressible in spoken language, then the only extant systems that meet this requirement are glottographic ones. To be sure, there are many highly complex notational systems that are arguably not glottographic, and which allow for a rich set of expressions: mathematical notation, dance and other movement notation systems, music (see various chapters in Daniels and Bright (1996)), and even the icon-based messages one frequently sees in (especially European) instruction manuals (Sampson, 1985, pages 31–32). All of these examples involve symbology that is conventional to a greater or lesser degree; all of them are clearly systems of communication that are complex to a greater or lesser degree; and all of them are able to communicate messages that can be quite complex, especially if one had to put them into words. But all of them are highly restricted in

[26] It would be a mistake, however, to view this as any kind of religious dogma in generative linguistics that is inculcated in succeeding generations of disciples. When I was a graduate student at MIT in the early 1980s, I do not recall writing systems being discussed in any form, either positively or negatively. Rather, the lack of attention to writing systems among generative linguists arises, I believe, simply because few in that tradition have thought much about the topic, and none have been encouraged to do so.

[27] Of course, as Harris (1995, page 45) rightly observes, the existence of Braille shows that the writing does not have to be visibly arranged, merely *spatially* arranged.

[28] Indeed, as we have seen, he goes much further than this, insisting that full writing systems must not only be glottographic, but at least to some degree phonographic.

the domain to which they apply, and this is, to take DeFrancis's position, the crux of the matter. To make the same point in a different way, while it may be painful to precisely express a complex mathematical expression using ordinary written English, this is something that could be done, just as one could read the expression aloud, and have it be understood by someone with sufficient mathematical knowledge. In contrast, it would be hard to see how one could represent the American *Declaration of Independence* using only the symbology of mathematics. Thus glottographic systems are general, whereas arguably semasiographic systems are restricted.

Should nonglottographic systems be considered writing? On the face of it this would appear to be purely a matter of definition, and hardly worth arguing about. However, there is one important property that nonglottographic systems such as mathematical notation share with (glottographic) written language, which neither of them share with speech, and that is the use of a two-dimensional surface: Speech is produced and processed over time, and therefore could be considered to be a one-dimensional signal; written forms, whether glottographic or otherwise, usually have two dimensions at their disposal and frequently make use of them in ways that have no parallel in speech.

For example, as Harris notes (pages 141–144), crucial use has been made in diverse mathematical traditions of *tabular* arrangements of symbols: multiplication tables and logarithm tables are just two modern instances of these. The tabular arrangement is crucial for representing the relevant mathematical concepts. For example, in a multiplication table, one understands the entries in each cell of the table as representing the product of the number heading the relevant column and the number heading the relevant row. Speech cannot adequately represent this two-dimensional structure. As Harris observes (page 144): "If mathematics had had to rely on speech as its cognitive mode, we should still be living in a primitive agricultural society."[29]

Similar uses of two-dimensional layout can also be found, of course, in glottographic writing. One case that Harris points to is pattern poetry, where words in the poem are arranged so as evoke a picture; there are also instances of "pattern prose"; the most famous of these in English is, perhaps, the mouse's tale/tail in Lewis Carroll's *Alice's Adventures in Wonderland*. A modern instance is the e-mail signature block, a made-up

[29] Having said this, it should also be pointed out that there are situations where one is forced to represent tabular information in speech. Such is the case of reading systems for the blind. One ingenious technical solution that circumvents some of the limitations of normal spoken language was developed by T.V. Raman (1994) in his text-preprocessing system named *Aster*. Raman's system renders LaTeXdocuments into speech (using the DECTalk TTS system), and it includes methods for rendering various levels of document structure, as well as mathematical expressions – including matrices, which are of course a kind of tabular representation. Tables are read left-to-right and top to bottom, with the position in the table being mimicked by the perceived position of the voice in the auditory field.

```
--------------------------------------------------------   ':'...''. ---
  Michael  Farber                  mfarber@lucent.com       '::.''''':;:
                                                           '::;       ;;:
  Lucent Technologies                                      :::,,       :;;
  1432 Pine St., 3D-403            Lucent Technologies     ;:;'        ;:;
  Liberty Corner                  Bell Labs Innovations     ;;:        .;:
  New Jersey, 07934                                          :;:,    ,:;:
  phone: 908-712-9993               fax: 908-712-9980          ':;;;:;:'
```

Figure 6.2. Two-dimensional layout in an e-mail signature

(but perfectly realistic) example of which is given in Figure 6.2; here we see the use of two-dimensional arrangement in the separation of the postal address from the name in the left-hand column, the e-mail address in the top right-hand column, and the integration of the verbiage from the company logo ("Lucent Technologies, Bell Labs Innovations") into the rest of the design. There are many other examples that could be given.

So nonglottographic forms of "writing" share with glottographic forms the property of using two-dimensional space in ways that have no direct counterpart in (one-dimensional) speech. Furthermore, this "layout analysis" (to borrow and somewhat adapt a term from document image processing) is clearly a field worthy of study in its own right. But what are we to make of this observation? Does it force us to view (e.g.) mathematical notation and ordinary written English as being two instances of the same class of object? And must the term "writing" apply to both? I fail to see why: Presumably one could restrict the term "writing" to glottographic representational systems, and use a separate term to denote forms of symbolic representation that make crucial use of two dimensions. Glottographic writing systems, in their full glory, would be instances of both; mathematical and other nonglottographic systems would be instances only of the latter. It comes down, after all, to a matter of definition.

Of course this view does entail that there are interesting aspects of (glottographic) writing that go beyond the way in which writing represents speech. This conclusion seems incontrovertible, but it is important to realize that this in no way contradicts the theory of writing systems presented in this book, which deals solely with the mapping between written and spoken form.

6.6 Postscript

I have presented a formal theory of orthography, making specific proposals about what linguistic objects are represented, what level of linguistic representation (what we have termed the ORL) may be represented, and what the constraints on the mapping between linguistic and graphical representation are. The question of what specific kinds of linguistic objects are represented is, of course, a topic that has occupied much of the literature on writing systems; the level of linguistic representation has only been discussed extensively in the psycholinguistic literature, and there only in superficial terms; constraints on the mapping between linguistic and written form have hardly been discussed at all. There is therefore some reason to believe that the current work is the most systematic formal proposal for a theory of writing systems presented to date. It is, nonetheless, only a beginning, and it is hoped that this work will serve as a stimulus for developing a much more complete theory of writing systems by a much wider group of researchers.

Such a theory is clearly necessary for a variety of reasons. Consider, for example, that orthographic evidence has been occasionally used by generative linguists to support one or another (usually) phonological theory. We have already discussed Chomsky and Halle's views on English spelling and its relation to their model of English phonology; one could add to this Steriade's (1982) and subsequently Miller's (1994) use of evidence from Linear B to support a model of syllable structure for Greek. Miller's study is broad in scope and systematic, but most use of orthographic evidence that one finds in the literature, including Steriade's and Chomsky and Halle's, is limited and mostly ad hoc. In some cases (plausibly Steriade's) the analysis may turn out to be correct; in others (Chomsky and Halle's) it is suspect. But the real point here is that a fortuitously selected orthographic fact held up as evidence for a particular linguistic claim cannot be readily evaluated in the absence of a serious theory of orthography. There is nothing special about orthography in this regard. In an entirely similar vein a phonological factoid brought in as evidence for a particular syntactic analysis should not be taken seriously without a good understanding of the relation between syntax and phonology. Orthography deserves the same level of respect.

A coherent theory of the relation between writing and linguistic form is also needed in speech technology, which was the starting point of our discussion. Many speech technology researchers, both in text-to-speech and automatic speech recognition, implicitly view the standard orthography for a language such as English as a poor kind of phonetic transcription. Thus one hears terms like "letter-to-sound rules" used as if somehow the sequence of letters <enough> was simply a lousy phonetic transcription of the sequence of sounds that would in standard IPA be represented by /ənʌf/. Recognizing that for a complex orthography such as English, the development of a letter-to-sound component is a major undertaking, there has been, over the past decade or so, a large amount of interest in automatic methods for acquiring letter-to-sound systems. Some of the better known instances of these are the works of Sejnowski and Rosenberg (1987), Luk and Damper (1993), Adamson and Damper (1996), Luk and Damper (1996), and Daelemans and van den Bosch (1997). Such systems can automatically "learn" the context-dependent transductions needed for a system like that of

English, so that one might expect *rough*, *trough*, and *through* to be correctly pronounced. (To date, though, nobody has yet demonstrated performance, for English, at the level of a more traditionally designed system including a dictionary plus morphological or phonological rules.) In so doing such systems take advantage of a crucial property of English orthography: While the mapping between a particular letter and a given sound is highly complex, one can almost always find a good answer by looking at the context within a fairly small window (say plus or minus four letters) around the target letter.

Even so, there is still a large amount of indeterminacy. Alternations such as *próduce* (noun) versus *prodúce* (verb), or *axes* /'æksəz/ (plural of *ax*) versus *axes* /'æksiz/ (plural of *axis*), demonstrate that one has to be prepared to make use of information not found in the letter string alone. In general one must use lexical, grammatical, or semantic information that can only be inferred from examining a wider context than just the individual word. Letter strings in English do encode pronunciation, but only in combination with other information that cannot be computed from the letter string alone.

So, to the extent that automatic methods of word pronunciation presume that all of the information needed to pronounce a word is found in its letter string, they are missing a basic point about how writing systems represent linguistic information. Orthography is not phonetic transcription; rather it is a guide to the native reader of the language that frequently gives a large amount of information about how to pronounce words, but also invariably assumes that the reader has other linguistic knowledge to bring to bear on the problem of decoding the message. This is a key reason why automatic TTS conversion is so hard to do right: Most of the linguistic knowledge that humans bring to bear on the task of reading is simply missing from TTS systems.

To further drive home this point, consider again the case of Russian orthography. As we have seen, Russian spelling is highly regular (much more so than English), but there is one crucial piece of information missing from the standard spelling, namely the lexical stress placement, without which one cannot predict the quality of various vowels in the word. In Russian, lexically determined stress placement of the kind illustrated by English *próduce*/*prodúce* is rampant. Stress placement information can be predicted from morphological information, and if such information were added to the strings (either by some dictionary-plus-rule-based procedure, or by some as-yet-to-be-developed high accuracy automatic inference procedure), then of course the various automatic schemes that have been proposed should have no trouble learning the relation between these annotated orthographic strings and the pronunciation. But this exercise would largely defeat the stated purpose of most work on automatic learning of "letter-to-sound" rules in that there would not be much savings of labor. On the one hand, developing the morphological analysis tools for Russian such that one can predict the appropriate morphological features to add to a given string is itself a major undertaking;[30] and once one has this portion of the system, developing the "letter-to-sound" rules is relatively straightforward. It should be added that to date there are no known methods by which the morphological system of a language as morphologically complex as Russian could be automatically learned; automatic methods thus fail to save labor precisely where the savings is needed most.

It should be clear that my goal is not to argue against the investigation of automatic methods for learning word pronunciation. On the contrary, investigation of these and similar machine-learning problems are an interesting and important line of inquiry. But such investigations should be grounded in a proper understanding of the phenomenon that one is attempting to investigate, and this understanding is frequently lacking in the speech technology community. As a result any regular attendee of speech technology conferences will be subjected to a series of quite surprising claims to the effect that since such-and-such an automatic method performs with (say) a 10% error rate on English word pronunciation (which is well known to be the hardest language, or so the supposition goes), the same technique can be applied to any other language, thus obviating the need for manual linguistic labor. Worse, since most regular attendees at speech conferences do not know any better, such claims do not raise the numbers of eyebrows that they ought to.

It is certainly optimistic to assume that a well-articulated formal theory of writing systems will ipso facto raise the general level of awareness of orthography and its relation to linguistic form. But it is also certain that without such a theory, writing systems will not generally be deemed worthy of serious study by theoretical linguists, nor will much attention be paid to their properties by speech technologists.

[30] In our experience, several months at least are required; see Sproat (1997b).

References

Adamson, Martin and Robert Damper. 1996. A recurrent network that learns to pronounce English text. In *Proceedings of the Fourth International Conference on Spoken Language Processing*, volume 3, pages 1704–1707, Philadelphia, PA. ICSLP.

Allen, Jonathan, M. Sharon Hunnicutt, and Dennis Klatt. 1987. *From Text to Speech: The MITalk System.* Cambridge University Press, Cambridge, UK.

Aronoff, Mark. 1976. *Word Formation in Generative Grammar.* MIT Press, Cambridge, MA.

Aronoff, Mark. 1985. Orthography and linguistic theory. *Language*, 61(1):28–72.

Aronson, Howard. 1996. Yiddish. In Peter Daniels and William Bright, editors, *The World's Writing Systems.* Oxford University Press, New York, pages 735–742.

Avanesov, R. I. 1974. *Russkaya Dialektnaya Fonetika (Russian Dialect Phonetics).* Prosveščenie, Moscow.

Avanesov, R. I., editor. 1983. *Orfoepicheskiy Slovar' Russkogo Yazyka (Orthoepic Dictionary of the Russian Language).* Russkiy Yazyk, Moscow.

Balota, David, Giovanni Flores d'Arcais, and Keith Rayner, editors. 1990. *Comprehension Processes in Reading.* Lawrence Erlbaum Associates, Hillsdale, NJ.

Baluch, B. and Derk Besner. 1991. Visual word recognition: Evidence for strategic control of lexical and nonlexical routines in oral reading. *Journal of Experimental Psychology: Learning, Memory, and Cognition*, 17:644–652.

Baxter, William. 1992. *A Handbook of Old Chinese Phonology.* Number 64 in Trends in Linguistics: Studies and Monographs. Mouton de Gruyter, Berlin.

Bell, Alexander Melville. 1867. *Visible Speech: The Science of Universal Alphabetics; or Self-Interpreting Physiological Letters, for the Writing of All Languages in One Alphabet.* Simpkin, Marshall, London.

Bennett, Emmett. 1996. Aegean scripts. In Peter Daniels and William Bright, editors, *The World's Writing Systems.* Oxford University Press, New York, pages 125–133.

Besner, Derk and D. Hildebrandt. 1987. Orthographic and phonological codes in the oral reading of Japanese kana. *Journal of Experimental Psychology: Learning, Memory, and Cognition*, 13:335–343.

Besner, Derk and Marilyn Chapnik Smith. 1992. Basic processes in reading: Is the orthographic depth hypothesis sinking? In Ram Frost and Leonard Katz, editors, *Orthography, Phonology, Morphology and Meaning*, number 94 in Advances in Psychology. North-Holland, Amsterdam, pages 45–66.

Bird, Steven. 1995. *Computational Phonology.* Cambridge University Press, Cambridge, UK.

Bird, Steven. 1999. Strategies for representing tone in African languages: A critical review. *Written Language and Literacy*, 2(1):1–44.

Bird, Steven and T. Mark Ellison. 1994. One-level phonology: Autosegmental representations and rules as finite automata. *Computational Linguistics*, 20(1):55–90.

Bird, Steven and Ewan Klein. 1994. Phonological analysis in typed feature structures. *Computational Linguistics*, 20:455–491.

Bird, Steven and Mark Liberman. 1999. A formal framework for linguistic annotation. Technical Report MS-CIS-99-01, Department of Computer and Information Science, University of Pennsylvania, Philadelphia.

Bloomfield, Leonard. 1933. *Language*. Holt, Rinehart and Winston, New York.

Bloomfield, Leonard and Clarence Barnhart. 1961. *Let's Read: A Linguistic Approach*. Wayne State University Press, Detroit, MI.

Bonfante, Larissa. 1996. The scripts of Italy. In Peter Daniels and William Bright, editors, *The World's Writing Systems*. Oxford University Press, New York, pages 297–311.

Booij, Geert. 1996. Verbindingsklanken in samenstellingen en de nieuwe spellingregeling. *Nederlandse Taalkunde*, 2:126–134.

Brandt Corstius, Hugo, editor. 1968. *Grammars for Number Names*. Number 7 in Foundations of Language, Supplementary Series. D. Reidel, Dordrecht.

Bright, William. 1996. The Devanagari script. In Peter Daniels and William Bright, editors, *The World's Writing Systems*. Oxford University Press, New York, pages 384–390.

Broderick, George. 1984a. *A Handbook of Late Spoken Manx: Dictionary*, volume 2. Max Niemeyer Verlag, Tübingen.

Broderick, George. 1984b. *A Handbook of Late Spoken Manx: Grammar and Texts*, volume 1. Max Niemeyer Verlag, Tübingen.

Browman, Catherine and Louis Goldstein. 1989. Articulatory gestures as phonological units. *Phonology*, 6:201–251.

Browne, Wayles. 1993. Serbo-Croat. In Bernard Comrie and Greville Corbett, editors, *The Slavonic Languages*. Routledge, London, pages 306–387.

Bunis, David. 1975. *A Guide to Reading and Writing Judezmo*. The Judezmo Society, Brooklyn, NY.

Cannon, Garland. 1989. Abbreviations and acronyms in English word-formation. *American Speech*, 64:99–127.

Carlton, Terence. 1990. *Introduction to the Phonological History of the Slavic Languages*. Slavica, Columbus, OH.

Chen, Hsuan-Chih and Ovid Tzeng, editors. 1992. *Language Processing in Chinese*. Number 90 in Advances in Psychology. North-Holland, Amsterdam.

Chomsky, Noam and Morris Halle. 1968. *The Sound Pattern of English*. Harper and Row, New York.

Chou, Phil. 1989. Recognition of equations using a two-dimensional stochastic context-free grammar. Technical report, AT&T Bell Laboratories, Murray Hill, NJ, August.

Church, Kenneth. 1980. *On memory limitations in natural language processing*. Master's thesis, Massachusetts Institute of Technology, Cambridge, MA.

Church, Kenneth and Patrick Hanks. 1989. Word association norms, mutual information and lexicography. In *27th Annual Meeting of the Association for Computational Linguistics*, pages 76–83, Morristown, NJ. Association for Computational Linguistics.

Ci Hai. 1979. *Ci Hai*. Shanghai Lexicon Publishing Society, Shanghai.

Clements, G. Nick. 1985. The geometry of phonological features. In C. Ewen and J. Anderson, editors, *Phonology Yearbook 2*. Cambridge University Press, Cambridge, UK, pages 225–252.

Coleman, John. 1998. *Phonological Representations: Their Names, Forms and Powers.* Number 85 in Cambridge Studies in Linguistics. Cambridge University Press, Cambridge, UK.

Coulmas, Florian. 1989. *The Writing Systems of the World.* Blackwell, Oxford.

Coulmas, Florian. 1994. Typology of writing systems. In Hugo Steger and Herbert Ernst Wiegand, editors, *Schrift und Schriftlichkeit/Writing and Its Use*, volume 2. Walter de Gruyter, Berlin, chapter 118, pages 1380–1387.

Cregeen, Archibald. 1835. *Fockleyr ny Gaelgey (A Dictionary of Manx).* Yn Cheshaght Ghailckagh, Douglas, Isle of Man. Reprinted in 1971.

Cubberley, Paul. 1996. The Slavic alphabets. In Peter Daniels and William Bright, editors, *The World's Writing Systems.* Oxford University Press, New York, pages 346–363.

Cummings, D. W. 1988. *American English Spelling: An Informal Description.* Johns Hopkins University Press, Baltimore, MD.

Daelemans, Walter and Antal van den Bosch. 1997. Language-independent data-oriented grapheme-to-phoneme conversion. In Jan van Santen, Richard Sproat, Joseph Olive, and Julia Hirschberg, editors, *Progress in Speech Synthesis.* Springer, New York, pages 77–89.

Daniels, Peter. 1991a. Is a structural graphemics possible? In *LACUS Forum*, volume 18, pages 528–37.

Daniels, Peter. 1991b. Reply to Herrick. In *LACUS Forum*, volume 21, pages 425–31.

Daniels, Peter. 1996a. Aramaic scripts for Aramaic languages. In Peter Daniels and William Bright, editors, *The World's Writing Systems.* Oxford University Press, New York, pages 499–514.

Daniels, Peter. 1996b. The study of writing systems. In Peter Daniels and William Bright, editors, *The World's Writing Systems.* Oxford University Press, New York, pages 3–17.

Daniels, Peter and William Bright. 1996. *The World's Writing Systems.* Oxford University Press, New York.

de Gelder, Beatrice and José Morais, editors. 1995. *Speech and Reading.* Erlbaum (UK) Taylor and Francis, Hove.

DeFrancis, John. 1984. *The Chinese Language: Fact and Fantasy.* University of Hawaii Press, Honolulu, HI.

DeFrancis, John. 1989. *Visible Speech: The Diverse Oneness of Writing Systems.* University of Hawaii Press, Honolulu, HI.

DeFrancis, John and J. Marshall Unger. 1994. Rejoinder to Geoffrey Sampson: "Chinese script and the diversity of writing systems." *Linguistics*, 32:549–554.

Diller, Anthony. 1996. Thai and Lao writing. In Peter Daniels and William Bright, editors, *The World's Writing Systems.* Oxford University Press, New York, pages 457–466.

Dutoit, Thierry. 1997. *An Introduction to Text-to-Speech Synthesis.* Kluwer, Dordrecht.

Faber, Alice. 1992. Phonemic segmentation as epiphenomenon. evidence from the history of alphabetic writing. In Pamela Downing, Susan Lima, and Michael Noonan, editors, *The Linguistics of Literacy.* John Benjamins, Amsterdam, pages 111–34.

Fano, R. 1961. *Transmission of Information.* MIT Press, Cambridge, MA.

Fant, Gunnar. 1960. *Acoustic Theory of Speech Production.* Mouton, The Hague.

Fischer, Steven. 1997a. *Glyphbreaker.* Copernicus, New York.

Fischer, Steven. 1997b. *Rongorongo: The Easter Island Script: History, Traditions, Texts*. Number 14 in Oxford Studies in Anthropological Linguistics. Oxford University Press, Oxford.

Flesch, Rudolf. 1981. *Why Johnny Still Can't Read: A New Look at the Scandal of Our Schools*. HarperCollins, New York.

Flores d'Arcais, Giovanni, Hirofumi Saito, and Masahiro Kawakami. 1995. Phonological and semantic activation in reading kanji characters. *Journal of Experimental Psychology*, 21(1):34–42.

Frost, Ram and Leonard Katz, editors. 1992. *Orthography, Phonology, Morphology and Meaning*. Number 94 in Advances in Psychology. North-Holland, Amsterdam.

Frost, Ram, Leonard Katz, and Shlomo Bentin. 1987. Strategies for visual word recognition and orthographical depth: A multilingual comparison. *Journal of Experimental Psychology: Human Perception and Performance*, 13:104–115.

Fujimura, Osamu and R. Kagaya. 1969. Structural patterns of Chinese characters. In *Proceedings of the International Conference on Computational Linguistics*, pages 131–148, Sånga-Säby, Sweden. International Conference on Computational Linguistics.

Gardiner, Alan. 1982. *Egyptian Grammar*. Griffith Institute, Ashmolean Museum, Oxford, third edition.

Gelb, Ignace. 1963. *A Study of Writing*. Chicago University Press, Chicago, 2nd edition.

Giammarressi, Dora and Antonio Restivo. 1997. Two-dimensional languages. In Grzegorz Rozenberg and Arto Salomaa, editors, *Handbook of Formal Languages*. Springer-Verlag, Berlin, pages 215–267.

Haas, W. 1983. Determining the level of a script. In Florian Coulmas and K. Ehlich, editors, *Writing in Focus*. Mouton, Berlin, pages 15–29.

Haile, Getatchew. 1996. Ethiopic writing. In Peter Daniels and William Bright, editors, *The World's Writing Systems*. Oxford University Press, New York, pages 569–576.

Harbaugh, Rick. 1998. *Chinese Characters: A Genealogy and Dictionary*. Zhongwen.com.

Harris, Roy. 1995. *Signs of Writing*. Routledge, London.

Harrison, Michael. 1978. *Introduction to Formal Language Theory*. Addison-Wesley, Reading, MA.

Hary, Benjamin. 1996. Adaptations of Hebrew script. In Peter Daniels and William Bright, editors, *The World's Writing Systems*. Oxford University Press, New York, pages 727–734.

Hopcroft, John and Jeffrey Ullman. 1979. *Introduction to Automata Theory, Languages and Computation*. Addison-Wesley, Reading, MA.

Horodeck, Richard. 1987. *The role of sound in reading and writing kanji*. Ph.D. thesis, Cornell University, Ithaca, NY.

Hung, Daisy, Ovid Tzeng, and Angela Tzeng. 1992. Automatic activation of linguistic information in Chinese character recognition. In Ram Frost and Leonard Katz, editors, *Orthography, Phonology, Morphology and Meaning*, number 94 in Advances in Psychology. North-Holland, Amsterdam, pages 119–130.

Hurford, James. 1975. *The Linguistic Theory of Numerals*. Cambridge University Press, Cambridge, UK.

Ifans, Dafydd and Robert Thomson. 1979. Edward Lhuyd's *Geirieu Manaweg*. *Studia Celtica*, 14:127–167.

Instituut voor Nederlandse Lexicologie. 1995. *Woordenlijst Nederlandse Taal*. Sdu Uitgevers, The Hague.

Johnson, C. Douglas. 1972. *Formal Aspects of Phonological Description*. Mouton, The Hague.

Kanwisher, N. 1987. Repetition blindness: Type recognition without token individuation. *Cognition*, 27:117–143.

Kaplan, Ronald and Martin Kay. 1994. Regular models of phonological rule systems. *Computational Linguistics*, 20:331–378.

Karttunen, Lauri. 1995. The replace operator. In *33rd Annual Meeting of the Association for Computational Linguistics*, pages 16–23, Cambridge, MA. ACL.

Karttunen, Lauri. 1998. The proper treatment of optimality in computational phonology. In Lauri Karttunen and Kemal Oflazer, editors, *FSMNLP '98: Proceedings of the International Workshop on Finite State Methods in Natural Language Processing*, pages 1–12, Bilkent University, Ankara.

Karttunen, Lauri and Kenneth Beesley. 1992. Two-level rule compiler. Technical Report P92–00149, Xerox Palo Alto Research Center.

Katz, Leonard and Laurie Feldman. 1983. Relation between pronunciation and recognition of printed words in deep and shallow orthographies. *Journal of Experimental Psychology: Learning, Memory and Cognition*, 9:157–166.

Katz, Leonard and Ram Frost. 1992. The reading process is different for different orthographies: The orthographic depth hypothesis. In Ram Frost and Leonard Katz, editors, *Orthography, Phonology, Morphology and Meaning*, number 94 in Advances in Psychology. North-Holland, Amsterdam, pages 67–84.

Kaye, Alan. 1996. Adaptations of Arabic script. In Peter Daniels and William Bright, editors, *The World's Writing Systems*. Oxford University Press, New York, pages 743–762.

King, Ross. 1996. Korean hankul. In Peter Daniels and William Bright, editors, *The World's Writing Systems*. Oxford University Press, New York, pages 218–227.

Kiraz, George. forthcoming. *Computational Approach to Non-Linear Morphology*. Cambridge University Press, Cambridge, UK.

Klima, Edward. 1972. How alphabets might reflect language. In James Kavanagh and Ignatius Mattingly, editors, *Language by Ear and by Eye: The Relationships between Speech and Reading*. MIT Press, Cambridge, MA, pages 57–80.

Knight, Stan. 1996. The roman alphabet. In Peter Daniels and William Bright, editors, *The World's Writing Systems*. Oxford University Press, New York, pages 312–332.

Koskenniemi, Kimmo. 1983. *Two-level morphology: A general computational model for word-form recognition and production*. Ph.D. thesis, University of Helsinki, Helsinki.

Krivickij, A. and A. Podluzhnyj. 1994. *Uchebnik Belorusskogo Yazyka*. Vyshejshaya Shkola, Minsk.

Kucera, H. and W. Francis. 1967. *Computational Analysis of Present-Day American English*. Brown University Press, Providence.

Law, Sam Po and Alfonso Caramazza. 1995. Cognitive processes in writing Chinese characters: Basic issues and some preliminary data. In Beatrice de Gelder and José Morais, editors, *Speech and Reading*. Erlbaum (UK) Taylor and Francis, Hove, pages 143–190.

Lehman, Winifred and Lloyd Faust, 1951. *A Grammar of Formal Written Japanese*, chapter supplement: Kokuji, by R. P. Alexander. Harvard University Press, Cambridge, MA.

Lejeune, Michel. 1974. *Manuel de la Langue Vénète*. Carl Winter, Heidelberg.

Levin, Esther and Roberto Pieraccini. 1991. Dynamic planar warping and planar hidden Markov modeling: From speech to optical character recognition. Technical report, AT&T Bell Laboratories, Murray Hill, NJ, November.

Lewis, Harry and Christos Papadimitriou. 1981. *Elements of the Theory of Computation*. Prentice-Hall, Englewood Cliffs, NJ.

Luk, Robert and Robert Damper. 1993. Experiments with silent-e and affix correspondences in stochastic phonographic transductions. In *Proceedings of the Third European Conference on Speech Communication and Technology*, volume 2, pages 917–920, Berlin. ESCA.

Luk, Robert and Robert Damper. 1996. Stochastic phonographic transduction for English. *Computer Speech and Language*, 10:133–153.

Lyosik, Yazep. 1926. *Gramatyka Belaruskae Movy: Fonetyka*. Published by the Author, Minsk.

MacMahon, Michael. 1996. Phonetic notation. In Peter Daniels and William Bright, editors, *The World's Writing Systems*. Oxford University Press, New York, pages 821–846.

Macri, Martha. 1996. Maya and other Mesoamerican scripts. In Peter Daniels and William Bright, editors, *The World's Writing Systems*. Oxford University Press, New York, pages 172–182.

Maksymiuk, Jan. 1999. An orthography on trial in Belarus. *Written Language and Literacy*, 2(1):141–144.

Marantz, Alec. 1982. Re reduplication. *Linguistic Inquiry*, 13:435–482.

Mastroianni, M. and Bob Carpenter. 1994. Constraint-based morphophonology. In *Proceedings of the First ACL SIGPHON Workshop*, pages 13–24, Las Cruces, NM. ACL.

Matsunaga, Sachiko. 1994. *The linguistic and psycholinguistic nature of kanji: Do kanji represent and trigger only meanings?* Ph.D. thesis, University of Hawaii, Honolulu, HI.

McManus, Damian. 1996. Celtic languages. In Peter Daniels and William Bright, editors, *The World's Writing Systems*. Oxford University Press, New York, pages 655–660.

Merrifield, William. 1968. Number names in four languages of Mexico. In Hugo Brandt Corstius, editor, *Grammars for Number Names*, number 7 in Foundations of Language, Supplementary Series. D. Reidel, Dordrecht, pages 91–102.

Miller, D. Gary. 1994. *Ancient Scripts and Phonological Knowledge*. Number 116 in Current Issues in Linguistic Theory. John Benjamins, Amsterdam.

Mohanan, K. P. 1986. *The Theory of Lexical Phonology*. D. Reidel, Dordrecht.

Mohri, Mehryar. 1994. Syntactic analysis by local grammars automata: An efficient algorithm. In *Papers in Computational Lexicography: COMPLEX '94*, pages 179–191, Budapest. Research Institute for Linguistics, Hungarian Academy of Sciences.

Mohri, Mehryar. 1997. Finite-state transducers in language and speech processing. *Computational Linguistics*, 23(2).

Mohri, Mehryar. 2000. *Finite-State Transducers*. MIT Press, Cambridge, MA.

Mohri, Mehryar and Richard Sproat. 1996. An efficient compiler for weighted rewrite rules. In *34th Annual Meeting of the Association for Computational Linguistics*, pages 231–238, Santa Cruz, CA. ACL.

Mountford, John. 1996. A functional classification. In Peter Daniels and William Bright, editors, *The World's Writing Systems*. Oxford University Press, New York, pages 627–632.

Myers, James. 1996. Prosodic structure in Chinese characters. Presented as a Poster at the 5th International Conference on Chinese Linguistics, Tsing Hua University, Taiwan, June.

Nanyang Siang Pau. 1984. *Learner's Chinese English Dictionary*. Nanyang Siang Pau, Umum Publisher, Singapore.

Needham, J. 1959. *Science and Civilisation in China: Vol. 3 – Mathematics and the Sciences of the Heavens and the Earth*. Cambridge University Press, Cambridge UK, with the collaboration of Wang Ling.

Neijt, Anneke and Anneke Nunn. 1997. The recent history of Dutch orthography: Problems solved and created. *Leuvense Bijdragen*, 86:1–26.

Nguyen, Dinh Hoa. 1959. Chū' nôm: The demotic system of writing in Vietnam. *Journal of the American Oriental Society*, 79(4):270–274.

Nunberg, Geoffrey. 1995. *The Linguistics of Punctuation*. CSLI (University of Chicago Press), Chicago, IL.

Nunn, Anneke. 1998. *Dutch Orthography: A Systematic Investigation of the Spelling of Dutch Words*. Number 6 in LOT International Series. Holland Academic Graphics, The Hague.

O'Connor, M. 1996. Epigraphic Semitic scripts. In Peter Daniels and William Bright, editors, *The World's Writing Systems*. Oxford University Press, New York, pages 88–107.

Packard, Jerome, editor. 1998. *New Approaches to Chinese Word Formation*. Number 105 in Trends in Linguistics, Studies and Monographs. Mouton de Gruyter, Berlin.

Perfetti, Charles and Li Hai Tan. 1998. The time course of graphic, phonological and semantic activation in Chinese character identification. *Journal of Experimental Psychology: Learning, Memory and Cognition*, 24(1):101–118.

Perfetti, Charles A., Laurence Rieben, and Michel Fayol, editors. 1997. *Learning to Spell: Research, Theory and Practice across Languages*. Lawrence Erlbaum Associates, Mahwah, NJ.

Pesetsky, David. 1979. Russian morphology and lexical theory. Manuscript. Massachusetts Institute of Technology.

Pettersson, John Sören. 1996. Numerical notation. In Peter Daniels and William Bright, editors, *The World's Writing Systems*. Oxford University Press, New York, pages 795–806.

Pinker, Steven and Alan Prince. 1988. On language and connectionism: Analysis of a parallel distributed processing model of language acquisition. In Steven Pinker and Jacques Mehler, editors, *Connections and Symbols*. MIT Press, pages 73–193. *Cognition* special issue.

Prince, Alan and Paul Smolensky. 1993. Optimality theory. Technical Report 2, Rutgers University, Piscataway, NJ.

Radzinski, Daniel. 1991. Chinese number-names, tree adjoining languages, and mild context-sensitivity. *Computational Linguistics*, 17(3):277–300.

Rajemisa-Raolison, Régis. 1971. *Grammaire Malgache*. Centre de Formation Pédagogique, Fianarantsoa, Madagascar, 7th edition.

Raman, T. V. 1994. *Audio system for technical readings*. Ph.D. thesis, Cornell University, Ithaca, NY.

Ratliff, Martha. 1996. The Pahawh Hmong script. In Peter Daniels and William Bright, editors, *The World's Writing Systems*. Oxford University Press, New York, pages 619–624.

Ritner, Robert. 1996. Egyptian writing. In Peter Daniels and William Bright, editors, *The World's Writing Systems*. Oxford University Press, New York, pages 73–84.

Römer, Jürgen. 1994. Abkürzungen. In Hugo Steger and Herbert Ernst Wiegand, editors, *Schrift und Schriftlichkeit/Writing and Its Use*, volume 2. Walter de Gruyter, Berlin, chapter 135, pages 1506–1515.

Rumelhart, David and James McClelland. 1986. On learning the past tense of English verbs. In James McClelland and David Rumelhart, editors, *Parallel Distributed Processing*. MIT Press, Cambridge, MA, Volume 2 pages 216–271.

Sagey, Elizabeth. 1986. *The representation of features and relations in non-linear phonology*. Ph.D. thesis, Massachusetts Institute of Technology, Cambridge, MA.

Salomon, Richard. 1996. South Asian writing systems (introduction). In Peter Daniels and William Bright, editors, *The World's Writing Systems*. Oxford University Press, New York, pages 371–372.

Sampson, Geoffrey. 1985. *Writing Systems*. Stanford University Press, Stanford, CA.

Sampson, Geoffrey. 1994. Chinese script and the diversity of writing systems. *Linguistics*, 32:117–132.

Schiller, Eric. 1996. Khmer writing. In Peter Daniels and William Bright, editors, *The World's Writing Systems*. Oxford University Press, New York, pages 467–473.

Schreuder, Robert, Anneke Neijt, Femke van der Weide, and R. Harald Baayen. 1998. Regular plurals in Dutch compounds: Linking graphemes or morphemes. *Language and Cognitive Processes*, 13:551–573.

Seidenberg, Mark. 1990. Lexical access: Another theoretical soupstone? In David Balota, Giovanni Flores d'Arcais, and Keith Rayner, editors, *Comprehension Processes in Reading*. Lawrence Erlbaum Associates, Hillsdale, NJ, pages 33–71.

Seidenberg, Mark. 1992. Beyond orthographic depth in reading: Equitable division of labor. In Ram Frost and Leonard Katz, editors, *Orthography, Phonology, Morphology and Meaning*, number 94 in Advances in Psychology. North-Holland, Amsterdam, pages 85–118.

Seidenberg, Mark. 1997. Language acquisition and use: Learning and applying probabilistic constraints. *Science*, 275:1599–1603, March 14.

Seidenberg, Mark., K. McRae, and D. Jared. 1988. Frequency and consistency of spelling-sound correspondences in naming. Presented at the 29th annual meeting of the Psychonomic Society, Chicago, November.

Seidenberg, Mark and James McClelland. 1989. A distributed, developmental model of visual word recognition and naming. *Psychological Review*, 96:523–568.

Sejnowski, Terence and C. Rosenberg. 1987. Parallel networks that learn to pronounce English text. *Complex Systems*, 1:145–168.

Serianni, Luca. 1989. *Grammatica Italiana: Italiano Comune e Lingua Letteraria*. UTET Libreria, Turin.

Shi, Dingxu. 1996. The Yi script. In Peter Daniels and William Bright, editors, *The World's Writing Systems*. Oxford University Press, New York, pages 239–243.

Skjærvø, Oktor. 1996. Aramaic scripts for Iranian languages. In Peter Daniels and William Bright, editors, *The World's Writing Systems*. Oxford University Press, New York, pages 515–535.

Smalley, William, Chia Koua Vang, and Gnia Yee Yang. 1990. *Mother of Writing: The Origin and Development of a Hmong Messianic Script*. University of Chicago Press, Chicago, IL.

Smith, Janet. 1996. Japanese writing. In Peter Daniels and William Bright, editors, *The World's Writing Systems*. Oxford University Press, New York, pages 209–217.

Sproat, Richard. 1992. *Morphology and Computation*. MIT Press, Cambridge, MA.

Sproat, Richard. 1997a. Multilingual text analysis for text-to-speech synthesis. *Journal of Natural Language Engineering*, 2(4):369–380.

Sproat, Richard, editor. 1997b. *Multilingual Text to Speech Synthesis: The Bell Labs Approach.* Kluwer Academic Publishers, Boston, MA.

Sproat, Richard and Chilin Shih. 1990. A statistical method for finding word boundaries in Chinese text. *Computer Processing of Chinese and Oriental Languages,* 4:336–351.

Sproat, Richard and Chilin Shih. 1995. A corpus-based analysis of Mandarin nominal root compounds. *Journal of East Asian Linguistics,* 4(1):1–23.

Sproat, Richard, Chilin Shih, William Gale, and Nancy Chang. 1996. A stochastic finite-state word-segmentation algorithm for Chinese. *Computational Linguistics,* 22:377–404.

Stampe, David. 1976. Cardinal number systems. In *Papers from the 12th Regional Meeting, Chicago Linguistic Society,* pages 594–609, Chicago, IL. Chicago Linguistic Society.

Steriade, Donca. 1982. *Greek prosodies and the nature of syllabification.* Ph.D. thesis, Massachusetts Institute of Technology, Cambridge, MA.

Steriade, Donca. 1999. Paradigm uniformity and the phonetics–phonology boundary. In Michael Broe and Janet Pierrehumbert, editors, *Papers in Laboratory Phonology V.* Cambridge University Press, Cambridge, UK.

Stone, Gregory and Guy Van Orden. 1994. Building a resonance framework for word recognition using design and system principles. *Journal of Experimental Psychology: Human Perception and Performance,* 20(6):1248–1268.

Talkin, David. 1995. A robust algorithm for pitch tracking (RAPT). In W. Kleijn and K. K. Paliwal, editors, *Speech Coding and Synthesis.* Elsevier, New York.

Taraban, R. and James McClelland. 1987. Conspiracy effects in word recognition. *Journal of Memory and Language,* 26:608–631.

Thomson, Robert. 1969. The study of Manx Gaelic. *Proceedings of the British Academy,* 60:179–210. Sir John Rhŷs Memorial Lecture.

Tzeng, Angela Ku-Yuan. 1994. *Comparative studies on word perception of Chinese and English: Evidence against an orthographic-specific hypothesis.* Ph.D. thesis, University of California, Riverside.

Vachek, Josef. 1973. *Written Language: General Problems and Problems of English.* Mouton, The Hague.

van den Bosch, Antal, Alain Content, Walter Daelemans, and Beatrice de Gelder. 1994. Measuring the complexity of writing systems. *Journal of Quantitative Linguistics,* 1:178–188.

Van Orden, Guy, Bruce Pennington, and Gregory Stone. 1990. Word identification in reading and the promise of subsymbolic psycholinguistics. *Psychological Review,* 97(4):488–522.

Venezky, Richard. 1970. *The Structure of English Orthography.* Number 82 in Janua Linguarum. Mouton, The Hague.

Voutilainen, Atro. 1994. *Three studies of grammar-based surface parsing of unrestricted English text.* Ph.D. thesis, University of Helsinki, Helsinki. Published as *Publications of the Department of General Linguistics, University of Helsinki, no. 24.*

Wade, Terence. 1992. *A Comprehensive Russian Grammar.* Blackwell, Oxford.

Wang, Jason. 1983. *Toward a generative grammar of Chinese character structure and stroke order.* Ph.D. thesis, University of Wisconsin, Madison, WI.

Wang, Jian, Albrecht Inhoff, and Hsuan-Chih Chen, editors. 1999. *Reading Chinese Script.* Lawrence Erlbaum Associates, Mahwah, NJ.

Wang, Kuijing. 1996. *Xiandai Hanyu Suolüeyu Cidian (A Dictionary of Present-Day Chinese Abbreviations).* Shangwu Printing House, Beijing.

Wells, J. C. 1982. *Accents of English 1: An Introduction.* Cambridge University Press, Cambridge, UK.

Wieger, L. 1965. *Chinese Characters.* Dover, New York. Republication of second edition, published 1927 by Catholic Mission Press.

Yarowsky, David. 1996. Homograph disambiguation in text-to-speech synthesis. In Jan van Santen, Richard Sproat, Joseph Olive, and Julia Hirschberg, editors, *Progress in Speech Synthesis.* Springer, New York, pages 157–172.

Subject Index

Language and Writing System Index

Name Index

Printed in the United States
65799LVS00004B/337-354

9 780521 034227